Alphabets of Good Life

Published by
Gita Publishing House
Sadhu Vaswani Mission,
10, Sadhu Vaswani Path, Pune – 411 001, (India).
gph@sadhuvaswani.org

© J.P. Vaswani
First Published - 3000 copies - August, 2018

ALPHABETS OF GOOD LIFE
ISBN 978-93-86004-09-3

No part of this book may be reproduced or utilised in
any form or by any means, electronic or
mechanical including photocopying, recording or by any
information storage and retrieval system,
without permission in writing from the Author.

Printed and bound in India by Thomson Press India Ltd.

ALPHABETS OF GOOD LIFE

J. P. VASWANI

Edited by:
Dr. (Mrs.) Prabha Sampath
&
Krishna Kumari

GITA PUBLISHING HOUSE
PUNE, (INDIA).
www.dadavaswanisbooks.org

Contents

Compilers' Note	7
1. Anger– Burn it!	9
2. Animal Rights	13
3. Anxiety– Dispel it!	17
4. Attachment– Free Yourself!	23
5. Attitude Counts!	30
6. Awakening	34
7. Begin the Day with God	38
8. Believe and Achieve!	42
9. Bhakti	46
10. Brahmacharya	52
11. Compassion	57
12. Contentment	60
13. Conversion	66
14. Courage	72
15. Dada Shyam	77
16. Death	82
17. Depression– Fight it!	85
18. Desire	90
19. Difficulties– Overcome them!	94
20. Disciple	100
21. Discipline	106
22. Duty	109
23. Education	117
24. Ego	123
25. Empower Yourself	126
26. Enemy Within– Beware!	132
27. Enlightenment	139
28. Environment	141
29. Equality	145
30. Faith	151
31. Fate & Free Will	154
32. Fear– Conquer it!	160
33. Freedom	166
34. Friendship	169
35. Give, Give, Give!	172
36. Goal	174
37. Gurmukh & Manmukh	179
38. Guru	184
39. Happiness	191
40. Health and Well-Being	195
41. Heaven and Hell	202
42. Here and Now	210
43. Humility	216
44. India	220
45. Inferiority Complex– Discard it!	227
46. Inner Peace	231
47. Irritation– Root it Out!	235
48. Joy Killers– Say No to Them!	239
49. Laughter	247
50. Law of Karma	254

51. Let Go, Let Go, Let God!	260
52. Let God In!	263
53. Life	271
54. Love	277
55. Make the Right Choice	284
56. Mantras for Peace of Mind	290
57. Marriage	293
58. Materialism	297
59. Mind Matters	305
60. Mother Earth	310
61. Mothers	314
62. Mukti: The Goal of Life	317
63. Name Divine	323
64. New Age	328
65. New You	333
66. Old Age	340
67. Optimism & Pessimism	343
68. Parents & Children	345
69. Patience	351
70. Prayer	357
71. Problems– Solve them!	361
72. Prosperity	367
73. Relationships	372
74. Religion	378
75. Respond– Don't Retaliate	384
76. Reverence for All Life	390
77. Risk: Learning to Take a Chance!	396
78. Sadhana	401
79. Satsang	404
80. Service	408
81. Shakti: The Power Within You	412
82. Silence	416
83. Simplicity	418
84. Sindhi Community	423
85. Spirituality	429
86. Stop Complaining!	432
87. Stress– Beat it!	438
88. Success	442
89. Suffering	446
90. Sufism and Sind	454
91. Surrender	458
92. Teachers	464
93. Temptation– Fight it!	470
94. Time	474
95. Truth	481
96. Understanding	485
97. Vegetarianism	490
98. World Peace	499
99. Yoga	507
100. You are Not this Body: Your are the Atman!	511
Glossary	514

Compilers' Note

When we decided to bring out a collection of one hundred aspects of Dada's teachings in connection with the much looked forward-to Centenary Celebrations, we stood baulked at the very outset by the difficulty in choosing! We brainstormed and pooled ideas over what 'topics' we could choose, and found ourselves simply overwhelmed by everybody's insistence on their favourite topics. If we were to do justice to readers' choice, we would have to compile a list of not one hundred, but one thousand topics and aspects of Dada's teachings!

And the trouble is that Dada would be the first to deny that he is a 'teacher' or a 'guru' and that he 'teaches' anything to anyone.

In a sense, this is true. Dada's life is his greatest message, the best 'book' that can motivate and inspire you! But he has spoken to us, written for us, and thousands of us treasure and value his teachings for the comfort, solace, support and inspiration they have brought into our lives!

Described as "a 21st century mystic who walks in the footsteps of the great Masters who come to this earth to teach and transform", Dada's words have reached and touched people from all walks of life, all over the world. He is the author of over 150 books; and as a writer, there are few subjects of human interest which he has left untouched; from karma to liberation, from simplicity to prosperity, from compassion to management, from friendship to parenting, from marriage to education, Dada's inimitable wisdom and humour has illumined every topic he deals with!

The gift of writing came to Dada very early on in life. Even as a college student, Dada edited no less than three monthly journals- the *Excelsior*, the *India Digest* and the *East and West Series*, all of them widely circulated and appreciated by his readers. Dada's writing is lucid, inspired, and free-flowing, much like his oratory. A unique feature of his books is that they are not the kind you read once and put away. Instead they are read and re-read to draw inspiration and spiritual strength. They are an inexhaustible source of wisdom and faith for countless readers. As for his mantras for the modern man, thousands of his chosen sayings are echoed across the globe by people seeking hope and faith: *I am not alone, God is with me! Not my will, but Thy will be done! Let go, let go, let God! Thank you God! I accept! Qabool, qabool, qabool! Yes Father, yes, and always yes!*

We cannot tell how many times people have repeated these words to themselves, how many times they have returned to Dada's books to rekindle their faith and find the courage to carry on!

We thought therefore, that we would compile one hundred aspects of Dada's wise and loving messages to us all, one hundred chosen life-lessons that would inspire us to live the kind of life that we ought to live. They are in Dada's own words, as he spoke them, wrote them, or gave them as answers to queries placed before him.

We have only scooped a handful of nectar from an ocean of Dada's wisdom!

Anger– Burn It!

Anger is a wildfire, a forest fire which spreads from shrub to shrub, from tree to tree, consuming everything that comes its way. In Hindi, we have a couplet which says: "Anger is the great inflictor of sorrow, the great sinner. First, it sets on fire its own mind, then the fire spreads to others." Anger creates a chain reaction. Someone gets mad at me– I must take it out on someone else, otherwise it will keep on seething within me. That someone else must have it out on yet someone else. And the chain reaction goes on!

Anger is so endemic today, wildly prevalent and inherent to our century that we could call it the 'age of anger'.

On the surface, we all are good and virtuous. But, within each one of us, there lie hidden so many weaknesses and imperfections, the worst elements within us, which are at times made manifest. Therefore, we must burn anger before anger burns us!

How many of us can truthfully say that we are masters of our anger? A little thing happens and we feel upset or irritated. A person speaks rudely to us and the colour of our countenance changes. We suffer losses in business, and our sleep is disturbed. Suddenly a dear one is snatched away from us and we lose our faith in God. This is the sad condition of so many of us.

Anger is more destructive than fire, more disastrous than an earthquake. In anger, individuals fight each other, leading to dire consequences. In anger, nations fight each other and thousands of young, precious, promising lives are lost.

But the good news is: anger can be controlled!

Why do people get angry?

The simple cause of anger, I believe, is self-will. Whenever I want something to be done in a particular way and it is done differently, I get angry. If only I can curb my self-will by surrendering it to the Will Divine, I will not be angry. Once I realise that everything that happens, happens according to the Will of God, and in the Will of God is my highest good, I shall never, never, get angry.

If only we realised that whatever happens, happens according to the Divine Will, we would never succumb to anger.

Can anger ever be justified?

Anger is a two-edged sword. There is a type of anger which drains energy and produces tension. There is another type that is a positive and creative life force, known as righteous anger. When it is my duty to be angry, and I become angry– that is righteous anger. A parent sometimes has to be angry with the child for the good of the child. A teacher sometimes has to be angry with a student for the good of the student. An employer sometimes has to be angry with an employee for the good of the organisation.

If you find a man molesting a woman, or ill treating an animal on the roadside, you have every right to be angry. Anger becomes righteous when you get angry to defend the rights of another, without any selfish motive. When a person feels it is his duty to get angry, he dissociates himself from his self-will. He himself becomes a spectator to his own anger. The historical example of righteous anger is given us in the New Testament. Jesus visits a temple and finds the priests desecrating it. He gets righteously angry and says to the priests, "What is it that you are doing? You have converted my Father's home into a commercial house."

This type of anger– righteous anger– will not degrade a man but will ennoble him.

What is the difference between suppression and control of anger?

There are three ways of handling anger. There is the way of expression, which so many of us follow. We feel angry and release it through our words and actions. Expression gives us relief, for we get some satisfaction at having given a piece of our mind to the person who upset us. This relief, however, is temporary. Resentments build up again, and we are ready for another spill out. Gradually, anger becomes a habit and the time comes when we become slaves to anger. We are controlled by anger, and anger is a terrible master. I read about a mother who, in a mood of anger, threw her own child into the fire!

The second way to handle anger is suppression. We suppress anger because we don't like to show people that we are angry. As psychologists tell us, suppression creates complexes which are not conducive to our mental well-being.

Then, there is the third, and the right way of handling anger. It is the way of forgivenes. When we forgive, we rise above anger.

Can anger affect our physical well-being?

Anger activates certain glands in the body, leading to an outpouring of adrenaline and other stress hormones, with noticeable physical consequences. The face reddens, blood pressure increases, the voice rises to a higher pitch, breathing becomes faster and deeper, heart-beats become harder, muscles of the arms and legs tighten. The body moves into an excited state.

If a person is given to constant ill temper, all these processes are constantly repeated and he will land himself in serious health problems.

The cumulative effect of the hormones released during anger episodes can increase the risk of coronary and other life-threatening diseases including strokes, ulcers, and high blood pressure. Stomach ulcers are caused by anger. They recur even after operations, if the resentment persists. It is, therefore, in your own interest that you learn to control, or at least reduce your anger.

Recent researches have found that people who are often prone to anger are at greater risk for heart attacks. On the other hand, when a person is calm, peaceful and happy, his internal systems work normally. Thus, when man comes under the influence of anger, the digestive processes are paralysed. Therefore, doctors recommend that you should be cheerful and in good humour when you eat.

Anger is a poison that affects the entire system; it throws poison into the bloodstream. I read about a mother who was given to frequent bouts of anger. Her infant received milk from her while she was in an angry mood. Soon the baby died.

Practical suggestions to overcome anger

1. The best and surest way of controlling anger is the way of self-realisation. Once you realise who you are, you will never be angry. This implies identification with your highest Self.

2. Develop the will to control anger. Realise the uselessness of anger. We may not harm the person with whom we feel angry but we surely harm ourselves.

3. Accept every incident and accident as God's Will. Rejoice in whatever His Will brings

to you. You will then arrive at a stage where nothing will upset you and make you angry.

4. Pray to God and seek the help of your guru to control your anger. Without their grace, you can achieve nothing.

5. Avoid occasions for anger. Whenever you find yourself in a situation which makes you angry, turn away from it.

6. Avoid haste– for haste is the mother of anger, even as hatred is its father.

7. Whenever you feel anger building, keep your mouth shut and your lips sealed. When you speak, make the effort to speak lovingly, softly, and gently. If you are unable to keep quiet, hum to yourself a simple tune. This will help you to relax and remain calm.

8. Count up to ten when you feel your anger rising; if you are very angry, count up to hundred. Drink a glass or two of cold water, or go out and take a brisk walk, or run or jog. Exercise will burn up your negative emotional energy.

If only anger could actually cement relationships, it would be worth our while to get angry. But anger only tends to drive a wedge into relationships, with the divide getting deeper and wider every time we succumb to it. The words that pour out of our lips and the decisions that arise from the dark cloud of anger, can only prove to be harmful and detrimental.

Over 70% of murder victims are either friends or relatives of the murderer, who committed the crime in anger that emerged from trifling quarrels. Holding on to anger is like grasping a hot coal in one's hand, with the intention of throwing it at the other, but burning one's own fingers in the process.

When the Buddha was asked, how not to react to the anger of friends and family, he replied, "When you get upset, your family and friends are not the cause; you become angry because you choose to be angry." It is you who makes the choice. You will not be punished because of your anger, you will be punished by your anger.

'Anger' is just one letter less than 'danger', so beware, avoid it and keep away from it.

Animal Rights

Today, wherever we go, we hear of animal welfare, but animal welfare is not enough! It is not the answer to exploitation and cruelty. Animal rights are needed! Men have their rights, but do they not have duties towards animals who have befriended them since the dawn of history? The time is come when we must get together and formulate a Charter of Animal Rights and a Charter of man's duties towards the animals. The first right of every animal is the right to live, for we cannot take away that which we cannot give. Since we cannot give life to a dead creature, we have no right to take away the life of a living one.

God has not created birds and beasts, fish and fowl to fulfill man's needs!

The ancient rishi of the *Ishopanishad* sang, "Ishavasyam idam sarvam." "All that is, is a vesture of the Lord!" God comes to us, putting on different vestures, different garments. Clad in different garbs, the Lord comes to test us, to find out if we truly love Him, as we say we do. Alas, we slay the Lord! We handle Him roughly, we treat Him harshly. We offer Him worship in temples and churches. We chant hymns to His glory, but out in the street we are cruel to Him. We slay Him and eat His flesh. We forget that the animal, too, is an image of God!

Much on earth is masked. But there is a strange, a mystic sense of fellowship with all that lives. This is what makes every life sacred.

Is vivisection justified?

In my opinion, it is meaningless to have so much dissection in college and university laboratories. This very work could be done by studying a model of a frog. Advances in technology have enabled access to life-like 3D models nowadays. It is not necessary to give pain to a frog or a cockroach.

Knowledge is not knowledge if it is obtained in cruel ways. Such ill-acquired knowledge is a curse: it unleashes the very forces of hell and will hurl humanity into a dark abyss of disease and death. Knowledge, if it is to be a source of blessing to humanity, must never be sought through the torturing of helpless creatures. True knowledge springs from compassion and love.

Man has yet to understand that there is only one life; the same life that is in him, is also in the frog. *Vedanta* teaches us the sanctity of this one life in all. This one life sleeps in the mineral, dreams in the plant, stirs in the animal, and wakes in man. I think the time has come when students should think of this matter and say, why kill when it is not necessary?

The same goes for animal testing too. The American Food and Drug Administration reports that 92 out of every 100 drugs that pass animal tests fail on human beings! How can such unethical tests be justified in a civilised society? Hundreds of cancer drugs have cured mice; yet none of them have effectively eliminated fatalities due to cancer in human beings. Is it not cruel and wasteful to continue such tests?

Our students are eloquent in debates over child labour, racial intolerance, and injustice against the working classes. All forms of exploitation must cease. But can we be silent on the subject of animal welfare and animal rights?

Animals have no press, no TV, no media, no representatives to voice their grievances. They need friends and supporters; they need articulate spokespersons. Our students should be encouraged to take on this challenging role!

Let me emphasise this again– animal welfare is not enough! We must speak of animal rights! Men have their rights; have animals no rights? The time has come for the younger generation to stand up and be counted for the inviolability of the right to life– both human and non-human.

"How can we worry about animal rights when it is a question of food and nutrition for the world's teaming population?"

First of all, this talk about overpopulation is irrelevant, because nature will provide for man's food. But if we take the law of nature in our own hands, then the responsibility devolves on us.

Secondly, due to breeding, the population of animals is growing today. If the population grew in a natural way there would be no problem at all; no bio-problem would occur.

Nature knows how to take care of its own creation. We are interfering with nature by adopting unnatural techniques to breed animals and poultry for food!

We use artificial methods for breeding animals to make money. Experts warn us that cows are given Stilbestrol injections during pregnancy so that they gain flesh, ensuring more money to the owner of the cow, for each pound of extra flesh! You do not know how many millions of animals are born through this process of unnatural breeding. We have to let nature take charge.

"But there is the concept of humane slaughter these days…"

Humane slaughter is a ridiculous contradiction in terms! We might as well talk of humane murder, as Sadhu Vaswani once remarked in outright rejection of this idea. We have adopted Ashoka's *dharma-chakra* as our symbol. Are we true to the spirit of Ashoka and Ashoka's ideals? Therefore I beg of you: stop all slaughter! Animals and birds have, alas, no language by which they can tell us of their suffering and pain. If we could but appreciate the poetry of animal life! Birds are a miracle of beauty in nature's wonderland. I have wondered how man can have the heart to catch and kill them!

Why do you observe November 25th as an 'International Meatless Day' and 'Animal Rights Day'?

Sadhu Vaswani was a voice of the voiceless, the dumb, the defenseless children of God who, alas are being slain by the millions in our soulless cities every day. "O, the sin of daily slaughter!" he exclaimed, and he added words with which many today will not be in sympathy. But he spoke with the foresight of a seer when he said, "Believe me, the day is coming when meat eating will be condemned as murder!" He also said, "I have seen God's image shining in birds and animals, and for me not to love bird and animal would be not to love the Lord!" It was therefore felt appropriate, that the 25th of November, the birthday of this humble, holy man of God, this prophet of reverence for all life, be observed, year after year, as an 'International Meatless Day' and 'Animal Rights Day'.

How can one day's observance help animal rights?

Just one day, because the idea is to create awareness in the minds of people in regard to the cruelties that are perpetrated on animals and birds day after day. When a delicious dish is placed before man, he eats it as a matter of course. He does not realise, he never thinks of the agony through which the slaughtered animal must have passed.

What is SAK?

The Meatless Day campaign was launched in 1986. Over the years, the campaign has grown from strength to strength. Today, the Movement has gathered momentum and has been renamed the SAK (Stop All Killing Association).

SAK aims at spreading awareness, and sensitising people to the concept of 'Reverence for All Life' as the first step to World Peace. To this end, The Mission and its Centres organise Peace Marches and adopt multi-pronged efforts to persuade people to accept this cause as their own. It also advocates the cause of animal rights, and launches active programmes to care for animals. Most important of all, the campaign promotes the ideal of vegetarianism and persuades people to eschew the food of violence, fish, flesh and fowl– at least on this one day– November 25. To this end, a SAK Newsletter is also published and widely circulated.

The 19th century gave black people their rights; the 20th century freed women from their shackles and was acclaimed a century of women's rights; the dawn of the new millennium will witness the triumph of animal rights! Is this not a glorious vision of peace, love and compassion? Do you know that on an average a human being eats 7,500 big and small animals during his lifetime? 7,500 animals, everyone of whom loves life as much as those who eat them up. Even as black people do not exist as resources for the whites, even as women do not exist as resources for men, even so animals do not exist as resources for human beings. The time is come when animals should be given, must be given, certain fundamental rights.

Anxiety- Dispel It!

Our age has been called the age of anxiety. Everyone has some anxiety or the other on his mind. Anxiety and modern life– they seem to go together. Every one of us has experienced a sleepless night due to anxiety and worry. Anxiety and worry are products of modern life. The way we live, the way we move, the way we do our daily work, contributes to anxiety. We are always in a hurry, we are always rushing, rushing about as though we carry the burden of the world on our shoulders. We are running, running all the time like squirrels in a cage. It is this type of life that leads to anxiety. Our anxieties keep on growing, our worries keep on multiplying, until the day comes when they manifest themselves in some physical ailment or the other. Our hospitals are filled with patients suffering from anxiety related disorders.

Let me give you an inspirational quote from the Bible:

Do not be anxious about anything, but by prayer and petition, with thanksgiving, present your requests to God. And the peace of God, which transcends all understanding, will guard your heart and mind…

(Philippians 4: 6-7)

In the Gospel, according to St. Luke (Ch.10, verses 38-42), Jesus visits the house of the sisters Martha and Mary. Martha gets busy attending to various household chores to make Jesus and his disciples comfortable. As for Mary, she sits at the feet of Jesus, listening eagerly to his words of wisdom. Martha complains about her sister– shouldn't she get up and do something to help? Jesus tells Martha, "You are worried and anxious about many things, but only one thing is needed. Mary has chosen what is better, and it will not be taken away from her."

What was it that freed Mary from the anxiety and the fretful activity that kept her sister so 'busy'? Mary chose to focus on Jesus– and on Jesus alone; to listen to his every word. In the process, she ignored the demands of hospitality. She was not being irresponsible; she was not trying to shirk her duties; she had her own priorities. She would listen to Jesus first– everything else could be done later.

This incident teaches us a valuable lesson. Put God first. He will automatically free us from our worries, and take care of all our 'concerns' and 'problems'. There is a beautiful line in the *Sukhmani Sahib,* a Sikh scripture which I love to meditate on:

Avar tyag tu tisay chitar...

Renounce everything; throw out everything; don't think of anything– but meditate on Him, concentrate on Him, think of Him, dedicate all your work to Him!

Avar tyag tu tisay chitar...

Fear, anxiety, and worry: The terrible trio!

We don't always try to categorise or label our feelings clinically when we suffer from anxiety attacks or panic disorders. Most of us tend to use the words fear, anxiety, worry, and panic interchangeably.

Worry and anxiety are responses to unknown, imprecise or ill-defined threats, often anticipatory in nature and created by the imagination. These threats are more associated with the need to be prepared. Worrying about potential problems in the future leads to feelings of anxiety.

Fear and panic are responses to known, precise, well-defined threats, which can be real or vividly imagined. Fear uses avoidance and escape to respond to these threats.

Fear and anxiety are similar, but there is one crucial difference between them: the cognitive component of fear is recognisable to us by perception or reasoning. It is the expectation of a clear and specific danger. On the other hand, anxiety is vague and unspecific. "Something awful may happen to me!" "Something terrible is about to happen!" is the typical reaction of anxiety or panic disorder. Fear is based on reality, or an exaggeration of a real danger. Anxiety is based on an irrational or formless danger.

Man is constantly given to worrying about the future. What does this anxiety do for us? It may not empty our tomorrows of sorrow, but it will certainly empty our today of its strength. And if the future should bring problems with it, this feeling of anxiety makes us unfit to cope with those problems. Therefore, it has been said, "Getting anxious about the future is like a rocking chair. It will keep on moving, but will not get you anywhere!" Such needless anxiety is like the advance interest you pay on troubles that may never come your way!

God has endowed us with the health and strength that we need. He has blessed us with the means and resources to tackle our life each day, as it comes. He gives us the strength and courage to face each day, each moment of our lives. Why then should we trouble ourselves over the future?

The endless cycle

"I am overwhelmed by constant anxiety," a sister said to me.

"What is it that you worry about?" I asked her.

"I'm worried about my daughter, who is expecting a baby," she began. "Also, I'm anxious to find a suitable girl for my only son."

"If that is your…" I began.

"That's not all," she interrupted. "I have only just begun."

"Do go on," I sighed.

"I'm worried about my husband's blood pressure," she continued. "And I'm constantly anxious about my old mother who lives all alone in the village. And I'm on edge at my workplace. I don't think my boss appreciates my work. And I'm dreadfully worried about the future! What will become of our savings with inflation rising so high, and interest rates falling constantly…"

I was reminded of the words of Seneca: "He grieves more than is necessary, who grieves before it is necessary."

Many people complain of anxiety, tension and nervous exhaustion. I am inclined to think that this is seldom the result of present trouble or work, but of trouble or work anticipated. It comes with the constant strain of looking ahead and climbing mountains before we ever reach the foothills.

"I'm so unhappy and worried this morning," one woman complained to another.

"What is it?" asked her friend sympathetically.

"I was worrying about something last night," said the woman, "and now I can't, for the life of me, remember what it was."

It is said that the first experimental steam engines actually wasted ninety percent of the energy of the coal they used. When the electric dynamo was designed, it was said to utilise ninety percent of the power, with the wastage reduced to ten percent. When we are reduced to a state of constant anxiety, we too, fritter away all our energy in fretting, fuming, in scolding and complaining.

It is in our hands to convert all our energy into power, vitality, and the sunshine of good cheer!

Anxiety is all-pervasive

Did you know that there are 'anxiety experts' who have done much research and analysis on worrying? I heard about 'anxiety experts' and 'worry professionals' from a friend who told me about an online 'worry club'. They even operate a 24-hour phone line where a worry professional will speak to you and help you to deal with your worry and anxiety.

A 'worry expert' remarks that people are so used to worrying that even when you save them from drowning, put them on the bank safe and dry, and offer them hot chocolate and muffins, they will begin to grow anxious that they may catch a cold!

I have spoken about this online club only to show you how all-pervasive worrying has become today!

People get anxious about small as well as big issues. Young people worry about their romantic relationships; young girls even worry about pimples on their faces; young men are anxious about dandruff on their scalp. To us, these might be laughing matters, but not to those who worry about these issues. Middle aged people are anxious about their insurance, investments, and repairs to their homes. Old people worry about slipping and falling in the bathroom. There is simply no limit to the worry-anxiety syndrome.

The trouble with anxiety is that once you allow it to enter your system, it often becomes a chronic condition; if you start worrying, you will find it very difficult to stop. Such is the chronic nature of worriers, that if they momentarily stop worrying, they imagine that there is a disaster about to strike them. In other words, they worry about not being worried! In this state of constant worry they are unable to relax– and in this state of stress and tension, they cannot find solutions to their problems, they cannot face up to the challenges of life!

The physical, emotional, and psychological effects of worry have been catalogued, analysed and documented by medical experts and counsellors. Worry and anxiety can lead to acidity and ulcers, and may even cause cardiac problems. We lose the joy of living; we fail to live life fully.

Little wonder that Benjamin Franklin described worry in the following terms: "A God, invisible but omnipotent, worry steals the bloom from the cheek and lightness from the pulse; it takes away the appetite and turns the hair grey…"

Anxiety is futile

We worry about things which may never happen. Why worry? Why be anxious?

They say that experts in the U.S.A. conducted a major survey among thousands of people to understand the causes of anxiety. Based on the survey's results, 40% of all our worries relate to things which may not happen. 30% of our worries relate to things that have already happened in the past, and we can do nothing about them now. But still we keep on worrying about them. 12% of our worries relate to illnesses, many of them are imagined afflictions which have been classified by doctors as a new disease, *symptomatic imaginitis*. Indeed, 82% of our worries are futile. Another 10% of our worries relate to our friends, our near and dear ones, relatives who are quite capable of taking care of themselves. However, we persist in worrying about them!

All of the above worries account for 92% of worries. The remaining 8% of worries are the only worries that may have some basis and that are worth any attention. Consider for yourself how absurd our situation is. 100 worries come to us, out of which only 8 require some little attention. However, we give the same importance to the other 92 trivial worries. I want to place this calculation before you in clear terms so that you may realise the futility of worrying, the folly of worrying, the absurdity of worrying. Why be anxious? Why be anxious? Why carry so many thoughts of anxiety in your hearts?

Ten steps towards an anxiety-free life

1. Realise once and for all the sheer uselessness of anxiety and worry. They are not going to solve your problems. They will only cloud your vision and make your brain dysfunctional.

2. Develop the will, NOT to get anxious. Every morning as you wake up, even before you open your eyes, say to yourself: here is a bright new day, which comes to me as a gift from the spotless hands of God. How am I going to spend it? By worrying or by not

worrying? The choice is mine! Choose not to get anxious.

3. All worries and anxieties are excess baggage that we are carrying. Dump the excess baggage! Travel light on the beautiful journey of life. Discard all worries and anxieties at the Lotus Feet of the Lord. Let Him take care of them!

4. Do not make mountains out of molehills. Develop a sense of proportion about your problems.

5. Learn to look at the bright side of things, the silver lining behind every cloud. There is a flip side to the worst of problems.

6. Shut the gates on the past; therefore quit agonising over past mistakes and tragedies.

7. Do not let your anxious mind become the devil's workshop. Therefore, keep busy all the time! Keep yourself constructively occupied. You must be so busy that you don't have time to worry!

8. Learn the art of true relaxation. If you are relaxed in body and mind, if you go about your work quietly, sweetly, gently, meeting people, speaking to them softly, you will find that worry will not be able to touch you.

9. Have faith in the goodness and in the caring power of God. When God is in charge of life, why should we worry?

10. Practise the 'therapy of thanksgiving'. Express your gratitude to God for the countless gifts he has bestowed on you. Gratitude nullifies all negative feelings like fear, worry, anxiety and despair!

Attachment- Free Yourself!

I would say that attachment to the body, clinging to worldly pleasures, slavery to the senses, the tendency to accumulate material wealth, and the craving for more and more, are fundamental causes of human unhappiness. Greed, one of the seven deadly sins, binds people with fetters that shackle their capacity for self-fulfilment and inner harmony. Once we become prisoners of desire, it becomes impossible to live our lives in joy and peace. Contentment becomes a distant dream within the restricting structures of materialism, greed and accumulation.

The Gita tells us that attachment of any kind leads to suffering. *Raga, abhinivesha* (clinging and attachment) as it is called, is an impediment– not only on the path of liberation, but also in the attainment of personal happiness. On the other hand, detachment is one of life's greatest lessons for those who seek the true joy of life.

You are not the body! You are the immortal soul within! Therefore, do not become a slave of the body. Do not keep running after the shadow shapes that come and go! The Light of lights shines in your Spirit! Kindle the Light within!

Attachment to wealth and possessions

Man keeps on accumulating. I ask some of the rich people I meet, "What are you going to do with the millions you have saved?" They tell me, "This is not the time to think of it. Now we are busy making millions. When the time comes, we will think of how to spend those millions." Alas, this is the tragedy of man– he thinks he has plenty of time! But suddenly, too suddenly, death pounces upon him. Leaving everything behind, man leaves the world. He had time for everything except self-realisation and awareness of the truth of life!

The more we are attached to a house, a car, a piece of jewellery or an object, the more we lay ourselves open and vulnerable to unhappiness. The desire to possess gradually leads to the impulse to accumulate and hoard. Invariably, we begin "keeping up with the Joneses" as they say in England– constantly comparing ourselves with our neighbours, and trying to be one level above them.

There is no lasting happiness to be found in the objects and pleasures of this material world. In God alone can we find true joy and peace.

Attachment to people

'Possessiveness' in personal relationships acts like poison. When we try to monopolise the affections of our near and dear ones, when we try to run their lives according to our rules, we are striking at the very root of our personal relationships. Therefore, it is necessary to cultivate 'detachment' even to the people we love.

Mothers get too attached to their sons, and lose the chance of a loving relationship with their daughters-in-law. Equally, wives get too attached to their husbands and develop needless antagonism towards his parents and family. Fathers are so possessive about their sons, that they want the youngsters to follow closely in their footsteps and become doctors/actors/politicians.

Detachment does not mean indifference or lack of care and concern. It only means you stop attempting to control others, and avoid judging others on your own terms. Here, as elsewhere, love is for giving– not for taking or demanding!

Attachment to the past

It does us no good to cling to the past, for the past is something which we can never return to in reality.

I read about a woman who fell on hard days when her husband died. Left to fend for herself and her two children, she regressed into her past– her childhood in which she had lived a comfortable life as the adored daughter of well-to-do parents. She began to relive the 1930s– dressing, talking, and behaving in the manner of those days to such an extent that she became the butt of people's ridicule.

It is a serious mistake to become a slave of your own past.

Attachment to one's 'image'

Some people become exceedingly obsessed with their physical appearance, bringing great misery upon themselves.

The Greek myths tell us of Narcissus, a handsome youth who was so carried away by his own good looks that he spent all his time gazing at his own reflection. Thus he broke the hearts of many young maids who loved him and longed to marry him. As a punishment for his self-centred, self-focussed attitude, he was turned into a flower that grew on the banks of ponds and streams– bending over to look at its own reflection in the water.

Today, 'narcissism' is a term psychologists use to describe an unhealthy obsession with oneself and one's own appearance.

A great Indian yogi puts it thus: "The saints tell us to treat this human body but as a temporary residence. Do not be attached to it or bound by it. Realise the infinite power of the immortal soul which dwells within this corpse of sensation."

Alas, we are unaware of this great truth. We are obsessed with the physical and the material. We look at the mirror, and we are dismayed by the wrinkles on our foreheads, and the grey hair on our heads. I am told that film stars suffer from severe stress and insecurity with each passing year, and that they are prepared to spend hundreds of thousands on cosmetic surgery, just to remove wrinkles and creases. Attachment and vanity result from excessive body-consciousness!

Is it not a paradox that when we cling to the body, it tends to wither and lose its shine? When we disregard the body and use it merely as an instrument of service, it begins to glow with health and radiance!

Freeing the self from identification with the body, we become aware of the truth that nothing belongs to us, no one belongs to us. Therefore, the multiplicity of conditions, the manifold problems that we confront in life will not overwhelm us anymore. We will remember Sri Krishna's words to Arjuna: *Nimitta matram savya sachin*– "O, Arjuna, be thou a mere instrument only."

This is indeed the best way to think of our physical form– as an instrument bestowed upon us to live life upon this earth.

Attachment to creed, dogma and ideology

Some people are so passionate about their beliefs, their values and what they consider to be right and wrong, that they resent anyone who disagrees with them.

There are very many fanatics who consider their religion as the true religion, their God as the true God, and their scripture as the only true scripture. They utter curses and damnation on all those who do not share their faith. This is of course, bigotry of the worst kind.

Attachment to winning

Everyone likes success– but success should not turn into an obsession.

Do you remember the wicked step mother in the fairy tale, who uttered the unforgettable lines:

Mirror, mirror on the wall, who's the fairest of us all?

As long as she 'won' the contest, and the mirror replied, "You!" she was very happy. But the moment she ceased to be "the fairest", she turned ugly– metaphorically speaking!

When we are obsessed with the need to win, we become incapable of enjoying the fame of life. The need to "win at all costs" led to one of the greatest political scandals of the 20th century: Watergate, which resulted in the disgraceful episode of the impeachment of a sitting American President, Richard Nixon.

Attachment to work

Some of us are excessively attached, nay, obsessed with the work we do!

Work is worship– and karma (action) is unavoidable for those who are born on this earth. But the secret of inner peace is to work without attachment to the results.

The laws of nature drive all of us to activity, for we cannot survive without action. But the wise ones act without attachment, with detachment, without looking for outcomes. Success and failure do not influence their attitude to their duty.

Of course, some of you are bound to ask, "Is it really possible for us to act without desiring any kind of results?"

There are people who are constantly chasing 'goals' and 'targets'– more money, a better job, higher pay, spectacular success, increased productivity, and greater satisfaction. Yet others grumble and complain all the time, because they feel their work is unrecognised, unrewarded, and unappreciated.

How may we avoid such disappointment, frustration, and this restless drive that arises from excessive attachment to our work?

Simply by surrendering the fruits of one's actions to the Lord! Let us stop chasing after 'personal satisfaction' and 'individual happiness.' Let us make our work, all our work, an offering to the Lord.

Do your best– and leave the rest to God! When you allow yourself to become an instrument of God, you will find that you can actually work more efficiently, and achieve greater success– for you will be freed from your own personal limitations.

When you rid yourself of the desire to 'achieve' results, when you are free from anxiety and stress that arises from expectations, you escape the twin perils of egoistic arrogance on one hand, and dejection or depression on the other.

Attachment can be deadly!

Do you know how monkeys are captured in the tropical jungles of the world? Not in traps or cages– for monkeys are too smart, too agile, too swift to be caught through trapping.

What their captors do is place peanuts, brazil nuts, and other 'monkey nuts' as they are called, in large jars with narrow mouths, and leave them about in the areas frequented by wild monkeys. The monkey sees the 'treasure' and hurriedly thrusts its paw inside the bottle to grab the nuts.

Too late, it realises that it cannot withdraw its paw which is now closed tight with the nuts inside the 'fist', caught at the bottom of the glass jar. Monkeys are 'primates'– our biological ancestors in the scale of evolution. They are intelligent enough to realise that if they let go of the nuts, they can somehow manage to squeeze their paws out of the glass jar with minimal damage. But alas, they are 'human' enough not to be able to let go!

All the monkey will have to do is drop its treasure– and it will regain its freedom. The trouble is that it cannot, and will not let go!

Such is the deadly power of attachments. If only we would let them go, we would be light, happy, and free!

Remedy for excessive attachment

You are not expected to renounce the world and go off to the *tapobana* to seek self-realisation. The trick is to be in the world, but not of it.

Therefore, mental, emotional renunciation– in other words, detachment– has to be cultivated. Love– yes, lust– no; money and savings to provide for the future– yes, amassing wealth beyond measure– no. A saint often pointed out, laughing, that a miser's wealth would only get squandered away by irresponsible sons and daughters, by thieves, or in property litigations!

Viveka and *vairagya* (discrimination between true and false and detachment) are recommended by Sri Krishna in the Gita, to cure us from the raging fever of desire and attachment. Indeed, they are remedies that all of us can adopt. They may sound tough, but like the best medicines, they heal us when they are taken seriously!

Camels on the rooftop

Jalaluddin Rumi speaks of King Ibrahim in whose heart was the longing to see God. But he was still attached to his kingship. One day, as he is about to fall asleep, he hears footsteps on his roof. Looking out of the window, he calls sharply, "Who goes there?" The answer comes from the rooftop, "I have lost my camels, and I am searching for them."

Half amused and half annoyed, the king cries, "What an idiot you must be, to search for camels on a rooftop!"

Back comes the answer, "No worse than you, O king, who, sitting on your throne, tries to seek union with God!"

The king's spiritual journey begins at this point. He renounces his kingdom and sets out to seek the truth.

How may we conquer attachment?

- Grow in the thought that nothing belongs to you, nothing is really yours. If something you value and cherish is lost or stolen, learn to say to yourself, as the philosopher Epictetus did, in similar circumstances, "I have given it back!"

Attachment – Free Yourself!

- Do not cling to your possessions! Cultivate what Huxley describes as the spirit of affective poverty– being indifferent to money. This is different from effective poverty– possessing no money. A man may have no money– and yet within him the craving may be strong for things which money can buy. Another man, like Raja Janak, may have the wealth of the entire kingdom, and yet be detached from possessions, power or position, which money can bring.

- Be detached! If you have an impulse to give something away, give it without hesitation, give it readily and cheerfully. Until we have learnt to give, we cannot grow in spiritual strength! Unless we learn to detach ourselves from the body, we cannot find the Light of Truth!

One final thought...

Who is the truly happy man? He who desires nothing, claims nothing, expects nothing, and is free from hatred and fear.

Attitude Counts!

When attitudes are right, there is no barrier we cannot cross, no dream we cannot realise, no goals we cannot achieve, no challenges we cannot overcome. Our living is determined not so much by what life brings to us, as by the attitude we bring to life. Our life is fashioned not by what happens to us, as by the way our mind perceives what happens. Attitude far supersedes our past, our education, money, circumstances, and skills.

We must be careful to see that we always have a positive attitude towards life. By this I do not mean that life does not have a negative side. But the man with a positive approach refuses to dwell on the unpleasant aspects of life. Surrounded by the most adverse conditions, he will look for a place to stand on. Conditions all around him may be frustrating, but he will not give up. He will continue to expect the best results, and this is an inviolable law of life– what you expect persistently, comes rushing to you. For you only draw to yourselves, that which you think of all the time. Your thoughts are magnets. Through your thoughts, you draw to yourself conditions and circumstances on which you contemplate constantly.

The Law of Attraction

The universe works like an echo. Whatever thoughts you think, will rebound on you. This is the Law of Attraction. You attract to yourself what you consistently think of.

No, we cannot change circumstances at will, but we can change our attitude to circumstances. And I firmly believe, you are not a failure until you give up trying. You cannot be defeated, except from within. There is no insurmountable barrier except your own weakness. There is no problem that you and God cannot handle together.

This therefore, is one of the crucial choices you must make: cultivate the right attitude! Change your attitude– and change your life! A man with the right mental attitude is unstoppable from achieving his goal. By the same token, no power on earth can assist a man who suffers from a wrong attitude of mind.

From the pages of recent history

Dr. S. Radhakrishnan, the great scholar and philosopher, and the then President of India, made his first visit to the United States when John F. Kennedy was the President. The weather was dark and stormy in Washington. When Dr. Radhakrishnan alighted from the plane, it began to pour cats and dogs, as the expression goes.

The young American President greeted his Indian counterpart with a warm handshake and a smile. "I'm so sorry we have such bad weather during your visit," he remarked courteously.

The philosopher statesman smiled. "We can't change bad things, Mr. President," he observed. "But we can change our attitude to them."

Our deep wounds and painful, emotional injuries arise not as much by other people and their harsh words, than by our own attitude and response to them.

Positive attitudes attract success

There are people who focus their attention only on problems and difficulties. Tell them of your dreams and plans, and they will say, "No, No! It is impossible! It will never work." They will point out all the drawbacks and weaknesses in your plan, and try their best to convince you that you cannot win. These are the people who can boast, "Bring me a solution and I will give you a problem!"

The truth is, there is no problem that does not have a solution. The man with a positive attitude thinks of the solution– while the man with a negative attitude only thinks of the problem. We need people who bring solutions to problems, not problems to solutions. Be positive in your approach and you will find solutions to all your problems. The man with a positive attitude may be surrounded by adverse conditions, yet he will seek a solution; he will expect the best results, and he will invariably succeed. Remember, this is the great law of life. That which you expect, always comes to you. It may come to you tomorrow, it may come to you fourteen years hence, but it will surely come to you. Therefore, why not expect the very best? Expect success and you will achieve success!

How attitudes influence our life

Many people ask me, "How can thinking change my life? How can it change the world around me which is the cause of all my problems?"

An attitude is born out of persistent thinking. And I say to you: Thoughts are forces; thoughts can influence our actions and change our personalities; thoughts are the building blocks of our life; thoughts are the foundation of our attitudes. A thought, if it is constantly held in the mind, will drive us to action. An action, which is repeated, creates a habit. The sum total of our habits forms our character, which determines our destiny. Therefore, if we wish to change our destiny, we must begin with the thought. Change the pattern of your thinking– and you can alter your life for the better!

Positive attitude to work

In a research on working women, it was found that even among those doing the same kind of jobs, some people viewed work as a series of hassles, while others saw it as a positive experience in which they were in control of their lives. Among those who felt positive about their work, satisfaction was 30% higher.

If you would see your work only as a 'job', then it drags you down. If you see it as a calling, a vocation, then it is no longer toil or trouble. It becomes an expression of yourself, a part of you.

Whether you are engaged in your own business or at a job, or engaged in house-work, you must exude optimism and positive thinking– and you will find it reflected right back at you!

There is a very small difference between people, but that small anomaly can lead to a major difference. That slight difference is attitude. The major difference lies in whether the attitude is positive or negative. Through a positive attitude, magically and effortlessly, we get connected to and perceive myriad opportunities, which previously had not been visible.

Choose a positive attitude

Here is an exercise that you can do to check your attitude:

1. Do you often use negative words or expressions in your conversation? (This can't be done, it's impossible, I can't make it and so on) If you think the answer is yes, switch to more positive words and expressions like, "Yes, I can", "Sure, it will be done" etc.

2. How often do you think well about yourself and others? Look out for things that you can be positive about. Find out aspects about yourself and others which you like.

3. How often do you smile? Smiling automatically puts you in a positive frame of mind.

How to cultivate a positive attitude

- A positive attitude cannot be taught, it must be caught. Therefore, be careful of the company you keep. If you move in the fellowship of people with positive attitude, their positive and beneficial vibrations and energy will influence you to develop an optimistic spirit.

- Shampoo your mind every day to sweep away all negative thoughts. Cleanse your mind of all adverse and detrimental thoughts and fill it with fresh, invigorating, positive thoughts.

- An expert tailor says that the best way to keep clothes in good shape is to make sure that the pockets are emptied when they are hung up. We may infer from this, that the best way to keep ourselves and our lives in good shape is to empty our minds of all worries, anxieties, tensions, and negative thoughts before we retire for the night. We can then begin the new day with energy, vigour and freshness.

- Whenever your mind is driving you towards negative thinking, affirm to yourself positive thoughts that will change the track of your thinking. Positive affirmations and positive visualisations make a world of difference to your thinking patterns.

- The world's scriptures are full of dynamic, positive, energetic thoughts which have the power to boost your morale and keep your spirits high. Choose any inspiring thought that appeals to you and repeat it to yourself constantly.

- Count your blessings and express gratitude for them! Gratitude is the best antidote to negative thinking.

The great psychiatrist, Karl Menninger, has said, "Think big. Men do not break down because they are defeated, but only because they think they are." Do not think and invite defeat; think victory. Think big, act big, believe big, pray big. This is the formula for a positive attitude!

The decision about the longevity of our lives does not lie with us, but we can surely choose how much life those years will hold. We may not be able to determine and manipulate the beauty of our face, but we can surely control our expression on it. We do not have any power over life's difficult and turbulent moments, but we can definitely choose to make life less difficult. We can in no way transform negative atmospheres of the world, but we have the ability to control the atmosphere that prevails in our mind. We slave and toil to bring those situations under our control which we are unable to, but seldom do we attempt to control that which is in our power to do so– our attitude.

Change your attitude– and change your life!

Awakening

Awakening is becoming aware of the world within. Every man is a carrier of tremendous energies. As long as he regards the external world as real, all these energies are being drained away into the external world. Once he awakens to his inner reality, once he shuts his eyes on the external and turns within, all these energies will lift him up to a state where he may experience the soundless bliss of the Eternal.

This is true awakening!

Awakening is not just waking up from slumber; it is also a dawn of awareness, of becoming consciously connected with the Divine within us! For this, you must cease to be a creature of the mind, and become aware of your link with a higher consciousness. Mere thinking becomes subservient to a higher consciousness!

True awakening is living with dynamic imagination, responding sincerely and courageously to opportunities, avoiding the temptation to fall prey to habits.

The *shakti* within

Gurudev Sadhu Vaswani often said to us, "You are not a weakling as some of you imagine yourselves to be. In you is a hidden *shakti*, an energy that is of Eternity."

The question is, how do we awaken this *shakti*? Consider Mahatma Gandhi. He was an ordinary man, just like you and me. But he had awakened the inner *shakti*, and hence could wage a successful battle, a battle without any weapons, a battle without bloodshed, against the mighty British Empire.

I once read the story of a beggar who lived under a tree. He sat there through rain and sunshine, day and night, summer and winter. He was homeless and lived in abject poverty. He ate whatever people threw into his begging bowl. One day he fell ill; his body was racked by pain and fever. He had no money to buy medicine or go to a doctor for treatment. He lay under the tree, ill and delirious until death released his soul from his wasted, emaciated body. A life of utter misery had come to an end. The municipal workers accorded him the last dignity of a destitute funeral. He had left the world, unwept, unhonoured, unlamented.

A few days passed. The plot of land which he had made his home was acquired by a construction company in order to build a commercial complex. Heavy equipment was brought to dig the ground and lay the foundation for a huge building. When they had dug deep under the tree, the construction workers found a pot filled with silver and gold coins. This poor beggar had been literally sitting on a pot of gold; yet he had lived a life of sheer deprivation. He was unaware of the treasure he was sitting on!

The power that can transform your life

Are we not like this poor beggar? An enormous treasure of *shakti* lies locked and hidden within us. But we go through life without ever unfolding this *shakti*, without using it for our own betterment. Little do we realise that we have the hidden potential that can transform our lives. There is a powerhouse within us, yet we live in a state of permanent power failure! Becoming aware of this power is awakening to the reality of the Self!

There is, within every one of us, a hidden soul that lies asleep.

Blessed is the man in whom the hidden soul awakens. He realises that the world with its pleasures, possessions and power, is a passing show.

He wants the Real.

As a pilgrim, he sets out in quest of God, he seeks God, he loves God. In love, he loses himself and finds the Beloved.

He becomes one with Him, one with the Universal Life— one with every animate or inanimate object.

The first thing we must do in order to awaken this *shakti*, is to turn the mind inward, towards the powerhouse within us. Turning inward is not easy, for our senses are constantly engaged in drawing the mind outward. Lured by the five senses, the mind roams far and wide, and begins to wander aimlessly, for these senses ignite desires, wants and needs. There is but one way to focus the mind inwards— the way of *abhyasa*, of meditation.

Meditation brings the awareness: "I am not this physical body that I wear. I am the eternal *atman*. My soul is not bound by this body or the senses. My life is precious. It is a gift from God, given to me for a specific purpose, a higher purpose." When this realisation dawns on us, we rise above our lower self, the ego-self, the self of passion and pride, of lust and hatred and greed. When we abandon this ego-self, we realise the *Vedic* injunction: *Tat Twam Asi!* That art thou! Is this not the ultimate awakening to the ultimate truth?

Reciting verses from the Holy scriptures and reflecting on them will also help us awaken to the higher Self. We will perceive the beautiful interior-space of our immortal souls. We will experience the kind of peace and joy that surpasses all worldly pleasures we have ever felt. We will discover the power of the Spirit within us. We will feel truly awakened.

Awakening can come in a variety of ways

Awakening comes in a variety of ways. But it is always a gift of grace.

When God or a God-man looks upon someone in grace, the soul within him is awakened. And he realises that the years spent in accumulating the wealth or honours of the earth were wasted in vain. The awakened soul turns its back on worldly pleasures and longs for union with the One Beloved. He lives a life of self-control and self-denial, without which no progress may be made on the path.

God's grace sometimes works through a shocking incident, and in that shock you awaken. Sadhu Vaswani used to give us the example of Raja Bhartrihari.

Bhartrihari was a noble, virtuous, kind and compassionate king. His subjects were happy under his benign rule. Once, a group of holy men visited him. They brought to him an *amarphal* (a fruit that bestows immortality). "O Raja, king of our hearts, please accept this rare and precious fruit from us. In the whole world, there is only one *amarphal*; and we wish that you, our noble king should have it. We have brought it to you because you are the one person who deserves to live for ever and ever more."

Bhartrihari accepted the fruit. But as he was about to eat it, he said to himself, "Of what use is life to me without my beloved? Let me give this *amarphal* to my wife, whom I love more than my life. Let her live for ever and ever more."

So the king passed the *amarphal* to his wife saying, "This is the fruit of immortality, eat it, and you, my beloved, will never die." The queen accepted the fruit. But as destiny would have it, she was secretly in love with the coachman. She said to herself, "Of what use will this fruit be to me if I live on, but my dear coachman perishes?" So she passed on the fruit to the coachman.

As for the coachman, he was in love with a prostitute. He handed over the fruit to the prostitute.

In a moment of rare introspection, the prostitute said to herself, "Of what use is life to me? The longer I live, the more sins I commit and the more I drag other people into a life of sinfulness. If there is anyone who deserves to live eternally, it is our great, good and just king, Raja Bhartrihari."

So back came the *amarphal* to Raja Bhartrihari. The king was amazed, he was dumbfounded! How did the fruit get into the hands of this prostitute? He made inquiries. He found that his wife had been unfaithful to him.

"What a fool I was to have placed my trust in the world and in a creature of this world!" he said to himself. "Let me lay all my trust in Him who never fails us. Let me set out in quest of the One and only One Beloved, the first and the only Fair, the Purest of the pure, the Spotless, the Stainless." Raja Bhartrihari renounced the world, and became a *jignasu*, a seeker after truth…

Now if you get a shock like this your sleeping soul wakes up. Or it may happen in a more quiet, calm mode. Say, you are sitting in a *satsang* and you hear a song, a line of which penetrates your heart and you look within; you say to yourself, what have I done with my life till now. So Sadhu Vaswani said to us, this awakening can come to us in a variety of ways…

I think of the Master's powerful words: "I have only one tongue but if I had a hundred tongues, with every one of those hundred tongues I would utter this one word: Awake! Awake! Awake! In our language: *Jago! Jago! Jago!*"

Begin the Day with God

The first thing we do on getting up in the morning shapes the entire day. Does it not stand to reason that we should begin the day right?

We must rise in the early hours of dawn, when divine vibrations are at their most positive and powerful, and spend a few minutes in silence. The *brahma muhurt* as it is called, is especially conducive to spiritual growth. What better way to nourish the soul than connecting with God at this sacred hour?

Begin the day well– and God will take care of the rest of the day!

Every day, as you wake up in the morning, let there be a simple prayer on your lips. Let me share with you the prayer that I offer to God:

O Lord! This new day comes to me as a gift from Thy spotless hands.
You have taken care of me throughout the night,
and I am sure You will keep watch over me throughout the day.
Praise be to Thee, O Lord. Blessed be Thy Name.
Blessed be Thy Name. Blessed be Thy Name!

You can reword this prayer if you like, in your own way. But make sure you begin the day by remembering God– with a prayer on your lips.

Daily appointment with God

Gurudev Sadhu Vaswani always emphasised that it was very important to pray, meditate and engage ourselves in a loving and intimate conversation with God. He called it "a daily appointment with God" which we must never forget.

There was a businessman who had risen to become one of the richest in the world. His days were always packed with meetings and visits. In spite of his busy schedule, he found time to speak with God first thing in the morning and before he went to sleep at night. Early one morning, he was told that he had an important visitor. "Let him wait in the anteroom," he said, "I have an appointment with God."

Why should we begin the day with God?

Every morning, as we awake, God gives us a precious, brand new day– 24 hours multiplied by 60 minutes multiplied again by 60 seconds! Let us spend each day to move closer to Him!

I have a personal preference for the early morning hour, and I have no hesitation in recommending it to you, too. The mind is quiet, peaceful, refreshed and rested after the night's sleep; all the negative impressions accumulated on the previous day have been erased, and you have a fresh, clean, blank page on which to begin writing. Above all, when you begin the day with God and meditate before you start your daily routine, you will not only find yourself spiritually and emotionally energised, you will also get a positive direction and power to take you through the rest of the day.

In silence, let us pray, meditate, repeat the Name Divine, do our spiritual thinking, engage ourselves in a loving and intimate conversation with God.

The secret of a saintly soul

There was a man of God who spread the sunshine of faith, hope, joy and optimism wherever he went. Whomsoever he met, he changed their lives for the better.

"What is the secret of this great joy that seems to radiate from your very presence?" they asked him.

In answer, he narrated the following incident from his life.

Years earlier, when he decided to leave home to tread the spiritual path, his mother walked along with him to the outskirts of the village, to bid him farewell, and to bestow her blessings on his spiritual quest.

Knowing that she would have to say goodbye to her loving son– perhaps never to see him again– she said to him, "Promise me one thing before your leave."

"What is it mother?" he asked her gently.

"Promise me first," she insisted.

"As you wish, dear mother," said the young man, "I promise to do as you wish."

"This is what I wish," said the mother earnestly. "Dear son, it is a wicked world into which you are going to seek your salvation. I want you to be safe from all harm and evil. Therefore, promise me this– begin every day with God; and close every day with God. This is all I ask of you." And she kissed him fondly on the forehead.

"It was this kiss– and this promise that my mother asked of me– that gave direction to my life," the holy man concluded. "My mother taught me the true secret of joy and peace– begin the day with God; and end the day with God."

A simple exercise for you

May I suggest a simple exercise to begin the day with God? Every morning, as you awaken, close your eyes and imagine the Life of God coursing through every part of your body, filling it through and through. The Life of God is already in us; we have to be conscious of it. Say to yourself: every moment, the Life of God, call Him by what name you will– Krishna, Buddha, Christ, Guru Nanak, is filling every nerve and cell and fibre of my being!

Our lives need to be renewed, daily, through contact with God. The rain of God's mercy pours every day; those of us who receive it are washed clean, renewed and re-energised to face the struggle of life, as servants of God.

The gardener who longed to see God

There was a poor gardener, whose dearest wish was to have a *darshan* of the Lord in his lifetime. He fasted and prayed and sent out his fervent aspirations that this boon may be granted to him. God, in His infinite mercy, heard the gardener's prayer, and conveyed to him the message that He would appear before His humble devotee in the garden where he worked, the following day. The man was overjoyed that his lifelong aspiration was to come true. He was excited and ecstatic; he felt that he simply would not be able to eat or sleep till that precious morrow arrived, when he would behold His God face to face.

That evening, a rich man came round to the hutment area in which the gardener lived. To celebrate the birth of a son, he distributed velvet blankets to all the poor people in the locality. Our gardener too, received a velvet blanket; he had never seen anything like it; it felt so soft and smooth and quite luxurious!

"Why, the Goddess of Fortune has begun to smile on me, at long last," he thought to himself. "Tomorrow, the Lord Himself is coming to visit me at my workplace. And today, He has sent me this rich gift for my personal comfort! I am indeed lucky!"

That night he covered himself in the velvet folds of the blanket and fell into a deep sleep. When the cock began to crow at daybreak, he covered his face and snuggled deeper inside the blanket. He did not get up in the early hours of the morning, as he usually did. In deep sleep, he muttered to himself, "The Lord can wait a bit for me…"

When he finally opened his eyes, it was too late. The Lord had already passed through the garden and he had missed the opportunity of having His *darshan*. The gardener wept and moaned and begged the Lord's pardon. Once again, in His infinite mercy, the Lord promised him that he would appear in his garden at the sacred hour of *brahma muhurt*. The gardener promised himself that he would get up at that holy hour and receive the blessings of the Lord. But the soft warmth of the velvet blanket made him too lazy to get out of the bed, leave his hut in the early hours of the dawn and walk to his garden for the promised *darshan* of the Lord. In this way, he lost the golden opportunity of experiencing the presence of God.

We may laugh at the gardener, but the truth is that many of us are like him. We are so wrapped up in worldly tasks and material pleasures, that we do not make the effort to grow and evolve spiritually.

Believe and Achieve!

There was a man who had set out on a mission to go around the world on his bicycle. He came to meet my beloved Master, Sadhu Vaswani, and said to him, "I have been on the road for over a year now. And during this year, there have been occasions when my spirits have fallen very low. I have felt discouraged and frustrated. Give me a few simple words that I can inscribe on my ring, so that whenever I feel depressed, I can look at the inscription and feel my spirits rising!"

Sadhu Vaswani thought for a brief while and then gave him these words: "Believe and achieve!"

These three words are one of the secrets of success– believe and achieve! Believe in yourself, believe in the work you have undertaken. Believe that you will succeed in your work. If you do not believe in yourself, how can you hope to succeed?

Believe and achieve! In order to do this, faith is essential. It is a triple faith that men need today– faith in oneself, faith in the world around, which is not merely just but essentially good, and above all, faith in God. If you cultivate this triple faith, you are bound to succeed in whatever you do!

Believe in yourself– but which self?

We must remember, there are two selves within every man. There is a lower self– the ego self, the empiric self, the self with which we are only too familiar in our day-to-day existence. It is the self of passion and pride, lust, hatred, greed, envy, jealousy, resentment, ill-will, selfishness and misery. Unfortunately, we have identified ourselves with this self. This is why in the world today, we have wars and violence, hatred and strife. The lower self sits on the threshold of our consciousness, and easily captures us, misleads us, leads us astray. And yet, it is just a tiny self. When you enter into the depths of meditation, you will realise that it is but a tiny speck of a speck of a speck of a speck. Because we have identified ourselves with it, we magnify it beyond all proportions and allow it to dominate our life.

There is another self within each one of us– the larger self, the nobler self, the radiant self, the true self, the 'Self Supreme' in the words of the Bhagavad Gita. In the measure in which you identify yourself with the higher self, in that measure success will come to you like an overflowing, ever-full river.

The story of Caruso, the great singer

Some of you may have heard of the great Italian operatic tenor, Enrico Caruso. He performed in major opera houses across Europe and the U.S.A., and was a singing sensation wherever he went. It is said of him, "Enrico Caruso was just not a singer, he was a miracle!"

Truly, Caruso was a miracle! It is said that when he sang with full-throated ease, the power of his voice, the vibrations of his music could actually shatter a glass to pieces. However, only a few people know that Caruso was an utter failure when he began his career. When he gave his first performance, we are told that the audience was so disappointed that they actually took sticks in their hands to drive him off the stage.

Caruso was not the one to give up easily. He was found pacing up and down his room, fervently uttering the words which became the very mantra of his life. What were those words? "You little me, get out of me! You big me, get into me! You little me, get out of me! You big me, get into me!"

Throw out the ego self, the lower self; invite the big self, the Self Supreme to come and take charge of your life. Surely, you will believe and achieve!

Let your heart get there first!

On a cold winter's day, with the temperature below zero, an old pilgrim was making his way to a shrine on the Himalayas.

"My man!" exclaimed a fellow traveller who passed by, "How will you ever get there in such cold weather?"

"My heart got there first," replied the man cheerfully. "It's easy for the rest of me to follow!"

Within each and every one of us is a tremendous potential to overcome obstacles and achieve success, to face difficulties and conquer them. There is just one thing we have to do to tap this vast potential, this tremendous power– we must believe in ourselves.

The strength of belief

Walter Davis was a great athlete who believed and achieved. As a boy, he contracted infantile paralysis, and the doctors feared that he might not be able to walk again.

His mother's loving care and attention put the boy back on his feet. As he began to walk slowly, he saw a boy doing high-jumps and thought to himself that it was something he would love to do. So he began practising high-jumps, until he became very good at it.

Nonetheless, his legs were still weak, and serious competition was out of the question for him. He kept up his painstaking efforts to strengthen them. When he married, his wife understood his aspirations and said to him, "Walter, it is not enough to have power in your legs. You must have power in your mind!"

She coined a new phrase for him: the strength of belief. This, she said, would bring greater strength to his legs.

The strength of belief took Walter Davis to great heights. At the 1952 Summer Olympics in Helsinki, he won the gold medal by setting a new world record at 6 ft $8^{1/4}$ in, propelled by his strength of belief. The boy they said might never walk again, became the champion high jumper of the world! Belief was his strength– he believed and achieved!

You become what you think!

"How can I become a better person?" a youngster once asked me.

I replied simply, "By being a better person, surely!"

Every one of us has some weaknesses, some imperfections, some undesirable qualities. We must try to assess our own weaknesses and work hard to eliminate them. If this seems daunting to you, select just one of your weak points to work on! If you try to tackle your flaws all at once, you may be disheartened by your lack of progress. Select just one weakness and focus your efforts on it. Do not dwell on the weakness itself– that will only fortify your weakness. Rather, focus on your resolution to conquer it.

For instance, if you are easily given to anger, you must not think of your short temper, but of its opposite quality– serenity, peace and tranquillity. The more you focus on these positive qualities, the sooner you will find that these qualities enter your being.

Remember, you become what you think! Think better thoughts, higher thoughts, and you will surely become a better person. You will really believe and achieve! And this will be your greatest victory, your greatest success– to conquer your lower self and overcome your own weaknesses!

Simple methods to believe and achieve

1. Do only that which you feel is right and true. Nothing in life brings about unhappiness and failure more surely than lack of integrity.

2. Do your best each day. Let this be the motto of your life: only the best is good enough for me! When you give to the world the best you have, the best will come back to you.

3. Fully trust in the Divine wisdom that designs and orders the scheme of things. There is a meaning of mercy in all that happens.

4. Plan carefully for each day. Budget your time. Take care of every minute of your time.

5. Begin the day right. Wake up each morning, full of hope and expectation.

6. Never give up! Persistence pays!

7. Tact is as important as talent. Therefore, speak politely, act courteously, respect everyone you meet.

8. Stay young at heart. Age is a state of mind.

9. Reach out to others. You succeed in the measure in which you help others to succeed.

10. Do not be daunted by failure. Failure is just a stepping stone to success.

Bhakti

What is *bhakti*? *Bhakti* is deep love and adoration for the Creator of this universe. This kind of love does not come suddenly. It is cultivated through *Naam Smaran*, through service to others, and by being kind to one and all. *Bhakti* is love for the sake of love. It is devoid of expectation and fear. *Bhakti* is that love which binds the devotee to the Lord. It is identified with deep yearning and longing. The experience of *bhakti* is love in its purest form.

When man begins to understand the reality of his existence, and the reality of the universe, he is mystified. He is in awe of the Supreme Creator and he begins to love Him. Love creates yearning and the yearning becomes a flame. Once the flame is lit, it grows into a sacred fire which destroys all that is evil and negative in our body and mind.

This love, this yearning, this pining and this pain of separation from the Beloved is a blessing which comes through the grace of the Guru. Life without this ache for the Beloved, without yearning for Him is indeed futile.

How can we grow closer to God?

My answer to this question is simple: grow in love. Love all life, for all life is sacred. Love animals, birds, trees, flowers, the sick and the distressed, the lonely and broken ones. This is true devotion, real *bhakti*; *bhakti* begins out of such love. Expand your heart to enfold the world in the embrace of your love, and you will indeed acquire the gift of *bhakti*.

If you wish to go closer to God, then follow the path of love. For at its best, *bhakti* is nothing but supreme love for the Supreme Being.

Bhakti is not taught

Just as God cannot be defined, *bhakti* cannot be explained by abstract reasoning or scholarly analysis. Let me give you an inspiring *sloka* from the *Nuri Granth*:

Love is Krishna
Love is the Light of heaven,
Love is the wisdom of the Gita
Love is God; Love is all…

In the Hindu way of life, the concept of *bhakti* denotes absolute devotion to the Lord. In its highest form, it is a truly sublime feeling, arising out of a pure heart and totally free from the contamination of desire for worldly goods or attainments. The true *bhakta* or devotee seeks God and God alone, for his only goal is liberation from worldly life and union with His beloved Lord. Love is tantamount to liberation. Love is the sole means of transcending time and to unravel the binding knot of existence.

Bhakti is not to be taught or discussed; it is to be caught, it is to be experienced. It is not a science or an art that needs to be learnt; it is an attitude to the Divine and the great gift of life that has been granted to us. It is not a toll-paid expressway meant for the exclusive and the elite; it is the simplest, swiftest and shortest route to God that is open to each one of us. *Bhakti* is a gift that is bestowed on us.

To be drenched in love is, to lose oneself in love, to walk the way of *bhakti*!

What are the requisites we need to attain to *bhakti*?

Degrees and diplomas are not required. Scholarly essays and treatises do not need to be submitted for assessment. Physical austerities or strict disciplines are not really essential. *Punditry* in scripture is not needed. All that we need is a love-filled heart. The Lord says so Himself: "Yet not by the Vedas, nor by austerities, nor by gifts, nor by sacrifices can you know Me. But by devotion to Me alone, devotion undivided, will you know Me and see Me and come unto Me!"

Bhakti Yoga– the path of devotion to the Lord– is in essence, the path of love– love that is unconditional, whole-hearted, selfless and completely fulfilling. Fill all your actions with love. Let your senses, emotions and action, express love.

What are the characteristics of a true *bhakta*?

Chapter XII of the Bhagavad Gita, simply entitled, "*Bhakti Yoga*" or "The Yoga of Devotion", is one of the shortest chapters of the Gita. Sri Krishna chooses to teach Arjuna about *bhakti* by outlining the qualities of His true *bhakta*. Thus this chapter becomes a manual of ideal living, appropriate conduct, and right attitude for those who aspire to walk the way of true devotion.

A *bhakta*, according to the Lord, is so sensitive, so compassionate, that he cannot bear the suffering of others. He shows no hatred or animosity; he has no enemies. He is unmoved by praise or blame. He is ever ready to help everyone in need. He is aware that service to humanity is service to the Lord Himself. He looks upon joy and sorrow with utter equanimity. Just as sweetness cannot be separated from sugar, *bhakti* and humility are conjoined and inseparable. Such a devotee is indeed an ideal human being in this imperfect world of ours.

As an imperfect seeker, how can I begin to walk the way of *bhakti*?

Although we may find it difficult to put into practice the qualities of the ideal *bhakta* outlined by Sri Krishna in this chapter, as seekers on the path, we can begin with simple exercises like repetition of the Name Divine, *kirtan* and meditation which can take us forward on the path. Constant engagements in *pooja* and *seva* also purify the mind. Offering flowers to the deity, lending a helping hand to our fellow human beings, showing kindness to those in distress, reading from the sacred scriptures, listening to stories from the great *puranas*– all these activities help to cleanse and purify the mind, and sow the seeds of *Bhakti Yoga* in us.

Jnana Yoga and *Karma Yoga* are difficult for ordinary mortals. But the ever-merciful Lord does not mean the rest of us to languish without a chance of liberation. Therefore, He recommends the easy way that most of us can take to reach Him– *bhakti marga* or the path of devotion.

In the Gita, the Lord also tells us about four different types of *bhaktas*, people who worship the Lord for different reasons– to seek success in their undertakings (*artharthi bhaktas*); to seek protection in distress (*artha bhaktas*); to seek illumination (*jignasu bhaktas*); and lastly, to seek Him, and Him alone (*jnani bhaktas*). The *jnana bhaktas* are truly the beloved of the Lord.

The *bhavas* of *bhakti*

Our saints and sages speak of five different attitudes or *bhavas* that a *bhakta* assumes in approaching God and building a relationship with Him.

Santa bhava, or calm and placid love for God, is best expressed in the profound piety of our great *acharyas* such as Shankara and Ramanuja, and great *puranic* heroes like Bhishma.

Dasya bhava, or the attitude of a humble servant of the Lord, is seen in the devotion of Hanuman for Sri Rama.

Sakhya bhava, or the attitude of a friend, is seen in Arjuna and the *gwalas* of Brindavan for Sri Krishna.

Vatsalya bhava, or the attitude of a loving parent (especially the mother), to God perceived as a child, is beautifully manifested in Ma Yashoda towards Bal Gopal.

Madhurya bhava, or *shringara bhava*– the attitude of a girl to her lover, is most beautifully exemplified in the Divine love of Radha for her beloved Sri Krishna.

Let me add, the *madhurya bhava* or the *shringara bhava* of *bhakti* is uncontaminated by lower passions like lust and physical attraction. There is no tinge of carnality or eroticism in this form of intimate devotion. Indeed, if one's mind and heart are mired in passion and sensuality, one becomes incapable of true *bhakti*.

What are the different ways in which we may express our *bhakti*?

1. Hearing the stories of the Divine *leela* and plays of Lord Vishnu: this is *shravanam*, and is what Maharaja Parikshit did, with great devotion and reverence, having the *Srimad Bhagavatam* narrated to him by Sage Shuka.

2. Singing or chanting the transcendental Holy Name and qualities of the Lord with heartfelt devotion: this is what we call *kirtan*, and the most well-known exponent of this mode of *bhakti* was Chaitanya Mahaprabhu.

3. Remembering, recalling and reflecting on His glory: this is known as *smaranam*. Bhakta Prahalada himself was the epitome of this mode of *bhakti*.

4. Serving the Lotus Feet of the Lord, or *pada sevanam*: an intense and devout form of *bhakti*, where the Lotus Feet of the Lord become the focus of the devotee's love and prayer. Bharata, who enthroned the sandals of Sri Rama on the throne of Ayodhya and lived with devotion for Rama's Lotus Feet, is the best example of this mode of *bhakti*.

5. Offering the Lord respectful worship: this is called *archanam*. In Hindu homes, this is simply known as *pooja* and is done in most families today.

6. Offering prayers to the Lord, or *vandanam*, as it is called. It is also a supreme form of reverence to the Lord. Many families practise this form of *bhakti*.

7. Becoming His servant in mind, body and Spirit: this is *dasyam* or *dasya kainkaryam*. This mode of *bhakti* is best exemplified by Hanuman.

8. Considering the Lord as one's best friend, developing friendship with Him: this is *sakhyam*. Kuchela Sudama offered this mode of *bhakti* to his beloved friend and fellow disciple, Sri Krishna, whom he had been blessed to know and love from the days of their *gurukul* at Rishi Sandipani's *ashrama*.

9. Surrendering everything to Him: this is *atma nivedanam*. This was what Mahabali offered to the Lord, when He appeared as Vamana, and asked for three paces of land from the great emperor.

These nine modes of *bhakti* are described in the *Prahlada Charitra*. "These nine processes," Prahlada concludes, "are the accepted modes of pure devotional service. One who has dedicated his life to the service of Krishna through these nine methods should be recognised as the most learned person, for he has acquired complete knowledge."

We can cultivate *bhakti* by engaging ourselves in any or all of these beautiful and meaningful devotional activities which will take us closer to God. But let us remember, ultimately, the form, the words, and the actions are secondary: what is most important is a pure and humble heart, free from ego and pride, filled with love for the Lord!

Practical modes of growing in the spirit of *bhakti*

1. Let us establish a link of love and devotion with Krishna or Rama, Buddha or Jesus, Mohammad or Mahavira or Moses, Zoroaster or Baha'u'llah, Nanak or Kabir, with a saint, a *satpurkha* who, to us, is God Himself. Every day, let us strengthen this link of love and devotion. Every day, let us pray to Him, let us kiss His Holy Feet, let us offer all our work to Him, let us, in moments of silence, converse with Him in love and with intimacy.

2. As we establish this link of love and devotion with God, we shall realise that, in everything

that happens, there is a meaning of God's mercy. Let us greet every happening with the words: I accept! I accept!

3. Be a blessing to others. God has blessed you with wealth and abundance, with position and power, so that you may be a blessing to others. Give out the best in you, in God's Name, for the good of others. Lend your helping hand to those who need it.

4. Let prayer become a habit. Pray, pray, and continue to pray.

5. Whatever you do– it may be a lowly act such as sweeping a room or a noble deed such as saving a life– do it wholly for the love of God.

6. Remember death every day. We live in a world of uncertainty. Remembering death will also reinforce the fact that you are not the body you wear. The body is only a cage. It will drop down.

7. Live in the company of fellow *bhaktas*. Hear the *leelas* of the Lord. Sing His glories and praise. The Name Divine uplifts and purifies our Spirit.

One final thought…

Significant are the words of Sadhu Vaswani, "Love is Krishna." When we fill our hearts with pure, selfless love for God and His Creation, we are filling our hearts with the pure, unalloyed energy of Krishna. Therefore, Sadhu Vaswani said to us, "God is the secret of man. Man never knows himself until he sees the God in himself. The deepest Self of man is God!"

Brahmacharya

All the major religions of the world talk about the necessity of self-discipline, especially the control of lower passions. However, the Hindu scriptures have attached a profound significance to the concept of *brahmacharya*. *Brahmacharya* in a literal and beautiful sense means 'walking with God', or 'living and moving with *Brahman*', the Absolute, Divine Self. In its highest form, it implies consciousness of the concept *Aham Brahmasmi*– I am *Brahman*. Thus, it relates to the effort to realise our divine potential.

In a more limited sense, *brahmacharya* implies the practice of celibacy and restraint of sexual indulgences. Thus in ancient India, young disciples and students learning at the feet of a guru in an *ashrama* were enjoined not to indulge in sensual pleasures and to observe strict celibacy, until they were old and mature enough to enter the next stage of life– the *grihastha ashrama* or married state.

Although celibacy and restraint are undoubtedly important aspects of *brahmacharya*, in a more profound sense they imply conquest over passions and sublimation of the merely biological instinct, leading to a profound perception of the Self in relation to the universe.

In its broadest sense, *brahmacharya* denotes purity of character, purity of thought, word, and deed. It indicates mastery over the mind and senses, especially over the sexual force. For when the latter is brought under control, all other aspects of our life are automatically brought under control. Such a state of self-discipline is conducive to our health, happiness, and spiritual progress. Indeed, *brahmacharya* is a virtue that will help us to lead an active and healthy life for a long period of time.

The secret is self-discipline!

A sage was sitting on the top of a mountain, silent, thoughtful, engrossed in deep meditation. His eyes were bright; his face was radiant. He seemed to glow with good health.

Placed before him was a jug of water.

A villager who saw the sage was so impressed by his effulgent appearance and the vibrations that emanated from him, that he begged the wise man, "O sir, tell me the secret of your wisdom and the sparkle in your eyes!"

The sage replied, "I fast, I meditate, I sip this water when I am thirsty– and that is all I do."

"The secret must be in the water!" exclaimed the villager. "O wise man! Give me some of that water– and name your price!"

Reluctantly, the sage agreed to give the man a pitcher of water in return for a gold coin.

The villager eagerly gulped down the water and waited for a miracle. Obviously, no miracle was forth coming. Reviewing his transaction gloomily, he concluded, "I was a fool to pay you for this water! I could have gone to the stream and got it for nothing!"

"Aha!" exclaimed the sage. "See, you are becoming wiser already!"

The secret of the sage's wisdom was not in the water– or indeed in the meditation or fasting– although people have always believed that these can lead to wisdom and emotional well-being. There is no doubt that they can, but the underlying principle of fasting and meditation is self-discipline.

Self-discipline is perhaps the most under-rated and least recognised virtue these days. I always say that self-discipline is the exercise of our spiritual muscles!

Brahmacharya is gender neutral

Brahmacharya in this broader sense, can be understood and practised by people of all ages, married and unmarried. When a married couple begins to realise that physical relationship is not an end in itself, they will find that they can relate to each other at a more profound and meaningful level. When we reach this state, we become capable of inner creativity and fulfillment. We grow in spiritual evolution and develop an intuitive intellect. The illusion of pleasure and deluding happiness of the world are left behind as we enter a stage of creative consciousness that is the Spirit.

In such a state, your thoughts will be clean, your mind more sensitive, and your soul in tune with the deep harmony of the universe. This is what yoga terms as *ojas shakti*– sublimated sexual energy.

What are the attributes of *ojas shakti*? A mind that vibrates spiritual strength and a radiance which surrounds you with an effulgent brilliance!

All happily married couples know that a meaningful relationship is one in which the partners learn to minimise selfish demands upon each other and acquire the virtues of patience, understanding, tolerance, and self-sacrifice. Thus, they promote their own spiritual evolution, and rise above the kind of superficial love that is only an entanglement.

The ideal of *brahmacharya* does not regard sex a shame and sin, but considers it as a creative force which is not to be squandered or abused. For when it is misused, sexual energy generates several negative qualities like pride, egoism, jealousy, anger, and greed in the human psyche.

Women and the ideal of purity

The Arabic word for woman is *hurma*, which means 'what is sacred'. Purity and chastity are a woman's natural virtues, and it is from women that men must learn them. Unfortunately, even as woman's spiritual strength is effulgent, so is her physical attraction to men. It is this attraction that makes men lose self-control and turn to aggression, violence, and molestation. I am not suggesting that women are responsible for these vile transgressions! I only urge them to be spiritually strong so that their inner purity may give them the power to protect themselves from harm. In respecting and elevating women, we respect and elevate ourselves; in abusing or degrading them, we degrade ourselves!

I have said to you that simplicity, sympathy, selfless service, and purity are the special qualities of women. When men imbibe these qualities, they get close to the Divine; when these qualities are totally absent in men, they become no better than beasts! To quote the words of Chanakya, "Purity of speech, of the mind, of the senses, and of the compassionate heart are needed by one who desires to rise to the level of the Divine."

The saint-poet Thiruvalluvar asks us: What greater treasure can there be, than a woman who has the abiding strength of purity? This 'purity' according to scholars greatly surpasses chastity or celibacy; it is an 'abiding moral tenacity' to never ever let evil enter her heart. Such a woman brings the triple blessing of virtue, wealth, and happiness to her family. Nor does this ancient treatise recommend that women be confined to a restricted life to protect her purity. The poet asks boldly: "Of what avail is close confinement? It is women's own discipline that is the best guardian of their virtue."

Much of what I have said to you regarding *brahmacharya*, self-discipline, and purity is most likely not acceptable to the 'free' thinkers of today. We are now beginning to uphold the qualities of 'tolerance' and 'understanding' for sexual and moral transgressions. I have heard arguments that sex is beautiful and that it should have no strings attached to it; I have also heard people insist that God made men and women for the sole purpose of enjoying each other 'in the flesh' and that any idea of attaching guilt and sin and shame to a sexual relationship outside marriage is indecent and bigoted.

I beg to differ. Perhaps the social restrictions placed on men and women are now having a contrary effect and pulling them in a reverse direction that can only be to their own detriment. Everybody chooses their own moral standards, their own values and ideals to live by; but we have no right to drag others' values and moral principles down to justify our own immoral preferences!

If all men would turn *brahmacharis*, would not humanity be extinct?

Gandhiji's answer to this question was simple: "Do not look for excuses! *Brahmacharis* are not to be had for the asking– for they are as rare and precious as diamonds. We only reveal our weakness and cowardice, when we look for such pretexts. Instead, we should keep this idea constantly before us, and try to achieve it to the utmost of our capacity."

Those who have practised *brahmacharya* even for a short period can vouch for the fact that body, mind, and Spirit gain strength and power. Their energy and enthusiasm is greater, and they attain to a higher form of joy which transcends the mind's quest for lower and lesser pleasures.

Brahmacharya in today's context

I am aware that people will find it strange that I talk about *brahmacharya*, which is associated especially with the practice of celibacy, in an age when sexual promiscuity has become rampant. I would only like to remind you that it was "free sex" of this sort that destroyed the ancient civilisations of Babylon, Greece, and Rome.

Brahmacharya in its highest sense leads to inner purification and awakening of the consciousness. Such a state of consciousness surely cannot tolerate moral aberrations like the legalisation of abortion and immoral relationships outside marriage.

What we need under the circumstances is a change of mind, a change of attitude, a transformation of the heart. Suppression or repression will harm us, while transformation of the mind will be a positive effort. And we would also do well to remember that an idle mind is the devil's workshop. An active, useful life with meditation and *naam japa* in leisure hours will help us lead a well-balanced life. The mind must be controlled and disciplined to promote mental well-being. Purity of mind is one of the greatest blessings a man or woman can achieve. Regularity, punctuality, clean habits, *sattvic* food, and yoga exercises are all beneficial in the practice of *brahmacharya*.

One final thought…

In ancient India, the two great ideals of purity and prayer were brought together in the one great concept of *brahmacharya*. *Brahmacharya* is not asceticisim, nor is it stoicism. The true *brahmachari* must be a man of purity and prayer. These two make the body and Spirit vital. They rejuvenate the outer body, breaking the barriers of weakness. They link man with God: and he finds a great *shakti* flowing through him. He becomes a channel for the outpouring upon others of the Spirit of Light!

Our saints and seers tell us that the body is a boat that can help us cross the *sansaar sagar*, the ocean of life. It was this boat that enabled great souls like Adi Shankara and Gautama Buddha to traverse the mighty ocean of humanity and enter the blessed realms of God-realisation. Truly do the Upanishads tell us: "God cannot be attained by the weak and the unhealthy."

Compassion

I would describe compassion as the crown of all virtues. I believe it is this quality that takes us closest to the Divine. When we practise– not just feel compassion, when we go out of ourselves to reach out to others and alleviate their suffering, we rise to the highest Self in us. At such times, negative feelings of strife and disharmony are totally nullified in our hearts and minds. When more and more of us practise the divine quality of compassion, our world will move towards lasting peace.

If we are indeed God's children, made in His likeness, coming from Him and destined to return to His Lotus Feet, then we need to cultivate qualities that make us worthy of being His children. We may not aspire to His power or His wisdom, but we can and must aspire to the one divine quality that we can all emulate– the quality of mercy, the spark of compassion which binds us to our fellow human beings and takes us closer to God Himself. *Daya dharam ka mool hai: naraka mool abhimaan*– compassion is the very soul, the very essence of religion. Compassion is the very root of religion, even as pride is the root of sin; therefore let us be kind, let us practise compassion till the very last breath of our being.

Compassion for all

Many of us are ready to sympathise with those who are close to us– relatives, friends, loved ones. We may go out of our way to help them. However, when it comes to strangers, do we rush to their help, or do we simply turn away? What about animals? How many of us kill animals to nourish our own lives? How can this be reconciled with true compassion? This is the true test of compassion.

My Master, Gurudev Sadhu Vaswani, taught and lived the life of universal compassion. The modern age, dominated by machinery and materialism, he said, can still be saved by the spirit of compassion and love, which has inspired the noblest philosophers, literatures, arts and idealisms of the East.

Sadhu Vaswani's compassion was not restricted to human beings. It extended to all of Creation, even to trees and flowers. He would not pluck flowers, for flowers, as he said, had their families, and they must not be separated from each other. Hence, he did not accept flower-garlands. The quality of his soul, his endless compassion was furthermore revealed through his treatment of animals. He could not resign himself to the sufferings of animals at the cruel hands of the butcher. "For me, not to love bird and animal would be not to love the Lord," he said, "For His children are birds and animals, no less than human beings."

Compassion is not selfish

Very often, our 'compassion' is born out of selfish motives. For example, when people leave the temple, they will ritualistically drop coins into the bowls of beggars lined up outside. This completes their visit to the temple, and they believe they gain *punya* from this act of charity. However, the same people will turn their face away from beggars who accost them in public places. Some of them even reproach the poor beggars, "Aren't you ashamed of begging?" or "Why don't you find some useful employment?"

We should live in such a manner that we do not bring harm to any being on our planet, through our thoughts, words, or deeds.

True compassion lies in embracing the misery of others as our own. How true it is that when we relieve the agony of others, we bring relief to ourselves.

Compassion is an inner desire which drives us to engage in good deeds, without expecting anything in return. The joy lies in just doing good to others!

A man of true compassion gives without judgement. He never asks if the others deserve his charity or compassion.

How can we walk the way of true compassion?

Let me offer you some practical suggestions:

1. Compassion begins in awareness– awareness that the One Life flows in all.

2. The second step of compassion is the acknowledgement that all Creation is One Family; all the people of the world, nay, even birds and animals are my younger brothers and sisters in the One Family of Creation.

3. Compassion begins in awareness, but it does not stop there! It is not enough to feel compassion, or express it through speech. Compassion should be expressed in action, in deeds of daily life, in little acts of kindness and love.

4. Selective compassion is selfish compassion! It is not enough to be kind and loving to those who are close to you, those whom you love, or those whom you consider your own. True compassion knows no barriers of caste, creed, race or faith. It falls like the gentle rain on all of humanity, all of Creation.

5. Compassion is not just giving of your money and your assets; true compassion is giving your love, giving yourself in an endless stream of sympathy that flows out to all.

6. Compassion is a divine attribute, and takes you closer to God. Therefore, compassion should be non-judgmental, and offered freely. When you begin to wonder whether people are worthy of your compassion, you are guilty of the kind of discrimination which even God does not practise against us, his erring children. Let the quality of your mercy be the determining factor in your acts of compassion– not the recipient's deserving.

The universal hymn of compassion

Compassion, kindness, and loving mercy must be the tune, the theme, the very soul of the song we all sing together. It must be the great ideal that binds humanity together– the great value that we must pass on to our children and our children's children. Compassion is the answer to all our unanswered questions, the solution to humanity's stifling, suffocating problems. Compassion to all living beings; compassion to our friends and family as well as our so-called foes and adversaries; compassion to all of Creation; compassion to the tiniest creatures that breathe the breath of life; when we have imbibed this great virtue into our lives and hearts, how can we allow violence, killing, and slaughter of animals? How can we give in to destructive forces like terrorism? How can we allow differences between rich and poor, black and white, Asian and African, American and European, Hindu and Muslim, Sikh and Christian?

Contentment

Santosha, or contentment, is a virtue we must all cultivate. When we overcome the craving for more money, more power, more material comforts, we become aware that there is nothing wrong in enjoying the pleasures and the delights of this beautiful world that God has created for us. God created this beautiful world as a vale of contentment, a garden of joy and beauty for us to live in!

Contentment is not to be equated with complacency and passivism; it is the dynamic realisation that what we are, and what we have, are part of God's Providence and God's Will for us. It is the awareness that we are with God in all circumstances and situations of life and therefore, lack nothing!

Contentment indeed is a rare and precious jewel! There is a Tamil proverb which tells us, "The mind that is content is the precious *parasmani* that turns everything into gold."

The five principal *niyamas* (dos or observances) recommended by Sage Patanjali are: *saucha* (purification); *santosha* (contentment); *tapas* (asceticism); *swadhyaya* (self-study); and *Ishwara pranidhana* (surrender to the Divine).

Santosha is the second of the five *niyamas*. It is the root of all happiness in life; its opposite, discontent, is the root of all unhappiness and suffering. *Santosha* is being content with what one has, what one is, where one is, and with what one is doing. It is a great blessing to have an attitude which allows us to find contentment in any situation.

Our saints and sages tell us that *santosha* is the key to all the *niyamas* and an obligatory condition for self-realisation. The practice and cultivation of contentment is not given to all of us. It is the ability to be at peace in any circumstances that we find ourselves in. This ability arises out of trusting that every situation is a learning opportunity, through which we gain valuable insights into the truth. *Santosha* stems from the knowledge that God is always with us, and that under His benign care and protection, we lack nothing.

A man of contentment is ever in the state of equanimity, extolled by Sri Krishna in the Gita. Whatever happens to him, he regards as a gift from God. He accepts it with gratitude. He neither complains nor blames anyone. Whatever the situation he finds himself in, whatever the misfortunes that may befall him, he does not question them or debate on their cause and effect. He never, ever doubts the supreme perfection of God and His

Divine Will. A man of contentment has a meditative mind, with a 'No Entry' sign for any negative and disturbing thoughts. He accepts everything with grace and humility.

Why are we discontented?

What makes a man discontent? It is that he is greedy for more! This may be due to our social values, which are materialistic. We place too much value on material possessions.

Let me tell you a story. A man had forty acres of land. He put an advertisement in the newspaper announcing that he would distribute his 40 acres of land to any man who was content with his life. As soon as the advertisement appeared, many people rushed to claim the land. The owner of the land asked each one of them the same question, "Are you content with your life?"

The answer was, "Yes, we are content and therefore we are here!"

"If you are content with your life, then why do you need more land?"

Logically, this is true. Even those people who are content and satisfied with what they have are tempted to have more, especially when it is given free! There is always the temptation to get more in life and to get more out of life. Discontentment always leads to greed.

Contentment does not lie in the fact that we are satisfied with what we have. Instead, contentment entails that what we do not have is what we do not require.

Discontentment leads to ingratitude

Some years ago, I met a woman who said confidently to me, "If I were God's assistant, I would help Him make a perfect plan for this world. Nobody would find anything to complain about; nothing would go wrong. The world He has created, and the way He governs it is pathetic."

Do we know better than God? Can we assume that we are superior to Him in managing the affairs of this world, including our own?

Is it not ironic that we criticise God, who gives us the freedom to say whatever we like? We abuse this freedom by negating its very source! How ungrateful we are! A man of contentment would not criticise God, nor would he find injustice in what happens to people; he would see the correlation between the circumstantial sufferings of man and his own karma. In other words, a man of faith would never feel or say that God is unfair and unjust. A man of contentment accepts everything as a gift from God. He perceives the best intentions in whatever is happening around him or even to him.

Contentment leads to grateful acceptance

Abu Usman was a distinguished man of God and a dervish par excellence. One day, as he and his disciples were walking on the street, a woman threw a basketful of ashes from the balcony. The ashes fell on the holy man's head. Abu Usman remained unperturbed. His disciples, however, became angry. "We will go up and teach that woman a lesson," they said. "You will do nothing of the sort," said Abu Usman. The ashes contained a few smouldering coals which had fallen directly on his head. How did Abu Usman react to this? "I am so great a sinner, that I deserve to be in flames. I am grateful to the woman, that she was kind enough to throw only ashes on me, she did not throw the burning coals that I deserved. God be praised!"

We are men of ingratitude. We fight back, we retaliate, we argue, we resist. We complain at the slightest irritation. We blame other people for our condition. We try to find fault with others, and hold them responsible for our misfortunes, our sorrow and misery. We refuse to accept our situation and unhappy circumstances as part of God's plan for us.

On the other hand, a man of contentment is ever ready to accept every misfortune, every unpleasant situation as having a meaning and a purpose. He therefore remains calm and composed.

Contentment takes criticism in the right spirit

To illustrate this, let me narrate to you the story of a well-known saint, who was called a mahatma. The mahatma did not lose his temper ever. A few people got together and conspired against him. They were bent on testing his patience and planned a strategy to provoke him. Two men were sent to him for this purpose. One of them said, "Give me *ganja*."

The mahatma calmly replied, "I do not have *ganja*."

"You cheat, you deceiver, give me tobacco. I'm sure enough that you sadhus like to go on a trip and get 'high'."

The mahatma maintained his composure. The harsh words had absolutely no effect on the saint.

As the two men quarrelled with the saint, a crowd of people gathered around them. Encouraged, one of the two men said, "He is a liar and a thief. He has been in jail. Look at my arms and the scars on them. This man whom you consider holy and divine, had a fight with me in jail. He hit me with an iron rod. It is my good fortune that I was saved, otherwise he would have killed me."

The mahatma remained calm. There was not a sign of a frown or a trace of irritation on his face. The abuses and false allegations failed to provoke him to anger. Everyone was surprised. The two men, who were sent with the task of angering the saint, felt ashamed of themselves. They fell at the feet of the mahatma and asked for forgiveness. The mahatma was truly a man of contentment, a man of emotional equanimity, a man above worldly quarrels, abuses and allegations. He was indeed one who lived on a higher plane of life, in the total faith and acceptance of God's goodness.

Saints and holy men, through their exemplary personal behaviour, teach us the art of living. They offer us 'lessons' free of charge, but sadly, there are very few takers. We find it difficult to accept this high order of contentment and live up to it.

The witness of Mansur

Once, Mansur, the spiritual paragon of Persia was asked, "What are the signs of a contented man?" He replied, "A contented man is one, whose hands and feet are cut off, who is hung on the cross, and still utters the magic words– *shukur, shukur!*" Mansur bore witness to these words, when later in his life, the non-believers did cut off his wrists and feet. What did this man of God do? He smeared his cheeks with the oozing blood. His disciples were surprised. "*Huzoor*, why did you do that?" Mansur, in all reverence to his Beloved, said, "The blood flowing out of my body will pale my face. I do not want to give people reason to say, 'Ah, that devotee of God, we tortured him to death and he died with a face as colourless as ashes.' Instead, they should say, that man died with the pink radiance of his Beloved on his face."

Contentment teaches us patience

Once, Mahatma Gandhi was travelling by train from Champaran to Bekhiyanagar, along with many other passengers. They occupied the seats in the compartment but left an entire berth for Mahatma Gandhi. Mahatma Gandhi had been on his walking trail since morning, and was very tired. His followers requested him to lie down on the berth reserved for him. Mahatma Gandhi agreed to occupy the berth and soon, he fell asleep. After a few hours, a rustic farmer entered the compartment at a wayside station. Seeing a man sleeping on the berth, he lost his patience. He rudely shook up Mahatma Gandhi, quarrelling with him and reprimanding him for occupying the full berth for himself, in a compartment that was so overcrowded. Mahatma Gandhi immediately sat up and gave place to the farmer. As the train moved, the farmer started singing popular patriotic songs and exclaiming slogans in favour of Mahatma Gandhi. Mahatma Gandhi watched this in silence and smiled.

The rustic farmer was actually going to Bekhiyanagar to have a *darshan* of Mahatma Gandhi.

In the morning as the train approached Bekhiyanagar, loud cheering could be heard, "Mahatma Gandhi *ki jai*!" The station platform was crowded. People from all walks of life had gathered there to welcome Mahatma Gandhi. It was then that the farmer realised that the man he had abused and had been rough with was none other than Mahatma Gandhi himself. The poor man began to cry and fell at Mahatma Gandhi's feet. Mahatma Gandhi immediately lifted him and embraced him. Mahatma Gandhi had shown what it is to be egoless. Although he was insulted and abused by the rustic farmer, he had maintained silence and remained calm and peaceful.

There are very few men like Mahatma Gandhi who are content to accept all that happens to them as gifts from God. They accept these gifts not just with calmness and equanimity, but with gratitude.

The man of contentment

- A man of contentment is known by his attitude to the things happening around him.

- In every situation, under all conditions he says, "Praised be the Lord! Whatever He does, whatever He gives me, is worthy of praise." This attitude of acceptance with gratitude should be genuine. It should come from the depths of your heart, then alone will you experience inner peace. A man of contentment will praise the Lord and express his gratitude even when he is passing through stormy weather or facing the worst crisis of life.

- A man of contentment is always at peace with himself and the world. He does not lose his temper, nor does he complain or blame others for his condition, because he knows that whatever God does has a meaning and purpose for him.

A man of contentment sings the song:

Tum hee sab kuchh jaanat preetam, teri ichha puran ho
Dukh mein sukh mein mere pritam, teri ichha puran ho!

Thy Will be done, O Lord!

Conversion

Psychologists are at a loss when accounting for the mindset and attitude that makes people convert to other faiths. They see such conversions as leaving the convert with a loss of his own sense of identity, leading to the breakup of families and the rich and plural ways of life and culture among people.

All sensitive and liberal, intellectual people in India and the rest of the world agree that freedom of faith and religion is not really freedom to convert others. In fact, Western psychologists and sociologists perceive conversion as an insidious attack made on the most vulnerable groups in society. This is true of the 'evangelical' work in tribal belts, fishing villages, and remote and interior areas of India where the underprivileged live. In the West too, it is observed that the target audiences for conversion are in the same category of vulnerable people, such as new immigrants. In the U.S., conversion is often from one denomination of Christianity to another– from Roman Catholicism to Unitarianism, or from Protestantism to Antibaptism and so on. Single mothers, divorced women, and economically underprivileged youngsters are 'persuaded' to embrace the faith of the proselytising groups who openly canvas for this end.

Gandhiji as St. Francis?

It is said that a professor of Philosophy from Poland named Stanislaw Krajewski once came to meet Gandhji. By then, Gandhiji was already very well known in Europe and America, as a saintly soul who was bringing about a bloodless and peaceful social and political revolution in British India. Professor Krajewski too, like others, admired and revered the Mahatma. In all earnestness, the professor said to him that Catholicism is the one true religion, and if only Gandhiji converted to the faith, he would be as great as St. Francis. Gandhiji had a simple question for him: Why can't a poor Hindu be St. Francis?

Yes, we should all follow our religion with faith and loyalty. We must appreciate the value of our own culture and its form of religious worship. We must all aim to be good human beings– as well as good Hindus, good Christians, good Muslims or good Jews. But asserting our faith must never degenerate into the very unholy act of heaping abuse and denigrating the culture and spiritual identity of other faiths.

How can intelligent, educated people ever believe that their God or His prophet is the only true Divinity, and claim that they have a monopoly on salvation and liberation for the whole of mankind?

Very few nations in the world today actually give people the fundamental freedom to practise their faith, and to 'choose their belief' or 'change their belief' at will. India is one among the few. But as far as India is concerned, many foreign missionary organisations view this as 'the right to preach', 'the right to proselytise' and 'the right to convert people to their own faith'. Once again, Gandhiji's words come to my mind: "I disbelieve in the conversion of one person by another. My effort should never be to undermine another's faith but to make him a better follower of his own faith. This implies the belief in the truth of all religions and respect for them."

A few uncomfortable questions

Can we 'use' God to degrade and convert followers of another belief system? Is only a particular religion regarded as the chosen one of the Lord? Is the Lord Himself someone who regards half the world as 'lesser' children?

And the means of conversion– can we use propaganda, fear psychosis, inducements, and brainwashing against vulnerable people whose very existence is precarious?

Gandhiji's words come to mind again: "No propaganda can be allowed which reviles other religions. The best way is to publicly condemn propaganda. And further, if I had the power and could legislate, I should stop all proselytising, it is the deadliest poison that ever sapped the fountain of truth."

Sri Aurobindo, one of India's great seers, was also disturbed by this inherent bigotry and posed this question about a certain religion: "You can live with a religion whose principle is toleration. But how is it possible to live with a religion whose principle is 'I will not tolerate you'? How are you going to have unity with these people?"

Faith is sacrosanct

There are some who believe that they have the one full and final revelation of the truth; so that those who stand outside the circle of their own faith must necessarily be in error. Again, there are some who approach religious issues without the spirit of sympathy; they fix their attention on what they regard as the aberrations and extravagancies of a particular religion and say, "This religion is a monstrosity!" Saddest of all, we have people who hurt and kill in the name of religion. They are ignorant of the fact that they are killing their own brothers and sisters!

Faith is a matter of the heart; faith relates to the Spirit; faith is conviction; faith is at the very core of our being. To attack, to cast doubts and aspersions on someone's faith is to hit him where it hurts most. It is violence of the worst kind.

In the wonderful environment of trust and tolerance that prevailed in ancient and medieval India, many faiths were welcomed and accepted on Indian soil. Hinduism, like Zoroastrianism and Conservative Judaism, is a non-converting faith. All three religions, therefore, do not interfere in the practice of other faiths. If our detractors were to say that the current environment in India is not one of peace and harmony, I would still say to them that the modern Hindu attitude is to live and let live, to follow his own faith and respect others' faith.

Conversions in ancient India

Conversion and interchange of faith within the Indic religions has always been a common phenomenon in India; the example of Emperor Ashoka is well known. We also know that the Chola and Pandya and Pallava kings of the South, switched over from Hinduism to Jainism and back, due to the powerful inspiration they derived from visiting Jain scholars and monks. One of the greatest intellectuals of the first century A.D., the saint-poet Thiruvalluvar, is thought to have been influenced by Jainism, and perhaps even converted to the faith.

In none of these cases can we suspect coercion, aggression or other devious means. No one would question a genuine and voluntary change of heart which is not forced on a man. Let me also stress, these kings were powerful and benevolent; they all exercised firm authority over their people, yet in no case were the people of these kingdoms ever induced to convert to the new faith embraced by the monarch. In fact, history tells us that their queens often remained firmly rooted in the faith they were born into!

It is said too, that Adi Shankara brought many atheists and fearsome *kaabalikas* back into the Hindu fold. In those days, we also had the tradition of great saints and scholars indulging in *tarka*, or philosophical debates which often lasted for days on end. The losers in these debates not only conceded defeat, but often embraced the faith of the winner, due to their own conviction. It is also said that they entered into such debates on the mutual agreement that if they lost their intellectual ability to convince the other, that would be grounds to accept the other's faith.

Aggressive conversions

As we can see, the scenario today is very different. Abuse and denigration is heaped on the Hindu faith, and vulnerable sections of society are offered inducements, or coerced through false promises or fear psychosis to convert. I am sure my readers will agree that this is not the same as voluntary change of heart.

One of the reasons given by aggressive coercers is that Hinduism is riddled with internal contradictions like the caste system, and that is why some sections convert willingly. I can easily point to you aspects of other faiths that are problematic and controversial: polygamy, women's status, exploitation of ignorance through so-called miracles and fear psychosis, inducement of a sense of guilt and shame, as well as threatening hell fire and damnation. Hindus know that such things exist in other faiths, and yet they have never capitalised on these weaknesses. It is no use telling a Hindu, "If you can, go out and convert others to your faith. It is a level and open-playing field!" This is a useless and futile offer which every thinking Hindu will reject, for we are simply not a converting faith! Hinduism just does not permit such intrusion, such violation of another's life and faith and dignity!

Hindus belonging to low castes are converted on the basis that their converters have liberated them from oppression, abuse, and segregation in Hindu society. Ironically, their own places of worship and local religious bodies continue to discriminate against them even after conversion! This should make them realise that casteism and untouchability (which incidentally has been banned under the Indian constitution) are social evils and social aberrations, not religious abominations. Else, how is it that these evils do not disappear instantaneously when they enter the new religious community into which they have converted?

Culture matters

The culture of any society is a delicate, rare, and beautiful fabric into which faith, religion, customs and traditions are woven integrally. To pull out the strands of belief and faith from the fabric of culture is to destroy and damage that culture beyond repair. We have allowed this to happen to the Mayan culture of South America; the ancient cultures of Egypt and Mesopotamia have disappeared without a trace; Greece, the cradle of modern thought is but a pale shadow of its past glory. The loss is not theirs alone, but the world's as a whole.

I repeat, freedom in religion does not include freedom to convert; it only assures that all of us may practise our faiths without interference and aggression from others.

Change of heart– or change of label?

A few years ago, when I was in the U.S., a lady came to meet me in Key West, Florida. She had attended several of my lectures over the years, and of her own accord, she had read the Srimad Bhagavat and the Gita. She was so inspired by these scriptures that she wanted to become a Hindu. She came to me for advice on how she should go about it.

I said to her, "You must give up this idea. You say you are inspired by Sri Krishna. You can never draw closer to Krishna simply by labelling yourself as a Hindu. What the Srimad Bhagavat offers is as valuable and as true as what the Bible offers. You must make an attempt to find it out and practise being a good Christian. A Christian can be equally dear to Sri Krishna as a Hindu. For in the Kingdom of God, there are no labels, no sects, and no denominations!"

May I humbly submit to you, true conversion is not just a change of label. When Jesus spoke of conversion, he did not mean a change of creed or dogma; he meant a change of heart, a change of mind and attitude. It is not entrance to a new church or mode of worship; it is inner transformation. How can we believe that God wants numbers from us? And how can we imagine that He wants us, imperfect creatures, to bring about the changes, perform actions that He Himself cannot achieve? Why should an omnipotent, omniscient, omnipresent Supreme Being require pathetic 'warriors' like us to fight and shoot and torture and kill others– that too, on His behalf? Is this not heresy of the worst order? Is this not an apostasy of true faith? And can we really bring ourselves to believe that we are walking on the primrose path to heaven and salvation by treading on the beliefs and sanctity of other people's convictions? Is this not a gross and serious transgression?

In the Kingdom of God, we will not be judged. In fact, we cannot even gain entry through our labels, but only by the lives we have led!

My plea

The topic of conversion has become an issue of heated debates both in my country, India, and elsewhere in the world, from the point of view of a culture, a society and way of life which has never believed in proselytisation or conversion. To me, the religion one is born into is like one's mother– can one change his or her mother?

One of my friends informed me last year that a court in the U.S. had actually permitted a child to change his parents– to revert from the family he was born into, and seek adoption from his foster parents on grounds of cruelty or ill-treatment.

I am sure you will agree with me, that this is an aberration, and not exactly the kind of example which we would wish to hold up for others to follow.

I once met an American-Christian brother in New York, who said to me, "Why can't they convert the Christians in America to true Christianity?"

All great religions are equally true. They are like branches of a tree– the tree of religion.

This, therefore, is the essence of my plea– that instead of conversion, we should try to be better human beings– Hindu, Christian or Muslim.

Courage

Courage is the key to a life well lived! To live a full life, to live according to God's plan, to live life purposefully and meaningfully, requires courage.

Life demands of us that we live with courage. Surely, courage must be the greatest of all virtues– because we cannot exhibit any other virtue without it. Without the courage to act, justice would be impossible. Without the courage to love, compassion and understanding would not exist. Without the courage to endure, faith and hope would not flourish!

Linguistic experts relate the English word courage to the French word *coeur*, meaning heart. Courage is born of the heart. It is the heart's response to the call of life.

Who are the real heroes?

When I talk to you of courage, I do not refer to the courage of Alexander the Great or Julius Caesar, who came and saw and conquered. I hold up as role models before you Sri Rama, Gautama Buddha, and Mahavira, who had the moral and spiritual courage to walk the way of truth and stand up for what they believed in. Buddha's message is one of hope and courage. Strive with desires! Conquer *trishna*! Be a hero in the strife!

Those who, like Ashoka, turn from war to peace, are the real heroes of humanity. When Ashoka accepted Buddha, he turned his back on war and sent missionaries of peace, far and wide. Ahsoka's son Mahinda, laid the foundation of a new civilisation of brotherhood and peace in Lanka.

The conquest that requires courage

I cannot help smiling when I read headlines such as: "So-and-so conquers Everest". Conquers Everest? Quite frankly, would we not be better off reporting that so-and-so has 'climbed' Everest or 'reached' the peak? Having reached Everest, can we even stay there overnight? Spend five or six hours there? No! We have to get back to one of the lower camps as fast as our legs will carry us in that harsh terrain. And yet we proudly claim that we have conquered Everest.

Please do not mistake me! I am filled with admiration for the heroes of mountaineering who have achieved this tremendous feat. Their discipline, determination, and dedication is worthy of emulation. I only wish to point out our attitude towards 'conquests'. I may say to you in passing, we are not here to 'conquer' nature; we are here to co-exist, to live in harmony with her. To realise this and put it into practice, requires courage.

It takes courage to live

Cowards die many times before their physical deaths; it takes courage to live life fully! Life is full of uncertainties, of the unknown and the unknowable. Experts recommend that we develop "a high tolerance for uncertainty" if we are to live in peace, while being aware that so much in our lives is outside our control. Losing control, living with uncertainty generates fear– and this fear can be conquered by courage and faith!

A stout heart and courageous spirit are vital if we are to live a life free from the fear generated by uncertainty. Dr. Johnson remarked, "Unless man has this primary virtue of courage, he has no guarantee of preserving any other."

An Arab folktale tells us of a wise, old man travelling on the desert road to Baghdad, when he met the figure of Pestilence hurrying ahead of him.

"Why are you in such a haste to reach Baghdad?" asked the old man.

"I am due to take five thousand lives in the city," Pestilence replied, before it went away.

Later, on the return journey, they chanced to meet again. "You lied to me," said the old man reproachfully. "You said you would take five thousand lives– but you took away ten thousand instead!"

"I did not do it!" Pestilence swore. "I took five thousand, and not one more. It was Fear who killed the rest!"

It takes courage to love

A wise thinker pointed out that there are two great sources of power, two great forces of strength in this world. One of them is vested in those who are not afraid to kill, hurt, wound, maim and destroy. The other is vested in those who are not afraid to love, forgive, heal and be reconciled.

Yes, we must be unafraid to love– for it requires courage. I have always believed that the power of love is far greater than the power of hatred; it is courage that gives this power to love. If we are to confront the dark forces of destruction and annihilation, we must use the greatest weapon in our possession– the courage to love.

It takes courage to forgive

If life and love require courage, it takes even greater courage to forgive. Gandhiji urged us to meet the tragedies of life with what he called "soul force". Forgiveness is not weak or naïve. It requires courage and clarity.

> *If you want to see the heroic look*
> *Look at those who can love*
> *In return for hatred*
> *If you want to see the brave*
> *Look at those who can forgive.*

Moral courage

We do not necessarily face life-and-death situations every day which require raw, physical courage. But life does throw difficult challenges at us without warning. A mother of two is told that she has to have an emergency surgery; the only earning member and head of a family is told that he is facing a lay-off; someone is told that he may have contracted a life-threatening illness; or it may be that you are simply surrounded by people who constantly undermine your faith and confidence and demoralise you!

Moral courage requires us to make the right choices, take the right decisions, even if it brings inconvenience or disruption to our lives. It demands that we don't submit to corruption– at the giving or receiving end. Think of a friend who has beaten the signal; the traffic policeman who knows his area well, is standing just round the corner to catch people like your friend. What would you tell your friend to do at this juncture? Squeeze a hundred rupee note into the constable's hand, apologise profusely and leave the place as quickly as he can? Or have the courage to make him draw out a receipt and pay the official Rs. 150 fine?

In order to make the right choices, we must stop and listen to the small, still voice of the conscience within. Listening to and obeying this still, small voice requires courage. How many of us can hear this voice in the stress, strain and clamour of this world? How many of us even remember that there is a thing such as the conscience within us?

It is imperative that we face the world with moral courage, even under the most difficult of circumstances. Courage is a choice which transforms our tragedies into triumphs.

It takes courage to achieve your goal

The yearning for freedom– political, social, intellectual, economic, racial or religious is imbedded so deeply in men, that people even risk their lives to achieve it. The world's greatest intellects, martyrs, and saints put their lives at stake by embracing courage. Socrates drank hemlock, calmly and dispassionately; Christ allowed himself to be crucified; Mahatma Gandhi faced his assassin's bullets with the Name of the Lord on his lips. These great souls cultivated the will to be unafraid, the will to conquer fear at all cost!

Develop moral courage

1. Convert fear into a catalyst! Fear is not merely an indication of cowardice, it is also an opportunity for courage. Fear should be used constructively, to overcome the weaknesses of the mind.

2. Accept change and uncertainty! Change and uncertainty are inevitable in human life. We can develop courage by relinquishing mental resistance to things we cannot control and simply accept all that comes our way. A better remedy is not just to accept, but to rejoice in all that comes our way, in faith that it happens by the Will of God!

3. Anchor your ship! Most of us are unsecured like floating vessels. We need to latch onto a power that is greater than ours. Life takes great courage and we may not have the strength to deal with its trials and tribulations alone. We need to anchor our ship to the Eternal Power, whom for want of a better word we call God. For He is the source of everything.

4. Seek inspiration! People like Mahatma Gandhi, Martin Luther King, Helen Keller and Swami Vivekananda were not born courageous. The lives of these illustrious people speak of tremendous challenges that they faced. It was their courage and their sheer grit to thwart fear that made them what they were. Seeking inspiration from great lives will help us to see that the problems we face are so trivial, and the fears we have so empty.

5. Follow your purpose! Fix a goal for yourself, then set out to achieve it. When you have fixed a goal, you will be able to motivate yourself to take on life and its challenges.

6. Don't wait for the future to happen, create it! Dreading the future simply draws attention to uncertainty and insecurity. When you set out to map your future and create your own destiny, you are executing your plan for success, instead of waiting for it to happen.

7. Learn to bend without breaking! Living courageously means you have to be resilient. This will help you adapt to circumstances with ease, when things don't go your way. Like bamboo, resilient ones bend but rarely break. You also have to learn to let go. The ability to let go makes you flexible and adaptable.

8. Learn to say NO! Saying yes may make for temporary peace and harmony, but it cannot always solve your problems. Saying no is tougher, but it protects you from poor decisions and their undesirable consequences. Say no to negatives! Say no to unhealthy addictions! Say no to people who exploit you and take you for granted.

Courage is not just about heroism, adventure, and conquest. It is about self-awareness, wisdom, and understanding your strengths, even in the face of adversity and uncertainty. Fortunately for us, these are personality traits that we can all cultivate.

Dada Shyam

One day, Gurudev Sadhu Vaswani shared with us the story of a good man who had been afflicted with unbearable pain and agony due to a debilitating illness. The physical suffering that he had to undergo was beyond human endurance. At the height of his affliction, he called out like a lost child, "Dada Shyam! Dada Shyam! Come to my aid!" As you may know, the word *Dada* in Sindhi means elder brother. The call of the distressed man obviously reached the Lord, whom we know to be the very spirit of compassion and love. *Deenabandhu, Deenanath* that He is, He responded to the call of the man in pain, and believe it or not, the man grew better and was finally cured completely of his painful condition.

Narrating this story to us, Gurudev Sadhu Vaswani urged us to look upon the Lord as our elder brother. "Call out to Him in love and fraternal affection! Look upon Him as your favourite elder brother! Trust to His loving care, and He will never let you down!" Gurudev said to us.

When Gurudev Sadhu Vaswani dropped his physical body, we took to this mantra spontaneously. We had been used to refer to our Gurudev as Dada, and it was natural that we should refer to God in the same affectionate and loving terms!

The Lord is our elder brother

One of the many *bhavas* in the Indian tradition of *bhakti* is the *vatsalya bhava* or the mode of affection for the Lord. The great saints of our country have called out to Sri Krishna as their child, their playmate, their father, and friend. We, the members of the Sadhu Vaswani *Satsang*, learnt to look upon Him as our elder brother! When the beautiful mantra 'Hare Krishna Hare Rama, Dada Shyam Dada Shyam' is chanted, we feel secure in the protective care and love of the Lord, who is as close to us as our own loving elder brother!

The story of Jatila

Jatila was a little boy who lived with his mother in a broken cottage at the edge of the forest. His school was at the other end of the forest. This meant that he had to cross the forest every day, on his own, to get to the school. When he left at dawn and returned at dusk, he would often hear roars and fearful sounds made by the wild animals in the threatening darkness of the forest. Sometimes, he was so overcome by nameless fright and terror that he would tremble with each step he took.

One day, he said to his mother, "Mother, I am so terrified of the forest! I die a thousand deaths every day, crossing the forest all alone. I don't want to go to school anymore!"

"My dear child, why must you worry?" the mother exclaimed. "Your elder brother lives in the forest. All you have to do is call out to him. He will take you across safely."

"My elder brother?" said the child, surprised. "Elder brother? Who is he? What does he look like? Where was he all this while? Why didn't you tell me about him earlier?"

"Your elder brother is called Krishna," said the mother. "Whenever you feel frightened, whenever you need anything, just call out to Him. He will appear in front of you. He will escort you all the way to school and back."

Jatila's eyes widened in surprise. All night, he dreamt of his elder brother, and the next morning, set off on his way through the forest, filled with curiosity to meet his elder brother and get to know him better. As he reached the dense heart of the forest, he cried out, "Dada! Krishna! Come to me and take me through this forest!"

There was no answer. But out of the fullness of his heart, the boy called out yet again, "Krishna! Krishna! If you are indeed my elder brother, come to me at once!"

Our saints and sages tell us that the Lord is ever at the beck and call of the truly devout. Pleased with the child's love and faith, Sri Krishna appeared before him in the form of a young cowherd and said to him, "Jatila, my brother, here I am. I will take you across the forest."

He held Jatila's hand and walked all the way through the forest, and took him within sight of the school. He said to the boy, "Jatila! You must never ever feel that you are alone, because I am always there to take care of you. All you have to do is call out to me, and I shall be with you."

This life that we live is also like a forest. Temptations surround us, fears daunt us, difficulties and problems overpower us; we often feel helpless, lonely and lost. All we need to do is to call out to Sri Krishna, as to our elder brother, with love and faith. He will surely come to our aid!

Bhakti is absolute faith

At its most basic level, *bhakti* is loving faith, childlike trust in God. A true *bhakta*, a true devotee, trusts in God completely and absolutely. He hands himself over, in loving childlike trust to the Lord. It is important that we become carefree and trusting just like a little child. It is then that no worry, fear, or anxiety can ever come close to us!

When man surrenders himself to God, then God takes upon Himself his entire responsibility. All we need to do is to hand ourselves over, in childlike trust to the Lord. And the angels of God will go ahead of us to clear the way. No obstacles will be too difficult, no barriers will be impossible for us to cross! For true faith, true devotion, is belief that whatever may happen, God loves me, He is always there for me! It is akin to the absolute, unconditional, complete trust that the child has in his mother.

Let me recall to you a beautiful incident from the life of Jesus. Once, people were bringing their little children to Jesus to have him touch them, but the disciples rebuked them. When Jesus saw this, he was indignant. He said to them, "Let the little children come to me, and do not hinder them, for the Kingdom of God belongs to such as these. Truly I tell you, whoever does not receive the Kingdom of God like a little child, will never enter it." And he placed his hands on them and blessed them.

Trust the Lord for all your needs

All of us can cultivate such childlike trust in the Lord. We only need to hold firmly to the truth that we are God's children, and that He is our loving Father who is too loving to punish us, and too wise to make a mistake. We must remember too, that God helps those who help themselves, and that our efforts and endeavours must operate in tandem with His Divine Will.

If we regard ourselves as His children, it goes without saying that the rest of mankind are our brothers and sisters, as indeed is the whole of Creation. Therefore, we must share whatever we can, with those whose need is greater than ours.

How may we cultivate such childlike trust in the Lord?

1. The first essential thing is a change of outlook. As it is, we depend too much on

ourselves, our efforts and endeavours. We keep God out of the picture. True, human effort has its place in life. But we need to understand that above all efforts is His Will. And He is the Giver of all that is! So let not our work be egotistic– but dedicated. Let us learn to work as His agents, the instruments of His Will. Our children are His children. We are here to serve them to the best of our ability and capacity. It is His responsibility to provide for them, maybe through us, or others. And His coffers are ever full!

2. The second essential thing is to share what we have with others. Let us set apart a portion, say one-tenth of our earnings, to be utilised in the service of God and His suffering Creation.

    To those who are unable to live on their income, this may appear a difficult thing to do. But even they will find that in the measure in which they share what little they have with others, they will be richly blessed. Out of the little that remains to them, they will get more, much more than they expected. This is what we in the Sindhi language call *barkat*.

    This is one of the laws of life– the more we give, the more we get out of the little that remains. Therefore, I tell my friends again and again: surrender all you are and all you have in God's safe hands. When you allow Him to take over, you have nothing to worry about!

3. Do not be scared of anything. Trust in the Lord and face the battle of life. There is no power on earth that can lay you low. Trust in Him. Turn to Him for everything you need. Make Him your Senior Partner– and success will flow into your life as rivers flow into the sea!

4. We must contact God again and again. It is necessary for us to consistently repeat His Name, to pray without ceasing. A prayer which may prove helpful is, "Lord! Make me a channel of Thy mercy!"

    To become a channel of His mercy, we must surrender all we are and all we have at His Lotus Feet. So may we become His instruments of help and healing in this world of suffering and pain.

    He who hath surrendered himself hath found the greatest security of life. And when one has surrendered, he does not need to wander anymore. All his cares and burdens are borne by the Lord Himself.

How beautiful are the words of the Gita:

They who worship Me
Depending on Me alone,
Thinking of none other– they are My sole responsibility!
Their burdens are My burdens!
To them I bring full security!

The more we meditate on the Lord's words, the more we shall grow in that true life which is a life of self-surrender. The life of child-like trust and true faith is a blessed, carefree life. It is a life free from the shackles of earthly "experience". To be truly free is to be born anew, to become a pure child of God. Such a one lives with God and walks with God and speaks to Him and hears Him speak.

Bhakti Yoga is the path of utter devotion, supreme love for God. It is pure and selfless love, which is far above worldly love. It does not involve bargaining with God over results; it is above all selfish motives. It is intense devotion and attachment to the Lord. It has to be felt, experienced– not talked about or discussed.

What are the marks of such a man who reaches out to God in childlike love?

- *Vatsalya bhava* pervades the devotee's heart, mind, and soul.
- In its intensity, all impurities of the mind are destroyed, reduced to ashes.
- It makes the devotee simple and childlike in his absolute trust in God.
- It has none of the weaknesses and defects of adult love such as selfishness, insincerity, attachment, and ego.
- It is the most pure and natural form of love– for we learn to love God even as a child loves its elders.

Death

Death is the one unalterable verity of human life. It is a cliché to say that all that is born must die; yet it is the truth. He who is born must die. But how many of us understand the meaning of death? What kind of experience brings down the curtain on the drama of our life? Truth be told, many of us are so superstitious about discussing death; we are frightened by the very word death.

What is death?

"What is death?" We put this question to Sadhu Vaswani once, and his reply was, "Death is a bridge!" When death comes, we leave the physical world and cross over the bridge to enter the astral world, which is a better, nobler, richer, more beautiful, more radiant world.

He also likened the death of the body to a sunset. He said to us, "Sunset is only an appearance, for what is sunset here is sunrise elsewhere. In reality, the sun never sets. Likewise, there is no death, death is only an illusion, an appearance. For death here is birth elsewhere."

Why do people fear death?

We fear the unknown. We do not know what our condition will be when death comes to lay its icy hands upon our body. We have always pictured the angel of death as a dark, sinister being, who will come and throttle us. The whole world is afraid of death. Everyone wishes to know what happens on the other side of death, but no one is prepared to die; it is one thing we all wish to avoid. Both the happy ones and the unhappy ones– even those that lead a miserable existence– do not wish to die.

Fear of death arises from the illusory notion that life on earth is pleasant, profitable, desirable and therefore worth clinging on to at all costs. Caught up in the toils of life, in the allurements and entanglements of the body, in the disappointments of yesterday, the problems of today and the anxieties of tomorrow, we are bounded, constricted by this world of multiplicity.

We should not be afraid of death; on the contrary, we should reflect on this wonderful phenomenon that takes us away from this world to an astral sphere. In a Trappist Monastery abroad, I saw written in bold letters the words, *Carpo Mori* meaning, 'Contemplate on Death'.

Death

Think of death every day.

Farid ud-Din was a great Sufi saint. In his youth, he was a wealthy man who owned a prosperous business of perfumes and herbal remedies, and was hence called Attar. It is said that his shop was the best and the most famous in the city where he lived.

One day, an unknown *fakir* came to Attar's shop. He stood in front of the shop and surveyed the premises carefully. His sharp glance took in everything, and missed nothing.

"What are you looking for?" enquired Farid ud-Din of the *fakir*.

The stranger replied, "I was wondering how you will be able to leave this prosperous business behind, when the Call of Time is upon you."

Farid ud-Din Attar too, was incensed at the words of the stranger who spoke so freely of death. Harshly, he said to the *fakir*, "Pray tell me, what would you do if death were to come upon you?"

The stranger smiled. He threw away the shawl that covered his body and lay down upon the ground. "When death comes to me," he said, "I shall depart, just like this!" With these words, he passed away then and there!

Farid ud-Din was profoundly moved by this incident. In him too, the slumbering Spirit awakened. He closed his prosperous business and set out in search of a guru who could show him the way onward.

Mrityorma amritam gamaya...

We are not the changeable, perishable, vulnerable body that we wear! We are the immortal Spirit within! We must all become aware that the *atman* is indestructible, imperishable. Therefore, there is no such thing as death of the *atman*. The destination of our life is not death, but the state that transcends death. It is eternity; it is the state of bliss that is our birthright; it is the state of union with our origin, which is pure divinity!

Sadhu Vaswani himself said to us, "I cannot die! It is the body that dies! And the body is but a garment, an instrument through which works the *atman*, the Spirit!"

I recall the mighty words of the Lord in the Bhagavad Gita:

He is never born, and he never dies. He is in Eternity, he is for evermore!
Birthless and deathless and changeless remaineth he forever.
He does not die when the body dies!

How can we prepare to meet death?

"Death is sure to come, but fortunate is he who has made preparations for that day." These are the meaningful words of my Master Sadhu Vaswani. We have to prepare for death, and when it comes, we must welcome it with open arms– for it takes us one step nearer to God.

We should live so that we have no fear of death!

Time and again, I have urged my friends to build a bond with the infinite. Build a strong, intimate, and loving relationship with God. See Him in any form which you desire, which is close to your heart. For, you will meet Him and realise Him in the form you have worshipped Him. This bond with the Infinite, helps us to go through what we call death. The messengers of death will not be the ones to touch us. It is the form in which you worship God, which will enfold you in its arms and take you safely out of the gross physical body. Let us build a bond with God.

Secondly, let us accept whatever life offers us, because every experience is God's gift to us. Let us acknowledge that gift and willingly accept the roller-coaster journey that is life– its ups and downs, its joys and sorrows, its pain and suffering, its moments of enlightenment and liberation.

Thirdly, let us serve the poor and the needy, feed the birds and animals. Let us serve them with the love of our heart. Let us keep away from all evil and do as much good as we can to as many as we can, in as many ways as we can, in the brief period that has been allotted to us on earth. This will help us to grow and evolve spiritually and emotionally.

Depression- Fight It!

Depression can be a serious setback for people. Adults and youngsters, men and women, suffer from depression. But in adults, their coping mechanisms are better, as also is their higher capacity for a mature response and reaction to stress. When young people are depressed, they tend to focus on all their negativities– their failures, their weaknesses, their disappointments and guilt. This is why suicidal tendencies are more common among youngsters.

Depression disables our mental make-up so that we are unable to see the positive side of things. As for recognising our own worth, our merits and our capabilities– we dismiss the very thought that we have such traits at all! In short, we are led to believe that things will never ever go well for us, ever again!

Inner feelings of doubt and inadequacy must be overcome. Depression exaggerates and expands on our weaknesses, ending up magnifying our misery.

The possibility of being happy, of laughing, being successful and content– all of this is utterly discounted, in this unhappy mental condition.

What is the cause of depression?

I believe the greatest killers of man are not heart attacks, cancer and accidents, but the clock, the calendar and the telephone. The price of financial success in modern times, an age of tensions, is mounting every day. The competitive spirit is cruel and ruthless, and drags many into depression.

There are various types and causes of depression– tension, anxiety, competitive struggle, failure, frustration, disappointment in love, a guilty conscience, isolation and lack of love and support.

People who live alone, people fighting major illnesses, people who have been bereaved, people who have suffered sudden financial losses are especially vulnerable. What can we do if our friends are put through such tests? Let us not think that these issues are too big for us to handle. Let us be there for them, offer whatever help we can, and extend the loving hand of friendship that can help them cross over to peace and security.

How can we recognise symptoms of depression in our near and dear ones?

If you read self-help medical guides, you will be quite startled by the common symptoms of clinical depression:

- Depressed mood during most of the day, especially in the morning
- A sense of fatigue, exhaustion or low energy levels almost every day
- Constant feelings of worthlessness or guilt
- Lack of concentration, inability to take firm decisions
- Excessive sleeping or lack of sleep
- Refusal to take an interest in the family/community
- Recurring thoughts of death or suicide
- A sense of restlessness
- Significant weight loss or gain

Experts say that if you have even five of these symptoms, you might be suffering from severe depression.

A friend who read these symptoms on a website said to me that he was startled to realise that he had most of them, almost every day!

The reason I have listed out these common symptoms is that you might learn to be sensitive to what are called "mood swings" or other warning signs in your friends' behaviour, therefore ensuring that they get your help and support and do not take rash decisions.

While we are on this subject, may I appeal to you to be a friend to all, be a friend of humanity in this sad world that is smitten with suffering! May the warmth of your friendship radiate towards all people who cross your path. May your good cheer and helpful attitude put a smile on their lips! May you be a helper and healer of all who suffer and are in pain!

Fight depression!

Depression must be fought even as we fight an infection or attack. It incapacitates us to such an extent that we are unable to think clearly and solve problems decisively. The more we succumb to depression, the more distorted our thought and perception becomes, so much so, we fail to realise that it is not really the situation which is so bad, but our depression which makes us believe so. In fact, mole hills appear to be mountains, problems seem insoluble, and it appears that there is no one, nothing that we can turn to!

Fortunately, such depression can be fought, conquered and cured with just a little effort. All we need to do is:

1. Open up to friends, family, and elders.
2. Connect with people whom we love and trust.
3. Avoid the company of negative, pessimistic people who aggravate our depression.
4. Seek counselling and guidance.
5. Avoid isolation and solitude by seeking the company of happy, pleasant people, or taking up some form of exercise, physical or creative activity.
6. Adopt a healthy diet, as junk food can negatively impact your mood.

One thing we must avoid at all cost: harbouring the thought of escape– or giving up on life!

Alternative prescriptions for depressed people

- Have you failed an exam? Think of youngsters who cannot afford their education.
- Have you been punished by your parents or teachers? Think of the countless orphans who live on the pavements and railway platforms.
- Have you been unsuccessful in a competition or an entrance test? Think of youngsters who are badly beaten up and tortured by the police.
- Do you feel unwanted or unloved? For a change, why don't you try to love and care for others?

Suicidal depression

I was once asked this question at a youth gathering: what do you think of the people who end their own life? Are they very, very brave, or are they just cowards?

I replied that it was not courage nor cowardice that make people attempt to end their own life. Rather, it is a result of a momentary insanity– a moment when these people feel that they have no one to turn to; that no one, nothing could help them out of their despair and depression.

I called it momentary insanity because their belief is patently false! How can anybody imagine that no power in the world can help them? How can they presume that their condition is so dire and difficult, and that the rest of the world is happy and peaceful?

There are millions upon millions of men, women and children for whom daily life is a struggle. They survive against all odds, they face challenges with fortitude. Should we not consider the plight of those who are far worse off than we are?

Why is suicide considered a crime and a sin? Is it not a human tragedy?

I am a Hindu, but I respect and revere all religions of the world– and believe me when I say, that all of them condemn suicide as vehemently as murder!

Suicide is not a solution to any of our problems. In fact, it only worsens our condition and will prolong our agony after death– and in the lives to come!

The fact of the matter is that we do not have the right to take away what we cannot give. We cannot give life; how then can we take it away, even from ourselves?

They tell me that there was a thought provoking play staged at London's West End, on a man's right to euthanasia, or mercy killing. The title of the play was a challenging question: "Whose life is it anyway?"

I can give you the answer to that question without hesitation: it is God's life– not yours or mine! As long as we wish to live here on God's good earth, it is of course our life; we can do as we please with it. But life is an asset entrusted to us for safe keeping. We cannot throw it away, and we do NOT have the right to bring it to an end!

How can we counsel people who have suicidal tendencies?

I would say to these friends, do not make the mistake of imagining that suicide is heroic, and that it will make people admire you or look up to you or feel sorry for you. Should you succeed in your attempt, what will their sorrow and regret do for you? The dead are dead; they can't live on their worldly anticipations and expectations.

Do not imagine either that you are 'punishing' your spouse, parents, friends, or teachers by taking away your own life. You are punishing yourself!

Do not be deceived into thinking that suicide is an escape, a solution, or an end to your misery. It is the worst sin against the Self, the Spirit, and God who created you.

To tell you the truth, I am agonised to read about the growing number of suicides these days, especially among young people. I am convinced that a person chooses suicide as an option only when he feels that there is nobody who understands him, nobody to support him or help him. Depression, isolation and a sense of alienation are rampant among the youth today. I can think of no better panacea for all these psychological ailments than faith in God, the loving support of the family, and the soothing, healing balm that friendship can offer.

Overcoming depression

1. We must never forget that depression is a temporary phase. Just as the sun goes into a sinking spell every night, but rises again the next morning, similarly, depression is temporary. Affirm to yourself again and again, "This too shall pass away!"

2. Take care to see that your tensions do not accumulate. Therefore, practise relaxation every day and learn to take your troubles to God.

3. Find someone to whom you can unburden yourself. Understanding and patient listeners are needed.

4. Count your blessings.

Desire

The word desire, we are told, is derived from the Latin *desiderare*, meaning 'to long or wish for'; this term derives from *de sidere*, or 'from the stars' whose original sense possibly was "await what the stars will bring"... It would be true to say we desire the very stars now!

Kama, meaning desire or longing, is one of the four *purusharthas*– goals of human life according to Hindu philosophy (the other three being *dharma*, *artha*, and *moksha*). Hindus believe that true self-realisation is possible by attaining and balancing these four goals. Perhaps each individual passes through stages of evolution during which each of these goals is sought. Thus, as we grow older and wiser, we overcome the desire to amass more and more wealth, or to seek after material pleasures. Our consciousness turns to the pursuit of the ultimate objective, *moksha* or liberation.

Many desires are good

Desires can be fulfilled in a state of awareness and through the right means. Desires are not always detrimental to our spiritual efforts; the desire for human happiness eventually leads us to the awareness that the world can never really satisfy our aspirations. Let us not forget too, that it is *kama* which motivates us to make friends, to marry and start a family, to relate to the people around us. Within the bounds of *dharma*, *kama* can lead to a life of joyous fulfilment. And when we have enjoyed some of these pleasures, we can be freed from bondage to *kama* and move ahead! A day will come when we will realise that earthly pleasures will no longer fulfill our needs, and we will strive for higher pleasures, more spiritual desires which we call aspirations. *Mumukshatwa*, the longing for *moksha*, in its early stage, is also an aspiration!

The function of desire

Psychologists tell us that it is desire that moves us, and, in moving us, gives us direction and meaning to our day-to-day worldly life. If you are reading these words, it is out of a desire to know something about yourself and the world! Desires arise like waves after waves within us; it is this continuous stream of desires that motivate us to act, to work and strive for our goals.

When we desire something deeply, we will it, and when the will is intense, we achieve it. A strong will makes it possible to achieve anything. A weak will makes us accomplish very little. Therefore more important than IQ (Intelligence Quotient) in our lives is WQ (Will Quotient) which drives us towards action and achievement.

If we were absolutely without desire, we would no longer be motivated to do anything, and life would come to a standstill! When people lose the ability to desire, they cease to act or aspire. An acute crisis of desire leads to boredom, and a chronic crisis to depression.

A deep desire for something alone can drive us towards achieving it. But despite our repeated efforts, if we fail to fulfil that desire, we fall into despair and depression.

Excessive desire

Significant are the words of the great lawgiver, Manu: "Desire is never satisfied by the enjoyment of the objects of desire. It grows from more to more, as does the fire to which fuel is added."

Even an aged and decrepit man approaching death, can still be filled with myriad desires. His feebleness leaves him incapable of fulfilling them, but the cravings still persist.

Desire, *trishna* or *moha*, is that well, that deep well, into which when a man falls, he is unable to come out. We all stand at the very edge of that well. You may be of high birth, you may have read the scriptures, you may have all the knowledge that books can give. But, once you fall prey to desire, once you are gripped by the craving to possess something, to indulge your craving, to satiate your passion, you cannot give up, you are unable to relent!

Emerson, while addressing graduates at Harvard University, cautioned them saying, "Young men, be careful of what you want, for you will surely get it."

Desires can also be destructive. Like fire, they are merely obscured by the smoke that emanates from it, but they can still burn and destroy.

How and when does pleasure turn to poison?

How is it that *kama*, one of the *purusharthas* sanctioned by the scriptures, becomes a *klesha*, or a deadly sin? The answer lies in the degree or the extent to which we pursue it: the key word here is 'excessive'. Even *kama* is legitimate within the prescribed limits.

It is when we exceed the limits that the pleasure turns to poison. In other words, unrestricted gratification defeats the purpose of true pleasure. *Kama* should not be allowed to dominate our life; it is an impulse which has to be restricted and disciplined. When there is no moderation, our wisdom is obscured, just like a mirror which is covered by dust.

Unrestrained indulgence in *kama* is condemned by all faiths and scriptures as a destructive and evil force. You may remember that the Gita warns us against excessive desire, which leads to delusion and bondage to the cycle of birth and death. In the context of the *purusharthas*, it represents the vital impulse to fulfil our legitimate desires without causing harm to others and without becoming slaves of passion. Here, as elsewhere, moderation and balance are essential.

True freedom from desires

It is very difficult, nay, almost impossible to satisfy desires. The more we try to satisfy them, the flames of its fire leap up higher as if oil is being poured into it. These flames then proceed to consume and destroy us.

Therefore, freedom from desires cannot be attained by gratifying them. It is only possible when the individual is able to gain control over them. The valiant individual who succeeds in overpowering his desires, is braver than the warrior who defeats his enemies in battle, for winning over desires is conquest over self!

Satisfying a desire merely results in the desire being replaced by another one. Gratification of desires only provides temporary and short-lived happiness.

When a boy meets a girl and holds her hand for the first time, the thrill that penetrates his entire being is inexplicable. He expects that sensation to persist the rest of his life, but a year later touching the girl means nothing, there is no more excitement. It is the innate nature of the mind to desire, and it is desire's nature to aspire for change.

Overcoming desires

It is not easy to overcome desires, but success on this path can be attained, to a great extent through *viveka*, which is the power and ability to discriminate, and *vairagya*, which is disinterest or non-attachment. Once the individual is able to discriminate between the 'real' and the unreal, he should just be a spectator.

Vairagya does not consist of abandoning one's worldly duties and responsibilities. It does not entail forgoing our worldly lives and living a life of solitude. It is an attitude of the mind, which detaches itself from the world. Through *vairagya*, realisation dawns that enjoyment of pleasures cannot give rise to genuine and lasting satisfaction. Now the individual can live in this world without being a part of it, discharge his duties, but with a sense of detachment. Such *vairagya* which is born of discrimination, sustains and endures.

Tips to overcoming desires

1. Do not let attachment bind you to anyone or anything. Be aware that attachment is the root cause of all misery.

2. Attending *satsang* regularly is most beneficial as it forms an impenetrable fortress around you, preventing the entry of any desires.

3. Selfless service cleanses and fortifies you, giving you the strength to say 'No' to desires.

Difficulties – Overcome Them!

Why do we face trials and difficulties? Why do bad things happen to good people? Why do good people suffer?

In truth, good people can never suffer. If a so-called good person suffers, it means that there is still a particle of evil lurking within him. An individual suffers so that the evil may be transmuted into good.

How does evil become good? How does gold get purified? By passing through fire! Even so, if there is some element of evil in a good person, he must pass through the fire of suffering.

Why difficulties and trials are sent to us

A little girl was learning to play the harmonium. As she practised the same lesson, over and over, she felt tired and her fingers hurt. She complained to her teacher who said to her, "I know it hurts the fingers but this kind of sustained practice will only strengthen your fingers." The little girl packed the philosophy of the ages in her reply, "Teacher, it seems that everything that strengthens, hurts!"

Significant are the words of C. S. Lewis: "God whispers to us in our pleasures, speaks to us in our consciences, but shouts in our pains."

"Whom God loves, He smites!" sings a poet-saint of my native land. Whoever would be a chosen one of God must gladly submit to a process of purification. He must be prepared to pass through the fire of suffering and be purified as thrice-burnished gold. He must be found worthy of facing trials and tribulations, of courting dishonours and disgrace for the love of God.

Beloved Gurudev Sadhu Vaswani said to us on one occasion, "Every great one of humanity has had to bear his cross. Krishna and Buddha and Jesus walked through the valley of the shadow of death. Who are we to say, 'We must escape sorrow, anguish, pain?' We, too, must bear our cross, bear and bleed. And when we bleed, let us remember the Will of God is working through us; and through suffering and pain, God's Will is purifying us, preparing us for the vision of the One Lord of life, light, and love in all that is around us, above us, below us, within us!"

God has created a wonderful world. He wants each one of us to be happy, prosperous, and successful, and to enjoy all the good things with which the universe is filled. If I am not happy, prosperous and successful, I may be sure that I have broken some natural law either in the present, or in an earlier incarnation. Nature does not have courts, judges, magistrates, or policemen who will arrest you when you infringe any of her laws. Nature works in a simple way. If your thoughts, words, actions are in obedience to the laws of nature, you may be sure of a happy and harmonious life, for nature is conquered by obedience to her laws.

Thoughts are forces, thoughts are things

Every thought I think is a force I generate for my good or evil. Every thought exists with form and colour. The thought may have the form of an angel or a demon, depending upon its contents. If I think a thought of peace, purity, prayer, love, joy, sympathy or service, it will stick to me wearing the form of an angel. If I think a thought of envy, jealousy, hatred, ill-will, resentment, greed, dishonesty, it will get attached to me wearing the form of a demon. Each one of us is surrounded by these forms, angelic or demonic, depending upon the type of thoughts we think.

Therefore I say to you: take care of your thoughts and fancies. With these you are building your own life. No one else is to blame for your present condition. You have built it with your own thoughts and desires generated in the near or distant past, in this birth or in one of your countless previous births. The forces that are around you have magnetic power. They draw to themselves forms of a like nature. If we are surrounded by angelic forms, they draw to themselves more angels. If we are surrounded by demonic forms, they attract to themselves many more demons.

We have heard of physically weak people performing heroic deeds of valour far beyond their physical strength. I read of a mother who weighed only 41 kilograms; in a moment of crisis, she lifted the wheel of an automobile beneath which her child had been caught. From where did she get all that strength? The seemingly impossible is accomplished when determination is accompanied by high purpose. Referring to Sir Galahad, Tennyson says, "His strength was as the strength of ten, because his heart was pure!"

Conversely, low and inferior thoughts have an evil and disturbing effect. Sometimes, in a fit of temper, we do things which we are otherwise not capable of. Later, as we repent for our evil deeds, we exclaim, "Some devil must have tempted me!" May I tell you, friends, we are not attacked by these entities, we attract them to us!

Face difficulties with faith!

There was a blacksmith who loved God deeply, even though he had to face many a trial, difficulty, and sickness. One of his acquaintances was an unbeliever. He said to the blacksmith, "How can you lay your trust in a God who sends such a series of difficulties and suffering and sickness to you?"

Quietly answered the blacksmith, "When I have to make an implement or a tool, I first take a piece of iron and put it into the fire. Then I strike it on the anvil to see if it will take temper. If it does, I know I can make something useful out of it. If not, I toss it on the scrapheap. This has made me pray to the Lord, again and again, "Lord! Put me into the fire of suffering, but pray, do not throw me onto the scrapheap."

In a passage of great beauty, the beloved poet of Sind, Shah Abdul Latif says, "I have known of no one who met the Beloved in happiness!" The Law of Love is the Law of the Cross, the Law of Sacrifice. And so Shah Adbul Latif sings:

They who embrace the Cross
And surrender their life breath–
To them is given the vision of God!

To the seeker after God, difficulties and dangers, trials and temptations come in an endless procession. He does not try to run away from them.

The man who tries to escape trouble finds himself, sooner or later, in more serious trouble. Such is the law.

No trial comes to us without a purpose. Every trial is a teacher, a guru; it comes to teach us a lesson we need to learn. Significant are the words of a Baul song: "By what path cometh thou, O guru? The mystery I cannot solve!" And again:

The welcome you receive is your Guru!
The agony inflicted on you is your Guru!
Every hammer-blow on your heart is your Guru!
What makes you shed tears is your Guru!

We have so many lessons to learn; these lessons differ from individual to individual. The lessons meant for me are not the lessons meant for you. Therefore, the trials God sends me are different from the trials He sends you.

Trials must not be resisted. To resist them or resent them is to add strength to them! Do not resist trials, but welcome them. Everything that we welcome is transformed. Suffering is transformed into strength. This is the great mystery of life.

Physical pain, mental agony, spiritual anguish– nothing lasts forever. Everything lasts for as long as it has a purpose to fulfil. When it has done its work, it falls away like the dead, dry leaves of autumn.

Many are the problems and perplexities that a seeker on the path has to face, as he treads the path. He knows that every one of them is necessary. He does not complain. He accepts difficulties as they come, makes them a part of his life, is nourished by them, and moves a few steps nearer the goal.

There are periods when a seeker finds himself surrounded by utter darkness. He finds it difficult to welcome trials and temptations with enthusiasm. In no case must he avoid them. Deep within him is the faith that though the situation may be exasperating, if only he will be patient and trusting, God will lead him out of danger into security, out of defeat into victory, out of darkness into Light!

Confront difficulties with courage

The one practical way to meet a difficult situation is to walk right up to it, look it in the face with courage and determination, and with the prayer, "So help me, God!" It is only when we are unwilling to meet a difficulty or are afraid to face it that it gets the better of us. When, trusting in God, we go forward to meet it, as we would meet a friend, the impossible happens. What was thought to be a trial, what appeared to be a source of danger and difficulty, is seen to be a blessing in disguise.

My thoughts go back to an incident which occurred in the days of my boyhood. It was a small incident to all appearances, but it taught me a lesson which I have not forgotten.

I was perhaps six years old at the time. I was a student in the primary school; a private tutor taught me English at home. I asked a friend to give me a story book and he promised to bring it on the *Holi* Day. The sacred day arrived. I heard a knock on the door. I eagerly moved forward to open it. The sight which greeted me was terrifying. I saw before me the fearful face of a lion. I screamed and ran into my home. Out of the lion's mouth issued words in a sweet, familiar voice, "Dear Jashan, don't be afraid! It's me, Govind, your dear friend! I have brought you the story book I promised..."

Immediately, fear vanished. I began to laugh. I moved forward to embrace my friend. I touched his face, which was covered with the mask. The fearful "lion's face" dropped down at a single touch, and my dear friend's familiar face stood revealed. Ever since this incident, I have tried to look at difficulties and dangers as friends who come to me wearing fearful masks, but always carrying rich blessings and gifts.

Meet every difficulty bravely. Do not try to avoid it. You will find that difficulties are gifts which God sends us for the enrichment of our inner life. He is the Lord of compassion and love: and His works are ever the works of mercy. If only we trust Him and surrender ourselves to Him, asking Him to lead us wherever He will, fearing nothing, avoiding nothing, but rejoicing in all that He sends us, no harm can ever come to us. Through every circumstance and situation will flow to us the love, joy, and peace of God.

Thank the Lord, always

We must always find some reason or the other for which to express gratitude to God. If there is one thing which God loves, it is a humble, thankful heart. Even in the darkest hours of life, if only we turn around, we shall not fail to find something for which we have to feel thankful to God.

A friend of mine lost an eye in an accident. He was taken to a hospital. Several friends visited him and sympathised with him in his irreparable loss. They found him cheerful as ever. To them he said, "I thank God that one eye still remains. The accident could have robbed me of both the eyes, but God chose to protect one of them. Blessed be His Name!"

One of the most moving stories which Beloved Gurudev Sadhu Vaswani told us is that of Bahram. He was a wealthy merchant. His caravans carried for sale in foreign lands, goods worth lakhs of rupees. One day, his caravans were looted by robbers. Bahram lost several lakhs. One of his friends came to console him in his great loss. It was a time of famine. Bahram thought his friend had come in the hope of getting a meal. Bahram asked his servant to serve some food. The friend said, "I am not in need of a meal. I only came to sympathise with you in your loss."

And Bahram said, "It is kind of you to have come. But I am not worrying over what has happened. I feel grateful to God that though the robbers looted my goods, I have looted none! The robbers have not touched the Treasure Imperishable, the treasure of faith in Allah, the Compassionate, for it is the true treasure of my life!"

The right way to take on trials

At the heart of everyone, everything, is goodness. And this is true of every experience, howsoever unpleasant it may appear to be. Life is a mixture of the "pleasant" and the "unpleasant", of joy and sorrow. As the great English poet, William Blake, says in one of his poems, "Joy and woe are woven fine, a clothing for the soul divine!" And as the Psalmist declares, "Weeping may endure for a night, but joy cometh in the morning!" Joy and sorrow follow each other as day follows night. But when suffering comes, the period of tribulation appears to be interminably long. A year of joy is but as a day: and a day of suffering appears longer than a year.

Trials and difficulties are an integral part of life, and every trial is a teacher. We would miss some of the best lessons of life, if these difficulties did not come to us. Many of us, alas, do not recognise this truth and do all that we possibly can to avoid a seemingly painful experience.

When trouble approaches, some of us try to run away from it; but trouble can never be dodged. The unpleasant experience recedes, only for a while, to return to us again, wearing a more formidable form. By avoiding trouble, we invite greater trouble at a later stage.

There are some who, knowing that trouble cannot be avoided, resign themselves to the experiences which fall to their lot. They do not resist: they give in to the inevitable. Often times, such persons are heard to say, "What cannot be cured must be endured!"

But there is a third way of meeting trouble, it is the only right way. The first way– the way of avoiding trouble– is folly. The second, the way of becoming resigned, is *avidya*, ignorance. The third is the way of greeting every unpleasant experience as a friend. Do not try to run away from trouble: you cannot do it. Do not endure trouble, simply because you must. But move forward to meet trouble, to greet it with the words, "Welcome, friend! What message do you bring to me from God?" And you will find that every trouble is a soiled packet, soiled on the outside, but which contains a precious gift. Every unpleasant experience is a package which hides a wealth of wisdom and strength.

The person who knows this greets trials and tribulations, problems and difficulties, with a smile. He is a true victor, and his way is the way of victory.

Disciple

Who is a true disciple?

Sadhu Vaswani tells us: He who loses himself in his guru, is the true disciple. The disciple surrenders his will to the will of his master, the disciple's will is blended with that of his master. So is the disciple released from the bondage of the ego, from the clutches of his carnal self, his lower self of pride and desires and appetites. The disciple is liberated and he enters into the life of freedom, the freedom which belongs to the sons of God. The disciple becomes a child of God. His travail is over; his journey is complete; he has reached the goal.

Qualities of a true disciple

He who follows his own will and his own desires is not a true disciple. He who doubts in his heart and is dominated by personal ambition may be intellectually strong; he who argues endlessly and emphasises the rightness of his own point of view may be an able debator– but a disciple he cannot be: for he is a worshipper of himself.

Gurudev Sadhu Vaswani outlined the following traits of a true disciple:

- Humility: When a true disciple was asked whether he was such-and-such-a one's disciple, he answered, "I am trying to be his disciple, so help me God!"

Humility helps us to avoid several obstacles and evils on the path of discipleship, such as ostentation and pretension.

Yes, the Kingdom of God, the *ashrama* of the guru, the path of discipleship is for the humble at heart. Unfortunately, many of us are proud, vain, and lost in ego! When we are lost in ego, we become blind to wisdom, and can only wander from darkness to darkness!

- Obedience to the teacher: The disciple must always remember that in obeying his guru, he obeys God.

The most essential mark of a true disciple is implicit obedience to the guru's wishes. "Not my will, but the guru's will be done," says the true disciple at every step. The more he is attuned to the guru's will, the more he will grow in the likeness of the guru, until, one blessed day, the disciple becomes a part of the guru's being. The disciple flows into the guru: the guru flows into the disciple. The twain are one, one in the One who is peace, joy, and bliss!

The teacher may put the pupil through severe tests. The worst may be this– he asks the disciple to be far away from him. A teacher knows that a raw fruit requires both sun shine and shadow, in order to ripen in maturity. So too, the disciple must have the double experience of fellowship and separation, for in separation too, there is union.

Spiritual obedience to the teacher, not physical nearness to him, is the mark of a true disciple!

Obedience has but one meaning– to obey. I may deliver a hundred discourses on obedience, and write multiple volumes on the subject, but I have not advanced a single step if I have not learnt to obey. The way of obedience is that which leads to the way of surrender, of which the Gita speaks in such rapturous terms.

- *Seva* or service: the disciple must serve the teacher whole heartedly.

The 'service' that we offer to our parents, friends, family, and other loved ones is service born out of our love and personal motivation to serve them and be of utmost help to them. In the service of the guru, there is, or should be, no such personal interest. In loving the guru, meditating upon the guru's form, in offering our devotion to the guru and in humbly serving him, we must remember– we are serving God in the form of the guru. Even when the disciple has attained self-realisation, he will continue to serve God and guru as before.

Does not the guru continue to serve his disciples all his life? He prays for them; he teaches them; he meditates with them; he aspires to bring them up to his level; this is his one aspiration all day, all night. The guru is like an angel with a lamp, constantly engaged in the service of awakening slumbering souls. He is the 'divine launderer' who is tirelessly engaged in the task of cleansing and purifying hearts and minds soiled with *vaasanas*. To the master who is constantly devoted to our spiritual progress and liberation, should we, too, not offer the loving service of our hearts?

Selfless service to the guru is also a form of *sadhana*.

A true disciple becomes less and less argumentative. When his legitimate questions have been answered, his genuine doubts cleared, he becomes more and more intuitive. He loses himself in the guru.

Daily practices on the path of discipleship

1. **Do not seek pleasure!** By this, I do not mean that you should become an ascetic. You have to live with the members of your family, live with them as one of them. Outwardly, there should appear to be no differences between you and them. It is your inner life, your inner attitude that should be different.

   Do not seek pleasure, do not desire anything. Accept whatever comes to you. If you find that a meal served to you is not to your liking, do not fret and fume, do not complain or criticise. Accept the food as *prasadam* from God.

2. **Do not cling to your possessions!** Attachment is an obstacle on the path of the seeker. Therefore, learn to be detached! If you have an impulse to give something away, give it without hesitation, give it readily and cheerfully. Until we have learnt to give, we cannot grow in spiritual strength!

3. **Claim nothing for yourself!** Learn to give without expecting anything in return. Give the love of your heart to all who come to you, and if they do not love you in return, let that not put you off.

4. **Do not be overanxious about anything**, even about your spiritual progress. For remember, He who is our Lord and Master, the *Satguru*, knows what is best for us, and if He wishes us to go slow, He knows best; there must be wisdom in it. Therefore, do not be anxious. To be anxious is to waste a lot of energy which may otherwise be used for a good purpose. Learn to resign yourself in His Will. "Thy Will be done!" Let this be the one prayer of your heart. "Not mine, but Thy Will be done, O Lord!"

I have shared with you four simple, spiritual practices that I found useful, when I set out on the path. They are easy to talk about, easy to list– but very difficult to follow, to act and to live.

For the sake of the guru!

The start of spiritual life consists of struggle and striving. We starve, and our hunger cannotbe satisfied by the most delicious dishes. We feel thirsty, and our thirst cannot be quenched by the choicest drinks on earth. Our hunger and thirst grow from more to more. It is then, that a yearning heart cries out, "O, for somone who may take me out of this little self into the larger life of the Spirit, someone who has drunk the elixir of life and tasted of the nectar of God's grace!"

Such a one, for want of a loftier name, we call Guru. I love to speak of him as the Beloved.

It is your greatest good fortune to come into contact with such a one on the pathways of life. You will look at him, he will look at you, he will look into you, he will read your heart as the pages of an open book. Each will recognise the other, and you will hear within your heart, his whisper, "Come, my child! Follow me!" And, without a single question, a single doubt, you will follow him wherever he leads you, to the very ends of the earth, even unto hell!

The way of the disciple

Our sages and saints have enumerated the stages a neophyte or aspirant has to travel on the spiritual path, before he attains to the highest Truth:

1. Wanderer: this is the first stage of worldly life before we realise and desire for the spiritual.

2. Pilgrim: here we begin to aspire towards the spiritual ideal.

3. Seeker: this aspiration leads to the quest for a guru.

4. Disciple: this is what we become when we find the guru.

5. *Sadhaka*: as a practitioner, we begin to walk the way of obedience.

6. *Shishu*: when one has done sufficient *sadhana* and cleansed the mirror of the heart, one becomes the child of the guru.

7. Guru: at this final stage we become the image of the guru. This is a stage reached by very few disciples.

Four kinds of disciples

A holy man once said there are four kinds of disciples:

1. The best disciple is like petrol. He will be ignited by a spark from the guru.

2. The second type of disciple is like camphor. He needs to be touched with fire and awakened by kindling the flame of spirituality in him.

3. The third disciple is like coal. The guru must take a lot of pain and effort in order to awaken his receptivity.

4. The fourth kind of disciple is like the plantain-stem. He remains cold and inert, unmoved by the guru's grace. No effort is of any avail with him.

The creed of a true disciple

1. He follows the guru's precepts to the letter and in the spirit.

2. He does not set out to 'judge' or 'criticise' the guru. He sees only the Divine in the guru– and does not try to fathom that which is unfathomable.

3. He approaches the guru in a spirit of reverence and humility.

4. He practises detachment, self-restraint and self-discipline. He attempts to free himself from lower passions, and keeps his mind and body pure at all times.

5. He attempts to grow above selfishness, by offering obedience, devotion and loving service to the guru. He always watches out for opportunities to be of service to the guru. And when the opportunity comes, he serves his guru humbly, willingly and devotedly.

6. As he grows in the spirit of obedience, he learns to eradicate the ego– the one major obstacle on the path.

7. He has absolute faith, confidence and trust in the guru. He lays bare the secrets of his heart before the guru.

8. The life of the guru is the disciple's loving model. He observes the guru, and learns from his every word, every gesture, every movement. The guru is his mentor, his ideal, and through constant association with the guru, he imbibes the guru's virtues.

9. The true disciple must be patient, earnest, and sincere. He cannot demand 'instant' enlightenment from the guru– he must earn it. Without sincerity and effort, he cannot attain the higher ideals of life.

One final thought…

We are told that when Michelangelo saw a barren rock or an abandoned slab of marble, he could see the vision of a beautiful figure which could be carved out of the inert mass of stone. But two things are necessary to make the imagined, beautiful sculpture, a reality. The first is to choose the right piece of marble; the second is an expert sculptor. And the piece of marble must be entrusted to the care of the sculptor, to be carved and chiselled at his will.

The true disciple must cleanse and purify himself and hand himself over to his master, to shape, mould, and make him into an image of the Divine!

Discipline

Discipline is the training by which we learn to obey rules or follow a certain code of behaviour in our daily lives. Discipline regulates our behaviour so as to follow certain moral and social obligations. It strengthens the body, enlightens the mind, and opens the heart.

True discipline is self-discipline. It was this kind of discipline that was inculcated in the *ashramas* of ancient India. The teacher, the guru, was not a taskmaster. He encouraged students to develop self-discipline. For, the teacher is not always with us, but we are always with ourselves. If we are trained to be self-disciplined, we will always be disciplined.

In my younger days, we were taught that there is the One who is watching us all the time. God is watching us. God is watching over us. Today, all this is forgotten. Even if God is a hypothesis, as so many people today declare, He is a very helpful hypothesis. However, contrary to their claims, God is not a mere hypothesis. God is real. God is actual.

Young people today value their sense of independence and self-worth. Their way is the way of questioning everything. They do not take orders from anyone; they believe in following their own way; they live and act by their "own sweet will". As such, discipline is becoming conspicuous by its fast disappearance in the world today! The values we worship are aggression, self-assertion, the ability to have one's own way, the strength to impose our will on others, the power to get everybody to do what we want them to do!

How can young people develop self-discipline?

When Benjamin Franklin was a boy, he divided his day and night into compartments of fifteen minutes each. Every hour had four compartments, and 24 hours yielded 96 compartments. Then he said, "So many compartments I will devote to sleep, so many compartmentsI will give to looking after the body, so many compartments I will give to eating, so many compartments I will give to studying, so many compartments I will give to games."

He led a disciplined life as a boy. Benjamin Franklin did not waver from the programme he had fixed for himself. Our way may not be the way of Benjamin Franklin; that was just an example. But, we must live a life of discipline.

In earlier days, we had discipline in our families, in our schools, with our teachers. Today, teachers are afraid of their students. The whole world has become topsy-turvy. Values have gone haywire.

Why is it necessary for us to be disciplined?

Without discipline, life would be chaos! Stability, structure, rule of law, and daily routine would be impossible without discipline. Responsibility, reliability, respect, and good governance would be lost without discipline!

Just imagine the busiest road junction in your city, at the peak hour traffic. Suppose the traffic signal was not working. Can you imagine what would happen? All cars, bikes, trucks, and pedestrians would try to move ahead irrespective of the other, and in a few minutes, there would be the most horrendous bottleneck and everyone would come to a standstill!

That is just an everyday example with which most of us are familiar. But on a more serious note, the observance of well-defined rules is the basis of orderly society. If there were no discipline, people would do whatever they pleased and would make other people's lives a veritable hell! It requires disciplined, good human behaviour to have an orderly society and make it an enjoyable place for everyone to live.

Athletes have to be disciplined and follow the rules of the game they are playing. Leaders have to be disciplined and not talk and act as they wish. Persons in authority have to observe self-restraint and discipline.

Without discipline there is no life at all. Without discipline you can achieve nothing, with a little discipline you can achieve little, but with total discipline, you can achieve all you wish to achieve. Therefore, always keep a watchful eye on yourself. Learn to say no to your passions and let your life speak the words you preach.

Discipline is doing what needs to be done, when it needs to be done, in the best way it needs to be done.

Discipline is not a curb on our freedom!

On the contrary, I would say that self-discipline is a form of freedom! It gives us freedom from lethargy, inertia, procrastination, and sheer laziness. It allows us the freedom to develop our individuality, our inner strength, our skills and talents. We become masters of ourselves, rather than remain slaves to our thoughts and emotions. It is said that the most powerful person is the one who has himself in his own power.

Discipline helps us to maintain our equilibrium. It enables us to live by our principles rather than succumbing to desires. It drives us to say no to our impulses rather than giving in to them.

Just as an ocean is made up of tiny drops of water, so also does our life comprise of millions of thoughts, thousands of words, and innumerable small deeds. To shore up our lives, we have to discipline all these countless thoughts, words, and actions.

Often, it is difficult to tread the right path. We are tempted to take the easy road. Many of us conveniently follow our minds in doing that which is in tune with what we want to do. But it takes discipline, will power, and courage to do what we ought to do, even though we may not want to do it. Doing the right thing at the right time, to the right person, in the right way– this is discipline.

Kop Kopmeyer, a legend in the field of success and achievement, has written four huge volumes on these subjects. When asked to choose among the numerous principles of success that he has written about, as to which was the most important and effective, with a smile he replied, "Do what you should do, when you should do it, whether you feel like it or not… We are caught in the grooves of our old habits and are unable to break away from them. It is only through discipline that we can be freed from the bondage to these unsavoury thoughts and deeds. That is real success."

Self-discipline is the key to personal greatness. It is the magic quality that opens all doors to you. We must discipline not only our intellect, but also our will and emotions. A truly disciplined man is in control of his actions. He ceases to be a slave to his impulses.

True education should help students to discipline their minds. However, discipline should be embraced, not through force, but by choice. Many of us resist adopting discipline in our lives, as it entails painful effort. But it is only a disciplined life that leads to happiness. Absence of discipline leads to suffering and misery.

Daily discipline ensures that a man is a master of his actions; he is not at the mercy of the moment.

Perfection is possible through self-discipline. We only have to stand unshaken, firm, and resolute in our resolve.

Duty

Swadharma, or the performance of one's own duty, is held up as the highest good in the Bhagavad Gita.

The Lord urges us not to neglect our own duty for any other task– however pleasant or superior it may appear to be. Never abandon your own duty, for this is what will lead you to *moksha*. In doing your duty, however humble it may be, you are not bound by action– your work will be as no-work. Go on doing your duty, however imperfect it may be at the start! This will purify your heart and will draw you nearer to the Divine.

When one acts, freed from the terrible strain of greed and desire, one finds that he is in harmony with the self. He is not pressurised by expectations, and therefore finds true fulfilment in what he does. This is the highest form of action, or *Karma Yoga*. *Swadharma* thus becomes the first step towards *nishkama karma*, or desire-less action. Gradually, his actions will be directed towards *loka sangraha*, service of humanity, and he will become a true karma yogi.

As a detached doer, you take up what duty bids you do. You perform actions prescribed by the scriptures, but unmoved by gain. You act impersonally, without attachment. You do an act, because it is due. You do your duty for duty's sake; you renounce all egotism, all attachments and all fruits.

The true karma yogi does not avoid humble or unpleasant tasks; nor is he specially attached to agreeable, pleasant, lofty tasks. He feels no emotion of repulsion or attachment towards his work. He does his task as a duty. Is the duty unpleasant? He does not hate it. Is the duty pleasant? He is not attached to it. He accepts life ungrudgingly. So is the teaching reaffirmed: "Arjuna! Play your part faithfully and courageously! Neither grieve nor glory! Submit to the Will of God! For His Will alone is fulfilled, not yours!"

The karma yogi does his duty, disregarding fruit, knowing that duty, well discharged, paves the way for liberation and illumination. He does his duty, setting the Law, the Wheel in motion. Do your duty and the Divine Law will operate. Leave the results to God's wisdom– trust in God and the Divine Law.

Duty first!

Thou shalt not fail in doing thy duty! Duty first! Does not the English poet say:

I slept and dreamt that life was beauty
I woke and found that life was duty.

We must do our duty. Duty is religion– even as work is worship.

"Do thy allotted work, Arjuna," the Lord tells His devoted disciple, "for action is better than inaction. Even the pilgrimage of the body is not possible without activity."

[Gita, III, 8.]

Work is a necessity of life! Even eating and talking are activities. It has been truly said that when God gave us each a mouth to feed ourselves, he also gave us two hands that can work to put food into that mouth.

Action is better than inaction. In the Bible we are told that Adam was condemned "to labour by the sweat of his brow". It is not a bad thing at all that we should all work– for work is a blessing, work is therapeutic, work is a tonic. An idle mind, we are told, is the devil's workshop. Even on the physical plane, idleness breeds illness.

But what kind of work?

Lokhayam karma-bandhanah: The world is in bondage to work, the Lord tells Arjuna– the world is imprisoned in selfish action. This is what most of us devote ourselves to; we work hard for the sake of power, pleasure and profit. This can hardly contribute to the welfare of society, or indeed our own true welfare. Therefore, the Lord recommends that Arjuna should act selflessly– without any thought of profit, without any sense of attachment, offering work as a sacrifice to the Lord.

"Therefore, without attachment, perform always the action which is thy duty; for by doing work without attachment, man verily reacheth the supreme," Arjuna is told.

If we have to renounce the results, why should we go through the burden of doing our duty or any other work for that matter?

Work is not an end in itself, it is only a means. I must do my work, with this in view that my interior self may be purified. This is the purpose of work, and that self-purification will come about only if I work and accept whatever result the Super Power sends me.

Many people think that everything is in their hands. Therefore, they are not able to accept the results if they are unsatisfactory. They complain, "I did my best. This is not fair. I deserve more." But, let me tell you that according to the teaching of the Gita, every work has five causes. Four causes are in man's hands– the doer, the field of work, the know-how, and the implements of work. The Gita says, there is a fifth factor which is not in the hands of man– *adrishta*, meaning the unseen.

For example, a peasant plows the land and sows the seed at the right time, but then he has to wait for the rains to fall. Now if the rains do not fall and the seed dries up, there can be no crop. There are two options open to the peasant– either to break his head against the wall, to weep, to tear his hair, call his family members and tell them to do likewise or to be positive and say, "There must be some good in it. Lord, I accept. But I am not going to give up this work. I am going to do it in the next season." Which is the better option?

How can we best do our duty?

A group of people were doing some construction work. As long as the supervisor was on the site, the workers were doing their duty. But, the moment he left, all of them stopped doing their work. The supervisor happened to have an artificial eye, so the next time he left, he took that eye and kept it on the table saying, "This eye will be watching you." One of the labourers had an idea. He took off his cap and placed it over the eye.

This is what we are doing. Duties are forgotten today. Nowadays, if we ask somebody, "Why don't you do your duty?" they reply, "It's no good. I don't get any pleasure out of it."

Learning to do one's duty as best as one can, is a matter of discipline.

Perform your duty first; abandoning your duty to pursue another's duty is both foolish and dangerous.

Each one of us has his duties, his obligations to fulfill. My duties may be 'high' or 'low'. It may be someone's duty to govern the nation; it may be another's duty to manage billions of dollars' worth of finances and investments; it may be your duty to teach a nursery class; it may be your friend's duty to tend a garden; it may be my duty to run an office efficiently; it may be my duty to sweep the roads clean…

It is not what we do that matters, it is the way we do it that matters.

If I do my duty sincerely and honestly, faithfully and conscientiously, the portals of perfection would be readily open, as easily open to me, as it is to the highest in the land! For the Lord makes no discrimination on the basis of caste or creed or social status. I may be the lowest of the low, but if I perform my duty to the best of my ability, the Lord will accept my work with loving grace.

Swadharma– not *paradharma*!

There is a very interesting fable which draws our attention to the distinction between *paradharma* (others' duties) and *swadharma* (one's own duties).

A poor villager had two household animals– a donkey and a dog. The donkey carried the man's burdens on his back every day. He was not stroked and petted by his master. The dog, on the other hand, stayed at his post at the doorstep, barking at all strangers. He wagged his tail at his master, who stroked him and lavished love and attention on him.

Enviously, the donkey said to the dog, "How I wish I could be you, even if for a short while!"

"Why not?" said the dog. "Let's exchange duties tonight. I shall lie down and snore, as you do every night. You can stay in my place and watch out for thieves."

"Sure," agreed the donkey. "But don't forget, you will have to carry the master's burdens tomorrow!"

The 'exchange' of duties was agreed upon and the animals took up their 'posts'. As luck would have it, a thief approached the cottage. Instinctively, the dog awakened, and urged the donkey, "Come on, do it now! Alert the master!"

The donkey started braying loudly. The master, who was in deep sleep, was so irritated by the harsh braying that he came out of the house and beat the donkey up severely. The thief of course, ran away with the commotion raised, so that the master did not even realise what the donkey had done for him!

The donkey, badly beaten up, groaned to the dog, "Enough is enough! You do your duty, and I shall do mine!"

The spirit of detachment and selflessness are impossible when you take on *paradharma*. Nor can it bring you real joy and satisfaction. On the other hand, doing your own duty will lead to a sense of satisfaction and fulfilment.

Swadharma performed without desire is truly fulfilling. For example if you are a teacher by choice, by natural inclination, you will find that you are teaching because you love it! On the other hand if you are teaching for the sake of the money you earn, then expectations and desires will cloud your joy.

There is no duty nobler than your own!

There are some people, who, out of the 'kindness of their hearts', as they call it, take up 'noble' duties, neglecting their own. Now, I am not suggesting that we should not undertake selfless actions. If you can spare the time, energy, and effort to do others' duties after performing your own duty to perfection– hats off to you! But this should not be an excuse or pretext to neglect your own duties!

There was a student who was very concerned about his best friend, who was unable to concentrate on his studies. He spent a lot of time with his friend, cheering him up, encouraging him, even trying to teach him. Both of them failed in the examinations!

There was a lady– a housewife and mother of three children– who was elected as the secretary of her Ladies Club. She devoted herself energetically to club activities and 'social service' programmes, neglecting her family. She told them to make their own breakfast, and order pizzas for dinner. This was surely a gross neglect of her duty!

The trouble with human nature is that many of us are dissatisfied with our own duties, and are apt to imagine that we can perform wonders and miracles everywhere else! Many people in India, for example, comment on the cricket team by saying, "If I were the captain of the Indian team…" But what about the homes, families, shops and offices where they are actually players or members?

Our students like to say, "If I were the principal/vice chancellor of a university/ education minister, I would declare more holidays and abolish all exams." What they need to do is attend to their duties as students, so that they can qualify themselves to become principals, vice chancellors and ministers in the future!

Our unsung heroine at home

Let us consider a mother. Who says her job is easy? She is the most unselfish person in the family, and also the most patient, the most understanding, and the least demanding. She always puts her family before herself. She does not look for rewards or recognition. As western nations are beginning to realise, she is like the Chief Executive Officer (CEO) or Managing Director (MD) of the organisation which we simply call H-O-M-E. Her duties include marketing, purchase, human resource management, administration, finance and budgeting. She is also the cook, chauffeur, housekeeper, nurse, laundry maid, cleaner, nutritionist, counsellor and hostess– all rolled in one. Some proud husbands even refer to their 'better half' as the 'Home Minister'.

And yet, hardly any mother has ever complained (seriously!) about her duties and responsibilities. Most of them accept these duties happily and willingly, and do their best for their families and homes. A mother is truly an inspiring example to us all!

The performance of one's *swadharma* or allotted duty, is not always pleasant or easy. But, as wise men say, the hardest duty can be smoothened, softened, 'oiled' with love.

Rights and duties: Our roles in the drama of life

There is a great cosmic drama of life which is being unfolded before us day after day. Each one of us has a part to play in this drama of life. Your role may be a major one, my role may be a minor one, but both of us need to perform well; both of us need to play our roles to perfection– otherwise, the drama will be a failure.

If each one of us attends to our duties in the right spirit, this world will surely be a Kingdom of God! If there is chaos, confusion, anarchy and indiscipline rampant in the world today, it is because the emphasis has changed from duties to rights. Today, everyone is claiming rights– workers, teachers, farmers, builders, investors, women, government servants, doctors and others– everyone is clamouring for their rights, but nobody talks of the duties that they have to attend to.

I feel that if each one of us gave first priority to our duties, if each one of us fulfilled our obligations conscientiously, everybody's rights would be automatically protected. If the employer fulfilled his duties well, the employees would have no reason to go on strike; if men fulfilled their duties conscientiously, rights would automatically accrue to women. There would be no fight against injustice, there would be no need to struggle for equality!

I am saddened when young married couples, in the guise of asserting their rights, actually impose their will on each other, and erect barriers between them! If a marriage is to be successful and happy, the partners must forget about their rights and concentrate on their duties.

Make your duty an offering to God

There are a hundred ways of doing the same thing. Some of these ways are right, some of these ways are wrong– but only one is the very best. We must do our duty in the best way possible, because it is our offering at the Lotus Feet of the Lord. How can we offer Him the second-best or worse? How can we not offer Him only the best?

Do your duty in the spirit of an offering to the Lord. This helps you grow in the awareness that you are an instrument of God, and that He is working through you!

When a strong bond, an irrevocable connection forms between our work and our inner self, then our work knows no limit, for our inner self is limitless.

The Lord urges us to perform all actions as dedications to Him. When you dedicate your duty to the Lord, you will indeed feel the difference!

1. When you surrender to His Will, and do your duty as an offering unto Him, you will not do anything that is harmful or evil.

2. When you allow yourself to become an instrument of God, your work will be better, more useful, more effective, for you are freed from your own limitations.

3. Doing your duty to God will also enable you to cultivate the virtues of perseverance and persistence, self-confidence and strength.

4. When you rid yourself of the desire for the fruits of action, when you are free from the anxiety about the result, you are content to leave it to the Lord. You also feel happy that you are acquiescing to His Will, and being a part of His Divine plan. You will find that the greatest good accrues to you, through utter surrender to God's Will.

5. You escape the great dangers of pride and arrogance on the one hand, and depression and dejection on the other. If your efforts meet with great success, it is His doing; if you should face failure, it is His Will.

6. You really put into practice the maxim: Work is Worship. Doing your duty thus becomes a

beautiful prayer. Performed in this spirit, work will always be a pleasant experience for you.

Not what you want– but what you ought to do! This is the mantra of duty.

When we learn to do our duty– selflessly, dispassionately, without desire, without expectation of a reward– we grow in the wonderful awareness, "I am not the doer; I do not expect, deserve, or depend on the fruit of action." This is selfless action at its best!

Education

'Education' according to its Latin origin, means 'drawing out'. That is what education is– a drawing out process. Alas, we have turned it upside down, into a pumping-in process!

The education that is being given in our schools and colleges today emphasises mere book-learning. Students are asked to study a few books, 'cram' certain facts, memorise them and reproduce them. We 'pump' dry facts and figures into their unresponsive heads, for we have forgotten the true meaning of the word education.

Modern education has sharpened the brain– but in the process, it seems to have hardened the heart! The bitter truth is that current education has failed in its most crucial task– the task of cultivating character, and instead emphasises advancement of the brain. Brain power is so well developed that we now create what is called 'artificial intelligence'. Technological progress has been tremendous; science has marched on rapidly. However, the problems we face today will not be solved by brain power alone!

Education of the true type must contribute to the health and happiness of the individual– and of humanity as a whole.

Sadhu Vaswani said, "Education is essentially a thing of the Spirit."

If education does not lead us from the darkness of fear, prejudice, greed and ignorance into the light of peace, joy, serenity, compassion, humanism, faith and love for all Creation, then it is not true education at all!

Even if one person is comforted by your words; even if one person's broken heart is healed by your understanding; even if someone's misery is wiped out by your kindness– you have made a difference! Your education has served its purpose.

A man is said to be truly educated when he is capable of living his life in the right way, when he shares unconditional love with all, and sustains his hope in the most difficult of situations. Above all, such a one makes God the centre of his life.

When does education begin?

Education is pre-natal. While the child is in the womb, the mother must think sublime thoughts. She must have no thoughts of resentment, ill-will, or jealousy, against anyone as this will influence the child in the womb.

A woman came to a sage and said to him, "My child is just born. When do I start educating him?" The sage told her, "You have already wasted nine months."

Bring God back into our schools!

I believe India will never be defeated, as long as her people are aware that God is the root of life. Turning away from God, we only wander from distraction to distraction. Therefore, this must be the first step in any value-based system of education: Turn back to God! Love God and love your fellow-men!

Let us bring God back into our schools and colleges. The current situation, in our country, has in several ways, repressed *dharma* in our system of education. How true are the words of the American philosopher: "If you throw God out of your schools and colleges, the vacuum thus created, will immediately be filled in by the Devil!"

It is not an exaggeration to say that a system of education in which God is absent, will be presided over by the devil. Unfortunately, this is what is happening in some of our educational institutions.

Therefore, I assert emphatically: we must educate our children, first and foremost, to know God and to love Him. If we make God a reality to our youth, we will surely find that they grow in those veritable qualities of character without which life has no meaning or significance.

What is your idea of 'well educated'?

A learned professor of Stanford University utterly rejects the notion that the first priority of education is intellectual development. According to him, "The main aim of education should be to produce competent, caring, loving, and lovable people."

Are you well educated? Are you competent, caring, loving and lovable?

Many people in the West feel that the chief aim of education should be to create and sustain a democratic society. There are also those who feel, equally strongly, that education should lead to economic development and corporate profits.

How many of you who are well educated will devote yourself to creating and sustaining a democratic society? And how many of you will put all your energy into maximising corporate profits?

Every aspiring student aims high and dreams of becoming a qualified 'professional'– say a doctor, an engineer, an architect or a software specialist. We look up, with great respect, to 'HR professionals', 'management professionals' and so on and so forth.

Let me ask you: is it not important that all these professionals including those professors who teach them and train them, should, above all, profess honesty, integrity, truth and idealism? Are these aspects of character not vital to every profession?

What professional education should emphasise

All I wish to stress here is that 'professions' should not be reduced to 'means of making more and more money'. Therefore, professional education, indeed, all forms of education should stress on the following:

- Life is larger than livelihood
- The end of knowledge is not just jobs and careers, or gains in silver and gold
- The end of knowledge is service and sacrifice

'Public life' and 'professional career' are terms much bandied about these days. What we expect of people in public life is probity, and what we want from our professionals is honesty and integrity. But what do we come across in real life? 'Cash for votes', 'multimillion-dollar scandal in banking', 'cybercrime fraud', 'corruption in defense deals' and so on and so forth!

Is this what we expect of 'educated' people?

Education in our age

Current education is dissatisfied with itself, and the dissatisfaction intensifies. As witnesses to this dissatisfaction, we have student unrest in India and other countries of the world. Classes are being boycotted, vice-chancellors are being *gheraoed*, teachers are being threatened and mishandled.

"Judge a tree by its fruits," said a great teacher of Palestine. Judged by its fruits, current education has failed miserably. This type of education cannot persist. A new type of education is needed– an education related to real life. Education must not be merely be academic or abstract. It must not aim at stuffing the student with information acquired from dead books or a set of sterile moralities and superficial values. True education should equip the student to cope adequately with life, with what lies ahead of him so that he may become a worthy participant in the adventure of life.

Current education, alas, is infected with the cult of the ego, the cult of pride and arrogance, vanity and show. What we need is a return to the ideals of simplicity and sacrifice, for in simplicity is true strength! Miseducation glorifies the ego. What we need is true education in values and ideals that will lead students to become exemplary human beings and good citizens of their motherland.

We have an elaborate infrastructure, we have a complex machinery of higher education– but I wish someone would tell me where I can find the soul, the true spirit of education in India today.

Current education has cut itself off from great ideals, from the all-pervading soul of nature, and from the great ones of humanity. That is why so many of our 'rising stars' succumb to the unholy temptations of power and wealth.

Today in India, forces of darkness seem to be choking the voices of Light. Today, both knowledge and power are being perverted into instruments of social chaos and destruction. Today, the moral base of life seems to have been shattered.

What we need then, is a system of education that will awaken the hearts of our youth. It is the heart that needs to be trained, for noble feelings and impulses that arise within it, guiding the intellect towards right actions. The heart is the master, the brain is but the servant. Of what use is an education that trains the servant, but neglects the master?

Why are students disillusioned with the system of education?

Students are no longer happy with learning from books which have no relation to real life. Nor are they interested in examinations which elevate text-books to the status of scriptures. They want answers to the pressing problems of life– problems which confront them in their day-to-day existence. They are eager to find out ways by which the world may be changed into a better, nobler, happier place. For no apparent fault of theirs, they find themselves in a world of injustice and exploitation, of cruelty and cut-throat competition, of hypocrisy and cant, of poverty and pain. And to their deep regret they find that the so-called elders take things for granted and do nothing to remedy the tragic situation.

What are the values that a New Education must emphasise?

I love to call them the five fingers of education.

The very first finger of education is character-building. Is it not true that the one urgent, the one piteous need of India today, is men and women of character? It is true, India needs foreign exchange and the goods which foreign exchange can buy. India needs technical know-how and a new social and economic planning. But more than all these things put together, India needs men and women of character. Men and women whom the lust of office will not betray, whom the gains of office will not lead astray, who will not scramble for power, but who will use all their power, in a spirit of humility, in the service of India's teeming millions.

Secondly, our education should lay emphasis on *seva*, the quality of service. Character is best built through altruistic living, living for others. Therefore, children must be trained not just to think of themselves, but spend their energies in giving comfort to those in need of comfort, in bringing joy into the lives of those that are joyless.

Thirdly, the emphasis must be on Indian ideals. Modern scientific knowledge is passed on to the students but they should not forget their rich heritage– the heritage which belongs to them as children of the ancient rishis. It is only with a blend of modern scientific knowledge and India's ageless wisdom that a new civilisation can be built.

In the fourth place, the necessity of international understanding must be realised. Lastly, there should be emphasis on cultivation of the soul. Man is essentially a soul. Our greatest blunder is that we have identified ourselves with the body that we wear, or, at best with the body-mind complex. New education should cultivate the soul.

Character, Compassion, Culture and Reverence for all Life, and Cultivation of the Soul: these values capture the ideal of right education.

The secret of good education

Reverence is the secret of education, and service is the fruit of education! Tennyson has said, "Let knowledge grow from more to more, but more of reverence in us dwell."

Reverence is of three types– reverence for what is above us, for what is beneath us, and for what is around us. Our education should inculcate the attitude of selfless service to all Creation.

Emerson, in his appreciation for Harvard College stated, "It has taught all the branches of learning." Though agreeing with him, Thoreau added, "Yes, all the branches but none of the roots."

Ego

If you were to trace the history of the word ego, you would come to know that in Latin, the word ego means self, or identity.

In modern parlance, ego has come to signify something else! It is an exaggerated sense of self-importance; an inflated feeling of pride in one's imagined superiority over others. When egoism manifests itself in outward behaviour, it becomes arrogance.

Is ego good or bad?

Experts tell us that ego is necessary to our survival insofar as facing challenges, tough situations, and crises in life is concerned. After all, the feeling that 'I-will-not-allow-myself-to-be-crushed' is what helps us come out of depression and failure. When you have to fight against odds, when you have to battle adversities, the ego is your greatest support. Personal care, good grooming and hygiene, doing well in your studies or excelling in your business, working for better recognition and appreciation, even achievement orientation are all, to a certain extent, motivated by the ego.

Some of you may be surprised to know that the following terms are used as synonyms for ego: self-esteem, self-regard, pride in oneself/one's abilities, faith in oneself, dignity, morale, self-confidence, self-assurance, and self-respect.

Negative ego

The negative ego– excessive ambition, insatiable craving and selfish drive– is the cause of all human unhappiness. Experts tell us that the negative ego is in a constant state of restlessness. It always imagines that there is a treasure of happiness and fulfilment somewhere out there, and can never feel fulfilled until this treasure is attained. Unfortunately, this elusive treasure is often a petty, selfish personal goal like money, wealth or personal power. The negative ego labours under the delusion that it is only the acquisition of this personal goal that can make it truly happy. Alas, such happiness is at best transient and fleeting. It may bring temporary satiation of desire, but the old restlessness and unhappiness will return to haunt us!

We can become servants of our ego, constantly striving to satisfy its many cravings and urges, making ourselves miserable every time the ego is defeated, and feeling vulnerable because the ego suffers massive wounds and hurts. Or we can become masters of the ego, not just its controllers and managers, but we can transcend the ego, let it go, and assert our identity as larger, complete beings.

Alas, for many of us, I'm afraid, the ego is unconquerable. Man has conquered space; man has conquered the sky; man has controlled even the courses of the rivers and the growth of the great forests– but man has not found it easy to control or conquer the ego.

The ego can make you its slave, if you do not learn to be its master!

Ego and the sense of separation

It is the ego which creates that subtle sense of separation between "me" and "others". When this sense of "me" or "I" assumes extravagant proportions, it becomes arrogance, pride, vanity and excessive egoism. At the other extreme, when it is defeated and thwarted and frustrated in its ambitions and desires, it leads to self-pity, victim syndrome, and paranoia.

I would say that the sense of separation, the sense of exclusion and isolation is what makes the ego a negative force. The stronger and more selfish the ego, the greater the sense of separation and the 'disconnect' that exists between us and others. When we become aware that as individual entities we are not apart from the universe, but an intrinsic part of a larger whole, then the sense of separation ceases to exist, and our personal goals are in tune with the common good of all humanity. In this state, the ego is a source of light; it ceases to weigh heavily on us; it becomes positive.

How to channelise the ego for our own good

Many psychologists argue that all work, all effort, all striving towards excellence is ego-driven. The very feeling that 'I must do my best, I must put my best foot forward', is derived from a strong sense of self-worth. As long as this effort is not derogatory to others' well being, ego is not a bad thing at all! What I am trying to say is that your self-impelled, self-fulfilling efforts can be aligned with selfless goals, if you are working for a common good!

One way of looking at higher awareness is to regard it as 'ego expansion'. For what is it but expansion of the self to become aware of the *Mahavakya, Aham Brahmasmi* or *Sohum*! If we were not capable of realising that we are not the limited, petty selves that we take ourselves to be, we would be trapped in our lowest self! Perhaps what is called for here is ego transcendence, rather than ego-expansion!

The highest form of 'ego-consciousness' is required to be able to assert the truth that all of us are princes and princesses, loving children of God, the King of kings. It takes a strong sense of the self to assert that as princes and princesses, there are certain things that we must never stoop to do!

The veil of the ego

The wise ones tell us that there are many veils that keep God hidden from our consciousness. Perhaps the most troublesome one is the veil of the ego. Sadhu Vaswani often said to us, "Remove the veil of ego, and you will behold the Light Divine." He, the omnipresent One is right here, standing before us. We are unable to see Him due to this stubborn, unyielding veil of the ego.

"God is right there, bright and illuminated. But the ego blurs our vision and we are unable to see the shining Divine Light," Sadhu Vaswani added. "An egoless man is one who walks the little way. His is the way of acceptance. He accepts everything. If he is asked to be the president of the country, he accepts it and holds the reins of the country. And when he is asked to be a sweeper, he accepts that too, in the same measure. A humble man asks no questions."

If we can remove the veil of the ego, we will truly behold the vision of the Beloved!

Break the tyranny of the ego

When in the midst of friends or strangers, refrain from pushing yourself forward.

1. Refrain from too much talk. Practise silent self-affirmation.

2. Learn to respect and appreciate others.

3. Remember– your real value lies not in your outer, empirical self, but in your inner, imperishable self.

4. Cultivate friendship with this inner self. Identify, understand and transcend the ego!

Empower Yourself

When I say "empower yourself", I mean discover the power, the *shakti* within you, that can transform your life. Uncover the potential in yourself to rewrite the story of your life. Take charge of your own life. Discover the joy that is your own birthright. Live life like a prince or princess, for you are a child of God, who is the King of kings!

Realise that you are the architect of your own destiny! Your life, your future, your dreams, your destiny are in your own safe and capable hands. To shape your life and your destiny, all you need to do is to empower yourself to bring about the positive transformation you seek.

God endowed each and every one of us with a free will, and each of us has the freedom to change our destiny at every step, in every round of life. In other words, each of us has the freedom of choice to act– to choose right or wrong. At every step of life, we can make the effort to improve our condition. Through our actions, we can actually succeed in changing our own karma and thus altering our own destiny.

Is this not true empowerment?

"When writing the story of your life, don't let anyone else hold the pen," a wise man tells us. Some of you may retort, "But I'm not writing my autobiography!" Believe me friends, every day, every hour, every moment, even right now, the story of your life is being lived, it is being written in the records of eternity, and the story of your life that is being written now will alter the course of your future! Every thought you think, every word you speak, every act you perform, is adding up to the story of your life. When I say "empower yourself" I mean, take charge of your life to make it meaningful, purposeful, worthwhile, useful to yourself and others, and above all, joyous and peaceful, so that you will wake up every morning, fresh as the proverbial morning rose newly washed in dew, eager to spread your fragrance all around.

Are you in charge of your own life?

Before we proceed further, let each one of us ask ourselves: am I in charge of my own life? Am I getting the best out of my life? Do I respond in a considered manner or just react hastily to people and events? Whom am I most eager to please– myself, my loved ones, my guru, or my superiors, my paymasters? Have I got serious complaints about the way my life is going? If yes, whom am I blaming for this– my subordinates, my family, my circumstances or God Himself? Do I retire to bed peaceful, contented and happy with my day's work, or do I fall asleep discontented, unhappy for no reason, and just ready to escape from the day's cares? Do I feel secure, contented and at peace with life, or am I beset with anxiety about the future?

Your own answers to these questions should reveal to you whether you have taken charge of your life, or you feel disempowered, unsure about who is running your life!

How can we take charge of ourselves and our lives? How can we empower ourselves to live a peaceful, joyous life?

Here are some approaches which can be applied to your daily life:

1. Embrace your life at this moment, here and now!

As the wise saying goes, today is the first day of the rest of your life, so make a new beginning here and now. Yesterday is a closed chapter. Therefore, do not waste your time regretting the past. The future is in God's safe hands. Why should you waste your energy interfering in His plans?

Let me share this anecdote that a friend narrated to me recently. There was a man who was walking in Central Park, lost in thought. He was worried about his business and unhappy about certain wrong decisions he had made in the recent past. As he turned into a secluded corner of the park, his attention was caught by a phone with the message: "For Direct Helpline to God, Pick up this Phone". Intrigued, he picked up the phone, and wonder of wonders, a beautiful melodious voice said to him, "Tell me my child, how can I help you?" The man was so desperate for help, he did not waste any time asking how or why. He blurted out, "Dear God, how can I live in the present? My regrets and fears and worries will never let me enjoy this moment! Can you please recommend a simple technique to sort this out?"

"That's easily done," said the loving voice. "Just focus on your breathing. Be aware of your breath as you inhale; breathe out fully and consciously when you exhale. When you focus on your breath, you can't focus on anything but the present. Why don't you just try it now?"

Shall we try it too? Focus on your breath. Take a deep breath; hold it for a few seconds; now breathe out, slowly, steadily, till your lungs have emptied. Now, breathe in…be aware of the breath that fills your lungs… hold your breath till you count 5… 1… 2… 3… 4… 5… Now breathe out… exhale fully… inhale… hold your breath… exhale… Did you have time to worry about the future or regret the past? Every time you feel overwhelmed by anxiety, try this deep breathing technique. You can do it even at your desk!

2. **Shift your focus!**

The thoughts, feelings, and emotions that are going on in your mind, manifest themselves as the screenplay of your life-story, played out, telecast on the wide screen of your everyday life. Friends, ask yourselves: are you thinking happy, cheerful, positive thoughts? Then you will see a wonderful, exciting life unfold in the future. Quit focussing on what is missing from your life; focus on your blessings. Visualise what you want to achieve. Do not dwell on fears and anxieties, do not dwell on your disappointments and frustrations. Why do you wish to relive your miseries? Don't create negative energy inside yourself. Therefore, stop criticising and judging others. I strongly believe that when you find fault with others, you are attracting their faults into your life!

Perhaps some of you are saying to yourselves: think positively; count your blessings; don't worry; stop criticising others– is all of this enough to shift focus and change our life?

Let me share with you what an aeronautical engineer once said to me. Imagine a pilot who is setting out on a transatlantic flight from New York to Paris. If his flight was just one degree off course, he would miss Europe altogether! Changing your life is not a matter of making radical shifts; small adjustments in attitude and thinking can bring about wonderful changes. So how about trying a one degree shift each day?

3. **Talking about screenplay and telecast, can the leading actor be left out?**

Acknowledge right now, that you are the hero/heroine of your life story, and determine that you will play your part well. Shakespeare spoke of seven ages of man. May I say to you, each and every day offers you a complex, challenging role to perform? Today, you might be the friend in need; tomorrow, you may have to be the comforting angel; later, the provider, the protector, even the defender of the defenseless, a champion of the underprivileged. No, I am not talking of earth-shaking, world-changing revolutions. I speak of the common, everyday occurrences of daily life. Whatever the role that comes to you, play your part well, for you are an actor in the karmic play of your life. How can your life be happy and successful if you do not play your role to perfection?

4. **Invest in optimism and faith!**

They are your safest insurance against misery, despair, and worry! When you place your faith in God and cultivate a spirit of optimism, believe me, the battle of life is almost won! Life cannot pose a question which faith cannot answer; life cannot present a problem which faith cannot solve; life cannot expose you to a sorrow or suffering which faith cannot surmount. Therefore, the great thinker and writer, Thomas Merton tells us: "Faith is the only key to the universe." Let me warn you, faith is not the equivalent of an Aladdin's lamp or an "Open sesame!" which will instantaneously produce before us, all that we desire. Nor does faith offer us the guarantee that we will never come face to face with sorrow, suffering, weakness, or disappointment. But faith can give us the courage, the right attitude, and the ability to face up to those problems and emerge victorious.

5. **Stay connected with the cosmic energy.**

Believe me, there are electrons of hope, joy, peace, and power floating all around us; make sure you pick up their frequency.

When we were little children, we were told that there were little angels floating about all around us, invisible to the eye, but very much there, hovering around us with protective vibrations. We were told that they kept saying *Tathasthu*! *Tathasthu*! So be it! So let it be! Now, just imagine: if you are thinking at this moment, I am miserable, nothing ever goes right for me, I am sure to fail, I am going to be bankrupt, I am going to lose this deal– what will happen if those little guardian angels say "So be it!" at that very moment? So let us think positive thoughts; let us tune in to the high frequency of joy and optimism that is alive in the universe. Let us think and feel and say, "Happiness is my birthright and I shall attain it! God wants me to be successful and I shall attain success with His grace and my hard work!" Repeat to yourself… "I want to be happy! I want to feel secure and contented! I wish to be successful! I want to love and be loved! So help me God!" I do hope you heard the angels proclaim: *Tathasthu*! So be it! So let it be!

6. **Switch on the sunshine of your smile!**

Spread happiness everywhere, for it is an immutable law of life that what goes out from you, must come back to you. Therefore, send out a smile, spread the sunshine of joy and laughter, and you will find your life flooded with more and more smiles and joy and laughter. If we are not happy, if we are not at peace with ourselves, we cannot share peace and joy with those around us. It is only when we begin to radiate peace and joy, that we spread positive vibrations around us.

7. **Get the balance right!**

Balance your perspective; balance work and life; balance your relationships; spend time on yourself and your interests. Spend less time on your cellphones and iPads and more time with yourself, your family and friends. I mean don't just text them, as you call it; talk to them, smile with them, look at their loving faces, not at their selfies or their Facebook profiles!

Today in the modern world, we all lead "extremely busy lives" as we love to tell everyone. "There's no time!" is the repeated refrain we hear all around us. We do not do much manual work anymore. But then, we do not seem to have any time for ourselves! Can I ask how many of you meditate daily? Can I ask how many of you sit in a silence-corner and recite your favourite *sloka* or mantra daily? Can I ask how many of you take time out to go for a walk? Create more time for yourself by rejecting non-essential activities!

8. **Draw on the greatest power source in the universe: and so, stay connected to God.**

God does not dwell in a distant heaven; He is with you, watching you, watching over you, here and now. Walk hand in hand with His unfailing presence. When He is with you, there can be no lack, no want, nothing missing in your life!

Dear friends, here on earth, all of us are not really in our element, if you acknowledge the fact that we are really spiritual beings! We are like deep sea divers who live and work outside their home environment. It is a strange, new, and sometimes, a threatening and dangerous environment; but if we are determined to make the most of our earthly lives, we must ensure that we stay connected to the Superpower above. Our living, breathing equipment for everyday life must consist of the lifeline of prayer, a regular, refreshing supply of meditation and reflection, and the abiding faith that we walk with God today and trust Him for the morrow. Just as expert divers check their equipment and their connections thoroughly before they dive, we too must begin the day by touching base with God, first thing in the morning. And just as they put away their gear safely after diving, we too must report back to God at the end of the day, in gratitude and devotion.

Any diver will tell you that he would be dead without his connection to the mothership! Any human being must know that life on earth would be unbearable without the vital connection to God!

Let God take over our lives, for He makes the impossible possible! All the time, while we are attending to our daily work, let our minds and hearts be fixed on God. Let the ship of the body move hither and thither, attend to its multifarious duties, but let the needle of the heart's compass be ever directed towards God. "For Thy sake, O, Lord!" Let this be the mantra of our life– and we will see that true happiness fills our lives!

Enemy Within- Beware!

Gurudev Sadhu Vaswani was often asked how he could advocate reverence for all life and *ahimsa* as absolute ideals, when the Hindu scriptures themselves supported animal sacrifice in *yajnas*. His answer was both simple and straightforward. "The soul of India," he declared, "has never countenanced the killing of creatures... when the Vedas speak of sacrifice, they refer to the internal sacrifice, the sacrifice of self-seeking impulses, the sacrifice of the animal within us... the sacrifice or *bali* of *kama*, *krodha* and the lower passions..."

The *yajna*, in its truest sense, is a form of worship that is essentially spiritual in practice. The whole concept of animal sacrifice is thus deeply symbolic, asking us to sacrifice or destroy in the fire of the spirit all that is base and ignoble within us! For these are the enemies within, which constitute impediments on the path of self-realisation, self-fulfilment, and achieving the true joy of life. It is this sacrifice that makes possible true inner cleansing, which is the firststep towards self-realisation. We have to deal with the enemies within, before we set out to deal with external factors!

Look within!

The Lord says to us in the Gita: Man can be his own best friend; he can also choose to be his own worst enemy!

When your mind makes itself a veritable hell, filled and cluttered with undesirable, negative thoughts, you lose the paradise of happiness which is your birthright.

We are responsible for our own happiness, and the quest for that happiness which is our birthright must begin from within us. What do you think you will find when you start looking within?

Sad to say, there are very many negative emotions that cause an imbalance in our lives, like jealousy, anger, envy, greed, sloth, shame, guilt, etc. Not only do they disrupt our energy system, but also lead to mental and physical disorders.

One thing is obvious: just as darkness is absence of light, evil is absence of goodness. Just as a tiny lamp can dispel darkness, so too, the assertion of good can destroy the negative tendencies in us. Therefore, we have the choice to conquer the negative traits that lead to unhappiness, evil or sin. All we have to do is to choose the positives, choose good, choose God. We have to conquer the enemies, the deadly thieves within us!

Keep away from those deadly thieves!

In one of Sant Kabir's *slokas* we have the following words:

O Kabir, during the dark nights, dark creatures are born,
Ready to go to the gallows; but God does not spare them…

Meaning: During the dark night, the black thieves venture out, unafraid of being caught. But they cannot escape the punishment given by God.

These immortal compositions truly take us back in time and space to the days when the great poets, saints lived and walked on this land. As we know, Kabir belongs to the 15th century. During those turbulent times, it was unsafe for people to travel on the highways, and at times, even to step out of the house at night. The roads were unsafe. Thieves loitered in dark alleys; dacoits, thugs and robbers roamed freely on the highways. Merchants and traders who travelled on horseback were easy prey for thieves. They were stopped, beaten and looted of all the money and goods they were carrying with them. Such were the conditions that dacoits and bandits became rich by stealing and plundering the wealth of rich men.

But let me hasten to add: Kabir's *doha* is not just a social reference to the times he lived in. As always, Kabir manages to pack in hidden depths of meaning into all these references. Men who carry money with them on dark nights are likely to be waylaid and robbed. But equally, men who live and walk in the darkness of ignorance and unawareness are also likely to be looted– only, the thieves and robbers in this case, are enemies from within us! And the treasure they loot is not material wealth, but the treasure of the Spirit.

Who are these thieves, who are these robbers, who plunder us ruthlessly in the darkness of the night?

Our scriptures use a special term to refer to these thieves: the *shadaripus* or six enemies within each one of us.

To be very specific, there are six thieves who carry traps to waylay us, ensnare us in their dark nets. Their favourite hiding place is in the darkness of our ignorance. These six thieves are *kama, krodha, lobha, moha, mada,* and *matsarya*– lust, anger, greed, attachment, ego, and jealousy. These six thieves are ever ready to capture us. We have to be cautious not to fall into their trap.

We are ever ready to blame other people, external factors, circumstances, fate, fortune, and at times even the good Lord Himself for our unhappiness, problems and failures. However, the truth is that we are responsible for our own lives, and it is time we become accountable to ourselves– hence the need to conquer the enemies within!

In Christian parlance, there is mention of "seven deadly sins" that are similar to the *shadaripus*: wrath, greed, sloth, pride, lust, envy, and gluttony. Buddhism too, talks of the three main roots of evil, called *mula priyaya* in Pali, which are greed, anger, and delusion or ignorance: *lobha, dosha, moha*. In Pali, these terms are closely interlinked; *lobha* is greed, desire, attachment; *dosha* is anger, hatred, hostility, aversion; *moha* is delusion, ignorance, lack of true knowledge.

Whoever you are, wherever you live, whatever your faith, enlightenment must replace delusion; the enemies within must be conquered. And yet, the fact remains, they are fed on our five senses and nourished by our own unworthy inclinations and desires! That is what makes them such deadly enemies.

Therefore Kabir warns us: the five sense organs– the eyes, the ears, the tongue, the nose and the skin– are supposed to be servants of the mind; but when they enslave the mind, they turn into our deadly enemies. "The mind surrenders before all sensory organs, but all these five sensory organs do not surrender before the mind," he laments. "In whichever direction I see, I find a fire of desires, and whichever direction I run to safeguard myself against it, I get the feeling of its heat." Says Kabir:

> *Man has to contend alone*
> *With five powerful enemies*
> *Each of them makes him dance*
> *Each as it pleases.*

Is this not true? These five senses become our enemies too, when we fail to control them; they overpower us so effortlessly, that we fall miserably before their onslaught.

The demons are within us!

Early in my life, I learnt the truth that we are not punished for our sins, but by our sins; that is, we suffer because of our failings, our weaknesses which are largely inner failures. What some people regard as sins, are essentially inner weaknesses which we can actually conquer, if we are willing to 'kill' the animals within! I think it is only because people were unwilling to take on this task of self-conquest that the barbaric practice of animal sacrifice came into vogue. Can I burn the anger within me? Difficult! How much easier to slaughter an innocent creature instead? Can I swallow my ego and arrogance? Far simpler to sacrifice a goat or chicken and swallow its flesh as *prasad*! Perhaps this is how animal sacrifice came into existence.

I cannot help thinking that the demons and evil forces depicted so powerfully in our epics and *puranas* are also symbolic representations of these negative forces, the enemies within, as we refer to them. In this sense, the Ramayana and Mahabharata are actually being enacted in the daily lives of us all! Ravana is nothing but a personification of the enemies within us— such as ego, lust, covetousness, envy, and pride. The Kurukshetra War is nothing but a metaphorical representation of the good and evil that is present within each one of us.

Conquering the enemies within is not a one-time battle in which you or I can emerge an all-time winner. It is a way of life, a mode of conduct, a discipline which we impose on ourselves to achieve the happiness that is our birthright as children of God.

The *shadaripus* or six enemies

Lust is such an aggressive compulsion that like a storm it sweeps over man and devastates him. Lust reduces man to the abysmal level of a wild animal. In the same way, anger also descends on him like a fury and ruins him. Greed leads man on to murder his own flesh and blood; it separates brother from brother, son from father, and friend from friend. Attachment is the main cause of suffering, but the worst vice is ego. Every man thinks that he is superior to others. Ego is the cause of self-pride. Man's biggest mistake is that he identifies himself with the body, with the mind, and with the ego! In reality, man is nothing but a combination of the five elements of nature. Little wonder then, that the Gita includes these deadly evils in its list of demonic qualities– the *asura sampadi*.

Pride, ego, and arrogance

Holy men and sages tell us that humility is the true mark of the evolving soul; and humility is not easy to attain, for it involves the utter effacement of the ego.

The dictionary definition tells us that egoism is "an inflated feeling of pride in your superiority to others". When egoism manifests itself in outward behaviour, it becomes arrogance or "overbearing pride evidenced by a superior manner toward inferiors".

The *asuras* or demons are standing examples of overweening pride and arrogance in Hindu mythology. Without exception, each one of the major demons like Hiranyakashipu, Ravana, Narakasura, and Kansa presumes that he is invincible and that no power on earth or in heaven can destroy him. The curious thing we learn about some of them is that they often put themselves through tough physical and spiritual austerities and offered their entire being to Gods like Brahma and Shiva to attain this invincibility. What we must note is that their spiritual disciplines and *sadhanas* failed to rid them of their ego and pride!

Let us therefore take note, that spiritual pride is as much a sin as physical or material pride! Who are we to assume that our piety, prayer, and *sadhana* make us superior to others? On the contrary, they should teach us the virtue of humility and make us realise that we are all dependent on God's grace and it is His mercy and kindness that help us against all odds!

Ahankara– the ego– is an abyss; it is the pit of pride, the pit of darkness, where dwells Satan, Gurudev Sadhu Vaswani taught us.

Swami Sivananda tells us, "*Guru-bhakti Yoga* is the surest and best *sadhana* to destroy arrogance and to dissolve the vicious ego." He compares arrogance and pride to deadly pests that ruin the harvest of our life; and the best 'germicide' to destroy *avidya* and *ahankara* (ignorance and pride), according to him, is this unique and peerless *Guru-bhakti Yoga*.

These pests and deadly germs become quite powerless to "afflict the fortunate soul who saturates himself with the spirit of *Guru-bhakti Yoga*. Blessed indeed is the man who earnestly takes to this yoga," Swamiji adds, "For he will obtain crowning success in all other yogas. To him will accrue the choicest fruits of perfection in karma, *bhakti*, *dhyana*, and *jnana*."

The failings of excessive desire: Lust, greed, and gluttony

For many of us, our so-called consciousness is limited to the bodily existence; we cannot rise beyond the level of the senses and the flesh; thus we are always subject to temptations, always at the mercy of forces beyond our control, desperate to snatch at 'pleasures' which offer gratification of the senses and the passions.

It is difficult to get rid of all desires. All we can do is try to minimise our wants and needs. As individuals, we may not find it easy to battle our own inner urges; but under the guidance of a realised soul who is desireless, who is positive, who is kind and compassionate, we may find the mental strength to conquer desire. Who better than Sri Krishna to show us the way? To conquer desire, and to find the perfect remedy against all sorrow and suffering, call upon Sri Krishna. Once Sri Krishna enters your life, those predatory desires, *trishna,* will lose its hold on you and let go of you. And you will progress towards a life of peace and harmony.

As for envy and jealousy, I cannot help thinking that these twin evils are the most demeaning emotions that human beings can ever give in to! They leave us unhappy on account of another's happiness, success or good fortune. In other words, we are constantly watching others and the way they are leading their lives, and burn with jealousy and bad feeling when good things happen to them. Truly demeaning!

Envy is closely allied to multiple negative traits: covetousness or *matsarya* (craving to possess what is not ours), jealousy or *asuya* (excessive fear of losing what we have, extreme attachment and possessiveness), resentment and bitterness at the good that happens to others.

Envy leads to ill-will, destructive thinking, constant criticism of others, disliking others for their good qualities, denying and negating their talents, skills and achievements, and rejoicing in the misfortune or downfall of others.

How to conquer the enemies within

1. What is impossible for man, is possible for God. Therefore pray to God constantly.

2. There are some battles which man cannot fight alone; therefore, choose the support

of your mentor, the guru, and arm yourself with the best protection: *Guru kripa*.

3. Let your mind be the master of your body: therefore, let the mind be disciplined and controlled. As the great Greek dramatist Euripides puts it, "The wavering mind is but a base possession."

4. Count your blessings! When you become aware of abundance in your own life, your attitude to circumstances will change and you will be ready to take on 'lean' and 'dark' days with a more positive and constructive attitude. This sense of 'abundance' will add to your faith and contribute to your inner balance and harmony.

5. Seek the association of good people with good, clean habits! Therefore, make *satsang* a regular habit. The positive vibrations and the sanctified ambience of the *satsang* is a remedy for many of life's evils!

Make a resolution now!

Tell yourself: I want to become New! I want to drop my old habits, negative ways of thought, and become quite, quite new! Imagine, you are inhaling the fresh air that God is sending out to you for each and every breath you take. Each and every breath is new and fresh! Each second, each moment of this life is fresh and new! Breathe in the fresh air! Inhale deeply and with each new breath you take, feel yourself becoming new and fresh! Tell yourself: I want to become new! I want to become new! Visualise yourself, radiant, happy and contented, deep within! See yourself smiling, joyful, at peace with yourself!

Enlightenment

What can I say to you about the ultimate experience: at-one-ment with the Divine? It is the vision that sets us on the path of freedom from this endless cycle of birth, death and rebirth; it is that shore of freedom that helps us emerge from the rising, threatening, drowning waves of the ocean which our sages called *sansaar sagar*. It is also the exhilarating realisation of our true identity as aspects of the Divine. It is the bliss of knowing the one Truth really worth knowing, the absolute and ultimate truth, that our real home is in the Eternal; it is our right to return there once and for all, permanely, for our dear Father awaits our arrival with deep love and longing!

Quick enlightenment

An anxious disciple went to a spiritual master and said, "A deep desire has arisen within me for God-realisation. Pray, show me the way to *mukti*– liberation. Grant me the gift of enlightenment."

The guru quietly replied, "In order to fulfil your wish, you will have to come and stay with me for a period of time, follow my instructions and surely you will attain enlightenment."

"This is the jet age," the disciple interrupted, "a computer age. Why can't you give me enlightenment right now?"

The guru thought for a moment and said to him, "I am glad you are eager to receive enlightenment. Let us first try to get a little familiar with each other. If you will permit me, tonight I will come and have dinner with you."

The aspirant jumped at the idea. At night the guru arrived at the residence of the aspirant. Immediately he said, "I am eager to eat. Kindly put all the dishes you have cooked into my begging bowl."

The aspirant looked into the begging bowl and saw that it already had some stale, left over articles of food.

"Let me wash the bowl first," he said.

"I am too hungry. I cannot wait. Forget about washing the bowl, be quick and serve me the food," the guru insisted.

"But I have made everything with so much effort– great care has been taken to cook a delicious meal for you. The good food will get polluted if it is put in this filthy, unwashed bowl!"

Quietly, the guru answered, "If this food can't be served until the vessel is clean, how can I put enlightenment– the food of knowledge– into your mind which is not pure? First purify the mind through practice of silence!"

What is enlightenment?

Many recent books and articles I have come across in recent years discuss something called "the enlightenment experience". They say it is characterised by bliss, oneness, unification, revelation, vision and epiphany. But these are mere words; and words, as we know, are sometimes weakened by repeated use and exaggerations! For even truly realised souls have found it impossible to describe the moment of union with the Oversoul!

The truth is that such an encounter, which many people have had the grace and good fortune to experience in this human life, cannot be expressed or understood with reference to our normal, everyday emotions and sensory perceptions. A busy working woman who comes home and sinks into her armchair with a cup of tea, exclaims, "Bliss!" An advertisement for a new brand of ice cream proclaims that it tastes "divine"! A good-looking film star is described as a "vision" in pink or black or blue. Where does this leave us with reference to enlightenment?

I have said to you earlier that each one of us must try our very best to seek a vision of the Divine in this lifetime. If we cannot attain to such a vision, we can seek the lotus feet of a holy one who has beheld such a vision! For even the glance, the grace, the blessing, the words of such a holy one can take us closer to the goal we seek!

Environment

I cherish every moment that I have been able to spend in the glorious environs of Mother Nature. Nature is beautiful; she is mysterious and powerful; her presence is healing, inspiring and uplifting. The philosophy of pantheism worships nature as Godly. The philosophy of transcendentalism believes that the spirit of God permeates all of nature. Our own *Isopanishad* tells us: *Ishavasyam Idam Sarvam*– All that is, is a vesture of the Lord.

Mother Nature is a magical healer. When we spend time in the lap of nature, walking in the woods, listening to the music of the birds, tending to our garden, or just looking at the evening sky, we feel revitalised and energised. When we breathe in the fresh air of open spaces and unpolluted surroundings, our flagging spirits revive.

Psychologists explain that when we are alone with nature, we let go of our social roles and worldly responsibilities, and therefore connect with the positive forces of the universe. This is why many people unconsciously choose the seaside, a mountain-resort, or some other natural location as their favourite holiday destination. Mother Nature can heal, inspire, and transform. She can work miracles on our tired psyche and exhausted physical frame, and restore us to a sense of harmony and well-being.

A blessed Mother to us all…

I have a confession to make. I am aware that the fashionable, trendy words to use today are 'ecology' or 'environment', but I deliberately choose the word nature, because it is close to my heart. It is a term that is known and loved by millions of men and women worldwide. It is associated with peace, purity, serenity, unspoiled beauty, tranquillity, and the transcendental spirit of the universe. It encompasses these myriad aspects of Creation, hundreds of thousands of living beings and organisms, stunningly beautiful landscapes, mountains, rivers, seas, forests, deserts, mangroves, lakes and plains that could have been created only by a Master Animator, whom, for want of a better word, we call God!

Our obligations to Mother Nature

Among all the creatures on earth, man alone has the capacity to interfere with the ecological balance. Elephants do not destroy forests and uproot trees; tigers and lions do not destroy their own habitats; birds and insects do not pollute the air, any more than fishes pollute rivers and seas.

But see how man treats nature.

It is man's responsibility to protect the environment. It is his sacred duty to see that the integrity and diversity of nature is maintained. For to destroy nature, is to destroy mankind.

Every day, in the span of 24 hours, 210 species become extinct. These are rare species of plants, animals and insects– living beings which were the products of millions of years of evolutionary process, and are now gone forever.

We generate thirteen to fifteen million tonnes of waste every day– much of which is non-biodegradable, toxic, and carcinogenic. We are exposing our ground water reserves and rivers to all this poison. We are polluting the air we breathe with all these deadly substances. Alas, we are asleep. When shall we hear the alarm bells ringing? When shall we wake up to the call of our own self destruction?

This is a time for conscious introspection…

For us in the third millennium A.D., natural disasters and calamities have become annual occurrences similar to summer vacations, Christmas, and the New Year. Hurricanes, El Niño, and Tsunamis– these 'new' disasters have been added to floods, earthquakes, volcanic eruptions, and landslides.

When I say that we have brought these disasters upon ourselves, some of my friends protest politely. "This is not our doing," they tell me. "Man is incapable of causing disasters of this magnitude. Besides, such natural disasters have occurred since the dawn of creation, starting with the melting of the planet in the Ice Age. How can man be held responsible for the unbridled fury of nature?"

With due respect to my friends, I beg to differ.

It is easy to view these disasters as "acts of God", as "unfortunate catastrophes," as "unpredictable events caused by unfathomable forces of nature". But we have to face the question: How far is mankind to be blamed for these disasters?

It is one thing to talk of 'natural disasters', but Mother Nature cannot be blamed altogether. The degree of destruction is the result of human negligence, human greed, and human selfishness.

Let us not forget that transgressing the laws of nature brings these disasters upon us, and if we do not learn from our mistakes, we shall be forced to repeat them!

Apart from such obvious natural calamities, experts tell us that Planet Earth is facing an unprecedented threat due to environmental degradation. Whole species are threatened with extinction; streams, rivers and even seas are becoming polluted; ground water is contaminated; the very air we breathe is choking our lungs. The ozone layer is being depleted, and the life-giving warmth of the sun, we are told, will soon cause skin cancer due to harmful ultraviolet rays. Summers are hotter, winters are colder, and it no longer rains– it pours, it floods cities!

We talk of 'conquering' lands and ruling the high seas; we wish to 'acquire' landed property and dabble in what we call real estate; we think we have 'subdued' nature and obtained sovereignty over her; we assume we are ready to 'annexe' space and the planets beyond earth; we claim ownership of forests and seashores and 'convert' them to money; we raze greenery and woods from mountain slopes and 'develop' these natural locations into resorts and villas; we pollute water sources and set up bottling plants to sell water to thirsty humans…

Alas, alas, when and where will our exploitations end? How far will we allow our greed to lead us? And how will the earth continue to tolerate our excessive acts?

What will happen to the earth? How will we survive? Where are we heading?

Let us mend our ways…

Reverence for nature is essential. Reverence for nature will help us to survive upon this planet. Reverence for nature will help us to preserve and protect this blessed earth for our children, and our children's children.

Reverence is essential– reverence for our rivers and forests; lakes and waterfalls; trees, plants, and the grass that grows beneath our feet; reverence for birds and beasts, whom I love to call our younger brothers and sisters.

Sadhu Vaswani spoke to us of the *Prakriti Sangha*– fellowship with nature– which he believed was essential to human happiness. There is a spiritual element in the beauty of nature, for nature is God's own expression in all its joy. It is the song, the dance of the Lord.

Nature is truly the environment of the *atman*– the eternal soul within each human being.

While going for a walk one evening with Gurudev Sadhu Vaswani, my eye fell on a pointed stone in the middle of the road. I felt grateful that my glance had fallen on it, for Gurudev could have tripped over it. I quickly went towards it and kicked it to the side of the road, satisfied that I had eliminated a possible fall.

I returned to his side, and to my dismay saw that there was an expression of pain and distress on his face. With diffidence I asked, "Please tell me, have I done something wrong? Have I displeased you in any way?"

Then in a wounded voice, Sadhu Vaswani said, "There is not a single atom of creation in which God does not exist. If God exists in the scripture, does He not exist in this stone? Therefore treat everything with reverence, touch everything with gentleness and love."

All life is one. All Creation is an organic whole.

We owe it to ourselves and the generations to come to conserve and protect the environment. Only then can our progeny be left with the legacy of a sustainable world which will be of benefit and use to all.

A nation that permits its soil to erode, is on a path of self-destruction. Forests are akin to the lungs of the land for they purify the air.

We have lost the sense of oneness with our environment and instead behave as though we own the environment and can treat it as we wish.

Neither are we superior to nor independent of our environment, we are just an integral part of it!

Equality

Equality! The word has a rhetorical, political, and social resonance! Since the French Revolution, equality has inspired mankind as a universal ideal.

'Equality' signifies a correspondence between a group of different people or objects. Equality is not similarity or familiarity. Thus, when we say, "All men are equal," we do not mean that they are identical or similar. Equality transcends similarity.

Philosophers will argue that the notion of 'complete' or 'absolute' equality is self-contradictory; for the concept of equality presumes a difference between the things under consideration. If things do not differ, they are merely identical.

Therefore, we can say: Equality assumes a difference; it teaches all of us to remember our common humanity despite all the differences of class, race, creed, colour and religion. It reminds us of Sadhu Vaswani's clarion call: Children of the earth, ye all are one!

Until the 18th century, so historians tell us, it was assumed that human beings are unequal by nature. The new ideas generated by the Age of Enlightenment stimulated great modern social movements and revolutions, and the immortal ideals of the French Revolution– Liberty, Equality and Fraternity– captured the imagination of mankind. Needless to say, the principle of equal dignity and respect is now accepted by all right-thinking people.

The Universal Declaration of Human Rights, which was passed by the U.N. in 1948, was directly inspired by the ideals of the French Revolution. In this crucial document, the concept of human rights was extended to include economic and social rights.

As with so many issues humanity faces, on paper, equality is assured to all of us. Alas, ground realities are different from constitutionally granted rights and privileges.

Look around you and what do you see? Unequal treatment is meted out to women, the girl child, the economically and socially deprived classes, and to racial and religious minorities. In George Orwell's classic novel of satire, *Animal Farm*, we read the dictum that referred to inequality amongst humans: "All animals are equal, but some are more equal than others!"

Equality must begin with us!

We do not have to interpret laws; we do not have to refer to the constitution. We can meet every human being we come across with the same respect. He may belong to a different creed or class or religion– but we must accord him the same respect that we would accord to any other human being! In other words, equality can begin with us, as individuals.

It was the German philosopher Goethe who said, "Treat a man as he is and he will remain as he is. Treat a man as he can be and should be– and he will become as he can be and should be."

Shakespeare's Prince Hamlet goes one step further. He rejects the idea of treating people according to their 'just deserts'. He asks sharply, "Treat a man as he deserves– and who shall escape whipping?" Therefore, treat them according to your own 'just deserts'.

The respect and dignity you accord to another should not depend on his status, his bank balance or his position, or the size of his car and his bungalow. Rather, it should be determined by your dignity and your sense of justice as a human being.

Why equality is vital in a democracy

According to what are called factors of economic development, a country's 'well-being' and 'prosperity' are determined not just by those statistics that we call gross national income (GNI), or even by what that country produces, the gross national product (GNP). We have to consider instead, a whole range of other factors such as 'quality of life', which my sensitive readers will realise, is much more than mere 'standard of living'. The nature of society and conditions of public life; the public services and amenities available to the people; life expectancy; education; family life and family welfare; community life; employment opportunities and job security; political freedom and social security; equality of genders; equitable distribution of wealth; opportunities for advancement; the sustenance and protection of the environment– these and other issues contribute to the overall well-being of the people.

End to racial discrimination

How can we even talk of equality when any one race regards itself as superior to another? Therefore, we must put an end to all forms of racial discrimination.

It is not without significance that the great-souled American leader, Martin Luther King Jr. was also a great admirer of Mahatma Gandhi, and his doctrine of non-violence and non-cooperation. He toured India to understand Gandhiji's life and ideals. He gave full credit to Mahatma Gandhi as the leader who inspired his protests, and vowed that he would continue to adopt Gandhian methods in his fight for racial equality.

Harmonious integration of pluralistic, multicultural, multiracial societies can only be achieved through good relations based on racial equality.

When we lose this sense of equality…

There was a time when we lost this sense of dignity and justice– and this led to the shameful practice of slavery.

Slavery was one of the worst forms of exploitation leading to unfair discrimination and inequality among people. In ethical terms, exploitation involves the treatment of human beings as mere 'objects' or as merely a means to serve others' ends. People are regarded as resources for utilisation without any consideration for their welfare or well-being.

I am of the firm opinion that all our transactions, all our relationships, should be based strictly on the principle of justice and equality. For exploitation in the long run leads only to hatred and conflict.

The French writer and thinker Voltaire rues the fact that many men, leaders, and rulers are born with a violent tendency for domination, wealth and pleasure; this is made worse by a strong taste for idleness. Consequently, he argues, men covet the money, land, and property belonging to other men– and this leads to subjugation and inequality.

From 1950 to 1990, the world witnessed a protracted period of civil unrest and popular rebellion, when people in several parts of the globe rose together against inequality and social injustice. This process of moving towards equality under the law was a long and painful process in countries like South Africa. In Northern Ireland, Catholics felt that they were denied equal rights; in Africa, blacks felt unequal under white regimes; even in America, the world's richest and most 'liberal' country, blacks demanded civil rights that were denied to them.

The notorious 'apartheid' regime of South Africa denied racial equality to blacks and 'coloured' people. The word apartheid literally means 'apartness' in the Afrikaans language.

It was a terrible system of racial segregation that was enforced in the Republic of South Africa from 1948 to 1984. Even before 1948, South Africa, which had long been ruled by whites, was racist in its policies and practices. Apartheid was designed to give legal sanction for continued economic and political dominance by people of European descent, while denying basic rights to native South Africans and 'coloured' people.

Today, the word apartheid, thankfully, is politically defunct. The apartheid regime has been rejected by the world community at large, and by native South Africans. The transition to a democratic republic, with power devolving to the black majority, is now a *fait accompli*.

The issue of women's equality also had to be fought for. While political equality– the right to vote– was accorded to women in the early 20th century, economic equality was not so easy to achieve.

Gender equality in India: The yeoman contribution of Mahatma Gandhi and Sadhu Vaswani

In India, Mahatma Gandhi was a seasoned crusader for women's equality. Under his leadership, women emerged from restriction to play leading roles in India's independence struggle. Gandhi never considered women to be unfit for any position or task. "To call women sex symbols is a libel," he wrote. "It is man's injustice to women." He also campaigned for women to become equal participants in family and social life. "The wife is not the husband's slave, but his companion, his helpmate and his equal partner in all his joys and sorrows," he asserted. "She is as free as the husband to choose her own path."

When I talk about Gandhi's respect for women, how could I fail to mention the quiet revolution brought about by my Master and Mentor, Sadhu Vaswani? In the days before the term "women's rights" was even coined, Sadhu Vaswani offered the *purdah*-clad, kitchen-bound women of Sind, spiritual liberation in the true sense of the term. His *Sakhi Satsang* (spiritual fellowship of sisters) enabled many women to become decision-makers for the first time in their personal lives– by the very act of voluntarily joining his *satsang*. It would be no exaggeration to say that he inducted Sindhi women into what had until then, been the domain of men– the practice of religion in the truest sense.

He did everything he could do to break the shackles of superstition and hidebound 'customs' that had kept Sindhi women restricted and confined for centuries. He spoke out against the *purdah* and the evil system of dowry.

I concur with Sadhu Vaswani's view that the future belongs to women. We live in a man-made civilisation and therefore, men are regarded as superior to women. But a new civilisation will dawn– a woman-made civilisation, based on the womanly ideals of simplicity, sympathy, service and sacrifice. I believe it is women who will have the *shakti* to rebuild the shattered world in the strength of their intuition, purity and the spirit of silent sacrifice. It is my firm belief that there is a new world in the making– the world of peace, harmony and unity– and of this world the builder will be the woman, not man!

A few words on casteism

The origin of the caste system, according to some scholars, is to be found in the *Manusmriti*. This text talks of the *varnas* or the four orders into which society is divided, in order to keep the life of the nation healthy and strong– the *Brahmins* (priestly class); the *Kshatriyas* (warriors); the *Vaishyas* (traders); the *Shudras* (not manual workers, but service providers, as we would call them today). The *varnas* as you know, are colours– and in this case, the hues that together make up the beautiful and durable fabric of society. Naturally, Manu's ideas of the status of women and his insistence on the superiority of *Brahmins* is totally unacceptable to us today. But we would do well to remember that these laws and codes were laid down at a time when Aryan society was in its earliest stages of evolution. As social conditions and cultural environments change, these codes of conduct and rules will have to be modified. In fact, it is clearly stated in the *Manusmriti*, that one should "reject such laws and rules that lead to unhappiness of other individuals or public resentment". The important thing is to follow the Spirit, rather than the letter of the law, and respect all types of contributions to society. There are no grounds whatsoever, to justify casteism, social inequality, and injustice as Hindu evils; they are social evils of the worst order and must be condemned as such.

As my Beloved Master, Gurudev Sadhu Vaswani explains, the classification of social order is based not on birthright, but the natural qualities of a man. If a nation is to be built and developed on the right lines, each one of the four orders must bring its contributions to the common weal. There is nothing great nor small about him who would be a helper of the state. All work is noble, all efforts are useful… differences make harmony. He who tills the soil or rears the cattle or carries on trade or digs the earth is as useful as he who fights for the State or governs it, or meditates in a quiet corner… A healthy, progressive society aims at a harmony, an integration of all orders.

One final thought...

The lessons of apartheid must always serve as a warning to mankind– that inequalities and discrimination perpetrated by force will only work towards the detriment of all people! Even in the post-*apartheid* regime, South Africa is still struggling to remove economic inequality and empower its black people.

Rascism, casteism, and all related practices must be condemned for the evils they perpetrate: discrimination against people founded on false notions of superiority and inferiority; discrimination on the grounds of descent, ethnicity, colour or physical characteristics; violent expressions of hostility, hate and bias; perpetuation of social injustice and inequality leading to intergenerational inequality.

I believe that hate cannot be conquered by hate; so too discrimination can only be wiped out if each one of us fosters tolerance, love, and understanding at home and at the work place.

Faith

What is faith?

Faith is belief in God and His goodness and grace. To believe in God is to know that He is present everywhere, in everything. In every man and woman and child is He; in every creature that breathes the breath of life; in everything animate and inanimate. Faith is knowing that God is too loving to punish and too wise to make a mistake, that all that happens to us, happens according to His Divine plan.

Faith is not blind, as some 'rationalists' would claim. Faith is seeing with the eyes of the heart. But alas, the eyes of the heart remain closed for many of us. When we open them, we will see that all that has happened has happened for the best, all that is happening is happening for the best, and all that will happen will happen for the best. There is a meaning of mercy in all that happens. God has a plan for every one of us, and there is Divine purpose in every little thing that happens to us. As the great American poet Whittier, put it, "When faith is lost… the man is dead!"

It has been said that faith sees the invisible, believes the incredible, and receives the impossible. Faith is believing that God loves each and every one of us. He will provide for all our needs. Faith is seeking refuge in the Lord, trusting Him fully, completely, entirely. For His is the One Light that shines, shines and ever shines! Though the storms howl and the darkness grows deeper, His Light will continue to shine on us!

It is a triple faith that men need today: faith in oneself, for only the person who has faith in oneself can have faith in others, faith in the world around us, which is not merely just but essentially good, and above all, faith in God. With faith in God there is no height you cannot reach, no distance you cannot traverse, no dream you cannot accomplish.

The great gift of faith

I am often asked: What is the one gift that you would ask of God if He were to appear before you and grant you a single boon?

I would ask God for the great gift of faith! Faith is the spirit that sustains life, it is the ray of sunshine that lightens up the dark, deep caverns of the human heart. Faith is the elixir of the soul.

Faith is the beautiful, fragrant flower that blooms even in the wilderness of despair and suffering. Faith is the one true source of support on which we can always rely in this rough and tough journey called life. Faith is the sustenance for all human endeavours. It is the greatest blessing that God can bestow upon us!

The power of faith

Man's life is powered by faith. We repose our faith in our parents when we are young. As we grow older, friends, family, spouses, partners are added to the list of people we trust. We have faith in the law of the land, in the system of justice and governance; we have faith in democracy; we have faith in medicine and doctors. How can we survive without the faith that subsumes all these faiths? How can we survive without faith in God?

It is the custom of pious Maharashtrian women, even now, to offer the food cooked by them as *naivedya* to the Lord in any nearby temple, before the family partakes of the food. Namdev's mother Janabai too had this habit. She would take a plate of freshly cooked food to the temple at Pandharpur, and offer it to Lord Vitthala, before the family sat down to eat lunch. Thus every meal was eaten as *prasad* in their devout family. One day, Janabai was unable to go to the temple herself, so she asked her young son, Namdev, to go in her place.

The young boy happily agreed to do so, and set off for the temple. He set the plate of food before the deity, tightly shut his eyes, and begged the Lord to accept the food he had brought. To his dismay, when he opened his eyes, he found the food on the plate, untouched. For him, *naivedya* was not just a show-and-take-away ritual. He closed his eyes once again, and implored the Lord to accept the food. When the food was still left untouched, the boy began to shed bitter tears. "Vitthala! Vitthala!" he called out piteously, "Don't you like me? Are you so angry with me, that you refuse to touch the food I have brought to you?"

Lord Vithoba, as we know, is tender-hearted! He could not bear the grief of His dear devotee, so he appeared in human form and promptly ate the food placed before him! Seeing the empty plate, Namdev was happy, and returned home to inform his mother that the food had indeed been offered to God.

To say that Janabai was mystified by the empty plate would be an understatement.

But she was a woman who never spoke in haste. She did not trouble her young son with the how and why and wherefore of the incident. The following day, she entrusted her son with the same errand, and secretly followed him to the temple to see what he did with the food. To her amazement, she saw Nama close his eyes and pray to Vitthala; and she saw the Lord appear in human form and eat the food placed before Him!

"To one who has faith, no explanation is necessary. To one without faith, no explanation is possible," said St. Thomas of Aquinas. Faith is idle when circumstances are right. It is only when circumstances are adverse that faith in God is tested. Faith, like muscles, grows strong when exercised. In faith we do not believe that God can, but believe that God will.

Faith liberates, faith empowers, faith encourages, faith heals. Life cannot present a problem which faith cannot solve; life cannot expose you to a situation which faith cannot surmount.

Truly, faith can move mountains!

Fate and Free Will

We have all been given the freedom of choice. If I choose to move on the path of good, I go forward; I progress; I evolve spiritually. If I choose to move on the path of evil, I regress; I am pushed backwards. If I choose wrong over right, evil over good, how can I blame God for what results from my action? It is I who must direct my steps towards God!

Karma and fate are not the same! Fate is an indifferent, neutral power and a concept of western thinking. Fate is blind; fate is arbitrary, in the Western view. The Hindu concept of karma is dynamic; we create our own karma and we have to reap what we sow. Our life now is the product of the karma that we have accumulated in previous births; simultaneously, this present life is also the seed of the future of our soul. We carry our past karmas with us; and this burden may have to be borne by us even as we journey from life to life. The good and bad karma that we accumulate are entered in the credit and debit column of the account of our life. The balance is carried forward from one life into the next. This credit and debit is what we commonly refer to as *punya* and *paap*.

Every living moment, we are creating our own karma, by the thoughts we think, the words we speak, and the deeds we perform. We choose our destiny!

Am I really free?

The question now arises: Is man a free agent? Or is he a puppet in the hands of destiny? Can he change his own fate?

There are some people who will tell you everything is already 'written', that you cannot change what is to happen. Whatever you do, whatever efforts you put in, you will not be able to change your destiny.

There are others who tell you, that man is endowed with a free will, man has the freedom to change his destiny at every step, in every round of life.

Let me repeat the two different answers given to our question. The first is that man is a prisoner of his own fate. No matter how valiant his efforts, he cannot change the contours of his destiny.

The second answer is that man is absolutely free. He has the freedom of choice to act—

to choose right or wrong. At every step of life, he can make the effort to improve his condition. Through his actions, he can actually succeed in changing his own karma and thus altering his own destiny.

I think that these two aspects of man's condition are like the twin blades of a pair of scissors. The first is *ichcha shakti*– the freedom of choice; the second is *Prarabdha Karma*– our accumulated karma. Only when the two go together, can we act in any sense of the term. When the two blades act together, the scissors do their job. You cannot cut a piece of cloth with just one blade of the scissors. Likewise, past karma and free will are both necessary for action.

Your past karma determines so many things that you cannot change. It determines the type of family into which you are born, your religion, your race, and the type of body in which you are born. These are things you cannot change.

I heard of a woman who spent lakhs of rupees to change the shape of her nose. The shape was changed through plastic surgery– but it was not to her satisfaction.

There was a man who spent a fortune trying to increase his height by a couple of inches. He could not achieve this; his height could not be increased even by one millimetre.

But there is a place for free will even in such cases. Whatever be your condition, you always have this choice– of reacting to it in a positive or negative manner. This is always within your power!

Prisoners or free birds?

I recall a memorable evening, when my Beloved Master Sadhu Vaswani was pacing up and down the terrace of Krishta Kunj– his residence in Karachi. As he looked down at the street below, he exclaimed, "Prisoners! Prisoners!"

I looked down too– but I saw no prisoners. I saw the traffic, and I saw a number of people who were going about their business. But there was no sign of prisoners!

Actually, Krishta Kunj was situated quite close to the Karachi District Jail, and prisoners would pass by the house from time to time, as they were led out by their wardens for labour routines, or accompanied by policemen to appear in court. But on this occasion, there were no prisoners to be seen. Surprised, I said to him, "But Dada, I see no prisoners here!"

Sadhu Vaswani's reply still echoes in my ears. For long have I meditated on the profound wisdom of his words to me that evening, "Prisoners, prisoners of desire are the people," he said. "Alas, they know not of their bondage!"

Prisoners of desire are we all! We are bound by our own joys and sorrows. We are happy with what the world gives us; we take great joy in our pleasures and possessions. We celebrate the birth of a child— and we mourn over his loss when he passes away. We weep for a while— and then we beget more children. We are not aware of the fetters that bind us!

Those of us who become aware of our bonds, make the effort to seek liberation. This state of awareness is known as *mumukshatwa*– the desire to attain liberation. In this condition, our deep consciousness is awakened and urges us on the path of liberation. This is a goal we can all achieve through our own efforts and the grace of the guru.

Have you seen caged birds being sold as pets on footpaths, pet shops, and public venues? People strike bargains with the bird sellers and take home the caged creatures, determined to love them and care for them!

To me a caged bird is deeply symbolic of man's plight. We are born free, like the birds. Freedom is our birthright. We should be flying in the open skies, and touching the splendour of rainbows. But we are caged by desires, by the 'bars' of 'ego'. We are prisoners of our own selves. We have to break free; we have to find our wings and fly away in order to seek liberation.

Instead we have locked ourselves into a tiny cage of the self, called 'EGO'. If anything binds us, it is our ego and the misdeeds that arise out of our ego.

Man's free will and God's Will: A subtle equation

In ancient India, a school of ascetics believed in pre-ordained fate, and taught their followers to take life as events presented themselves, for individual effort was useless under the circumstances. Newer faiths like Buddhism and Jainism dismissed the whole concept of fate and placed the utmost emphasis on individual effort. It is only Hinduism that combines the ideals of free will and Divine Will to show that although man is the architect of his own destiny, he must always submit to the Divine Will. If we realise that God is the prime mover, and the source of all action, it becomes easy for us to surrender to His Divine Will, and thus become free from the clutches of the ego.

The *Gayatri Mantra* which is recited with piety and devotion by millions of Hindus, is at once an adoration, a meditation and prayer, acknowledging the power of the Divine Will. Here is a free translation of this powerful mantra:

Oh God, the Protector, the basis of all life, Who is self-existent, Who is free from all pains and Whose contact frees the soul from all troubles, Who pervades the universe and sustains all, the Creator and Energiser of the whole Universe, the Giver of happiness, Who is worthy of acceptance, the most excellent, Who is pure and the Purifier of all, let us embrace that very God, so that He may direct our mental faculties in the right direction.

Surrender your will to God; dedicate your efforts to Him, and He will redirect your energy and efforts to bring you the liberation you seek!

Our ancient epics and *puranas* too illustrate the power of Divine Will and free will. Thus the Pandavas represent human free will operating in consonance with Divine Will, while the Kauravas represent human free will set against Divine Will. So it is that the Kurukshetra War is described as a battle between good and evil, *dharma* and *adharma*. When Arjuna wavers momentarily before the battle, the Lord gives His Divine teachings to him. Significantly, towards the end of his discourse, Sri Krishna actually tells Arjuna: *Yathechchasi tatha kuru*– "I have told you all that I had to say. Do as you desire to do."

Arjuna was merely the instrument; Sri Krishna was the Doer. So too with most of us: our actions, events and incidents are pre-determined according to the Divine Will. Our reaction, our response, our attitude to these events and incidents is of our free will. Our karma is determined not so much by our actions, as by the attitude with which we perform actions.

Why do things go wrong in our lives?

Look around you and you are sure to come across many such cases, where people make choices in good faith, in the light of their insight and wisdom, and yet things go wrong. Marriages that began as rosy dreams end in divorce; Engineering/Medical seats 'bought' at a premium by doting fathers are abandoned when their sons decide to pursue their dreams in other directions. Dear ones are entrusted to the care of the best surgeons for a major surgery after positive prognostications and reassurances by doctors and hospital administrators. Though the surgery is successful the patient does not survive! Property, real estate, farmlands bought with lifetime savings turn out to be legal nightmares. The list is endless.

Does all this mean we cannot escape 'fate' or 'destiny'? Does this mean our so called free will is just a myth?

God gave us free will and the right to choose. If we choose wrong, even unwittingly, we face the consequences. But in such cases, we must face the effects of our choice in the spirit of humility and acceptance. The wrong choice has been made so that we may learn a few necessary lessons from life. There is little to be gained by blaming ourselves and even less to be gained by blaming God for all our ills. God is too loving to punish; too wise to make a mistake!

How to ensure that our choice is in consonance with the Divine Will

1. To be able to make the right choice, you must quieten your mind, calm your senses, and open your heart. Clear out all preconceived notions and prejudices. Then invite God into your mind and heart, so that you may receive His grace to decide what is best!

2. You must practise the presence of God. Practising the presence means striking a relationship with God. Make God your father, brother or friend. He is even prepared to be your mother. I tell businessmen to make God their Senior Partner! Go to God again and again. Talk to God as you would to a relation or a friend. Feel that God is all the time by your side. When the mind wanders, practise the presence by repeating a simple prayer like: "I love you God!" Or simply utter, "God, God, God."

3. The Prayer of Affirmation also helps when you face a major choice. After carefully considering what are the desirable and undesirable results of the choice you are about to make, think deeply of what you want and what you don't want out of your choice. Then affirm to yourself, "Dear God, our lives are safe in Your hands. My children/my family/ my business/my life is under Your Divine protection. I have no fear for them. I have cast out all fear, for I have surrendered my life into Your safe hands. I know You will take

care of my dear ones at every step, every round of life. Please accept my thanks for protecting my dear ones."

4. Repeating affirmations are also helpful. You must affirm what you want, and not what you don't want. Your affirmation should always be a positive one. There is the Law of Attraction which states that the universe is a huge copy machine. It does not judge whether what you desire is right or wrong. It just draws you closer to what you desire. Very simply stated, the Law of Attraction is the belief that the universe creates and provides for you that which your thoughts are focused on. Positive thoughts lead to positive outcomes and persistently negative thoughts lead to negative consequences.

Let me express a few positive affirmations to help you make the right choice:

- I shall trust and listen to my inner voice
- I shall cultivate and cherish loving relationships
- I shall change my thinking– and change my life
- I shall face life with courage
- I shall cultivate the attitude of gratitude
- I shall practise the virtue of forgiveness that heals me and others
- I shall choose kindness

Let this be your choice, made out of your own free will: surrender the thread of your life into His safe hands!

Fear- Conquer It!

Fear casts its dark shadow over our lives at some time or the other. We are prone to fear almost instinctively. Neither the highest nor the lowest of us is exempt from fear. The most powerful nations fear their rivals and neighbours. Politicians are afraid of losing elections. Students are afraid of failing in examinations. Mothers are afraid about their children's safety… The list is endless.

Fear is the one mark that characterises us, children of a skeptical age. We are afraid of the future, afraid of poverty, afraid of unemployment, afraid of dishonour and disgrace, afraid of disease and death– it seems to me that sometimes, we are afraid of life itself!

We live in fear; we work in fear; we walk in fear; we talk in fear. We move through life from one fear to another, crushed beneath the weight of a woeful existence!

What is fear?

The dictionary defines fear as "a feeling of anxiety concerning the outcome of something or the safety of someone" or "the likelihood of something unwelcome happening". The synonyms are apprehension, anxiety, alarm, dread. Fear is based on reality, or an exaggeration of a real danger.

There is a wide range of situations that spell danger– and there is an equally wide range of fear responses. We accept our fears as 'normal' fears or 'founded' fears, when the fear is in proportion to the degree of danger in a situation. But if the fear response is out of proportion to the danger, it becomes an abnormal fear or phobia.

Psychiatrists tell us that only two fears are present at birth: the fear of falling, and the fear of loud noises.

How is it then that we build up so many fears later on in life? Does fear have an organic basis? Or is it simply built on our own unconscious processes?

We have so much to fear…

The 'logic' of fear is truly illogical. We are afraid of losing our jobs– but we are even more afraid to go out and seek new positions. I know some people who are terrified of contracting a major illness– but they are even more scared to meet a specialist and go through a series of tests. Some young women are afraid of marriage, as they feel that they would lose their identity– but the idea of remaining single makes them feel insecure! Many old people worry about the years that lie ahead of them– but they are haunted by the fear of death!

As I said, we are afraid to die– and we are afraid to live, because life has become so complicated, risky and insecure!

"A ship in the harbour is safe," goes the saying. But that is not what ships are built for!

Fear can be positive or negative. Positive fear is the aspect of fear which acts as a signal to warn against danger, or that which motivates us to improve our performance and prevent our downfall. The fear of not being accepted by society causes us to conform to norms and discipline our lives. These kinds of fears are considered 'necessary'.

Negative fears are imaginary, exaggerated, illogical and extremely corrosive. These fears make us anticipate imaginary, non-existent problems and blur our vision of reality. They are barriers between people and reality. Negative fears are either conditioned through people and situations or acquired through traumatic experiences. When fed, these negative fears grow monstrously and don the form of anxiety and depression.

Fear keeps us safe

People often think that fear is a destructive emotion. This is not entirely true. Fear is natural to human beings in many situations. It teaches us to be cautious and helps us create safeguards for ourselves. It is what keeps us safe and secure. When we are afraid of things thattruly threaten our security, such fear is protective. In fact, I would go so far as to say that man is fortunate to have learnt to fear certain things– or else, the human species would have been wiped out long ago.

For example, it is normal and human to have legitimate fears that help us deal with the everyday challenges of life. Such fears foster a sense of self-preservation. If it were not for these fears, we would be walking into speeding cars, putting our hands into fire, rebelling against authority, and so on. These fears are in proportion to the dangers posed. For example, when one hears thunderstorm, sees lightning, and as a result stays indoors from fear of being struck by lightning, the fear is caused by the survival instinct! It is the disproportionate, negative fears that turn into phobias.

Fear is all-pervasive

Fear permeates all aspects of our life on earth. Fear is not only present in us– it seems to exist in the very fabric of our institutions.

Fear exists within the family– we are afraid of the safety and well-being of our close relatives. Fear exists in the workplace– the executive who is called to meet the big boss is often petrified. Fear exists in our schools and colleges– the student who has not done his homework is frightened of the teacher and afraid of punishment. You can almost smell fear in hospitals– patients are afraid of their own constitutions and the unknown, unforeseen health complications they may fall prey to. Alas, children are afraid of parents– and worse, some parents are actually afraid of their children!

Competition and rivalry have made professional life a veritable rat race. A world fired by the spirit of rivalry and competition is a world built on the foundation of fear. Performance, evaluation, comparison– everything arouses fear. The fear of failure, the fear of losing a match or a contest, is one of the worst kind of fears that haunts an individual. The stigma of failure makes us lose faith in ourselves. We are afraid of becoming unacceptable.

Types of fear identified by experts

A leading psychologist identifies five basic fears, from which almost all of our fears arise:

1. **Extinction**– the fear of annihilation, of ceasing to exist. This is what we call "fear of death" in common parlance.

2. **Mutilation**– the fear of losing any part of our body, of losing the integrity of any organ, or natural function. Anxiety about animals, such as bugs, spiders, snakes, and other creepy creatures arises from fear of mutilation.

3. **Loss of autonomy**– the fear of being immobilised, paralysed, restricted, entrapped, imprisoned, or otherwise controlled by circumstances beyond our control. In the spatial sense, this is commonly known as claustrophobia, but it also extends to our social interactions and relationships.

4. **Separation**– the fear of abandonment, rejection, of becoming a non-person, not wanted,

respected, or valued by anyone else. When this kind of rejection is imposed by a group of which we are members, it can have a devastating psychological effect on us.

5. **Ego-death**– the fear of humiliation, shame, or any other mechanism of profound self-disapproval that threatens integrity of the self or yields loss of self-image and self-worth.

Why do we fear?

- Many fears are learned. They are caused by conditioning from parents, peers, educators, media, society and culture. They are also a product of social standards. They are absorbed by the pattern in which people around us react to dangers, calamities or even simple problems. Fears of darkness, spiders, plane crashes, fear of illness, fear of drowning etc. are common examples. Fear of the unknown is a fear that is most common.

- Some fears are acquired as a response to unhappy childhood incidents. For example, a child locked up in a room as a punishment may develop claustrophobia, a fear of enclosures.

- Fears can also develop in later years as a repercussion to some trauma. For example, if a person sees a car crash, he becomes fearful of driving.

The roots of fear

"The mind is its own place," wrote Milton, "and in itself can create heaven of hell, or hell of heaven." There is great meaning in these words. If fear has to be eradicated, it has to be uprooted from the mind.

A turbulent mind causes uneasiness, fear, and anxiety. The mind has to be stilled, and its restless energy must be harnessed and channelised into constructive thoughts and plans. The conquered mind is a source of poise and serenity. When there is an inner sense of calm, people and events will not agitate us. The desire for things to always go our way leads to disappointments and fears! Selfish thoughts should be replaced by positive, accepting, and selfless thoughts.

2,500 years ago, when people approached the Buddha with their problems, his solution was the same. They said to him, "We have fears and worries! What should we do?"

"If you want to be happy and fearless, then train your mind!" he answered.

The effects of fear

- When we allow fear to grow, it paralyses our faculties. It makes us feel powerless against situations.

- Fear causes immense physical damage, ranging from acidity and ulcers to fainting. In many cases, extreme shock and fear in the form of terror has even caused cardiac arrests.

- Panic attacks bring symptoms such as palpitations, choking, numbness, breathlessness, nausea, and sweating.

Identifying fear

The first step to deal with fear is awareness. It is very important to identify fear and feel its presence in your body and mind. Every situation that triggers fear should be recognised.

Understand what you fear! Analyse it– break it down! What is it? Is it a monster that is real or a fabrication of the mind? Is it rational?

One way to look at fear is to observe its incidence. If one person is afraid of the dark and another is not, the second is afraid of cats and the third is not, that means there is nothing in the dark nor in the cats that is inherently fear-causing! The fear is only our response! Therefore, once we establish that our fear is irrational, its tyranny on the mind will be broken.

Becoming aware of the potential harm caused by fear is a concrete step in overcoming fear. When fear grips us, our faculty of reason, our performance level, our efficiency and our ability to make decisions are all lost!

Fear and faith cannot coexist!

Fear and faith repel each other. Where there is true faith, there can never be fear. Therefore, the best antidote to fear is faith.

Faith is the most powerful emotion known to man. Faith is not the blind belief that God grants all our prayers. Faith is knowing that all that happens is part of a Divine plan. Faith is

Fear – Conquer it!

believing without doubt that everything was perfect in the past, that everything is perfect in the present, and that everything will be perfect in the future. It is faith in the universe, faith in all that is true and virtuous in this world, or faith in that power which for want of a better word, we call God.

The Persian poet Saadi said, "I fear God, and next to God, I fear most of all, him who fears Him not."

When a little child is thrown up into the air by his father, the child giggles with joy! For the child has implicit and utter faith in his father and he knows full well that when his father has thrown him up, he will surely catch him! This is true for us with our Divine Father too; if he puts us to test it is He who will hold us! If our faith in Him is unconditional and absolute, He will never let us down!

Faith is the surest way to conquer fear!

Freedom

What is Freedom? Freedom is not the license to do as you please. Freedom is the choice you make, to do what you have to do! True freedom is of the inner self. True freedom does not mean you break away from society or your family and live like a vagabond. True freedom is not lack of responsibility or accountability. True freedom is the spiritual insight that sets us free from the bondage to desires.

May I ask you, what is your idea of true freedom? Is it to live and act and do whatever you please? Is it to fulfil all your aspirations and desires? Is it to indulge your every whim and fancy? Is it to throw off all restrictions and regulations that keep you chained, confined to a routine that you resent? Or is it something that transcends all this?

The desire to be free, to feel free to pursue one's goals and desires is an innate human aspiration. For some, this desire is materialistic– they wish to be free from financial restrictions, to be able to possess whatever they crave for. This may be a new car, a better job, or even an expensive holiday abroad. For others, the desire is more mature, more elevated– they wish to achieve true peace, joy, or love. Whether it is freedom from want or freedom from worldly cares, the desire to be free is simply part of human nature.

What prevents us from achieving this freedom?

We all know of convicts and offenders who are locked in physical prisons, behind metal bars under the law of the land; naturally they crave to be released from confinement. But there is another type of imprisonment that many of us are subject to. I believe that many of us are locked in a mental prison of our own making; we feel restricted, confined, by our own oppressing thoughts and emotions, and crave to be free from such crippling negative energies. To be still, to taste a beautiful moment of calm, to feel the central core of peace and bliss that is within, is to be truly happy!

Remez Sasson, the inspirational writer, says that we are all trapped, imprisoned by the conditioning of our own incessant thinking. Freedom from the compulsion of constant and endless thinking is real freedom. Our minds are constantly grappling with thoughts, from the moment we wake up in the morning, until we fall asleep at night. We do not have even a moment's freedom from our thoughts in our waking hours. Thoughts create more thoughts, and also receive thoughts from the external world around us. This habit is so strong and deeply embedded that nobody even thinks of overcoming it.

Now ask yourself: can you really consider yourself free in such a state? You may be a free citizen living in a free country; you may be financially independent; you may exercise your choice in daily decision making; and yet, your mind keeps you chained to an incessant flow of thoughts and mental images, many of which are useless and futile, and some of which are actually negative and depressing. Outwardly, you are free; but deep within, you are enslaved by your own thought processes.

Inner freedom comes with the adoption of the spiritual ideal.

What is this spiritual ideal? "Be desireless, but be duty bound." Release yourself from the chains of desire, and be free to fly back to your native home, the Realm of Light! Do your duty by the weaker, the ignorant, the needy, the helpless ones; do so in the awareness that all life is one, and that you are expanding your inner sky in reaching out to those in need of you!

Sat Chit Ananda, the peace and bliss that no ending knows, is the true condition of the soul! Unending peace, joy, and love is the natural state of the human being, but we are not always 'free' to access this happy state and savour its joy.

Freedom and discipline

In the 1960s and '70s, 'discipline' was regarded as an unhealthy word. The cult of 'self-expression' was fashionable. People would say, "Don't restrain your child. Don't discipline him. Let him express himself freely." Consequently, children, especially in the affluent West, were allowed to do as they pleased. Even infants had their 'freedom'; they were fed only when they cried– and not as per a regular time-schedule. Child-specialists called this 'demand-feeding'! Children were not scolded or reprimanded; they were allowed to 'be themselves'.

But what kind of 'self' is that which seeks free expression and defies discipline? Surely, it is not the higher Self in the being. Such 'freedom' leads not to license, but to licentiousness; it feeds and waters the lower self, the ego– the self of desire and unruly passions, of cravings and animal appetites. When a child is indulged and allowed to surrender to his whims and fancies, he begins to throw tantrums, he loses his temper and behaves as he pleases. This is not true freedom or creative, 'free' expression; it is just misbehaviour!

Freedom to choose

We have all been given the freedom of choice. God has bestowed on each and every individual, the right of freedom– the same degree of freedom that God has kept for Himself. Man is free to choose– between vice and virtue, good and evil, selfishness and service. Man can choose to be selfish or unselfish. He can choose to be a sinner or a saint. He can choose to move on the path of evil, even become a criminal. He can choose to become a thief or a murderer. Equally, he can choose to move on the way of virtue, he can become a God on earth. The choice is entirely his.

But remember, if the right to freedom of choice is vested within him, it follows that the responsibility for his actions also rests with him; for we cannot have rights without responsibilities. At every step on the road of life, we have the freedom to choose the direction in which we move.

Freedom comes with responsibility, for freedom without responsibility is anarchy; and true freedom exists only in doing what is good and right and morally acceptable. This is why we say, freedom is not the right to do what we want, but to do as we ought!

Friendship

Friendship is not easy to define or even describe. Companionship, camaraderie, fellowship, amity– these may be good synonyms as far as dictionary use is concerned, but friendship is something special for those who are blessed with it! I am told that the Eskimos have a hundred different words for snow. How I wish the English language could offer us those many options for the words that we use so lovingly! All we have are adjectives to describe different kinds of friends– such as close friend, best friend, childhood friend, school friend, trusted friend and so on.

Friendship is special to all of us, and friends are treasured people in our lives. It was a wise man who pointed out that we can't pick or choose our family, and we are severely limited in the number of family members. But there is no limit to the number of friends we can choose and keep for life!

The ideal friendship is selfless and undemanding, expects no material benefits, transcends all barriers of class, caste and social status, and yet sustains the highest values of mutual care and affection. Genuine friendship allows for open and free communication without flattery or hypocrisy, and brings joy of pure affection, free from ulterior motives.

What value do friends bring into our lives?

1. Friends bring real happiness into our lives. Companionship, caring and sharing add to this happiness.

2. Friends bring out the best in us, adding to our sense of self-worth and self-esteem.

3. Friends encourage us, inspire us to reach our goals, help us cope with problems, and enable us to live longer and healthier lives.

4. In childhood, friendships enhance our learning process and improve our life skills; as young adults, our social skills are honed by friends.

5. When we foster friendship with those whose interests are different from ours, we learn new things, acquire new perspectives. Such friends broaden our horizons and add a fresh hue to our lives. We break the age-old cliché: "Birds of a feather flock together"!

6. Good friendship multiplies itself! Friends help you acquire more friends. The larger our friends' circle, the richer our lives! Of course, some friends will always remain special, but having a large group of friends adds value to living.

7. Friendship nurtures some of the best qualities in us, such as being sociable, helpful and supportive.

8. Friendship is the best antidote to joy-killer feelings including loneliness, depression and insecurity. These are unhealthy and harmful tendencies that can come upon us at any time in our lives. Good friends keep these negativities at bay.

9. Friends help us to be grounded, by keeping a reality check on us. Many of us tend to get carried away by impractical goals and ambitions. A friend who knows us well can hold us back from disastrous flights of fancy.

10. All of us have the aspiration to make this world a better place, at least in our own small way. Friends can help us bring about this change for the better, for as a team or a group, we can achieve much more! Whether it is standing up for a cause we believe in, fighting against a social evil, or just raising funds for charity, friends offer us invaluable help and support.

Offering and receiving the great gift of friendship is one of the greatest joys of a well-lived life. Our friends need us, even as we need them. The effort we add in making friends and keeping them will surely render our lives rewarding and fulfilling.

How to honour true friendship

- Allow your friends to be themselves. Accept them as they are, along with their imperfections.
- Give your friends their personal space. Respect their privacy, even as you retain your own. Friendship loves free space and will not thrive when enclosed.
- Always be ready to help your friends.
- Do not offer advice unless it is asked for, and offer only constructive advice.
- Be loyal to your friends– see them through good times as well as bad times. We can all do without 'fair weather friends'.
- Learn to praise your friends and appreciate their achievements.
- Always be honest with your friends, speak out your feelings. Do not bottle up anger

or resentment, for clearing the air will help relationships to grow and flourish. However, also bear in mind that some things are best left unsaid.
- Learn to trust time-tested friends. Never ever doubt their loyalty or goodness.

How to be your own best friend

Friendship with oneself is all important; without it we cannot be friends with others.

1. Realise that you are unique– you have been created with certain traits and gifts that are special to you. Simply because you are not aware of them, does not mean you are worthless. Try and unearth your special strengths and gifts.

2. Think of what you enjoy doing– singing, dancing, storytelling, drawing, calligraphy, cooking, gardening… Recreate the sense of pleasure and enjoyment that you derive from these activities, and add more such activities to your daily routine.

3. Participate in the social activities of your group, your community and your neighbourhood. Do not allow yourself to become isolated from your neighbours and friends. Connecting with others, participating in such activities draws you out and brings awareness that you are part of a cosmic whole.

4. Give more meaning to your life by finding a worthy cause to which you can devote your energies– it may be an NGO, a *satsang*, a social service group, or anything you believe in.

5. Learn to be kind to yourself! Do not criticise yourself or call yourself names constantly! Take good care of yourself physically and mentally.

6. Avoid the company of people who put you down constantly. Do not allow others' criticism to affect your self-image.

7. Make a difference to others– and you will see what a difference it makes in your attitude and personal life! Therefore, go out of your way to help others and make life better for them.

8. Above all, always remember that God loves you and created you to fulfil His special purpose. When you know that He loves you and trusts you, how can you think poorly of yourself?

Give, Give, Give!

When God sent man to the earth, He sent him with the command: "Give!"

Man is meant to be a giver. We must give all we have– our time and talents, our experience and wisdom, our influence, our wealth, our life itself– to those in need. It is only then that we will experience *ananda*– the joy that no ending knows.

We make a living by what we receive, but we live a true life by what we give. The most wasted of all days is the one in which we have not shared something with someone who cannot pay us back.

Give without any expectations, conditions or boundaries. Give not for show or public ostentation, give for the joy of giving. We give little when we give of our possession. It is only when we give of ourselves that we truly give. When you give, do not think that you are obliging others. On the contrary, feel grateful to God that he has given you this wonderful opportunity of serving others.

We cannot live for ourselves alone. A thousand fibres connect us with all creation. God in his abundance has showered on us so many blessings. Everything we have is a loan given to us, to share with those whose need is greater than ours. Man becomes selfish, not by pursuing his own good, but by neglecting the good of his neighbours. We think of ourselves alone and choke our growth. Let us become unselfish.

Give, give, give! Those that give, live; those that give not, are no better than dead souls!

Everything in nature gives; only man continues to take. We too, should learn to give with total detachment and renunciation, with the feeling that nothing belongs to us. If we have nothing to give, let us at least give a smile, let us share a few some sweet, kind words, and let us refrain from hurting, harming others.

Three types of giving

The first kind of giving is like the flint, two pieces of which have to be rubbed together over and over again to emit even a tiny spark.

The second is akin to a sponge, which has to be squeezed, till the last drop of water comes out.

Give, Give, Give!

The third and the best form of giving is like the honeycomb, from which sweetness freely oozes out.

Such unrestricted and overflowing giving is the true form of giving. A beggar once came to the door of Thomas Carlyle, when he was a boy. His parents were not at home and he was in a dilemma. He did not want the beggar to go away disappointed. In his boyish enthusiasm, he rushed to his room and brought out his piggy bank. He smashed it to smithereens and handed over its entire contents to the beggar.

On recalling this incident Carlyle said that never before had he experienced such bliss and satisfaction. Such is the inexplicable joy of giving!

Sadhu Vaswani often said, "I have but one tongue, but even if I had a million tongues, I would but utter this one word 'Give, Give, Give'!" True religion is to bring joy and happiness in the lives of others. You cannot always be happy, but you can always give happiness!

Sadhu Vaswani embodied the spirit of giving. Just 48 hours before he left his physical body, a leper couple walked into the Mission Campus seeking help. The Master learnt that they required 15 rupees to return to their village. Lovingly, he gave them 25 rupees and sought their blessings. On return to his room, he beckoned me and asked me to keep only two sets of clothes for him and to distribute the rest among the poor and needy.

Do not hoard, but scatter the wealth of your heart and your loving service, and relieve the agony of the world, was his message to us all.

Goal

You are unique. God made you for a special purpose. Discover that special purpose. Make it your goal and once you have fixed that goal, you must keep your eyes fixed always on that goal. This is one of the secrets of making the most of life– fix your goal!

Arise! Awake! This is the call of the Gita to all of us. This arousing call occurs also in the *Kathopanishad*, where young Nachiketas is advised: "Arise! Awake! Approach the great and learn."

"Arise, awake, and stop not till the goal is reached!" was Swami Vivekananda's clarion call to the youth of India. Sadhu Vaswani too, was inspired by this great message of awakening in our Scriptures. "Arise! Awake!" he called to us again and again. "How long will you in slumber lie?"

Arjuna heeded Sri Krishna's call to awaken on the battlefield of Kurukshetra. Nachiketas was an apt pupil who learnt the great truth about life and death from Lord Yamaraj. Alas, we mortals are so reluctant to awake, arise, and strive towards our goal!

If I were to ask you right now, "What is it that you want out of life? What do you wish to achieve?" Not many of you will be able to give me an answer straight away. But if I were to phrase the same question in a negative manner, "What is it that you feel you cannot achieve?" many of you will have ready answers. Some of you will say to me, "Achievement does not run in our family. My father achieved nothing, my brother achieved nothing, I shall achieve nothing." Perhaps others will say, "I do not have the power, the education, or the influence and the resources to achieve whatever I want." Yet others might say, "My brother has all the brains in the family and my sister has all the good looks, I have nothing, so I cannot do anything."

Excuses, excuses, and more excuses!

To each of you I would say, you must fix your goal. To start with, you must affirm to yourself what you want or what you wish to be. Only then can you proceed with what you must do to move forward in that direction.

The goal of this human birth

The *jivatma* has but one destination: merging with the *Paramatma*.

If life is a game, attaining to God is the goal; if life is an examination, union with the Creator is the desired 'passing' with Distinction; if life is a journey, God is the desired destination. Every step I take, every move I make, every moment I live and breathe must remind me of who I am and where I am headed: God is my chosen goal and destination.

My journey upon this earth must ever take me onward, forward, Godward.

The goal of perfection

In the Bhagavad Gita, Lord Sri Krishna tells His devoted disciple Arjuna, "Birthless and deathless are you, O, Arjuna! Birth and death belong to the body. You are of the Spirit– immutable, immortal, eternal!"

The teaching is echoed in our Vedas: "You are Divine! *Tat Twam Asi*!"

Let me also remind you of the words of Jesus, as recorded in Matthew 5:48– "Therefore ye are to be perfect, as your heavenly Father is perfect."

The goal that every one of us must place before ourselves is to be a perfect human being. It does not matter if perfection seems an impossible goal to attain; what matters is that we strive towards it, and in the striving lies the essence of our higher aspirations– that we try to be like Him who is the epitome of all that is good and wise and perfect!

Perfection is defined as a state of completeness and flawlessness. The ancient Greek philosophers saw perfection as a state of perfect rest, a detached stasis, as opposed to frantic and restless wandering, movement and hectic action. The Stoics interpreted perfection as harmony– harmony with nature, reason, and with man himself. They held that such harmony– such perfection– was attainable for anyone.

It was George Fisher who said, "When you aim for perfection, you discover it's a moving target." In other words, it is not easy to be a perfect man. It is a long, difficult journey, on which one has to surmount many obstacles and cross many hurdles. This difficulty is compounded by the fact that man, by nature, is restless. Man, by temperament, tends to wander aimlessly, pushed by desires and fuelled by ambition.

Nevertheless, the pursuit of perfection is a worthy goal, and all of us must strive for it.

Stop drifting!

Liberation and perfection are the highest goals we can strive for. But there are other goals we can choose to make our lives successful, joyous, and peaceful. Life goals give value and worth to our lives. We can vow to make our marriages successful; we can aim to be the best athlete or student in our peer group; we can strive to make our relationships meaningful and purposeful.

We forget that each of us is unique. They say that there are a hundred million people in India today. Just imagine, among those hundred million people there is no one exactly like you! Why, amongst the billions of people who inhabit the earth, there is no other person who is like you!

We are just moving; we are just drifting. But if we wish to succeed; we must fix our goal!

You have heard the name of Jesse Owens, the black American athlete who won three Olympic gold medals and created a record at the Munich games. Jesse was born with scrawny legs, lean, weak, bony legs. But one day, the man who was known as the fastest runner in the world, Charlie Paddock, came to his school. Addressing the boys, Paddock said, "You can be what you want to be in life. Decide what you want to be, then go to God and ask Him to help you to become what you want to be."

These words penetrated young Jesse's consciousness. After the lecture, he went up on the dais to meet Charlie Paddock and said to him, "Will you shake hands with me?" Paddock smiled and shook hands with him, and Jesse felt as if an electric current passed through his entire being. He went out to the playground and started jumping. He kept on jumping, and in this upbeat mood, he met the sports coach and said to him, "I have a dream! I have a dream!" The coach asked him, "My boy, what is your dream?" Jesse Owens, the boy with the scrawny legs, replied, "I want to be the fastest man alive, like Charlie Paddock!"

The coach patted the boy on the shoulder and said to him, "It is good to have a dream, but you must build a ladder to reach the dream!"

The ladder that one must build to fulfil his dream is made up of four rungs– determination, dedication, discipline and a positive attitude.

Jesse Owens built this ladder, and the dream he cherished did come true one day. Jesse entered the Olympic Games. He ran the 100 meters, and won gold; he ran the 400 meters, and won gold. As for the high jump, he not only won gold, but created an Olympic record that remained unbeaten for several years to come!

Just imagine, a weak boy with scrawny legs set a goal for himself, and achieved it! Yet we complain, "I don't have the strength… I don't have the resources… I don't have the influence to achieve what I want!"

Fix a goal and keep an unwavering focus on it all the time!

Most people live life on the surface. They live a superficial life, unaware of the goal or the meaning of their life. A man who lives his life without any purpose is akin to a rudderless ship, moving with no direction. Once you fix your purpose, keep it steadfast, and through your strength of mind, go ahead and achieve it.

If you wish to achieve your goals, whether they are material or spiritual, you need to act. If you want to change your life, you need to put the teachings of the great ones into practice. Pick up one or two simple ideals that appeal to you, and make them a part of your life. A holy man once said, "If you have spent your whole life in gaining one good quality and giving up one bad one, you have not lived in vain."

Start now!

There are some days when you don't feel like doing whatever it is you are supposed to do that day to move towards your goal. Well, instead of thinking about how hard it is, and how long it will take, tell yourself that you just have to start. Once you start, it is never as hard as you thought it would be.

Try it now:

- Identify the most important thing you have to do today to achieve your goal.
- Decide to do just the first little part of it– just the first minute or two. Getting started is the only thing that matters now.
- Clear away distractions. Turn everything off. Close all programmes. It should just be you, and your task towards achieving your goal.

- Pay attention to your mind, as it begins to have urges to switch to another task. You will feel compelled to check your email or Facebook, Twitter, or your favourite website. You will want to play a game or make a call or do something else. Notice these urges.
- Notice the urges, but sit still, and let them pass. Urges build up in intensity, then pass, like a wave. Let each one pass.
- Notice also your mind trying to justify not doing the task. Let these self-rationalising thoughts pass.
- Now, just take one small action to get started– as tiny a step as possible. Get started and the rest will flow.

One final thought…

All thinking, seeking people ask themselves this crucial question: Who am I? What is the purpose of my existence here?

I would not be wrong if I were to tell you that you rise or fall to the level of your answer to this question! You will rise or fall depending on the goal you have set for yourself! For you set your own goal: you create your own benchmark, and you reach it by your own efforts. If like the ancient decadents, you decide that the sole purpose of existence is to eat, drink, and be merry until you drop dead, that is a goal which will not demand too much of effort on your part. If, like some ambitious businessman, you decide that the sole aim of your existence is to make millions and millions, your task is clear cut– you will require a great deal of business acumen, sound sense, and the efforts to succeed in your business. If you make up your mind to settle for a steady 9 to 5 job and a quiet evening watching TV in your own living room, well then, you have your work cut out. But if you are looking for something that transcends all this, if you are looking for what we call self-realisation or God-realisation, you have set the highest possible goal that any human being can aspire to, and you must work very hard to achieve it. This goal is indeed worthy, and the efforts you put in to achieving it can only take you higher and higher up on the ladder of spiritual growth.

Gurmukh and Manmukh

There are two kinds of people: *gurmukh* and *manmukh*. *Gurmukh* are those whose face is always turned towards the guru, even as the sunflower follows the direction of the sun as it traverses the sky. Such people are always living, moving, speaking, thinking, and acting in the consciousness of the guru's presence with them, within them. They will never ever do anything of which they think the guru would disapprove. The guru might be thousands of miles away, but their minds and hearts are focussed on him all the time, under all circumstances. Before every decision, before every deed, they ask themselves: what would the guru have me do in this situation? And they act accordingly. *Manmukh* are those people who tend to be led away by their worldly desires; they are always looking towards the world and its many illusions of power, possessions and pleasure. They often fall prey to their own greed, covetousness, lust, hatred, and the like.

Gurmukh and *Manmukh* are concepts expressed repeatedly in the sacred *Guru Granth Sahib*. Although the word *gurmukh* (*gur* = Guru; *mukh* = face), has several connotations, we use the word here to signify someone who is God-conscious, devoted to the guru, God-inspired or guru-inspired who, imbued with the Word, is crowned with glory at the Lord's portal. In direct contrast, the *manmukh* is self-centred and self-willed, and his face is turned towards the world and its allurements.

The *manmukh* imagines he is happy, but he is not genuinely content. He may have all the wealth of the world, but true happiness will elude him. The *gurmukh* may be poor in the wealth of the world, but he will always be happy. Most of us run after worldly things. There are very few who realise the value of spiritual wealth, and try to grow in it.

It is natural for the mind to be attached to a person, position, material wealth, or even one's work. This attachment leads to bondage and suffering. Fortunately, the guru can create conditions which help you to be detached. The guru has the *shakti*, the power, to break free his disciple from attachment to any relationship. He is the only one who can help to recreate and redefine your karma. The unique relationship with the guru releases you from bondage to this world.

I often think of the guru as an expert ophthalmologist, who specialises in cataract surgery. Using a sharp instrument, he extricates his disciple's blinding cataract of ego and attachment. Today, we have advanced laser technology for eye surgeries. Similarly, the guru too, has his own subtle methods to cure us of the ego. He does not wish to inflict insufferable pain on his disciple. Like God, the guru is ever merciful. Hence, devotees and disciples should be God-loving and guru-loving, not God and guru-fearing.

"Don't make me *manmukh*, make me *gurmukh*." This should be the silent aspiration of each one of us! This must be the mantra that each parent should pass on to his child! "Don't make me *manmukh*, make me *gurmukh*."

Two opposing ways of life

The *gurmukh* is one who follows the way of life prescribed by the guru and abides constantly by his precepts. In this sense, he has his "face turned towards the guru."

The *gurmukh* is inspired by the guru's spirit. He scrupulously follows the guru's teaching and lives as the master bids, for he is "merged in the guru's Word". He stands for truth and righteousness. His adherence to truth has cleansed his soul and made him pure. To such a man alone is the Truth revealed, for he is rid of doubt, delusion and pride– *Gurmukhi hovai su sojhi pae haumai maia bharamu gavae* (GGS- 1058-59). His is an illumined mind– free from ignorance and doubts. *Vivek*, or discrimination, is his special trait.

The *gurmukh* always dwells upon the Name of God. He constantly meditates through *simran* and thus acquires stability of mind. Freedom from attachment characterises his conduct. The *gurmukh* carries out actions, but he himself transcends them. He is above the dualities of pleasure and pain.

The *Gurbani* is full of praise for the *Gurmukh*. *Jnani, sant, brahma jnani* are some of the words used in the scripture to describe the *gurmukh*.

The word *manmukh* is made up of two terms: (*man* = mind, lower self; *mukh* = face). Thus, the *manmukh* is an ego-centred man whose face is always turned to the world away from the guru. Filled with ego, he is obsessed with the self and its sensual needs.

Oblivious of God and impervious to His Will, the *manmukh* puts himself into karmic bondage, for he becomes a slave of his base passions and lower impulses. He has no respect for the word or the precepts of the guru. Allowing himself to be ruled by the senses, he is unreceptive of God's saving grace.

Why the guru's glance of grace is so special...

Pawan guru paani pita maata dharat mahat.

This is the beautiful opening line of the *sloka* with which the *Japji* concludes.

The guru is our air…we can survive without water for a few days, we can survive without food for a few weeks; but can we survive without breathing? And yet we take the breath for granted. We are hardly aware of the breath, and of the oxygen in the air which God has supplied for our benefit so bountifully…

I can only express the pious hope that we do not become such *manmukhs* who take the guru for granted! For, as the *sloka* tells us, the guru is as precious to us as the vital breath we take in. He is as essential for our true life, the life of the Spirit, as air is to staying alive. He is the visible aspect of God— the living, moving presence of God in our lives. Thus the most important, the most vital status is accorded to the guru.

Let me share with you the beautiful words of Sadhu Vaswani from his "gleanings" of the *Guru Granth Sahib*:

Beautiful and fair beyond compare,
Is the palace of my Lord!
Adorned with gems, with pearls and gold
Is the palace of the Purest One:
His castle is enchanting!
Without a ladder how may I ascend?
The Guru is the Ladder.

Without a boat there is no road on the sea:
The Guru is the Boat!
Without the Guru, there is darkness:
Without the Nama, The Name, the word,
there is no understanding

If I abide within the Name,
The Name doth come and dwell within my heart!
The Guru utters the word, the Name,
And death dwells not where the Word abides!
"I am a sacrifice unto the Guru for it is he who has revealed Govind to me."

The witness of Sri Ramakrishna

Sri Ramakrishna once said, "There are two kinds of devotees. One has the nature of a kitten– absolute dependence on the mother. It only knows how to meow. It does not know where it is going, or what it will do. In the same way, a devotee gives the power of attorney to God, freeing himself from any anxiety. The second type of devotee has the nature of a young monkey, who holds onto its mother with all its strength."

In simple words, there are disciples who cling to their master. They do not wish to go away, they stay with their master, with their muru. Later, the muru, with his grace, helps them to reach the final goal.

Whichever type of disciple you may be, it is most important to surrender yourself to the master. Hence, keep uttering: *Na hum, Na hum, Tu ho, Tu ho*! Not me, but Thee and Thee alone! The more you proceed towards God, the more you will see that God Himself has become everything, that it is He who is doing everything. He is the guru and He Himself is the spiritual ideal. It is He Himself who has granted you spiritual knowledge and love for God.

The story of Padmapada

Padmapada is the sterling example of the disciple who, by his intense devotion and implicit obedience to the guru, attains perfect receptivity and becomes capable of assimilating the guru's teachings completely.

Even as a young man, he had turned away from worldly life and longed to find a guru who could show him the way to liberation. Adi Shankara recognised his deep and intense longing and accepted him as a disciple. He was initiated into *sanyasa* and given the name Sanandana. So earnest was his desire to learn at the feet of the guru, that it is said that Adi Shankara would often explain the great truths of the Vedas to Sanandana thrice over, causing other disciples to wonder why he was singled out for the guru's special attention.

Sanandana was envied by the other disciples, who felt that he was being groomed as the dearest disciple of the guru. They thought that he did not deserve this honour. Adi Shankara heard them expressing their resentment, and decided to reveal Sanandana's true worth and set their doubts to rest.

One day, as the master and his disciples were walking along the banks of the River Ganga,

Adi Shankara called out to Sanandana; the guru was on one side of the river and the disciple was on the opposite bank. On hearing the guru's call, without even a moment's hesitation, Sanandana closed his eyes, and started walking across the swirling waters of the Ganga.

It was the rainy season, and the river was in spate. The other disciples watched in disbelief as Sanandana rushed across the flowing waters, to reach the guru as quickly as he could. Ganga *Mata* was so full of admiration for the young disciple's intense devotion that she made a lotus bloom at every step he took across the river. Stepping across a veritable bridge of lotuses, Sanandana rushed to be by his guru's side.

All the disciples who saw this blessed event were wonderstruck by the earnest *sadhaka's* miraculous feat. Blissfully unaware of the impact he was creating, unconcerned for his own safety, Sanandana reached the other shore swiftly and fell at his guru's feet, breathless but ready to be of service.

Adi Shankara embraced him and bestowed on him the beautiful name, Padmapada– he at whose feet lotuses spring!

Padmapada was a *gurmukh*. The guru's word, the guru's command, was to him the ultimate duty. Therefore, he was the most beloved disciple of his guru.

The *manmukhs* are to be pitied

The Gurbani tells us:

Manmukh har har kar thakay mail na sakee dhoi.
Man mailai bhagat na hova-ee naam na paa-i-aa jaa-ay.
Manmukh mailay mailay mu-ay jaasan pat gavaa-ay.

The self-willed *manmukhs* have grown weary of chanting the Name of the Lord, *Har, Har*,
but their filth cannot be removed.
With a polluted mind, devotional service cannot be performed,
and the *Naam*, the Name of the Lord, cannot be obtained.
The filthy, self-willed *manmukhs* die in filth, and they depart in disgrace.

[G G S p. 39]

The choice is ours: to walk the way of *gurmukh* or *manmukh*!

Guru

The Guru is the ladder, the dinghy, the boat, the raft by means of which one reaches God;
The Guru is the lake, the ocean, the sacred place of pilgrimage, the river,
Without the Guru, there can be no bhakti, no love…

Beautiful are these words of Guru Nanak! Truly blessed are those who come into contact with a realised soul, an evolved soul who will point out to them the way to true freedom, emancipation and liberation. Such a one will take us out of the darkness of *avidya* (ignorance) into the realms of *jnana* (wisdom); out of *dukha* (suffering and misery) he will lead us on to *Sat Chit Ananda*– the bliss that no ending knows.

A stage comes in the life of every spiritual aspirant when he realises the need for a Guru– someone who can hold him by the hand and take him onward, forward, inward, upward, Godward. When he feels this need, all he needs to do is to pray to the Lord, "O Lord, put me into contact with someone, a man of Light, with someone who can connect me with You, with someone who has known You, with someone who knows the way."

The Guru, Sadhu Vaswani taught us, is much more than an 'instructor' or 'advisor'. He is a dynamic person with a transforming power– for spirituality is a tremendous *shakti*, and the true Guru is a man of *shakti*. By the method of evocation, the Guru draws out the disciple's spiritual energy. Therefore, we read in the ancient texts: "The Guru leads forth the pupil to himself!" It is in this process of 'leading forth', drawing the disciple to himself– not in merely communicating information– that lies the secret of the Guru's *shakti*.

The word Guru, as we all know, is derived from two Sanskrit root words: 'Gu' means darkness, 'ru' means light. Thus, the Guru leads us from darkness to light.

I have also come across other such interesting etymological derivations. Let me share a few of them with you.

1. Some scholars think that 'gu' stands for *guptam*– that which is hidden; 'ru' derives from *roopayati*– giving form or shape. Hence the Guru is one who gives a form and shape to the indwelling God, who reveals God to us.

2. 'Gu' is also thought to refer to *goodham*– a mysterious secret; and 'ru' to *rauti*– to proclaim. The Guru is one who proclaims the reality to us.

3. A Punjabi scholar traces the word Guru to *gur*– which means two different things: 1) to raise, to lift up and also 2) to hurt, to kill. Accordingly, he explains a Guru is so called because he kills, indeed destroys the ego and ignorance of the disciple and elevates him to *moksha*, or liberation.

May I humbly submit that these derivations and definitions cannot convey to you the true nature of a Guru. They can only indicate some of the many facets of a Guru, who is a soul beyond definitions. When you have found your Guru– when he has found you, and allowed you to 'discover' him, the bliss of that experience alone can convey to you what my poor words cannot convey!

Do I really need a Guru?

In an age of self-help books, self-improvement practices, and do-it-yourself ideas, it is not surprising that people should raise the question: Why do we need a Guru? Is not self-realisation possible with individual effort? Can we not seek liberation for ourselves?

Let me say to you, there are some great ones who have reached God without being formally initiated by a guru. Lord Buddha was one such great soul, who was not initiated by a Master, and we all know that he attained enlightenment. There are many others like him, too!

There are people who refer to the words of the ancient text to strengthen their case: *Aham Brahmasmi*. I am Brahman. If that is so, and God is the indweller within me, why should I need someone like the Guru on the outside, to lead me inward and Godward?

True, the Light of the *Paramatma* shines within each one of us. But alas, we live in the outer darkness, unaware of the Light within. Let me repeat, the Light inextinguishable dwells within each one of us, but we cannot see it, for it is hidden behind veils of ignorance, veils of mind and matter. The great wall of the ego stands between us and the *Paramatma*– and we cannot see the Light Divine. It is the Guru who can destroy the great wall of the ego, and lead us from darkness to light.

The *Satguru*, the True Teacher, is in the heart already. He speaks to us from there. But while we are trapped in this illusory world of the senses, we cannot hear his soft, sweet voice– for our hearing is drowned in the trumpet-like blaring of the phenomenal world. This is why we need an 'external' Guru, whom we can see and hear and understand even in our human form.

Why do we need a Guru? The Guru is the great cleanser, a great purifier– not merely a great teacher. Caught in the web of *maya*, caught in the snare of sensual desires and worldly pleasures, we accumulate bad karma, birth after birth after birth. Alas, our poor efforts are not enough to cleanse these impurities. It is the Guru's grace that can cleanse us and lead us towards the Divine Light of God

The "Third Eye", the Inner Eye of the Spirit remains closed for most of us, its vision impaired by our negative karma. The cataract of the ego, the wheels of arrogance and pride, have covered this inner eye completely. The Guru is the 'eye' surgeon, who can restore our inner vision.

The Guru reaches out to us, and with his grace, annihilates the ego. He tears away the wheels of ignorance which shield us from self-realisation. He reveals our true identity to us– *Tat Twam Asi*! That art Thou! It is his grace that liberates us from bondage to the circle of life and death. This gift of grace has devolved on the Guru from God Himself– for God knows that the world is in dire need of grace. His Presence is of course universal. He gives us the Guru, for our individual benefit, for our personal liberation. This is why our ancient scriptures enjoin us to venerate the Guru as God:

Gurur Brahma, Gurur Vishnu
Gurur Devo Maheshwara…..

In this human birth, we cannot see God in person, but it is our good fortune that we can see the Guru, hear his *upadesh*, associate ourselves with daily *satsang*, accept his gracious *prasad*– indeed, grasp his holy feet firmly– and through him, all God's blessings and all God's grace will come to us!

How may we recognise the true guru?

Many of my friends– especially my young friends– ask me how they can recognise a true Guru. To them I always say, that for those of us who live on a lower level, it is difficult to make decisions about more evolved souls who dwell on a higher plane. However, there are certain marks which may serve as indicators of a true Guru.

1. The true Guru wants nothing for himself. He will not take anything from you. He has come to the earth only to give. Sadhu Vaswani would often say, "Today's Gurus have become *ghurus*." In Sindhi, the word *ghurus* means takers.

2. A true Guru has transcended the ego. It does not exist in him. He is humble, childlike, innocent, and pure.

3. A true Guru lives in the Light and the Light lives in him. His presence is radiant, and it illuminates your soul.

   The *jignasus* of ancient India constantly prayed: *"Tamaso ma jyotir gamaya!"*– "From darkness, lead me into the Light!" This light indeed is the Light of the Spirit. The Guru can kindle this light in the heart of a receptive disciple. Therefore, the Guru is revered as a "Light bringer".

4. The true Master does not call himself a Master. The true Guru will not describe himself as a Guru. He will say to you, "I too am a seeker, a disciple like any one of you."

   The great Sufi Saint Hazrat Nizamuddin used to say, "It is the privilege of the disciple to decide who will be his Guru. It is not the privilege of the Guru to decide who will be his disciple."

5. The true Guru must be a devotee of the Lord. He should be one who submits to the Will Divine, and urges his disciples too, to do the same.

6. It is the sacred duty of the Guru to lead us on the path of *shreya*, to impart spiritual wisdom to us, not worldly knowledge.

7. The Guru should instill in us an awareness of the truth that is imperishable, and not dwell on transient matters that pass. Knowledge of the *atman*, awareness of the presence of God– these are permanent and lasting matters, and the Guru should always remind us of the life eternal.

8. The Guru should not use his knowledge of the scriptures or his wisdom to earn his livelihood or for his own personal benefit. Indeed, there is no such creature as a "professional Guru".

9. The Guru should teach by precept as well as practice. He should be a living, walking scripture, and his life should be his message. He must reflect the teachings of the scriptures in his actions and speech. He must bear witness to the Vedas and the Gita in deeds of daily living.

10. The Guru must be a *jitendriya*, one who has controlled and mastered his senses.

11. Finally, in the words of the *Srimad Bhagavatam*: "The symptoms of the true sadhu are that he is tolerant, merciful, and friendly to all living entities. He has no enemies, he is peaceful, he abides by the scriptures, and all his characteristics are sublime."

The Guru is then, a man of saintly qualities. He is free from sensuality and the drag of the flesh. He is a picture of purity. He is free from greed. He has no desire for wealth or worldly possessions. He does not seek earthly greatness. He does not even desire to increase the number of his followers. In his heart, there is no feeling of hatred or enmity towards anyone. He has conquered the weaknesses of the flesh and the mind. He has, specially, these three marks: love, humility, and wisdom.

Sadhu Vaswani was such a one! His love drew us to him even as a magnet draws needles. No one could resist the power of his love which flowed out alike to the saint and the sinner, to friend and foe. As for his humility, it defied description. It was the humility of one who had reduced himself to naught. "*Na hum, Na hum! Tu ho, Tu ho!*" He said this again and again: "I am nothing! Thou alone art, O Lord!" In his life, he revealed what it was to become nothing, no-thing. As Jesus said, "The empty alone are filled." Sadhu Vaswani became empty of the self, the ego, and the Lord filled him with love and wisdom. He had the wisdom of the truly wise, of those who had touched the root of life and unravelled the secrets of the Spirit. This is why he could express the most profound truths in a language so simple that even a child could understand!

Guru and *shishya*: The perfect relationship

From birth until death, human beings are sustained by a network of relationships: parents-children; brothers-sisters; uncles-aunts-cousins; friends-neighbours; husbands-wives; partners-colleagues-associates; superiors-authorities-subordinates; buyers-sellers… the relationships form an endless link.

Among them all, the Guru-*shishya* relationship is unique. It is ordained by Divine grace; it is born out of inner conviction and inner need; in its genuine form it is a pure, selfless, spiritual relationship which lifts human beings on to a higher plane, far above the mundane relationships of this world.

The Guru is the true awakener who can shake us awake from the deep slumber we are in.

He is the "kindly light" who can lead us away from the encircling gloom to the Eternal Radiance which is our true nature and our true home.

What is it that the Guru does for us?

The Guru creates us anew. We are reborn in the Spirit, when we surrender to him. He is much more than an 'instructor', 'advisor', or 'professor'. He is an 'enlightener' with a transforming power. Spirituality is, as we have seen, a tremendous *shakti*. And the Guru's *shakti* lies in this– that he leads forth the disciple not only towards liberation, but towards himself, so that the disciple becomes a teacher in his own right.

The Guru's words of wisdom, his *bani*, charged with divine and holy meaning, enter the heart and shine there as jewels bright; they lead the disciple to the presence Divine. The Guru's words are the disciple's torch in darkness, they are the disciple's source of true happiness in the strife of this broken life.

How can I find my ideal Guru, among so many who call themselves by that name?

I strongly believe that you cannot 'find' your Guru: it is he who will come and find you. And when you meet him at that special moment of 'discovery', you will surely feel, "This is my Guru! He is the one I have been waiting for all these years! My blessed Master, why were you away from me for so long?"

Yes, the Guru, in his grace, will find you, when you feel the need for him.

A Guru becomes necessary only when you feel that he is necessary– not otherwise. Spiritual aspirations come to all of us at one stage or another; we cannot rest content with what the world gives– and what the world takes away. The yearning grows in our heart to seek the wealth that is eternal, the wealth that cannot be looted or lost.

You do not go out in quest of the Guru. The Guru will come to you himself. You will see him– and you will realise that he is a teacher meant for you, ordained by God's Will for you. For this is the law of the spiritual life– whatever you aspire for, will come to you. Only, that aspiration, that longing, that yearning of the heart should be strong and deep. That yearning takes the form of a cloud, and when the cloud becomes heavy with rain, it starts to shower its blessings– and out of this shower of grace will come your Guru.

Is not the guru's power revealed to us by the 'miracles' and other extraordinary deeds that he performs?

My Master believed– and also taught us to believe– that one's spiritual *shakti* should not be channelised into performing extraordinary deeds for the sake of demonstrating such power. And so I would say, no, you cannot recognise a true Guru by the 'extraordinary' deeds that he performs.

Having said that, let me also add, I regard the Guru as a miracle worker– in a different sense. He performs the miracle of transforming the life of a true disciple, does he not? What can compare to the miracle that he works on our hearts and souls?

Let me tell you too, about another distinguishing mark which will help you recognise your Guru. You will be overwhelmed by the spontaneity of the love and affection that flow from him to you. This is the surest sign that he has seen the same Divine Spirit that resides in himself, reflected in you. This leads on to the next 'sign'– the beautiful, vibrant atmosphere of bliss that emanates from him, and extends to everyone in his presence.

One final thought…

The Guru is one who is singularly free from *kama*, *krodha*, and *lobha*– lust, anger, and greed. He is compassion incarnate, love personified, radiance in visible form. He is also purity, wisdom, tranquility, and spirituality. He does not have to talk to you all the time; his silence itself speaks volumes. His vibrations fill you with peace and joy. When you are in his presence, you think of nothing, you want nothing. To be in his vicinity is ecstasy; to listen to his *upadesh* is upliftment and inspiration of the highest order. But we need to be receptive– or we will remain ignorant, like the fish which kept looking for water, even while it lived in the mighty ocean.

Happiness

Happiness, true happiness, is an inner quality, it is a state of mind. If your mind is at peace, and you have nothing else, you can still be happy. If you have everything the world can give– pleasure, possessions, power– but lack peace of mind, you can never be happy. So it was that a holy man exclaimed, "Nothing in the morn have I; and nothing do I have at night. And yet there is none on earth happier than I."

I repeat: happiness does not depend on outer things. Happiness is essentially an inner quality!

How can we 'find' happiness?

Happiness, in itself, is an abstract noun! You cannot see it or touch it! It does not exist in material terms. Only by being happy within yourself, can you find it!

Unfortunately, we probe the entire world over for happiness. Even if we search until our last breath, we are not going to find happiness 'out there somewhere'. We cannot wish for it; we cannot buy it; nobody can hand it over to us on a platter. It is a very personal feeling– and it must come from within!

Does this mean that most of us will never find happiness? After all, very few of us ever learn to look within!

The answer is: No! We all are capable of experiencing happiness. No matter who you are, no matter your circumstances, you must realise that happiness, without any conditions, is your birthright.

You cannot depend on someone else to make you happy or 'give' you happiness. This will place a tremendous strain on both of you. On the other hand, if you are sincerely happy within, and allow the other person to feel the same, both of you will bring happiness to each other… without any expectations, without any pre-conditions, without any anticipations.

Happiness has no existence or value in itself. It is not an object, which we can pursue or possess, or attain as a prize. Rather, it comes as the effect of appropriate actions; it is almost incidental– a bonus, which we receive in the act of self-fulfilment through right thought, right attitude and right actions. When what you think, say, and do, are in harmony, it brings about a state of happiness.

'Wanting' happiness

There was a businessman who led a contented, busy life. He had a comfortable home, a lovely wife and children, a reasonable income and a thriving business. He drove a large family car, which he was very fond of.

One day, he saw a neighbour driving a Mercedes Benz. "What a beautiful car that is!" he thought to himself. "How I wish I could own such a car!"

The man became restless, and driven to buy a new car. He moved heaven and earth, spent lakhs of rupees till he possessed a Mercedes Benz. And– he was happy!

Consider this– the man was happy to begin with, or at least, he was not unhappy. Then, he developed a desire. He did not wish to be happy; he wished for a car. He attached a great deal of value to the car, and did everything he could to obtain the car. Finally, he got the car. He was happy– or he was no longer unhappy– in other words, he was back where he started.

We may not all want Benz cars, but we are no different than this businessman. We are fine, we are content, we are happy– until we want something. Our happiness is replaced by a craving for something. "I want something." We pay a certain price and get what we want. We say, "I've got it." We are happy– just as we were, before we wanted something.

So ask yourself– is it the Benz, the thing that you wanted, that brings happiness? Does happiness actually come from a Benz, a bungalow or a diamond necklace? By themselves, none of these things can 'generate' happiness. You create a cavity, a depression in your mind, when you want something. When you get it, the cavity is filled. However, you yourself created the hole, you filled it, and you tell yourself, "I'm happy now."

In reality, you threw away the happiness you had when you created the 'want' cavity. When you don't want anything, when you rise above wants, your original state of happiness remains intact. For it is not how much we have, but how much we enjoy what we already have or already are, that determines our happiness.

Your true nature is *ananda*!

God is Bliss Supreme– *Sat Chit Ananda*. God has made us in His image. As His image, are we not also happiness personified? You are supreme joy and you are eternal bliss. It is only when you forget your true nature that you lose your happiness. You forget that you are an aspect of the Divine. It is this lack of self-knowledge, this *avidya* that makes you unhappy.

With an unhappy and dissatisfied mind, how can you look for happiness? How can you hope to find it outside, when your 'inside' is dark and clouded?

Don't forget your true nature! If you do, you will find happiness and unhappiness rising in waves, and beating on the shores of your life. You will be lashed by disappointments, failures and frustrations. In the end, you will give up and say, "I've had enough. I don't want anything anymore."

Renounce wants and desires; forsake everything else– and you will find God. God is true happiness.

Secrets of happiness

May I teach you a little prayer?

Dear Lord, so bless me that I may bring happiness to someone today. I know that You made all of us so that we may live happily in this beautiful world that You created. Give me a heart filled with gratitude and a positive attitude so that everything I do and everything I say brings happiness to others. I am happy because I am me, and I know I am connected to You, dear God, who is the source of all happiness and peace. May I always reflect this happiness and peace to everyone who crosses my path.

This then, is the first secret to always be happy: If you want to be happy, make others happy!

The second secret is: have an open mind! Do not bear grudges; do not blame others for your unhappiness.

The third secret is: cherish your relationships!

Fourthly, appreciate everyone you meet!

Lastly, forgive and forget– for forgiveness is divine!

Let the change begin with you!

This is a wonderful universe we live in and everything in it is good. All is for the best, in this best of all possible worlds. Why should we set out to change the universe or anything in God's Creation? It would be far better to change ourselves. When we are negative, selfish, unforgiving, when we bear a grudge, when we blame others, we are perceiving the world through our own distorted lens. It is our attitude or disposition that makes us unhappy. Many people carry the notion that they have enemies everywhere. Their colleagues, neighbours, business rivals, bankers, lawyers, employees– everyone seems to be out to get them. May I say to you, we cannot hope to 'conquer' so many enemies! The easier and quicker option would be to change so-called enemies into friends! We must replace grudge with generosity; bitterness with sweetness; hate with love…and then we will experience the happiness that no ending knows!

Health and Well-Being

Health and happiness are twin goals that mankind has always pursued. Many of us know that we must be healthy in order to be happy; but very few of us realise that we must strive to be happy in order to be healthy!

The Sanskrit word for health is *swasthya*, which literally means 'to be oneself'. You cannot be yourself when you are ill! Health also means "whole". A healthy person is whole– his life is balanced and his energy moves in rhythm. A healthy person is happy, within and without.

Good health is the basis of all that we value and cherish in human life– success, achievement, financial prosperity, emotional security, and above all, spiritual unfoldment and inner peace.

What is good health?

Good health does not necessarily mean extending one's lifespan. Longevity is not the primary goal of human life. We are told that life expectancy has increased in our times, due to better health care and advances made in medicine and allied sciences. But a longer life is not what all of us seek. A life of pain, disease, and medical treatment can only be a miserable burden, when it is prolonged. There are incurable diseases and people who are 'clinically dead' being put on life-support systems in the ICUs of hospitals. This is hardly the kind of treatment or 'life' that we aspire to!

Good health has been described as the complete integration of body, mind, and soul. Americans describe good health as "wellness", defined by experts as a decision that we all have to make in order to maximise our life's potential. Wellness encompasses the major areas of life– the physical, emotional, social, intellectual, vocational and spiritual spheres. Wellness sets a new standard for life; it calls for continuing improvement and self-renewal in all areas of life. Wellness is much more than the absence of illness. It is total well-being– in body, mind, and spirit.

Since the beginning of the 20th century, we have believed in what is known as psychosomatic unity of the human being. 'Psyche' means mind or soul; 'soma' means body, suggesting that we are not just bodies, but an entirety that includes body, mind, and spirit, functioning in a symbiotic relationship in which a separation is impossible to make.

True health and well-being encompasses man's physical, mental, intellectual and spiritual states. When there is harmony and integrity between all these states, man is in good health. This is the concept of holistic health that we need now.

Good health is your birthright!

Many of us have come to accept ill-health as a matter of course. Pain, sickness, ulcers, aches, abnormal growths, exhaustion– all these have become as inevitable as inflation, taxation, and bad weather.

There is no need to accept ill-health with such a sense of stoicism and helplessness. We can and must take matters into our own hands!

It is a clinically-proven fact that your body reacts to your attitude. I know bankers and financiers who suffered a heart-attack when their investments proved to be damaging. Equally, I know about chronically ill patients who miraculously revive when a marriage is announced or a baby is born into their family. Bad news can make you ill and good news can make you well. Negative emotions create an imbalance in your body, leading to ill-health; positive emotions restore the balance, bringing good health. Your body reacts to your attitude and changes your state of health. If you wish to change your life, you only have to change your attitude. You can change your attitude and choose good health!

Sickness is not a punishment. It is the effect of a cause for which you are responsible. By choosing tension instead of tranquillity, stress instead of serenity, indulgence instead of moderation, bad instead of good, we make ourselves ill!

Some of our attitudes cause disease, while some of them promote good health. The body has its own excellent self-healing mechanism, and it prefers to be in a healthy condition at all times. Therefore, it is up to us to choose good health– by choosing the right attitude to life.

Four doctors

When I was a little boy, I caught a severe cold, and was sent to see a doctor. On the way, I halted at the *kutiya* of a holy man. When he learnt that I was on my way to see a doctor, he said to me, "I always consult four doctors whose treatment I rely on." I was taken aback. "But sir," I said to him, "I don't think I am so ill that I need to consult four doctors. I believe one is enough for me."

HEALTH AND WELL-BEING

The holy man smiled and explained to me that these four doctors are very special– Dr. Diet, Dr. Quiet, Dr. Sunshine, and Dr. Laughter.

Let us cultivate better acquaintance with these eminent specialists, for they are always available for our benefit, and they cost nothing!

Dr. Quiet: Beautiful and serene is the silence of the Spirit! When we enter its realm, we experience peace, harmony and a sense of well-being. Our ego gives way to Divine love. Our stress and tension melt away. In this condition, we can listen to our inner voice, which can help us solve the most difficult problems of life.

Alas, in the mechanical rush of the modern world, we have lost touch with the cultivation of silence and solitude. Our lives are getting increasingly complicated; the list of things to be done gets longer, while 24 hours seem to get shorter! At the end of the day, we feel drained, exhausted, emotionally and mentally weary. Where can we find retreat from this spiritual exhaustion? The Roman philosopher Marcus Aurelius has the answer: Nowhere can man find a quieter or more untroubled retreat than in his own soul.

Dr. Sunshine: Sun-treatment, natural healing as a whole, is as old as humanity itself. *Surya-namaskar* was part of our daily routine in India since time immemorial. Sunlight and fresh air are of tremendous help both to the healthy and the sick. People in good health grow stronger and become less prone to diseases; people who are unwell are cured by the healing rays of the sun and coolness of the air. There is an old saying: "Where air and sunlight enter, the doctor has no place."

Air and light are two elements which enfold us, and without which we cannot exist. It will do us tremendous good to live in contact with the vitalising forces of both. We must try to let as much air and light as possible to enter our homes and workplaces– even though 'civilisation' has forced many of us to live and work in premises which are air-conditioned and artificially cut off from natural light and air!

Dr. Laughter: Laughter is not only a medicine, it is a tonic; it is the best physical, mental and spiritual exercise you can perform! Always see that your face wears a smile. As Mahatma Gandhi said, your dress is incomplete unless your face wears a smile!

The *Readers Digest*, one of the most well-loved magazines in the world, had a long running column called *Laughter: The Best Medicine*. I could not agree more! Laughter is at once a physical, mental and spiritual tonic. Laughter heals the sick; laughter improves the mood and relieves the tension of the healthy. Laughter is infectious– a smile is always mirrored in the face of the one you smile at! A few minutes spent laughing works wonders for our morale.

Dr. Diet: Eat less, speak little– this was the injunction given by *Hakim* Luqman, a healer from antiquity. We must learn to eat in moderation. Some people think they need to eat till their stomachs are full. In reality, our stomach must be only half-filled with food; the other half should be air and water. If we fill our stomach with fast food, junk food, or an excess of carbohydrates and fats, we are bound to suffer from the ills of overeating. I recommend to my friends that all cooked food should be eaten in moderation; and uncooked food like salads and fresh fruits should be eaten in plenty– I call this my "sun-cooked" food!

He who lives to eat is a sinner; he who eats to live is a saint. We should not be obsessed by food; nor should we crave for a particular food. Rather, we should choose the right foods that will enable us to keep up good health of body, mind, and spirit.

Ancient Hindus regarded all food as *prasadam*– a gift of God. Therefore, they partook of food in a spirit of humble acceptance and gratitude.

Positive secrets of good health

1. **Be aware of your breath**: Not many of us are aware of the value of breath in building up a healthy body and a happy mind. Every time I breathe in, I breathe in that subtle element which has been called *prana*. *Prana* is the vital force of life, though many of us take it for granted! When we take in air through the nostrils into our lungs, we take in precious, life-giving, life-sustaining oxygen. Breath is life!

   Breathing has the most profound influence on every part of our system, including the brain. It exercises the muscles, stimulates the action of the heart, improves circulation, regularises elimination, washes out harmful carbon dioxide from the blood, and lowers stress. Healthy exercise and healthy breathing are inextricably bound together. This enables the lungs to absorb optimum levels of oxygen so as to purify the blood, and eases strain on the heart. Deep breathing brings immense benefits to us, including a stable mind, steady thinking, inner peace and a long life.

2. **A healthy mind in a healthy body**: This has become a clichéd expression. But, like so many clichés it reminds us of a neglected truth: One cannot enjoy physical well-being

without mental well-being. Nutritious food, fresh air, regular exercise, good habits, clean environment and a sober lifestyle are all essential to our well-being, but the right attitude, the right state of mind and right thinking are indispensable. For man is not just the body– he is a composite of body, mind, intellect, and spirit.

Great thinkers and philosophers down the ages have differed on several issues, but they have agreed unanimously on one point: We become what we think.

3. **Exercise adequately**: How many of us are physically fit? How many of us devote at least a little time every day to physical activity– walking or cycling or swimming or some form of sport?

"Where is the time for all that?" some of us ask in exasperation. "I am exhausted when I get home, I can't be expected to trudge out at six in the evening!" some people may say. Yet others have their own excuses: I don't like to sweat; I don't look good in track pants; it's too boring, and so on and so forth.

All of us have used these excuses at one time or another. The truth is we are reluctant to take up any form of exercise.

A lady doctor once asked me if I took vitamin supplements. I answered in the affirmative. "Do you take the real vitamins?" she persisted.

"Real vitamins?" I said, "I have heard of vitamins A, B, C, D, E and K. Which of them is the real vitamin?"

"None of them," she replied. "The real vitamins are the vitamins W– Water and Walking!"

There are no two ways about it– physical activity of some kind is vital for good health. Physical activity must be regular, for its beneficial effects cannot be stored. Exercise must become a habitual part of our daily life.

'Exercise' sounds complicated. It may require special garments– shorts, track suits, leotards. It may need special equipment– treadmill, weights, exercise-bikes etc. All this means spending money, and we all know we do not always use all that we buy.

To everyone of you who is put off by the word 'exercise', my advice is, "Forget exercise. Just walk!"

Walking does not demand any expensive equipment. It can be done in any loose-fitting, comfortable clothes that you are used to wearing. Walking is easy and simple, and can be done practically anywhere! It is the best form of exercise for all of us.

It is not without reason that walking has been described as the queen of exercises!

4. **Drink plenty of water**: It would be befitting to mention the importance of water. In the absence of food, man can subsist on water alone for several days. This is because over 70% of the human body is composed of water. In fact, 70% of all the food we eat consists of water too.

   Unfortunately, we fail to drink enough water every day. We further fail to pay attention to the purification of the water we drink. Impure water, or water from contaminated sources can harm the system. The water we drink should therefore be boiled, filtered, and stored in a clean container. We live in a world where people pay to get bottled drinking water– something that would have shocked our ancestors beyond belief!

   Water helps to flush out the toxic wastes in our body. It controls the body temperature by being emitted as perspiration. Experts have calculated that there is a daily loss of four and a half pints of water through our skin, lungs, kidneys and alimentary canal. Needless to say, this loss must be replenished.

   It is good to drink water whenever you are thirsty. However, it is better to drink water after a meal than with it.

   It was a wise man who said, "Drink your food and eat your water." No, he hadn't got his verbs mixed up! What he meant was that food should be chewed, masticated so well that it glides down like a liquid when we swallow it. And water should not be gulped down hastily, but sipped, savoured and taken in slowly!

5. **Practise *Brahmacharya***: *Brahmacharya* is not just celibacy or asceticism. In its purest form, *brahmacharya* is literally "walking with God".

   In its broadest sense, *brahmacharya* denotes purity of character, purity of thought, word and deed. It indicates mastery over the mind and senses, especially over the sexual force. For when the latter is brought under control, all other aspects of our life are automatically brought under control. Such a state of self-discipline is conducive to our health, happiness and spiritual progress. Indeed, *brahmacharya* is a virtue that will help us to lead an active and healthy life for a long period of time.

I am aware that people will find it strange that I talk about *brahmacharya*, which is associated especially with the practice of celibacy, in an age when sexual promiscuity has become rampant. I would only like to remind you that it was "free sex" of this sort that destroyed the ancient civilisations of Babylon, Greece and Rome.

The mind and body must be controlled and disciplined to promote mental and physical well-being. Purity of mind is one of the greatest blessings a man or woman can achieve. Regularity, punctuality, clean habits, *sattvic* food and *yoga* exercises are all beneficial in the practice of *brahmacharya*.

One final thought...

Lester Sauvage, M.D., is a specialist in open-heart surgery. Dealing with patients from every religious background, he realised that it was not enough for him to merely extend or prolong the life of his patients. It was not enough to provide them with medical care and physical comforts; their healing process would not be complete until their spiritual needs were also fulfilled. After all, these people were not just case numbers or hospital records, they were human beings with spiritual dimensions.

Dr. Sauvage found it helpful to ask them to answer three questions, when he had successfully completed open heart surgery on them, and they were ready to resume their lives:

1. What do you plan to do with the added years that you have been given after the surgery?
2. How will you make these extra years happier and more meaningful?
3. What does happiness mean to you?

He found that reflecting on these questions helped his patients to focus on their spiritual needs, and discover the true purpose of living. It also enabled them to get better soon, and evolve towards better health in a holistic way. Together, he and his patients evolved a three-step plan that would make their lives more meaningful:

1. To live in the present
2. To be in constant communion with God
3. To serve God by serving humanity

Like so many other aspects of your life, good health too is a choice you make!

Heaven and Hell

The English word heaven was originally derived from a term of reference to the sky or firmament. As time passed, it assumed a deeper philosophical meaning as a state of afterlife. Subsequently, it came to refer to the place where God dwells. Although there are as many different concepts of heaven as there are different religious faiths, I must say the opposite of heaven– hell– has pretty much the same connotation across all religious distinctions. Whether they are Hindus, Christians, or Muslims, people will agree that hell is a state or a place where God is absent.

The Hindu concepts of *swarga* and *moksha*

When it comes to Hindu belief, heaven is NOT the highest goal we can achieve! In Hinduism, *moksha* (liberation) or *mukti* (release) is considered far superior to heaven (*swarga loka*), which at best, can only give us rewards for all the good we have done. When we have reaped the fruit of all our good karma, we must go back to re-enter the cycle of birth and death. Far superior to heaven is *moksha*, ultimate liberation from the cycle of death and rebirth.

For most Hindus, *moksha* is the highest goal. It means liberation and release from the world of *sansaar*, the eternal cycle of birth, suffering, death, and rebirth. It is a state of union with God.

There is a path– the path of light and liberation– that will take us to the abode of the Highest, from where none returns. It is the abode of the Supreme, the abode of *Brahman*, the abode of the Eternal. Here, you will touch the plane of the pure white Light, the radiance that casts no shadow, and you will be free, liberated from the cycle of birth and death.

What is heaven? And what is hell?

I am afraid Hindu scholars would tell you there is no place called hell. Theologians frighten us with the thought that the sinner is doomed to eternal punishment, that the sinner must burn eternally in the fires of hell. Nothing is farther from the truth.

God is all love and compassion. Indeed, God is Love. Love is not an attribute of God, love is not a quality of God. Love is God and God is Love. And love cannot bear to see anyone suffer. However, love would wish each one of us to ascend higher and higher in the scale of evolution.

Love would wish each one of us to grow in purity and unselfishness. Therefore, if there are any fires, they are chastening fires, purifying fires. The moment a soul is sufficiently purified, it need not be in the fire.

Where dwelleth God?

In a question and answer session with our young Bridge Builders group, a young girl asked me, "Where is heaven?"

"Heaven is here," I replied. Being young and immature, she could not grasp the meaning of my words.

"Here?" she asked, wondering how heaven could descend on earth.

"Heaven is where God is. And God is everywhere. He is omnipresent."

"But God is in the heavens above," she said, pointing to the sky.

If God lived in the sky above, the birds that fly would be in heaven. If God were in the depths of an ocean, then the fish and the whales would be in the serenity of heaven.

If, like many people, you also cherish the fond belief that heaven is a place "up above there, somewhere", then, let me tell you, you need not give into despair about the 'heights' to which you would be obliged to 'climb'. I believe God created us mortals with two very special wings– faith and hope.

The truth is that God is in the sky above. God is in the depths of the oceans too. God walks on this earth. God is present in every grain of sand. God is in every shrub, plant, and tree. And God most certainly lives in the hearts of his devotees! God is omnipresent. Nothing can exist without him.

Gateway to heaven

If there is indeed a 'gateway' we have to pass through in order to reach heaven, what are the 'entrance procedures' which will operate? And what kinds of gates are we talking about?

Sometime ago, a sister who has been fighting a life-long battle against overweight, remarkedto me that she had decided to give a spiritual dimension to her diet regime. She put up a sticker on her fridge which read: The gates of heaven are narrow!

I told her that she was closer to the truth than she imagined, for had not Jesus said to his followers: "It is easier for a camel to go through the eye of a needle than for a rich man to enter the Kingdom of God."

On a more serious note, the eye-of-the-needle metaphor suggests that the gates of heaven are not a free-for-all passage, allowing all comers to enter at will. Nor are there VIP passes or special bookings, nor any reservations, or free permits to cross the gates.

What, according to Hindu belief, happens at the portals of heaven?

According to Hindu scriptures, Yama's brother and chief dispenser of justice, Chitragupta, stands at the portals of heaven, and is in possession of that significant ledger wherein are maintained the most minute details of our 'credit' and 'debit'– in short, the good and bad karmas we have accumulated in this lifetime. *Jaisi karni vaisi bharni*– as we sow, so shall we reap. "Go thou to heaven or to earth, according to thy merit…" so say our ancient scriptures.

What have we been up to, in our hectic lives? More pointedly, what exactly have we done with our lives? At the gates of heaven, we will face a moment of truth, a moment of reckoning, when we are forced to contemplate the answer to this deeply personal question. What is our deserving? What is our claim to merit?

Entrance "qualifications" for heaven

If you are applying for a job, you can produce an impressive CV or biodata, listing your academic achievements and your work experience.

If you are applying for a government license to start a new business, you can put together a remarkable list of your assets, contacts, and skills.

If you are hoping to earn a place for yourself in the *Forbes* 'Fortune 500', your bank accounts, stocks and shares, capital and movable/immovable properties will take you a long way.

But heaven is a different proposition! Your Ph.D., your BMW, your farmhouse, your MNC, your influence, and your power are not going to open those gates for you! Heaven is far more democratic, far more egalitarian than most of our countries on earth. We all have a free, fair, and equal chance of making it across those sought-after gates.

Life after death: The astral world

The *atman*, or the soul, after the death of the body, falls into sleep. It is a deep and peaceful sleep, from which the soul awakes, refreshed, with the problems of the earth far behind, like a young child's memories of the previous day.

The soul is now ready to embark upon a new phase of existence, for it finds itself in a new world– the astral world. The soul is now clothed in the astral body and dwells in the astral world. It is a wonderful world. I wish I could describe the infinite beauty of the astral world. Truly, it is more beautiful than the most beautiful place on earth– more lovely than Kashmir or Switzerland.

Levels in the astral world

The astral world is a vast region. Even as on the earth-plane we have, on the one hand, palaces and beautiful mansions, and on the other hand, dilapidated slums, even so in the astral world, there are different sections. Each man finds his own place in the astral world. The utterly coarsened creature– selfish, cruel, malignant– will find himself in the lowest and densest regions of the astral world, surrounded by creations of his own desires and cravings.

The man who has lived the right type of life on earth, who has always aspired to the true, the good, the beautiful, who has lived a life of service and sacrifice, of love and compassion, will find himself, after death, in beautiful regions of the astral world.

How does the soul find its own place in the astral world?

In the astral world, there are no policemen to tell you where you belong, to guide you to the place where you will have to stay. How, then, does the soul find its own place?

While we are on earth, the soul dwells within the physical body and acquires a certain vibration. Each soul vibrates to its own frequency, depending upon the degree of its unselfishness, love and compassion, its purity and prayerfulness. The more unselfish a soul, the more pure and prayerful it is, the greater the frequency of its vibrations. When the soul is separated from the body, it goes straight to that part of the astral world which has the same vibrations as that of the migrating soul. Thus, each soul finds its own place in the astral world.

The astral world is an infinite world. There are levels upon levels in the astral world, and there are no restrictions placed on the movement of souls. A soul is free to go where it will. A soul can ascend to higher levels, it can descend to lower levels. No passports are needed, no visas are required to enter higher or lower regions of the astral world.

A soul can move to the highest regions— regions which are higher in light and happiness than the one which it occupies. But what happens is, when a soul goes to a higher region, it finds itself vibrating to a higher frequency. It finds it too bright, and the light hurts its eyes. The vibrations are so refined that it cannot respond to them. It feels choked, it feels suffocated. It cannot stay there. Back must it return to the level to which it belongs, where the vibrations are in tune with its own. This is how each soul finds its own place in the astral world.

What about hell?

There is no hell, but we may say that there is *naraka*– a sort of a psychic, purgatorial quarantine– where some souls are required to remain for some time to be cleansed, washed, purified, before they proceed in their onward march.

It should be remembered that *naraka* is not punitive, nor is it eternal. There is no idea of punishment behind purgatory. Purgatory is only a temporary phase through which a number of souls have to pass to be cleansed and purified.

How does this process of purification take place?

In *naraka loka*, the soul is forced to face its own record. All the sins of omission and commission that a person has committed during his sojourn on earth, stand before him. The soul reacts to its own record.

The soul realises that the life it has lived has been so far from the ideal. Immediately, within the soul, a conflict takes place between its higher and lower aspects. This conflict is what is called purgatory.

Purgatory is simply the forced realisation of the significance of our own misdeeds. No one catches hold of us and drags us to purgatory. It should be noted that heaven and hell or purgatory are not places, but states of consciousness. And because in the astral world, all those with the same outlook, the same rate of vibration, draw together, heaven and purgatory, for all practical purposes, have definite astral locations. In purgatory, each individual soul learns that sin brings inevitable sufferings, sin carries within itself the seed of suffering. Sin leads to suffering. Pleasure leads to pain.

In the *naraka loka*, the soul is purified, even as gold is heated in the crucible, until all its dross is burnt away. However, all impurity that a soul brings with itself is not burnt away. Only a few souls are so pure and strong that they can endure so severe a trial. Therefore, the soul, at a single purgation, is purified only as much as it can bear– and no more. The soul thereby wipes out only a part of its karma and, in due course, comes back to earth with the rest still clinging to it. It is this unexpired karma that causes it to suffer in the next life.

If we can cure ourselves of our evil tendencies, we will not need to visit purgatory at all, for purgatory is meant only to purify us, to heal the wounds of the soul. If the soul has no wounds, a visit to purgatory will be uncalled for.

What is the heaven-world?

If purgatory is a hospital for the healing of sick souls, going to the heaven-world is like visiting a hill station. There is so much beauty and peace there.

In the heaven-world, our unfulfilled desires of a higher nature find expression. Heaven is a world of wish-fulfilment.

Every one of us has a number of wishes of a higher type, which for some reason or the other, we are unable to fulfil during our stay on earth. Those wishes are fulfilled in heaven.

Compared to the physical, the astral world is a place of exhilarated consciousness. There is a stepping-up of emotional life to very high levels. In the astral world, our creative faculties are given free play. One creates naturally and readily in astral matter, for it is mobile and plastic and responds instantaneously to feeling, thought, and will. Whatever you think of, you create for yourself.

Thus, for instance, in the heaven-world there is no rain. If you want rain, all you have to do is think of rain and rain will begin to pour! But it will be your personal, private rain! Only those who wish for it will get it.

In the heaven-world, your wish is immediately granted. Therefore, in the heaven-world, there is no envy, no greed, no feeling of "You've got more than I have". Because the moment you want anything, it is there. In the heaven-world, we realise how creative the mind is. Whatever the mind thinks of, it immediately creates. Therefore, the things which we have wished for but failed to attain in our earth-life, are achieved in heaven.

We create our own heaven

The Zen scholar Ajahn Brahmavamso tells us a wonderful little story about two monks who lived together in a monastery for many years. They were good friends and companions in devotion and meditative practices. They were always supportive of each other.

Then they died within a few months of each other. One of them was reborn in the heaven realms, and the other was reborn as a worm in a dung pile. The one up in the heaven realms was having a wonderful time, enjoying all the heavenly pleasures. But he started thinking about his friend, "I wonder where my old mate has gone." He scanned all of the heaven realms, but could not find a trace of his friend. Then he searched the realm of human beings, but could not find his friend there either, so he looked in the realm of animals, and then of insects. Finally he found him, reborn as a worm in a dung pile… Unbelievable! He thought, "I am going to help my friend. I am going to go down there to that dung pile and bring him up to the heavenly realm so he too can enjoy the heavenly pleasures and bliss of living here."

So he went down to the dung pile and called his mate. The little worm wriggled out and said, "Who are you?" "I am your friend. We used to be monks together in the past life, and I have come to take you up to the heaven realms where life is wonderful and blissful." But the worm retorted, "Go away, get lost!" "But I am your friend, and I live in the heaven realms," and he described the heaven realms to the worm. But the worm replied, "No thank you, I am quite happy here in my dung pile. Please go away." The heavenly being thought to himself, "If I could only just snatch him and take him up to the heaven realms, he could see for himself." So he grabbed the worm and started tugging at him. The harder he tugged, the harder the worm clung to his pile of dung. Like this worm, we are all attached to our pile of dung.

Suggestions to prepare for the afterlife

1. Every night, before you retire, recollect all that you have thought, said, and done during the day– in reverse order. Repent for all the sins of omission and commission of the day. Repentance brings about a change of heart. Out of the heart arise the issues of life.

   When the heart changes, man becomes new. He longs to dedicate his life to God. Man becomes a child of God. It is ideal to not commit a sin. But having committed it, penitence is infinitely better than not asking for forgiveness. Ask God to forgive you for your sins, your misdeeds, and ask Him to give you the strength to become new.

2. Ask for forgiveness. But do not forget that before you ask for forgiveness, you must forgive those that have wronged you. Jesus taught a beautiful prayer to his disciples: "Forgive us our trespasses, even as we forgive those that trespass against us!"

   Until we have forgiven those who have wronged us, we cannot ask God to forgive us. Before we can ask our Heavenly Father to forgive us our wrongs, we must forgive those who have wronged us, who have spoken ill of us, who have abused us, maligned us, criticised us, condemned us, who have treated us with hatred and scorn.

   Therefore, learn to forgive even before forgiveness is asked. Let our forgiveness be liberal. There are some people whose forgiveness is so miserly that they will never let you forget that they have forgiven you. Let our forgiveness be generous and bountiful, making us forget completely the wrong that has been done to us.

3. While on earth, let us learn the language of the astral world. It is the language of love– pure, passionless, selfless love. In every thought, in every word, in every deed, let us express the pure, unselfish love of our heart.

   To love is to serve, to love is to give, to love is to go out of one's way to bring comfort to another, to love is to sacrifice everything for the sake of those that suffer and are in pain. The noblest of men are those who serve, who live for others, whose lives are an oblation to God at the altar of suffering Creation.

Here and Now

Life is here and now! We all know that life is often compared to a book, each chapter representing one particular phase of our life; but there is one major difference between my life and a book; I cannot turn back the pages of my life! I cannot revisit the past! Nor can I read the final chapter of my life before its due time. Life has to be lived in the present!

The past is over and done with; the future is in God's hands; the best that anyone can do is to live in the present, wisely and well. As the proverb says, "Sufficient unto the day is the evil thereof." In other words, the day will have its own share of challenges, difficulties, rewards, and achievements. Why should we complicate matters by dragging our regrets of the past and fears of the future into the present?

One of the unalterable laws of life is described in the following verse:

Beete ko chitvo naheen, Aage karo na shok
Vartmaan se vart lo, Taa ganeye nar dukh

Literally translated, it means, "The past has no meaning, do not cry over it; make friends with the present and sorrow will not affect you."

It may take you some time to understand this verse; it will take you a long time and considerable effort to assimilate the true meaning of this verse in deeds of daily life! But the trouble you take will be well worth the effort.

Let go of the past!

Have you heard the story of an old man who was found to be sobbing bitterly on his deathbed? His friends asked him why he was crying so broken-heartedly. He said to them, "In my youth, I threw away a fortune worth crores of rupees due to my licentious living and evil ways. Isn't that cause enough for sorrow?"

"We understand," said one of his friends, a wise man. "Can you get back your crores by crying now?"

The old man retorted, "How can I get back all that money now?"

Here and Now

"Then why should you cry over spilt milk?"

There was no answer.

Most of us live in the past. We cling to the memory of all those unhappy moments in our life. The trouble with most of us is, we hardly ever dwell on the happy experiences that we have had in the past. Most of us seem to harbour a permanent love affair with the sorrows and regrets and failures of the past! We embrace these bitter memories to ourselves constantly, refusing to let go of the bitter past.

Some people get accustomed to bitterness through this habit of pondering negative memories. They get so used to sadness and depression that hope and joy cannot 'agree' with them anymore. As I have said to you repeatedly, we are what we think. Our thoughts become patterns; these patterns influence our actions; our actions, when repeated, become habits; our habits gradually constitute our behaviour; and our behaviour over a period of time, colours our character and personalities. Now go back and realise how negative thinking and unhappy memories may discolour our lives! In fact, such behaviour and such thought patterns will only ensure that our future becomes just a mirror image of the past!

There is no need to spend a lifetime regretting all our past mistakes. True, we must repent for them, and wherever possible, make amends; but above all, we should learn from our mistakes. There are no irreversible failures in life, only different experiences. And every experience comes to teach us a lesson. Therefore, it is futile to dwell constantly on the past. We must make the best of the present moment.

Yesterday is history. Tomorrow is a mystery. Today is a gift. That is why we call it the present.

How to make the most of the present

When we train ourselves to live in the present, we appreciate the joy and the very act of living; we involve ourselves in life and discover its beauty. We learn to focus. We must make every moment count; we must embrace every moment, cherish the living present!

Are you awake, aware, and mindful– are you in the here and now?

Nutritionists will tell you that it is essential to chew your food slowly, relish every morsel, and taste each flavour in every spoonful of food you pick up from your plate and put into your mouth. This is essential, they say, both from the point of view of enjoying the food, and for absorbing all the nutrients and learning to eat moderately for your satisfaction. Life is a tasty meal that has been laid before you. Shouldn't you savour, enjoy, live every moment of this great gift?

Mindfulness, living in the present moment, allows you to enjoy the richness and the treasure that every second offers you. If you are worried about the past, anxious for the future, irritated by circumstances, or just annoyed with someone, you throw away this treasure! Mindfulness gives you greater control, greater awareness of how you interact with people and react to situations. You realise that it is wasteful to lash out in anger, or be consumed by fear. You learn to regulate your behaviour. You become less aggressive, less resentful, and more peaceful.

The ancient Romans unfortunately misinterpreted this attitude. They developed the philosophy of Epicureanism, which they erroneously assumed was the best way to live. To them, living in the present only meant hedonistic indulgence in pleasure– eat, drink, and be merry, for tomorrow we die!

Many of you may think that if we have to live in the present, then we should enjoy it to the hilt. We should make the most of the present moment, living a life of mindless, ceaseless pleasure. This is very foolish. This kind of pleasure is only bound to lead you to pain. Stay away from such pleasures. Fill the present moment with the beauty of faith and the joy of doing your duty well.

Live in simplicity. Do not waste your energies in useless talk. Do not discuss or debate trivialities of existence. Do not be obsessed with your appearance, mode of dressing, and the external glamour. Be free of the emotional baggage that such futile living brings.

You can try this little exercise if you like: when you find yourself indulging in daydreaming, reflection or idle thought, catch yourself and become aware of what you are thinking of. Are you dwelling on the past? Are you going over your own mistakes and failures? Are you trying to visualise how things might have been different if you had acted differently?

People often assume that daydreams are about the future. They will be amazed to learn how their past experiences colour their future dreams!

Surprisingly, business leaders are also stressing this principle now: do not cling to past practices; do not adopt age-old strategies; do not dwell in the past if you want to succeed in the present. The 21st century, which is barely twenty years old now, is vastly different from the 20th century. The IT Age is simply not the same as the old 'Industrial' Age. The emphasis now is on networking and building business relationships. If we go by past attitudes and practices (even those that succeeded in the past), these moves might just backfire on our own business interests.

Adapt to present conditions

There were two sisters who were travelling by long distance train from Jammu to Kanyakumari. Due to adverse weather conditions, the train had to be halted at a station in central India, until conditions improved, and the tracks were cleared. The passengers were stuck on the train for hours together. The elder sister was annoyed, irritated and frustrated; she railed and ranted; she complained bitterly to the TTE and the conductors, who were helpless themselves; she sulked endlessly and became a source of annoyance to all her fellow travellers.

The younger sister, on the other hand, refused to allow her spirits to be dampened by the delay. She went around cheerfully, making friends with the others, exchanging jokes, playing with children, starting singing sessions in different carriages, conducting quiz contests to keep young people occupied, and generally spreading good cheer all around. Strangers responded to her, sharing their food with her, inviting her to join their group, and enthusiastically joining her efforts to organise games for the entertainment of all. When the train finally reached its destination, the elder sister was morose, depressed, and tired. She felt that her days had been wasted. As for the younger sister, she had the time of her life! She made so many new friends, she had such new experiences, and she managed to retain her good mood and her good humour all along. She enjoyed the journey, despite the delays and the setbacks and all the little inconveniences. She had made the most of the present.

Maximise the moment

Living in the present maximises all the possibilities that life offers to us. We are able to focus on what is happening around us, and savour all those little joys and pleasures that are available in the here-and-now. Let us take the everyday example of someone who goes to bed after a long day of hard work. As everyone will agree, the moment when one puts ones head on the pillow is indeed a wonderful and welcome moment. We feel that we have 'earned' the rest and repose that is now rightfully ours. I, for one, recommend to my friends that this should be a moment of peace, reflection, and prayer. I urge them to go over the day that is done, quickly remembering their acts of commission and omission, thank God for all the day has brought to them, and then slip into sleep, surrendering the thread of their life in God's hands. Go through the day– but do not dwell on the day's errors and mishaps! I do not ask you to erase the past; but you must not continue to dwell on the past to the detriment of the present and the future. Chances are, if you go over the events of the day again and again, you will lose a peaceful night's sleep!

The same can be said of waking up to a new day: let us assume you have a tough, busy day ahead. Do not let the tension of your busy schedule grip you the moment you awaken from sleep! Savour all the joy and promise that the new day holds for you, as you come into wakefulness. Realise what it means to have a brand new day gifted to you by God– surely, it is a sign of His hope for you, an opportunity to move closer to your goal in life! So begin the day with gratitude to the Lord, and a short prayer to Him! Do not forget too, that a new day is breaking in all its splendour and glory just outside your window. Savour the beauty of the dawn, the music of the birds, and the fresh air of early morning. Why should anyone throw away these golden moments just because there are a few meetings and business deals ahead?

Walk with God today

May I offer a few recommendations on how you can choose the joy of living in the present moment?

1. Let me begin with the Zen proverb: When walking, walk. When eating, eat. Do not try to talk on the phone when you are driving. Do not sit on the sofa with your dinner plate to watch TV. Do only one thing at a time. When you are talking to someone, give him your full attention. It may be just a little matter– but it gives you a sense of the people around you. Give your best to what you are doing. Let all your energy and attention be focused on the task at hand. When the mind is one pointed it is capable of concentration and is free from tension.

2. Take time to live, because life has so much to give! Do not rush through your tasks. Slow down your pace if you are one of those hyperactive, rushed-off-their-feet people. We do not have to be lazy; but we must avoid needless hurry. As the proverb tells us, "Haste makes Waste". And a lesser-known Spanish saying warns us, "He who pours water hastily into a bottle spills more than what goes in".

3. Learn to be kind to yourself; therefore, learn to do less rather than more! Divide your work day into one-hour compartments. Draw a circle to represent a one-hour compartment. Pour into it all the work you can comfortably do in the next one hour. Do not think of the work that remains to be done– it can wait. All your attention must be focussed on the work that you can do during the next one hour. But one thing you must do– you must see that you finish the work you have assigned yourself before you move to the next compartment.

4. Stop agonising over the past as well as worrying about the future. I tell people again and again: you should not make yourself miserable by thinking of the past or the future. Live in the present moment. You will feel more focussed, more peaceful. It was Lao-tzu who said:

   If you are depressed, you are living in the past
   If you are anxious, you are living in the future
   If you are at peace, you are living in the present

5. Take time out for yourself. Spend at least five minutes a day in silence. Do nothing. Just focus on your breath. Notice the world around you. Be at peace within! Pause periodically and observe your own breath.

   Repeat to yourself the words: "I am made for this day. It is the happiest day of my life– it can be the most successful day, if God so wills!"

Humility

The word humility is derived from the Latin *humilitas*, which means 'grounded', or from the root *humus*, the earth which is beneath us.

This derivation is particularly appealing to us in India, as we consider Mother Earth, *Bhumata*, as the most gentle, uncomplaining and compassionate mother who allows us to literally trample all over her. Indeed, magnanimity, the ability to treat others with generosity, the tendency to put others before oneself, is a characteristic feature of humility.

Humility is a virtue associated with modesty, lack of pride, and reverence for others. Therefore, it is highly regarded by all religions. It is associated with egolessness– and is therefore the best antidote to *ahankara* or self-pride, which is an evil that all of us must avoid.

Humility does not consist in hiding our talents and virtues, or in thinking of ourselves as being worse than we really are; but in realising that all that we are, and all that we have, are freely given to us by God.

What is true humility?

Asked to spell out the difference between pride and humility, a holy man said, "Pride says to God: Let my will be done. Humility says: Let Thy Will be done!"

No one reaches God except through the path of humility. Humility, by revealing to us what we are, teaches us that by ourselves we can do nothing: for we are nothing. All the good we do is done through us by God. Humility, therefore, means utter surrender to God and to God alone.

The best thing that man can do is to hand himself over to God, to accept everything including disgrace and disease, trouble and tribulation, misfortune and misery, as coming from God. Whatever comes from God is good. It comes to purify. Therefore, rejoice in every situation and circumstance of life, giving gratitude to Him whose works are ever the works of mercy.

Humility and leadership

I am afraid, in the modern age we do not think very highly of this virtue! "Humility is all very well," we proclaim. "No doubt it is an admirable quality. But this world is for fighters and pushers. Seek to have a low profile, and the pushers and shovers will walk all over you. If you want to get anywhere, cultivate aggression. Otherwise you will be regarded as a loser."

Thus we prefer to pay lip service to humility, rather than recommend it for practice in deeds of daily living!

"This is a competitive world, Dada," a brother said to me. "Humility is a virtue of past ages. It is not a quality which I would suggest an entrepreneur or a business leader to have."

I feel pained to say that we urge our children to be pushy, competitive, aggressive and self-centred from an early age. We are convinced that arrogance, pride, and ego are necessary for self-esteem, for survival in this world. "Put yourself first," seems to be the mantra we instill into them.

Some of you will be surprised to know that humility is now being studied as a virtue necessary for the best leaders, in management circles. It is not perceived as lack of self-esteem or lack of confidence, but an attitude which allows for others' greatness. This helps the manager create the right environment for him not just to manage, direct and order people– but to help them discover their best potential, by helping them transform themselves.

Respect for others

It was a wise man who reminded us: "It is well to remember that the entire population of the universe, with one trifling exception, is composed of others." People who are genuinely humble, know that the 'others' are significant; they know that many of these 'others' can be quite intelligent and interesting. They know that there is a lot they can learn from other people; therefore, they treat everyone with respect and courtesy. They are keen and eager to discover what others have to offer. They are fascinated by how others think, feel differently, and what different approaches they adopt to solving problems.

We can be confident and self-assured. Humility is not false modesty; it does not mean that we must think of ourselves as low or wanting. We just have to become sensitive to people, respect others as much as we respect ourselves, and we become aware that everyone can contribute something worthwhile to the cause we believe in!

We gain from others when we realise that as human beings, we are all interdependent.

We learn from others when we realise that we need their help, and seek the same with humility. At such times, we come to realise how little we know, and how we cannot get on without others. However, we would miss these valuable insights, if our pride and ego stand in our way.

There is so much wisdom to be gained from the people around us! Life offers so many opportunities for us to evolve emotionally and intellectually. Some of us are blessed with material wealth and riches; some of us are blessed with business acumen; some are gifted with an artistic bent and creativity; yet others stand apart with their caring and compassionate attitude; a few of us are efficient and capable administrators; sincerity and devotion mark the efforts of some people. The world needs us all.

Beware of false humility

Let me warn you against false or superficial humility. People often assume false humility for a particular purpose. Thus subordinates bow and scrape before their superiors. When you assume false humility for a selfish objective, it is not really humility at all– but hypocrisy!

Even as we become humble, this egoistic thought creeps into our minds, "I am so humble, and these people are so proud!" This is the pride of humility. When I regard myself as better than another, it is pride. When I regard myself as the lowliest of the low, that is true humility and non-egoism.

Above all, it would benefit us to remember that humility does not dwell in the face; it dwells in the heart. It is not in sanctimonious actions, in false modesty, that humility emerges. We may convince people of our fake humility, but they will soon come to know that it is not the genuine thing!

The 'hum' of humility is humiliation

A man of humility is unconcerned about the reaction of other people. He is not hurt by criticism. He remains calm even when criticised or mocked at. What happens to us when someone criticises or casts aspersions on us? We get angry. Our immediate reaction is to confront and retaliate. Our instant impulse is to seek vengeance from the opponent; tit-for-tat is what we believe in. A single word of criticism ruffles us to no end. We do not have the humility to forgive and forget. We do not have the humility to accept the criticism or a harmless joke at our expense. Every single unkind word hurts our ego.

Let us learn to be humble. Let us aspire to the virtue of humility; and let us not commit the fatal error of assuming that we are perfect. If we have even a trace of humility, it is not due to our achievement, but thanks to the grace of the Lord.

The light of God shines in all of us, in every creature that breathes the breath of life. But in some of us, the Divine Light is hidden behind many veils, so that we cannot behold its radiance. These are the veils of pride and ego. When these veils are torn asunder, we can see the Divine Light shining in all its glory. Humility will surely help us to attain the Lotus Feet of the Lord.

India

India was one of the greatest civilisations of the ancient world. At a time when darkness brooded over Western Civilisation, India was strong and vital. She was acclaimed as the leader of the nations, a builder of civilisation. Much has she suffered through the centuries. Great has been her agony. And today, she is struggling to rebuild herself and assert her greatness. But India's greatness is essentially her spirituality! As long as she holds on to this ideal of *atma shakti*, India cannot be defeated. And India will never be defeated, as long as her people cling to the vision of the sages who saw that the root of life is God. Turning away from Him, we but wander from distraction to distraction.

The question is this: will India stand true to the ideals that made her great in the long ago?

What is the essence of India's culture?

The essence of India's culture is the vision of the One-in-all. India's greatest message to the nations is that life is one. The same life that is in you, is in me. We are not apart from one another. Electricity may flow through a bulb of 5-watts or 500-watts, but the electricity is the same. A 5-watt bulb will give you a little light and the 500-watt bulb will give you a blaze of light, but the power, the *shakti*, the light element that passes through both, is the same.

Out of this vision of the One-in-all grows the spirit of reverence for all life. There are three kinds of reverence: reverence for what is above us, reverence for what is around us, and reverence for what is beneath us. By reverence for what is around us and above us, we mean reverence for God, our spiritual elders, senior citizens, our friends, and our compatriots. Reverence for what is beneath us includes reverence for the poor, the broken ones, the handicapped, birds, and animals.

Reverence for all life signifies unity of life. Creation is One Family. In this One Family of Creation, birds and animals are man's younger brothers and sisters. This is India's culture. Indian music, dances and other elements of culture have grown out of this vision of the One-in-all. For instance, all music is harmony which grows out of the understanding of the One-in-all. If there is One-in-all, we must harmonise with all.

A friend once asked me: "At a time when India is set to become an economic superpower and play a significant role in the world's power politics, how does your viewpoint continue to emphasise spirituality?"

This question took me back to my youth, to an era of idealism and hope, patriotism and public spirit, when the political and personal came together in the quest for freedom, for independence from the colonial yoke. They were tough times; they were difficult times which called for sacrifice and selfless action. But they were also days of incredible enthusiasm and positive energy. In undivided India, "the empire on which the sun never sets" finally saw its sunset!

I was privileged to be a witness to this "tryst with destiny"; and if this was not honour enough, I was overly blessed to be in the sacred company of Gurudev Sadhu Vaswani, who played his own uniquely constructive and political role in the great national drama that was unfolding around us, involved in our day-to-day lives.

In Sind, our homeland, Sadhu Vaswani was one of the most respected spiritual leaders and leading lights of the Independence Movement. His role in mobilising public opinion in favour of the freedom struggle was, indeed significant. As far as Sind was concerned, he was the foremost interpreter, and in India, one of the earliest advocates of Mahatma Gandhi's Non-Cooperation Movement. At the Sind Political Conference of the Indian National Congress, he was chosen to move the resolution on the policy and programme of Non-Cooperation. It would be no exaggeration to say that it was thanks to his stature and influence that the resolution was carried and passed, despite united opposition from veteran Sindhi leaders! Gurudev Sadhu Vaswani's inspiring presence and wholehearted support ensured that Sind was pledged to Mahatma Gandhi's movement.

It is crucial to note that Gurudev Sadhu Vaswani's belief in the *Satyagraha* Movement was not just patriotic and nationalistic; it was essentially spiritual! He genuinely believed that it would spiritualise the life of India's people. It is the living, flaming spirit of his wonderful ideals that continues to inspire my faith in India as a spiritual superpower!

Sadhu Vaswani's 'politics' for India

Let me give you Gurudev's reply to this question which was often posed to him: "My politics, you ask? Service of the poor, is my answer in brief. The divine urge of freedom cannot be killed. It must grow from more to more. A state is not free until the poor have come into their own. How may we build such a state? The problem is beyond politics."

For years together, he kept on sounding a note of warning– that if, in our enthusiasm for political freedom, we neglect other aspects of freedom, politics will fail in its purpose, and the nation will only wander from darkness to darkness. Alas, this became painfully true in the years following our independence.

Why do we Indians imitate the West when we have such a rich heritage of philosophy, culture and spiritualism?

For over ten centuries, India has lived in subjugation. Little wonder then, that as a nation, we suffer from an inferiority complex. The external glamour and affluence of Western nations easily dupes us, and we feel happy imitating them. However, all imitation and emasculation is weakness.

As India grows in strength, she will press forward to a new dynamic march of her eternal genius, her own destiny. India has a mission to fulfil in the coming days. She has to reveal to the nations that there can be no true freedom without spirituality. India has much to learn of the West and vice versa. When the Indians learn to absorb the best of life in the West and share with the western nations the truths of her ancient culture, she will shine once again in the splendour of the new morning sun; she will be respected as a leader of the nations, a builder of a new civilisation of simplicity and strength, brotherliness and fellowship, sympathy and service.

How is it that you still continue to have an optimistic picture of India?

Sadhu Vaswani believed that the intellectualism and scientific explorations of Europe have been infected with calculated self-interest and narrow nationalism. India, among the nations of the earth, still has a vision of the *atman*, the one Universal Self in all, still believes in *daridra narayan* (the divine Spirit in the poor), still adores God's vision in all races and religions, in all scriptures and sages. India holds the key to the future of the world, for India still thrills to the message of love and brotherhood, "He that loves not, lives not, and he that beholdeth the One-in-all and the All-in-one– he hath eternal life!"

Sadhu Vaswani was a prophet of new India. The dream that clung to him was the dream of an India of the truly strong and free, an India which would go out upon her mission of help and healing to the nations of the East and the West. He asked the young to strive after the ideal of sacrifice, not ambition; to be simple; to cooperate with all and not let differences in creed or political opinion stand in the way of solidarity; to help in reconstruction of village-life; and to accept the creative ideal which regards humanity as one and service as the end of all knowledge.

Sadhu Vaswani's message to the people was, "Unite and build". He urged that the one piteous need of India was unity. Its salvation lay in unity. Without India, he said, where would the world be? And without unity where would India be? "It is the duty of every Indian to bear witness, in deeds of daily living, to the great ideals of India's sages and saints. Through the example of his life, the Indian must awaken the love of God and the spirit of service of the poor and lowly in the hearts of those around him."

My Gurudev's clarion call still echoes in my heart; therefore I am positive and optimistic about the future of this nation and its people.

India is the land of saints and sages, rishis and holy beings. Still, why is there so much pain and suffering in this country?

It is because of the rishis, gurus and saints that the people have the strength to accept everything with a smile. They believe that suffering comes not without a purpose. It is not something to be shunned.

The emphasis in the teachings of the great spiritual leaders of India is not on the outer things of life, the glamour and enticement of the world, but in unfolding the inner powers, the *atma shakti*. It is because of this, *atma shakti*, the inner soul power, that India has been able to ride many a storm and quell many a tempest of time and history. When all other ancient civilisations have perished, India alone lives on!

What is the reason that we have not produced great-souled leaders like Mahatma Gandhi, Sardar Patel, and the Titans of the Freedom Struggle?

Where are the Gandhis, the Sardar Patels, the Maulana Azads and the Nehrus who can lead the youth and engage them in this constructive task, you might ask me. May I say to you, Mohandas was only a timid, frail youth who went abroad for his higher education so that he may restore the family's fortunes. He did what his family expected him to do, but he did much more– he transformed the destiny of the nation!

Maulana Azad was a precocious scholar, a poet and a linguist, and actually dabbled in atheism and rationalism before he embraced Indian nationalism.

Sardar Vallabhbhai Patel worked very hard to go to London, where he topped his class in the famous Inner Temple to become one of the cleverest and most successful barristers in Ahmedabad, given to western clothes and a leisured lifestyle, and showed no interest in national politics until he was forty-two years of age.

Jawaharlal Nehru once described his own childhood and formative years as "sheltered and uneventful". He was brought up in an atmosphere of privilege and luxury, educated by private governesses and tutors. It was reading about the Boer War and the Russo-Japanese War that fired his imagination and enthused him to become a fiery nationalist.

My message to my dear young men and women of India is this: it is from among you that the Gandhis and Sardar Patels and Maulana Azads and Jawaharlal Nehrus of the future will rise!

What is the role you envisage for the youth of this country?

The task before us is to build India anew.

"New India," Gurudev Sadhu Vaswani said, "will be built not in the Rajya Sabha or the Lok Sabha, the Assembly or the Parliament, but in the school and the home…"

How true! Our youth represent the future of the country, the future of the world; in them lies the hope for humanity. They will be the builders of a new India, the architects of a new world order. If only we are able to produce a generation of truly educated youth, young men and women of character, we can not only build India anew, we can transform the face of the world, we can change the future of humanity!

We need young men and women who are imbued with this great ideal. We want builders and architects who will take up the task of nation building.

In fact, this is my appeal to all Indians: Awake! Awake, India! The future calls to you! The voice of the future calls all Indians to dedicate themselves to the task of serving this great nation, to take it to the heights of glory which is its destiny and your destiny!

Practical suggestions to build the India of the future

1. Let us imbibe the message of simplicity! Is it not significant that Saraswati is also known

as Bharati, the embodiment of the spirit of *Bharata*, the nation? And to me, Bharati, Saraswati, is the embodiment of purity and simplicity– two virtues that all of us need to cultivate. In simplicity is true beauty; in purity is the seed of perfection. Let us aspire to these great ideals. I ask you to be simple in dress, diet and daily habits. Imbibe this message of simplicity.

2. Seek not power, seek service! India needs *sipahis* and *sevaks,* soldiers and servants. It is only in compassionate, altruistic living that we can discover the best that we are capable of. Are you ready to answer the Mother's call to you? India needs volunteers– volunteers for the nation.

3. Avoid the cult of imitation. Ours is a glorious culture, but our education system would be no better than a prison cell if it keeps you blind to the glory of India's culture and the beauty of Indian ideals. We may have come out of colonial slavery; now it is time to come out of mental, moral and intellectual slavery. Take pride in being Indian. Express yourself. Express India! Let us stand up as true Indians in mind, body, and spirit.

4. Learn science, which is control over matter, but do not neglect self-control! When scientific knowledge is 'applied', it becomes a source of power, a force which may be both beneficial and destructive, depending on how we use it. Science education should help us make better, more informed and more ethical choices– or it may actually wipe out civilisation as we know it today. This is where the heart comes in; this is where self-discipline and self-control are needed. If the heart is kind, pure, compassionate, it will never make wrong decisions.

5. Let your focus be on the poor. May I call upon the youth of this country: focus on the poor people of this country. Focus on the farmer, the labourer, the homeless and the hungry; anything that does not benefit them, cannot benefit the country in the long run! The aim of education is not gains in silver and gold. The aim of education is service of the poor and the suffering ones. If we wish to build a new India, we must put the villages first; we must put the rural millions, the farmers and landless labourers first.

6. Remember the great Indian ideal: in spirituality is true strength. Spirituality should reinforce your faith in God! Make God a reality in your life. Make Him a friend, a partner, a guide, a guardian, a parent, and invite Him to watch over all that you do. Spend a little time in prayer, in introspection and in silent communion with God. Do not live for yourself alone, for that will make life small and selfish. Learn to live for others, and you

will find that life blooms like a beautiful flower! Offer your *aahuti*, your mite, to the great *yajna* of nation-building, and you will be richly blessed!

One final thought...

We are still thinking in terms of Gujaratis and Punjabis, Maharashtrians and Biharis; we still consider ourselves Hindus, Christians and Muslims. We need to be Indians, we need to become volunteers for India, truly Indian volunteers who will put India first. India first! India first! This must be the watchword of everyone who will be a volunteer for India!

Would you be these volunteers, these helpers, healers, builders and soldiers? Then undertake the *tapasya* of nation-building; the *yajna* of true patriotism. For make no mistake, it is a *tapasya*, a test of sacrifice; it is an ordeal by fire! Do you have the courage, the idealism, the spiritual strength that this great task calls for? If you do, then this country is truly blessed! And to all of you who wish to be India's volunteers, I end with this message: Put India First!

Inferiority Complex – Discard It!

Most of us understand inferiority complex to be an intense feeling of inferiority, resulting in a personality characterised either by extreme reticence or, as a result of overcompensation, by extreme aggressiveness. In common parlance, it refers to lack of self-esteem, feeling of inadequacy, lack of self-confidence, and low self-worth.

The term 'complex' in psychoanalysis refers to a combination of emotions and impulses that have been obscured from awareness, but still influence a person's behaviour. It is a state of thinking, an attitude with which we have not really come to terms. The tendency of the complex is to draw unrelated ideas into itself. The word has now come to mean simply, "an exaggerated or obsessive concern or fear".

All of us occasionally go through feelings of inferiority. Many students, for instance, feel a sense of inadequacy and fear when they see others writing fast and furiously during examinations. Competitors in a race feel stressed when they see rivals rushing past them. Debators awaiting their turn at the podium, become nervous and insecure when they hear their competitors holding forth eloquently to the cheers and applause of the audience. Such a feeling is normal and can often act as an incentive for higher achievements.

But a complex is something far more deep-seated; it is firmly rooted in the subconscious, causing the individual to overcompensate through aggression or retreat.

Why theory?

I must tell my dear readers that I am no expert in neurotic theory! I share some of these theories that I have read of merely to help laymen like us understand what this painful and debilitating complex is all about; and also to help us treat our children, siblings, and friends with understanding and appreciation, so that they do not feel such inadequacy and helplessness! We are not all trained counsellors that we can recognise symptoms and offer appropriate therapy, but surely we are all capable of becoming understanding, sensitive individuals who care for the welfare of others!

What are the causes of inferiority complex?

Psychologists talk of four broad reasons:

1. **Parental attitudes**: Children who are brought up in authoritarian families and are subjected to constant fault-finding and criticism often grow up with an inferiority complex. Many of them grow up in the belief that they are 'inadequate, incompetent, and inferior', to quote an expert.

2. **Physical defects:** Any physical deformity or even non-critical defects like squint or thin legs, abnormal facial features, and speech defects give rise to excessive emotional reactions, and become compounded with earlier unpleasant experiences.

3. **Mental limitations**: Insecurity and low self-worth are created when unfair comparisons are made with other 'superior' people and their achievements.

4. **Social disadvantages**: The background, class, family, and status of an individual may also aggravate feelings of inferiority.

Psychological theory cannot account satisfactorily for all aspects of human nature and human behaviour! We have many strong-willed, emotionally balanced people with pronounced physical defects; we have great leaders and entrepreneurs coming from disadvantaged sections of society, who have never let their background hamper them. The reasons cited above are only to be taken as indicative factors, and not the only causes of inferiority complex.

How can we recognise inferiority complex manifested in behaviour?

There are basically two modes of such behavioural symptoms: withdrawal or aggression. In the first case, the individual becomes extremely self-conscious and sensitive, and keeps aloof from social contacts. In the second case, as if to overcompensate for his own feeling of inadequacy, the individual becomes aggressive, seeks attention, criticises others, or tends to overdo his part. Withdrawal is far more common than aggression in individuals who are victims of this complex. Other observable attributes include:

- Extreme embarrassment or shyness
- Timidity
- Fear and bewilderment in company of peers and others
- Sensitivity to all forms of criticism
- Resentment of criticism
- Rebellion against corrections/suggestions for improvement
- Desire for praise

- Defense of their own actions
- Aloofness from social contacts
- Day-dreaming/ fantasising
- Pretended illness
- Bitterness towards others
- Constant irritability
- Undue worry

My only purpose in sharing the above information is to help my readers recognise these symptoms in friends and acquaintances and deal with such issues sensitively. As I said earlier, all of us feel inadequate or inferior on some occasion or the other. We may even notice some of the above symptoms in ourselves! The point is to become aware of them, deal with them effectively, and stop them from becoming impediments to our own inner peace, sense of balance, and personal happiness.

Let me repeat my mantra: happiness is our birthright as children of God! It is our duty to attain to this true happiness by conquering our weaknesses and promoting our true strengths.

For parents: Prevention in childhood

1. We should treat our children with love and sensitivity. We should not make them unhappy by constant unfavourable comparisons with their peers.

2. We should not set unreal standards and levels of success for them to achieve.

3. We must offer encouragement and appreciation instead of merely insisting on competition.

4. We must create opportunities of success in the child's area of interest instead of insisting that he should succeed in our area of focus. For instance, we may want the child to stand first in class; but he may want to dance, sing, or paint.

5. We can give the child responsibilities at home that he can fulfil and reward him with praise for every job that is well done.

6. We should encourage the child to develop skills that will contribute to his sense of self-worth.

Let me give you a small example: stammering is a common speech defect among many children. The therapy practised by many parents is patience, love, and constant training for the child in repetition of the utterances and slowing down of speech. Thus, what could become a major embarrassment for the child is successfully averted by simple measures at home. Only when we identify and recognise our weaknesses can we deal with them and overcome them successfully.

It is said that the child's greatest security lies in the personal feeling of affection and love shared by the parents at home. Let me add too, that love for God, prayer, and childhood training in spiritual exercises like *kirtan,* yoga, and meditation can do wonders for the wholesome development of our children!

Dealing with our loved ones

1. Encourage them to talk about themselves, vent their suppressed feelings– especially their past hurts– in an environment that is non-judgemental and free from fault-finding.

2. Allow them to express their fears and frustrations and deal with these in a spirit of compassion and understanding.

3. Help them appreciate their own gifts and unique talents.

4. Assure them that they have something valuable to offer to the world.

5. Strong and loyal friendship is the best support that you can give people with an inferiority complex. Spending time in the company of a positive friend can be the best way of improving the self-esteem of such people.

6. If at first, the individual refuses to open up to you, you can gift inspirational books or CDs to him, so that he becomes aware that he can help himself.

7. Assure them that they have something valuable to offer to the world.

One final thought…

Remember, you are unique!

There is no one quite like you in the whole wide world! Therefore, stop comparing yourself with others. Stop all negative self-talk– "Nobody likes me." "I am too short." "She is laughing at my clumsiness," Instead, try positive visualisation. Picture yourself happy, laughing, confident, doing your work well. Be yourself! Do not try to live your life imitating others. Recognise and celebrate your achievements and victories, however small they may be.

Inner Peace

Peace! It is as if we have become indifferent to this word! Although it is frequently in use, it seems so alien to us in reality. But is not peace the ultimate quest of every human heart? Peace is what we all crave. Peace is what humanity has piteously cried for, age after age. Peace, peace, peace– in this one word you have the secret, the answer to all your questions, the solutions to all your problems.

I think of the great rishis of India, the great rishis of *Aryavarta*, who held peace very dear in their hearts. This is why, at the end of every *Vedic* prayer we have the sacred chant– *Om Shanti Shanti Shanti!*

Scholars tell us that this sacred word *shanti* is uttered thrice to heal us, protect us, and give us freedom from three kinds of ills that destroy our peace:

- *Adhyatmikam*– the mental, physical, and spiritual troubles that we cause ourselves.
- *Adhibhautikam*– the troubles brought to us by others, outside of us.
- *Aadhidhaivikam*– the troubles caused by natural phenomena such as rain, storm, thunder, lightning, fire, floods, etc.

The three-fold recital *Om Shanti Shanti Shanti* brings us peace by relieving us from all three evils.

What is peace?

All descriptions will fall short and you will not understand peace until you have felt it in the heart within! Like love, peace must be felt!

One of the questions people ask me most often is: Do you think it is possible for anyone to lead a life of peace in these troubled times?

My reply is, it is not only possible; it is your birthright. Yes, *ananda,* bliss, the peace that passeth, nay, surpasseth understanding, is your birthright! You are a child of God– and He is the source of eternal, unending bliss. The moment you realise that you are a child of God, you will let nothing affect you. All you need to do is forget yourself– and realise your true Self as a child of God. When we forget this outer self, and transcend the phenomenal, material world, we draw closer to the real, inner self, which is peace.

Why do we lose our peace of mind?

This happens because our wishes, our desires, are crossed. We want a particular thing to be done in a particular manner. When it happens in a different way, perhaps in exactly the opposite way, our peace is lost.

Why do we feel upset, frustrated, disappointed?

We are too attached, too involved in this worldly life. If I do my work, if I live my life as if I am playing a part, I would not be upset.

There is one way of achieving true peace of mind– it is to attain the realisation that all that happens, happens according to the Will of God. Once you realise and live by this understanding, there will be no more frustration, no more unhappiness. You will abide in a state of tranquility and peace.

Peace within

Peace is our original nature. We are made of peace. Each one of us is *Sat Chit Ananda*. *Ananda* is the joy, the bliss that no ending knows. This is our original state– we have only to get back to it!

It is only because we are so self-centred that our peace is disturbed.

I am sure you must have seen on several occasions that when your mind is disturbed, and you do a little painting, play a little tune, or sing a song, you find that peace fills you all at once. Why? Because you forget yourself in this creative work. Likewise, when we move out of ourselves and give joy to those who are in need of it, we forget to be self-centred– and peace is ours!

May I offer you now, eight steps to interior peace?

Step 1: **Begin the day with God**! When we begin the day with God, we harness ourselves to the source of the highest power and energy in the universe. We give ourselves the best start that we are capable of. We reiterate our utter dependence on God and ensure that He is with us in all that we do. Begin the day with God, hold fast to Him throughout the day, and He will fill your day with peace.

Inner Peace

Step 2: Let your mind rest in God! *Ashantasya Kutah Sukham!* A disturbed mind is far from peace. How can it mediate? How can it even be happy unless it is established in God? How can we hope to find happiness in the world outside, when we fail to realise that it is centred within our own mind?

Resting your mind in the Divine presence, as it were, focusses the mind, energises and vitalises your intellectual abilities so that you are able to give your best to the situation at hand.

The perfect man is one whose wandering has ceased! We may not attain this perfection overnight; but we can and must attempt to focus the wandering mind so that we may harness its power for our own good. I read an anonymous statement which said: Focus on God puts you in touch with the Infinite, so that your mind can grapple with the finite successfully.

Step 3: Be a lion, not a dog! When I was a school boy growing up in Karachi, a holy man visited the city. I often went to sit at his feet and listen to his teachings.

Once when I took leave of him, I said to him, "Baba, please give me a teaching." And he said to me, "*Sher bano, kutta nahi bano.*" Be a lion, don't be a dog.

I was thoroughly bewildered. I said to him hesitantly, "Baba, I think I am a lion, because I was born under the sign of Leo. But what do you mean by saying don't be a dog?"

The holy man explained, "If you throw a ball at a dog, he runs after the ball! If you throw anything at a lion, he will ignore that object and go after you. He will go after the thrower, not the object that is thrown."

We always think about what has been thrown at us, about the circumstances and conditions in which we live, about the changing vicissitudes of life, the passing shows of life. We do not think of Him, the Thrower who has thrown all these things at us!

Step 4: Don't concentrate on problems, concentrate on solutions! Problems are a mark of life, a sign of life. If you ever go through a day without having to face a single problem, you will be well advised to read the obituary column of your newspaper to find out if your name appears there. It is only the dead who don't face problems!

What is the right way to handle problems, you may ask. I will tell you: Don't look at the problem, look at the solution! The greatest satisfaction in life comes to you not in running away from problems, not in the dereliction of tough duties– but in meeting and solving problems, in facing up to challenges as a dependable, responsible individual.

Problems are not stumbling blocks, but stepping stones to a richer and more beautiful life. If I may say so, problems are opportunities presented to you. It was a wise man who remarked: "Each problem has hidden in it an opportunity so powerful that it literally dwarfs the problem. The greatest success stories were created by people who recognised a problem and turned it into an opportunity!"

When problems surface, insights disappear. When insights surface, problems disappear!

Step 5: Count your blessings! Should we not feel grateful to God for the gifts He has bestowed on us– two eyes with which to see the beauty of the world around us, two ears with which to hear music, song, conversation and children's laughter; two hands with which to do a thousand things; two feet which can take us wherever we choose to walk! And that is not all. He has given us people who love us– family, brothers and sisters, friends and well-wishers!

Step 6: Accept God's Will! May I pass on to you a mantra which is sure to bring you peace? It is a prayer which a saint, a holy man of God used to offer again and again. Inscribe it on the tablet of your heart. Repeat it again and again– remember it by day and night, for it is really simple: *Yes Father, yes Father– yes and always yes! Yes Father, yes Father– yes and always yes!*

The world is safe in the hands of God! Why then should we lose our sleep and peace of mind?

Step 7: Do your best– leave the rest to God! He who has surrendered himself to God finds the greatest security of life. He need wander no more. All his cares and burdens are borne by the Lord Himself.

Step 8: Pray without ceasing! If you would have inner peace, pray without ceasing! This is one spiritual discipline that can go on forever! Praying ceaselessly is not a ritual; it is not about words or gestures. It has been described as a constant state of awareness of our oneness with God. You may of course, ask for all the good things you need– and you may gain the faith that it is all obtainable to you; for all prayer is effective, but ceaseless prayer has multiplied effect.

May your life be peace-filled!

Irritation– Root It Out!

Irritations are inevitable. We are going to encounter them wherever we are, in whatever we do. If we are wise and mature, we will learn to handle them without paying a heavy price in terms of frayed nerves and acute emotions. By giving in to irritation, we allow our energy levels to drain; our efficiency drastically lowers, and we also lay ourselves open to worse problems that are sure to follow. Have you seen the comic strip where an irate driver kicks the flat tyre of his car– and then howls in pain as his foot is sprained by the kick?

A mindful person learns to face life's daily irritations without being upset. We should learn to block out irritations altogether, by adopting a tolerant, easygoing attitude towards people and events.

The life of modern man!

It has been truly said that modern man is so busy earning a living that he has no time left to live!

Fast, faster, fastest! We want everything instantly. We have fast food, fast cars, instant messaging, lightning trunk-calls, non-stop flights, speed dialing, and short cuts for everything. We beat the red signal at traffic lights, we overtake others at great risk to ourselves, we simply cannot bear to wait!

Where is all this hurry taking us? Where are we dashing at such a bolting speed?

I must remind you of one of those golden, old proverbs which characterised life in the good old days: slow and steady wins the race. I wonder how many of you believe in its efficacy, wisdom and sound sense!

A Victorian poet, Matthew Arnold, wrote about life in the pre-industrial age, which "ran gaily, as the sparkling Thames". Poets have always compared the passage of life to the flow of the river– gently, steadily, tirelessly, the stream flows on and on.

You only have to visualise rivers today to realise that the metaphor will not hold accurate any longer! Our rivers no longer run clear and steady. They are muddied, polluted, poisoned by chemicals and industrial effluents. Often they are in spate, overflowing their banks, causing enormous tragedies with loss of numerous lives and damage to property.

Fast, faster, fastest– we are hurtling through life at a breakneck speed. Our favourite 'rides' are roller coasters on which people pay money to ride, and then scream in fear as they are plunged through loops and falls and steep drops! What are we looking for? What do we hope to find in such breathtaking pastimes?

Slow and steady– this was the pace of life, over fifty years ago– and this was how men and women, old and young, lived their lives. The speed of 'instant' modes has entered our lives too, and we pay the price with stress, tension, neurosis and unheard of physical ailments. Experts say human nerves are unable to withstand the stress and strain associated with modern life.

Hurry, hurry, hurry! Today, mothers are virtually on roller skates, dropping children at school, going off to work themselves, attending meetings, calling on doctors and bankers and plumbers and electricians, and attending to household chores.

In earlier days, everything was done in such a leisurely manner. We walked to school, to the park and to the library. We spent hours poring over books! We played long games unhurriedly, indoors and outdoors. We prayed together, laughed and talked together, as extended families. Uncles and aunts visited us, and were our honoured and cherished guests.

You will not believe me when I say this– we had time for everything those days! We had time for people; we had time to listen to others; we had time to devote to meaningful activities and relaxing, happy hobbies. And yet, we had the same 24 hours per day as you have now!

Do not let irritation sap your energy!

The greatest malady of modern life is that man permanently seems to be on a treadmill! He is on the move all the time, running, running, running– and still in the same place!

Executives are jet setting across the globe– visiting customers in Nigeria today; meeting with bankers in London tomorrow; trade conferences in Buenos Aires the day after; off to Chicago for a new collaboration afterwards …

Tiny tots in primary schools go to swimming lessons before school, tennis practice after and computer classes in the late evening…

Under these circumstances, is it at all surprising that we are constantly prone to irritations and annoyances? One of my friends, who is a doctor, said to me the other day that many of his patients come to him with sudden outbreaks of high blood pressure. Outwardly they are calm, quiet, dignified individuals. But inwardly the daily frustrations and irritations of life are taking a toll on these men!

People easily feel upset, irritated, annoyed, unhappy. A chauffeur is slightly delayed in reporting for work– and his master is driven into a frenzy. Frenzy is fine, if it is going to bring the chauffeur to his door at once. But he knows it cannot– so who is the loser?

Irritation and annoyance are now all-pervasive

When we say "irritation" or "annoyance" we always associate these terms with trifles, petty issues, events and situations with what we call "nuisance value". So, you might ask, why do we have to take irritation and annoyance so seriously? Have we not agreed that they are, after all, trifling and petty?

A middle-aged housewife was asked to list all situations that added to her list of everyday irritations. She wrote down the following list:

1. The ringing of the morning alarm just when she is sinking into a deep and dreamless sleep.
2. Getting the family members up, one after the other, running around to get them ready for school/work/college/business.
3. The constant ringing of the telephone/doorbell.
4. Dealing with the household help and the provocations they bring.
5. Waiting interminably for the bus/public transport.
6. Carrying a load of shopping home.
7. Cooking breakfasts/lunches/dinners and other meals, day after day, after day...

Taken individually, these are no doubt trifles. But taken collectively, they represent continuous little snips and cuts which will eventually make one's peace of mind and serenity wear thin. They may be minor or superficial nuisances, but they undermine your effectiveness and add raw, sharp edges to your personality. Before long, you begin to snap and lose your temper with your near and dear ones, and the petty annoyance we started with, becomes a veritable contagion! Our capacity for patience and tolerance is torn to shreds, and serenity and calm fly away from us!

When major crises and tough trials loom before us, we tend to tackle them with great courage, fortitude and resourcefulness. But when trifling irritations and constant frustrations assail us, we tend to lose our cool.

When we focus our mind constantly on irritations, we only allow them to linger on and become festering annoyances. The trick is to snap out of irritations and recover our calm and serenity.

Patience is the key!

Patience is the formula which can help you black out, shut out every kind of irritation! Learn to have an objective, detached and dispassionate attitude to problems. Try to understand why some people behave as they do, and you will find that their behaviour no longer upsets you. Instead, you will find yourself sympathising with them and trying to help them in any way you can!

Granted, it is a human tendency to want to hit back at whatever– or whoever– has annoyed you. But it can be an even more satisfying experience when you control your resentment and become the master, not only over yourself, but the situation. And remember, the man who can master a situation by self-control, always wins the battles of life!

Overcoming irritation

I would like to pass on to you ten practical suggestions:

1. Believe in the Higher Power watching you and giving you strength.
2. Always be relaxed in body and mind.
3. Do not neglect your daily appointment with God!
4. Always see the bright side of things.
5. Count your blessings!
6. Keep yourself busy doing something creative.
7. Smile, smile, all the while!
8. Don't hold on to your grudges.
9. Practise the technique of Tonglen– breathing in all negativity and breathing out serenity, calm, peace and tranquillity.
10. Help others.

Joy Killers– Say No to Them!

If you wish to have the real joy of life, banish joy-killers from your heart and your life! And what are these joy-killers that lurk within you and make you miserable? They are fear, hatred, jealousy, envy, resentment and negative thinking.

Put an end to these joy-killers. Give them no place in your mind and heart. If you feel you get no joy out of life, sure as the sun rises in the East, there is some joy-killer lurking somewhere in your consciousness.

Once, a man with a cavity in one of his teeth, came to a dentist. As the dentist was cleaning the cavity, the end of his drill broke off. The dentist ensured that every little piece of metal was removed from the patient's mouth. However, about three years later, the man began to complain of a pain in his neck. The doctors could not find anything. About six years later, he developed a severe pain in the shoulder, and again the doctors could not find anything. About twelve years later, the man complained of a pain in the jaws and, this time, the X-rays revealed a small foreign substance, which proved to be a tiny fragment of the dentist's drill. This had been causing him pain for twelve years.

Similarly, a man may have some fear, hatred, jealousy, envy, resentment lurking in his consciousness. If joy is absent from his life, he must find out and eliminate the joy-killer, howsoever tiny it be, that he carries about with himself in his subconscious.

Man seeks happiness

"Every man, whatsoever his condition, desires to be happy," said St. Augustine. "Indeed, man wishes to be happy even when he so lives as to make happiness impossible…"

True this is, that everyone wants to have the joy of life, at all times, in all conditions and circumstances of life. Everyone wishes to be happy. Since the dawn of civilisation, man has searched for happiness. The search has continued down the long corridor of time. Man has discovered that pleasure leads to pain, riches vanish, fame is fleeting, success is an illusion. How, then, is man to be happy? How is he to have the true joy of life?

Many years ago, we had a terrible earthquake in Sind Province, Pakistan. It left everyone shaken and scared. Pandemonium prevailed. Some people ran out of their houses, some shrieked in terror, some fainted. Some grabbed their jewellery boxes and tried to lay their hands on all valuables they possessed. Mothers carried their little children and rushed out into the streets.

Amidst all this panic and confusion, there was one– it was dear Sister Shanti, adopted daughter of Gurudev Sadhu Vaswani– who remained serene and unperturbed.

"Were you not afraid?" she was asked. "No," she answered. "I was thrilled and happy to know that I have a God who can shake the world!"

There spoke a person who had the joy of life in full measure.

The quest for happiness

Let me tell you the story of three men. They were all in quest of happiness. "Where is happiness?" they asked. "What is the secret of happiness? How may man have the true joy of life?"

The first man felt that the true joy of life abided in pleasure. He was convinced that he could find joy only where there is pleasure. He was a wealthy man. He built for himself a wonderful palace and filled it with treasures of art. He lived a life of ease and luxury, ate rich foods, and drank the choicest wines. To his court came wise men from different parts of the world, for he enjoyed their discourse, as well as great painters, musicians, artists. His library contained the best and most beautiful books in the literatures of the world. He met the world's prettiest women, and the pleasure-seeking luxury of his home became a legend.

As a young man, he found life supremely interesting, but as he grew older, he discovered that within every pleasure was a seed of pain. Life given to mere pursuit of pleasure was full of boredom, when the pleasure became excessive. As he was about to pass away, he confessed that despite pleasures and luxuries, his life was empty to the core. It was a life not worth living. He had not found the true joy of life. He had not found happiness.

Who could have been brought up in more luxury than Prince Siddhartha who, later, become Gautama Buddha, and showed to millions the way to true, abiding happiness? He was the only son of King Suddhodana. The king built for his son, not one, but three palaces in which the prince lived during summer, winter, and the rainy seasons. He had everything that the world could give. But within his heart there awoke, again and again, the question, "Where is true, abiding happiness?"

Joy Killers– Say No to Them!

Gautama was married to one of the most charming girls in the realm, Princess Yashodhara. A son was born to them. Gautama named him Rahula, meaning "fetter", something that binds one to a place or action.

Gautama felt he could not carry on; he felt fettered. He kept telling himself, "I want to be free! I want to set out in quest of happiness. Where is real, abiding happiness? Where is the true joy of life?"

In the dark of the night, when his wife, child, and many servants were fast asleep, Gautama quietly slipped out of the palace. He became a wandering mendicant. In his heart recurred the question, "What is the secret of true happiness?"

Similar to the first man in our story, Gautama found that true happiness is not in a life of pleasure. The second man in the story realised very early in life that pleasure is transient, ephemeral, transitory. Pleasure is like a bubble that bursts. It is an illusion, and it is unsatisfying. He was sure that happiness could be found only by withdrawing into oneself, avoiding the world, its trials and tribulations, and retiring into absolute solitude. He became a hermit who had nothing to do with the world. No one could reach him, he sought the company of no one.

But he, too, was unable to find happiness. For life without human companionship is barren as the sands of a desert. The hermit's way is not the road to a life abundant, to a life of joy and happiness.

The third man in the story avoided the two extremes. He did not embrace pleasure to the exclusion of everything else. He did not cut himself off from the world, realising that where there is no battle, there can be no victory. He devoted his life to duty– the duty of his daily task, the duty he owed to his family, his community, to humanity and to brother birds and animals. He realised that Creation is One Family. Birds and animals too, are man's younger brothers and sisters in the One Family of Creation.

He did his duty by everyone. He gave his love to everyone. He loved God and he loved every child of God. He loved trees and flowers, rivers and rocks, stars and streams. He loved birds and animals, ants and insects. And he had the true joy of life. He made the great discovery that when your heart is full of love, your life is full of joy. He did not turn away from pleasures; he enjoyed as many simple pleasures as his life would allow. And every day, he spent some time in silence, in solitude. He withdrew from men and, in silence, communed with the Wonder of the Ages, the Wonder that is radiant in the sun, the moon, the stars, in every atom and in the *atman* within. Every day, he spent some time in silence and sought to understand the meaning of the mystery of the endless adventure of existence.

Thus he lived, and when he was about to pass away, he said, "I die a happy man!" Those that were around him too, said the same thing, "He was truly a happy man!"

The lesson is so obvious that it is superfluous to emphasise it. Yet men and women all the world over have failed to take the lesson to heart. Some restlessly pursue unsatisfying pleasures. Others, disillusioned by life, seek comfort in solitude. Very few tread the path between the two extremes, devoting themselves to a life of good ideals and right action.

The age of gloom

Very few of us know how to live life simply and live life right. Thus for many people, life seems to have lost its flavour; an ever-increasing number of young men and women complain, "Life is not worth living!" We seem to be entering into an age of gloom. It is true, science is advancing. We seem to have reached the very zenith of technological brilliance. Man stands on a planet of limitless promise. He has probed the secrets of the atom, the depths of the sea, the vast expanses of space. He has unravelled the mysteries of his own mind and body. Yet is he unaware of his real being and purpose. He is faced with a terrible loneliness, and his mind is filled with a thousand fears which he cannot name.

The great historian, Arnold Toynbee, was a man gifted with many deep insights into men and matters. He observed that with the rise of the industrial civilisation, man had received many benefits, but for them he has had to pay a terrible price– his peace of mind. As we have grown in material and technical know-how, peace of mind has declined. An industrial civilisation has come to stay– we cannot, at this stage, abandon it. But we must figure out a way so that, living in this computer age, this age of networking and connectivity, we may find a new happiness and a new ability to get true joy out of our lives.

How may we get the true joy of life?

Let me pass on to you some means to attain the true joy of life. These are not merely to be heard or read, but to be put into practice. The ground rule is: **If you wish to have joy of life, keep away from all joy-killers.**

And what, you may ask, are the joy-killers?

Joy Killers – Say No to Them!

- The first of the joy-killers is hatred. Let there be no feeling of hatred in your heart.

A man met me. His face was black as coal, as he said to me, "There is a fire burning within me. The flames will not be quenched, until I have shot the man who caused my father's death."

There you have it. Hatred is a fire. So long as fire burns within you, you cannot have joy of life. As the Buddha said, "Hatred ceaseth not by hatred, hatred ceaseth by love!"

When a thought of hatred comes to you, trample it under-foot and breathe out a thought of love and good-will.

There was a man who led a depraved life. His wife and children sought spiritual solace at Gurudev Sadhu Vaswani's *satsang*. One day, the man came to Gurudev and shook his fist at the Master. In hot rage he said to Gurudev, "If you only knew how much I hate you!"

Beloved Gurudev looked at the man lovingly and said to him, "If you only knew how much I love you!"

What magic, what healing power was there in Gurudev's words, I cannot say! The man fell at his feet and, with tears in his eyes, begged forgiveness. His life was transformed in that miraculous moment. He turned away from his evil ways. He accompanied his wife and children to the *satsang*, every evening.

When Jesus was crucified, we know he prayed for his persecutors. There he was, tied to the Cross: nail after nail was struck into his hands, his feet, his throat. Blood flowed out of his gentle, pure body, a body that had never caused harm to anyone. And on his lips was the prayer, "Father, forgive them, for they know not what they do!"

Rishi Dayanand had been poisoned by his cook, Jagannath. The foolish man had been bribed to kill his great master. On his deathbed, Rishi Dayanand called Jagannath and said to him, "Here is money for your ticket to Nepal. Escape, before my disciples find out what you have done, else they may tear your body to pieces."

Such is the witness of all the great ones of humanity. They have met hatred with love and shown that the true joy of life is in loving. If you would be truly happy, love one another. Meet hatred with love and forgiveness.

- Yet another joy-killer is resentment. So long as we have feelings of resentment within us, we do not, we cannot get the joy of life. Our daily life is full of little irritations which cause resentment, and this is what keeps us away from the true joy of life.

    No one who clings to his resentments can ever hope to be happy. In fact, by refusing to forgive and forget, he will harm himself irreparably, walking the way of spiritual death. On the other hand, the person who forgives, enters a new life of gentle peace and quiet, inner joy. I always emphasise that forgiveness is its own reward; it is the forgiver rather than the forgiven, who receives the greater benefit.

    If you have not forgiven someone who has harmed you, if you are harbouring resentment in the heart within, let me say to you: you have not experienced the most sublime joy of life. Let us forgive one another here and now– today! For a day may come when the opportunity to forgive will be taken away from us.

    No negative emotion is ever appeased by indulgence– it demands more and more until it consumes you. So is it with anger, resentment, revenge, and retaliation. The more you feed them, the more they will destroy your peace of mind.

    "For every minute you remain resentful," a wise man says, "you give up sixty seconds of joy and peace."

    Forgiveness actually empowers you to lead a more meaningful life. It helps you to overcome the vicious cycle of resentment and revenge and enter the realms of unity, peace, and harmony.

- Yet another joy-killer is fear. It has been rightly said, there is no medicine for fear. The ancient *Vedic* rishi prayed, "May I be fearless of the friend, fearless of the foe; fearless of the known, fearless of the unknown; may our nights be without fear, our days without fear!" When fear gripped the mind of the Buddha, he said, "I never stood still, nor sat nor lay down until, pacing to and fro, I had mastered that fear and terror."

    To have the real joy of life, we must develop the spirit of courage that can vanquish the joy-killer that is fear.

    "What is it that rescues man in all danger?" Yudhishthira was asked. And he answered, "Courage!" It is courage that comes to the rescue of man in all types of danger. So it is that

Joy Killers— Say No to Them!

Cervantes said, "He who loses wealth loses much, he who loses a friend loses more, but he that loses his courage loses all."

- One of the worst of all the joy-killers is the habit of thinking and talking negatively. I read of a businessman who carried a card in his pocket. On the card were written the words, "I shall not speak any negative words today. I shall not think any negative thoughts today."

The businessman takes a new card every morning and writes the words afresh. He has been doing this daily for about a year and, as a result, he says, "My conversation is almost cleared of negatives. Before I started this practice, I spoke negatively about almost everything, and I found that there was no fun in life. Today, life is so full of joy that I sometimes feel thatI may burst."

Life is full of joy to the man who thinks positively and speaks positively. Many of us have the habit of thinking negative thoughts. We exaggerate misfortunes which may never come to us at all.

There is the amusing story of a man and his wife who set out to visit a friend, whose house was some miles distant from their own. On the way, they remembered that they would have to cross a bridge which was very old and was considered unsafe. The woman began to worry about it.

"What shall we do about that bridge?" she asked her husband. "I shall never dare to go over it, and there is no boat that can take us across the river."

"Oh," said the man, "I never thought of the bridge. It is most unsafe to cross it. Suppose it should give way while we are on it! We would be drowned!"

"Or suppose," said the wife, "you step on a rotten plank and break your leg, who would take care of me and the children?"

"I don't know," said the man, "what would become of us, if I broke a leg. Perhaps, we would all starve to death."

And so it went on. Both of them kept on worrying, imagining all sorts of misfortunes, until they reached the bridge, and found that a new bridge had already been built. They crossed over it in safety.

One final thought...

We all need to become aware that life is too precious to be frittered away in what I have called "joy-killers"– hatred, fear, envy, resentment and negative thinking. If this involves a change of mindset at the micro level, the larger transformation lies in our entire attitude towards our faith in God as a positive force– as a source of joy and peace. Let God take charge of all your affairs! If only you can do this, you will find miracles happen in your daily life.

Laughter

Many of our problems can be solved, if only we relearn the gift of laughter. The tragedy of modern man is that he does not laugh enough. Laughter, I always say, is a powerful tonic; it vitalises the body, mind, and spirit. It is an excellent dry-cleaner– it cleanses you from inside. The source of genuine humour is not the head. Instead, it springs from the heart. Its core and essence is love.

There is something funny about all of us– we are sometimes ridiculous, sometimes even absurd! Each one of us has his faults and failings, his quirks and oddities. So let us learn to laugh at ourselves first. When we learn to laugh at ourselves, we will never be offended when others laugh at us.

The holistic benefits of laughter have been well researched and well-documented. Laughter relaxes the muscles, expands the blood vessels, enhances respiration, improves circulation, and reduces the level of stress causing hormones. Above all, laughter exercises your facial muscles, improving your "face value"! Laughter, especially the ability to laugh at oneself, is the greatest gift we can have. For humour tempers our faith, even as carbon tempers iron, to produce a tougher, more resistant substance. The day on which laughter does not fill, enhance, and colour us, is a wasted day indeed!

Laughter: The feel-good, look-good therapy of cheerfulness

Cheerfulness, we now believe, is the greatest lubricant of the wheels of life. It diminishes pain, fights disease, mitigates misfortunes, lightens burdens, and eases one's life.

It has been calculated that it takes 42 muscles to frown; a scowl causes lines and wrinkles to form on your skin. Whereas you use just 17 muscles to smile, which in fact reduces wrinkles, tightens your chin, and makes you look younger. So what will you choose– a scowl or a smile?

When you feel sad, depressed, and tensed, just look at your face in a mirror. It seems so serious, so constricted, so tight that you will not want others to see it! The stress and strain reflected on your face is obviously due to negative emotions that are playing havoc inside you.

Cheerfulness is the new wonder drug. Doctors tell us that our blood molecules contain receptors which receive signals from the brain. When you are happy, cheerful, and contended, the receptors transmit these signals of happiness and a healing process within you is accelerated. Indeed, modern medicine assures us that if we laugh more, we grow healthier! Jolly physicians are better than pills! A sense of humour plays an important role in positive and effective leadership. It greases the cogs and wheels in getting things done smoothly and also in amicably getting along with others. If one can be capable of discovering humour even in painful situations, then one can easily survive them.

There are many therapies, many 'pathies'. They include allopathy, homoeopathy, chromopathy, naturopathy. There is the ayurvedic system of medicine. There is *yogic* therapy. There is also the therapy of cheerfulness– the therapy that tells us that if only we are cheerful and happy all the time, we will not fall ill, and even if we do, we will recover rapidly.

One expert refers to laughter as 'internal jogging'. It stimulates the internal organs. Laughter is also akin to an effective tranquiliser, with no accompanying side effects.

Did you know that many of the great ones of humanity were also lovers of laughter?

Socrates, St. Francis of Assisi, St. Teresa of Avila, Sri Ramakrishna Paramhansa, Sri Ramana Maharishi, Swami Ramdas, Mahatma Gandhi, and Sadhu Vaswani– to name but a few– all of them possessed a lovely sense of humour.

Mahatma Gandhi said, "If I didn't have a sense of humour, I would have committed suicide long ago!"

When Swami Vivekananda visited America, during the close of the last century, he could not understand why clergymen wore solemn and serious faces. They believed that it was irreligious to laugh in public. Swami Vivekananda was a child of joy. He was so spontaneous; he did not restrain himself from laughing at public meetings when the occasion demanded. The American clergymen did not approve of this conduct which they thought was 'frivolous'. Swami Vivekananda thundered at them, "What business do you have with clouded faces? It is terrible. If you have clouded faces, do not go out that day; shut yourself up in your room. What right have you to carry this disease out into the world?"

One recalls the admonition of St. Francis of Assisi to his disciples: "You must not behave outwardly like melancholy hypocrites. You must go about wearing smiling, fresh, gay, agreeable faces." You must learn to laugh, again and again. We are told, in fact, that St. Francis called his brother Friars in the Franciscan Order "Jesters of the Lord".

St. Teresa of Avila too, had a beautiful sense of humour. One day, she had walked quite a distance, and felt tired. Someone offered her an ass to ride. She rode a short distance when, suddenly, the ass collapsed and dropped down dead. She heard a Voice whisper in her ears, "Teresa, this is how I treat my friends."

Immediately Teresa retorted, "Lord, this is why You have so few friends!"

Swami Ramdas said, "I do not have to shed tears. I laugh my way to God."

Dr. Albert Schweitzer's famous hospital was in Lamberne, in Equatorial Africa, where the climate is hot and humid. The doctors who assisted him came from Europe and felt quite uncomfortable with the weather, which often threw them into a dour mood. Dr. Schweitzer applied the therapy of cheerfulness on his medical staff. The therapy worked wonders on his young doctors and nurses, invigorating their sagging spirits and giving relief to their taut nerves. Everyone looked forward to meal times at which Dr. Schweitzer would relate to them amusing stories, humorous anecdotes, and make witty remarks.

My Beloved Master, Sadhu Vaswani, had a sparkling sense of humour, which often made us burst out in laughter. I remember one day, a doctor-friend who thought very highly of himself, came to Sadhu Vaswani and said, "I have decided to give up my practice and devote all my time to the service of the country."

Sadhu Vaswani said to us, "I am not sure if he has given up his practice or his practice has given him up!"

Does God laugh?

My answer is: Yes, God does laugh! He does not laugh at our weaknesses and imperfections, our heartaches and failures. But he does laugh at the ungodly world which thinks it can efface God out of existence.

He laughs at our schools and colleges where, in the name of secularism, a God-less education is given to our boys and girls, the "builders of tomorrow".

God also laughs when some of us remark that we can teach God how to make a better world. I find it amusing that many people swear that they wish to serve God– but they all want to serve Him in an advisory capacity!

There is a wealthy woman who rejoices in saying, "I wish God made me His secretary. I would teach Him how to make the world better and happier!" Imagine what a lovely sense of humour God must have to put up with these kinds of comments day after day!

I believe it was Sri Ramakrishna Paramhansa who said: God laughs when a doctor assures his patient that if he takes his medicine, he will recover soon. God laughs, for He knows that the man is going to die that very night. God also laughs, when two brothers draw a line and say, this property is mine and that is yours. God laughs, for He knows that all 'landed property' belongs to Mother Earth.

The therapy of cheerfulness

1. Wake up in the morning with a smile on your face and the words, "Good morning, Lord!" on your lips.

   These three words form the title of a book written by an American businessman. He says he gets up with these words on his lips, every morning. He has been doing so for a long period and claims that, by merely doing so, he has added a new dimension to his life.

   See that your face always wears a smile. It was Mahatma Gandhi who said, "You are not completely dressed until your face wears a smile!" It has been said, wear a smile and you have friends: wear a scowl and you have wrinkles. Which would you have?

2. A smile is infectious. It is mirrored in the face of the one you smile at. Therefore, wherever you go, keep on smiling. Be careful to see that your smiles always announce sweetness and goodness, never portray sarcasm, bitterness or pride.

3. Give a hearty laugh at least three times every day– once before breakfast, once before lunch, and once before dinner. If you find it difficult to laugh, look into the mirror and make funny faces. A family I know follows this principle. Before dinner, each member of the family relates something which makes the others laugh. Only then do all the members partake of their meals.

4. Develop a healthy sense of humour. A sense of humour will save you from many difficult

situations.

Two American senators got into an argument. One of them was tall and hefty, the other was short and slim. The former lost his temper and said, "If I liked, I could swallow you up!"

The other answered with a smile, "If you did so, you would have more brains in your stomach than in your head!"

Two people happened to pass through a passage from opposite directions. The passage was too narrow for both to pass at the same time. Where they met, one said rudely to the other, "Make way for me!"

The other gently answered, "I was about to say the same to you." To which the first retorted, "I never make way for a fool!"

The other quietly stepped aside and said: "I always do!"

5. Learn to laugh at yourself. We often laugh at the oddities and weaknesses of others but not at our own. We must learn to laugh at ourselves. It has been rightly said that the person who can laugh at himself is a delight to be with; he applies to his ills and errors the most soothing balm the human spirit desires– laughter. Many of us think that we are the acme of perfection. But each one of us has so many oddities at which we can laugh.

The great sculptor, Daniel Chester, carved a statue of Emerson. Every day, Emerson sat in front of the artist while he was at work. One day, looking at the statue, the sage of Concord exclaimed, "The more it resembles me, the worse it appears!"

6. Always look at the bright side of things. Everything has two sides– the bright and the dark or, as I would wish to put it, the bright and the less bright.

A king had a dream in which he found that all his teeth had fallen out. He wanted an interpretation of the dream. A dream interpreter was sent for. He consulted the ancient books and said to the king, "Sir, this is the most unfortunate dream. It signifies that all your dear ones– your children, wife, and relatives– will die during your lifetime."

The king was disappointed and ordered that the soothsayer be thrown into prison.

Another dream interpreter was called for. He, too, consulted the same ancient books and said, "O king, this is the most fortunate dream. It signifies that you will survive all your dear ones. Long live the king!"

The king felt happy and richly rewarded the soothsayer.

Both statements have the same meaning. It is the way you put information across or the way you look at it that matters!

7. Be sure that God is in charge of the universe. He is the controller of the destinies of individuals and nations, and nothing can ever go wrong.

So many things happen to us, and we are unable to understand the 'why' of them. Our dear ones are suddenly snatched away from us. Misfortunes hit us. Calamities befall us. Losses ruin us. If only we have the faith that God is too loving to punish and too wise to make a mistake, we shall not be upset. As I always say, there is a meaning of mercy in all the incidents and accidents of life. Therefore let us accept everything with the mantra, "Yes father, yes, and always, yes!"

Think about it...

- In the instants of laughter, there is a tendency to remain in the present moment. In this way, one forgets the worries of the future and the pain of the past.

- When people laugh together, it brings them closer and improves relations. It also helps to enhance communication.

- Laughter stimulates both sides of the brain. It helps to keep the person alert and also helps to retain more information.

A joke to laugh our way to cheerfulness!

There was a town in which they wished to build a temple with a school attached to it as well as a dispensary where the poor would receive free medical aid. The entire project was estimated to cost a crore of rupees.

Members of the fundraising committee approached a rich *sethia* for a donation. The *sethia* was parsimonious by nature. They said to him, "We want you to be the first to contribute to the Temple Project. God has blessed you with rich abundance. Give us at least 1% of the total estimated cost of the project."

"How much would that be?" asked the *sethia*.

"The entire project is estimated to cost a crore of rupees," they explained to him. "1% would work out to a lakh of rupees."

Immediately, the *sethia* took out his cheque-book and wrote out a cheque for Rs. 1,00,000 and, handing it over to them, left the house.

The members were taken aback. They were not ready for this quick response. They had thought that if they asked for a lakh of rupees, they would only receive Rs. 10,000.

Suddenly, one of the members discovered that the cheque was not signed. They rushed to the *sethia* and said to him, "Sir, by mistake, you have forgotten to sign the cheque."

"It is not a mistake," said the *sethia*. "The scriptures teach that donations to charitable causes should be anonymous. Let my donation, too, be anonymous."

The Law of Karma

The law of karma, simply stated, is the law of cause and effect. It is a scientific law. It is a universal law. It is, in fact, built up of two universal laws: (1) As you think, so you become; and (2) As you sow, so shall you reap. You cannot sow thorns and reap apples. The law of karma is universal in its application. It applies equally to all. We are sowing seeds every day in the field of life. Every thought I think, every word I utter, every deed I perform, every emotion I arouse within me, every feeling, fancy, wish that awakens within me, are seeds I am sowing in the field of life. In due course, the seeds will germinate and grow into trees, and yield fruit– bitter or sweet– which I shall have to eat. No one else can do that for me.

Are there different types of karma which bind us?

In order to understand this balance of cosmic justice, it is necessary for us to grasp three different aspects– three different types of karma:

1. The first type of karma is *kriyaman* or *agami karma*. This is the karma of action and instant reaction. For example, you are thirsty and you drink water. Drinking water is an effort, an action. It produces an effect immediately: your thirst is quenched. The reaction cancels out the action and the karma is settled, on the spot; there is no residue to be carried over. *Kriyaman karma* is that which cancels itself there and then. You take a bath; it is an action by which your body is cleansed; this is the effect which is immediately achieved. Causes subside, when the effect is produced. Action comes to an end, when the reaction sets in. Thus, *kriyaman karma* is not carried forward. Any action of yours that leads to immediate result is *kriyaman karma*. Action and reaction– *kriya* and *pratikriya* are both completed; they have no effect on your future actions.

2. The second is *sanchita karma*, the sum total and store of all our actions, good and bad, in the sequence of innumerable lives that we have lived. All of this is recorded and preserved. I repeat, *sanchita karma* is the karma that we have accumulated through numerous lives. All the actions we have performed– physical, mental, verbal– contribute to create this storehouse of karma. However, all this karma does not fructify, does not bear fruit at once. Only a small part of it fructifies in any one birth or embodiment. The rest of it remains accumulated– awaiting its fructification.

Let me give you a simple example. You appear for an examination: you do not get the result immediately. You have to wait for two or three months– in some cases, up to six months before your results are declared. So, your appearing for an exam becomes a sort of *sanchita karma*, which does not produce its effect immediately. Karma which does not fructify immediately is *sanchita karma*. Our *sanchita karma* keeps on growing. In fact it grows from birth to birth; it has been accumulating on a spiritual record through innumerable lives from time immemorial. The load of *sanchita karma* which each one of us carries is tremendous– indeed, a heavy load! All those karmas which do not produce their effect immediately are held in deposit– they are added to our accounts of karma.

I remember, a few years ago, the Sadhu Vaswani Mission had instituted a prize to be awarded to anyone who could recite the 700 *slokas* of the Bhagavad Gita by heart. So far, no one has come to claim this prize. The amount is still lying in deposit. It is a *sanchita* prize.

3. The third type of karma is that part of our karma which matures, comes to fruition in one particular birth. This is *prarabdha karma*– and it is this karma which is the basis of our present birth, our present embodiment. Those of us who have been given the gift of human birth, we may be sure that this is the result of very good karma. Thus *prarabdha karma* on which our present existence is based, is often referred to as fate, destiny or luck, in popular language.

Prarabdha karma is a part, or a fragment of *sanchita karma* which has fructified in this birth. Our *sanchita karma*, accumulated over hundreds of births, is like a mountain; in each *janma*, we are adding to the store. Of this vast store, the *prarabdha*– the inevitable– is but a fragment. It is that portion of our karma assigned to us to be worked out in our present existence. It is also called ripe karma, for it is a debt which has become overdue, and must be paid back.

It is *prarabdha karma* which determines the family into which you are born. It determines the race, the nation in which you take birth; it also determines your sex, the type of body you will acquire, etc. Remember this– your wealth is pre-determined. You may keep working all day, all night to get more money– but only that much money will come to you, which is permitted by *prarabdha*. Even if you get more, you will lose it through speculation, theft, etc.

There is inequality in this world, wherever we turn. Is this fair?

We are told, all men are created equal. No one can be so blind or foolish as to imagine that there is actual equality of ability or environment or conditions of birth for all. Why, even in the same family, all children do not have equality of ability or intelligence. There is a family of which the eldest son is an IAS officer and the younger is unable to pass the SSC examination.

We have a proverb in Sindhi which says, "The mother gives birth to children, each brings with himself his destiny." In other words, each one brings his karma with himself.

There is a family of which the youngest son is a multimillionaire, while the eldest is so poor that he and his children are virtually starving, literally begging for food.

Two questions arise: 1) Is this inequality the result of karma? 2) And if so, is it fair? The answer to both, as the great teachers of India have taught us, is in the affirmative. You are the architect of your own destiny. You are the builder of your own life. Every thought, emotion, wish, and action creates karma, and we have been creating karma for thousands, perhaps millions of years. If our thoughts, emotions, and actions are benevolent, so called good karma results. If they are malevolent, evil or difficult bad karma is created. The good or evil we generate attaches its effect to us and remains in our current life until we have satisfied it by balancing it out.

If all that happens today is the result of our past karmas, does it mean that everything is pre-destined?

No, certainly not! We are the architects of our own destiny. We are the builders of our future. Many of us blame fate, *kismet*, for our misfortune. But let me tell you, dear friends, that you are the builders of your own fate. Therefore, be careful especially of your thoughts. We pay scant attention to our thoughts, believing that they are of no consequence. We say, after all, it was only a thought, what does it matter? Every thought is a seed you are sowing in the field of life, and what you sow today, you will have to reap tomorrow.

This 'destiny' is not something imposed on you from outside– you have built your own destiny through the efforts of yesterday. Yesterday's effort is today's destiny. Equally, today's effort is going to be tomorrow's destiny. Thus it is you yourself who is responsible for what is happening to you. The family into which you are born, your relatives, your friends, your spouse, your children, your religion, your race, your environment, your work, your status, your wealth– all these are controlled by *prarabdha karma*.

God has created a universe of beauty, fullness, happiness, and harmony. Each one of us is a child of God. God wishes each one of us to be happy, healthy, prosperous, successful, and to enjoy all the good things He has created. We keep ourselves away from all those bounties because of our karma. Change your karma and you will change the conditions in which you live. You can change your karma by adopting a new pattern of thinking.

Is there a contradiction between karma and man's free will?

When God created man, He gave to man the very freedom that He kept for Himself. Man has a choice to use freedom in the right or wrong way. Freedom entails responsibility and your choice creates your karma. Remember, what I am today, is the result of the choices I made yesterday. What choices I make today, will determine what I will be tomorrow.

How to live a life that bears witness to the law of karma

Let me pass on to you a few suggestions that can be helpful in daily life:

1. Always be aware of your thoughts. As you think, so you become. Every time an evil thought approaches you, push it out of your mind. An effective way of pushing out a thought is to slap or pinch yourself the moment an undesirable thought enters your mind.

2. As you sow, so shall you reap. Therefore, be aware of every little thing that you do. Every day, spend some time in silence, preferably at the same time and at the same place. Sitting in silence, go over all that you did during the earlier twenty four hours. It is helpful if you go over your actions in the reverse order– think first of what you did a little while ago, then of what you did a little while earlier, and so on. You will surely find that there were things which you did which you should not have done, as there are things which you did not do but should have done– many errors of commission and omission. Repent for them all and pray to the Lord for wisdom and strength to never to do such things again.

3. Take care of your *sangha*– the people with whom you associate. If you move in the company of holy ones, something of their holiness will penetrate your life and fill you with holy aspirations and vibrations. Hence the value of daily *satsang*.

4. Develop the spirit of detachment. Attend to your duties and be inwardly detached, knowing that nothing, nobody belongs to you. You are only an actor– and also a spectator– in the ever unfolding, cosmic drama of life. You have to play this double role of an actor and a spectator.

5. Grow in the spirit of surrender to God, "Not my will, but Thy Will be done, O Lord!" Repeat the Name Divine, and pray with a sincere heart that you may rise above the *dwandas* (the pairs of opposites), above pleasure and pain, loss and gain, for it is only then that suffering will not be able to touch you– and you shall be at peace with yourself and with those around you.

6. Be vigilant. Be watchful, live in awareness all the time. It was the Buddha who said to his disciples on one occasion, "O *bhikkhus*, if you are not vigilant, desire will enter your heart even as rain enters a room through a leaky roof."

7. Do as much good as you can, to as many as you can, in as many ways as you can. Help as many as you can, to lift the load on the rough road of life. The day on which we have not helped a brother here, a sister there, a bird here, an animal there, is a lost day, indeed.

Is there no short cut to the ending of karma?

Yes. There are three ways. The first is the way of self-inquiry, to understand who you are.

You are not the body, nor the mind. You are not the *buddhi*. You are that which cannot be touched by karma. Once you arrive at that stage, all karma drops out.

The other is the way of self-surrender.

The third is the way of selfless service.

Those are the three ways by which the store of karma can be burnt. But even then, the *prarabdha karma* that you have brought has to be worked out. But the *sanchita karma*, the storehouse of karma, gets burnt.

In the law of evolution, can a human being be reborn as an animal?

When the law of karma finds that a person is so incorrigible that he will not be reformed until he goes back to the stage of the animal, and begins again– it is only in such cases that a human being is reborn as an animal.

I sometimes think about a classmate of mine. When I was in the first standard, he was in the fourth. I came to the second, he was still in the fourth standard. I went to the third and he continued to be in the fourth. I went to the fourth and he was my classmate. I went to the fifth and the teachers said, "We must do something. This boy has been in the fourth standard for so many years, let us send him back to the third, so that he can gather some momentum."

I do not feel that anyone of you could have had that experience. But it does happen in very few cases, where people commit mortal crimes, for example, kill little children. Then perhaps, the law of karma gives us the body of an animal so that we can restart the process. But it is always for our own good.

Let go, Let go, Let God!

Let go, let go, let God– is my mantra for troubled souls. Why have you clung to your burdens all these years? Drop them. Draw strength from the words of the Gita, the voice of the Lord that comes floating to us across the centuries: "Renouncing all rites and writ duties, come to Me for single refuge, and I shall liberate you from bondage to suffering and sin. Of this have no doubt."

The secret of true faith is in three words: "Let it go!"

Let it go! Let go of your fears, your guilt, your problems and your frustrations. Let go in God's name! For He is the support and sustenance of your life. There are no obstacles on your path that He cannot clear; no problems that He, in His mercy and wisdom cannot solve!

If you want to be at peace, if you want to feel that God is watching over your life, if you want to feel the abundant love of God in your heart, if you wish to live in the present moment, then just let go of all your anxieties and worries, let go of all the constraints which are oppressing you; hand your life over to God, and watch miracles happen!

Let go, let go, let God!

Make this your mantra of faith.

If you are frustrated, disappointed, hurt, unhappy, if you find that, in spite of putting forth your best efforts, you have failed, then let me say this to you: Let go, let go, let God! Let go of everything, and let God take charge of all your affairs! If only you can do this, you will find miracles happen in your daily life. You will see limitations washed away and new opportunities open. God will work through you to bring your highest good into visible expression in your life.

Begin right now to repeat the words, let go, let go, let God! As you continue to repeat this mystic formula, either silently or audibly, it will open the way for the flow of Divine power, and you will be blessed.

A man fell seriously ill. The best of doctors could do nothing to help him recover. His wife wept, shed tears, prayed to the Lord. There was no answer. The man's condition became more and more critical. Then someone suggested to the wife, "Let go, let go, let God!"

"What do you mean?" she asked.

"Let go of your husband," she was told. "Do not cling to him. He does not belong to you. He belongs to God. Surrender him to the Lord and let Him do what He will."

The wife followed the advice and soon her husband's health began improving. Today, he is hale and hearty.

Letting go permits Divine ideas to flow, Divine light to shine, Divine power to work, Divine order and rightness to bless your mind, body and affairs.

What is the secret of a faith-filled life?

The secret of a faith-filled life, a life of joy, peace and relaxation is in the three words, "Let it go!" Life is full of incidents, both pleasant and unpleasant. When an unpleasant thing happens, we are apt to lose our balance; this creates a negative emotion which expresses itself in a feeling of frustration, sadness or depression. An effective way of dealing with such a situationis to go to the root of the matter and "let go" of what is causing the negative emotion. Let it go! Let everything go!

Has my sister failed to understand me? Let it go! Has my brother spoken ill of me? Let it go! Has my best friend turned against me? Let it go! Have I suffered loss in business? Let it go! Have my plans been upset? Let it go! Have I been treated with disrespect? Let it go! Has a dear one passed away? Let it go! Has my health suffered a setback? Let it go! Have I been cheated, robbed, or deceived by someone in whom I have placed my trust? Let it go!

In this world of impermanence, a world in which things come and go and nothing abides, is there anything worth worrying over? Let it go! The more we let go, the more do we conserve our energies for the constructive and creative tasks of life.

Live a stress-free life

There was a woman of ninety. People marvelled at the fact that they had never ever seen her stressed or upset over anything. She was never tensed, always serene and calm, and her face was tranquil as the waters of a lake on a windless day. She was always at peace with God, with those around her, and with herself.

Someone asked her how she could be so composed in all conditions and circumstances of life. She answered, "I think it is because I become a little child every night!"

"What do you mean?" she was asked.

She answered, "Every night, I go to my silence-corner. I look at my Beloved, Sri Krishna. I place all my worries and anxieties and problems of the day, one by one, at His Lotus Feet. If I am feeling guilty about something I have done, which might have inadvertently hurt or caused grief to someone, I ask for His forgiveness and then accept it. If I am worried about anything, I hand over the problems to Him and let go of them then and there. If I feel lonely or unwanted, I tell Him so and He enfolds me in His loving arms. Always, after letting go, a deep peace settles over me and tensions disappear…"

Is there no limit to letting go?

Think of the people who have endured rape, abuse, violence and psychological torture. Is it right to tell them, "Forgive and forget! Let go, let God!"?

Yes, yes, yes! The perpetrators of evil will have to face their karmic consequences in ways and means that we may never know. But the victims, the injured innocent ones must heal themselves, make themselves whole and carry on with their lives.

And no, I am not being arbitrary or insensitive or uncaring! I don't want you to live with the terrible woes and festering wounds from your past! You need to be free from pain and lifelong anguish. Therefore I beseech you earnestly, choose the way of compassion, forgiveness and healing. You owe it to yourself. The person who wronged you committed the offence in the past; will you continue to relive the anguish for a lifetime? Will you continue to wrong yourself, redoubling the hurt and the suffering? No! Let go, let go, let God take over your life and heal you!

Let us hand our anxiety and care over to the Lord. Let us let go, let go, let God! Let God take care of our loved ones, let Him solve our problems, let Him take charge of our lives. What seems insurmountable and impossible to us, is possible, indeed, effortless for God! So why are we holding on to grief and anxiety and fear? Let us discard these negative feelings at the Lotus Feet of Him who can turn the impossible to I-am-possible!

Let go, let go, let God!

Let God In!

Many philosophers and thinkers have suggested that the moral and cultural decay of the present age can be stopped if man brings God back into his life. These five words are the panacea to all the ills of life: bring God back into your life. We don't have to wander in this quest; we don't have to go in search of Him. He is everywhere. He is omnipresent. He is the Indweller of our hearts! Just let God into your life!

Take refuge in God. Call out to Him in absolute faith. All your problems will be solved. When man takes refuge in God, a process of transformation begins. First of all he realises this: that he is not alone. God is with him. This realisation brings new hope, new *shakti* and new energy. He is rejuvenated and he gains the confidence to achieve his goal. He is ready to take on the challenges of life.

"I am not alone, God is with me. The universe is with me." Affirm this and let me assure you, you can surmount any obstacle; you can face any challenge. You can face every difficulty and solve every problem.

The further man moves away from God, the more restless and hollow he will feel. God is our Sustainer. The physical body and mind cannot function without the soul. So too, man should be linked with his inner higher self, which is, after all, an aspect of God. If man wants to live a healthy life physically and mentally, then he should be connected with the source-soul, the Supreme Self. Those who have rejected God from their life have experienced an intense agony and restlessness. Their life is tortured by their own desires– like walking bare foot on the hot sands of a desert in summer.

Life has a purpose!

There is a beautiful design behind the magnificence of Creation. Our scriptures tell us that it was God's intention– *Bhagavad sankalpa*– that was the force behind the creation of this universe. Therefore, everything in this universe is well ordered, well designed, and created with a specific purpose. There is nothing random about Creation. As a great scientist once remarked, "God does not throw dice."

This applies to us, as human beings too. Each of us is born with a purpose. We may not be readily aware of it. This purpose is revealed to us at the proper time, when we have evolved in awareness or consciousness. As children we might think that the goal of our life is to become a pilot, a sailor, an engine driver or doctor; these are only job or career goals. But these are at best short term or even long term goals. What I am talking about is the purpose for which we were born, the purpose for which we have been given this gift of the human birth.

I believe the purpose of this human birth is to know God, to make Him real in our lives, and to grow in perfection so that we may be reunited with Him, our Source and our Destination.

Face the challenges of life

Till we discover this purpose, life raises many questions, poses many problems, and throws many challenges at us. The highway of life hardly gives anyone a smooth ride, although we are all apt to imagine that others have it easy! If truth were to be told, the journey of life is beset by obstacles, difficulties and challenges. There is none here who can say his life has been a joy ride, without bumps, without ups and downs.

Difficulties and misfortunes too, come with a purpose. For whatever happens, there is a reason! There is a hidden meaning, a meaning of mercy in all that happens to us. All incidents, events, and accidents happen according to a divinely ordained plan. If we make mistakes and are forced to pay a heavy price for them, this too has a learning purpose. Problems and challenges are thrown in our way by the Divine power to test our inner strength, to help us grow in spirit, and discover the true meaning of life.

Perhaps we are not aware that within every one of us there is a source of spiritual strength, which when tapped, can move mountains. Every one of us– poor or rich, frail or strong, disabled or fully able, ill or healthy– has the *atmic shakti*, the inner strength, which when awakened can help us face every obstacle, meet every challenge, and overcome every difficulty. Successful men and women have used this inner strength and achieved great heights.

God is!

"Who is God? Where is God? Can I see Him? What is the scientific evidence you can offer to prove his presence?" These are some of the questions I get asked frequently by lay people.

If we are going to talk of scientific evidence, let me tell you, the most famous scientists of the past have had faith in God. These include Copernicus, Kepler, Galileo, Blaise Pascal, Mendel, and many others. And while we are on the subject, I must refer in particular to two of

Let God In!

the greatest scientists in human civilisation. One of them, Sir Isaac Newton who discovered the law of gravity was also a devout believer. A man of true genius involved in the study of physics and mathematics, he once said, "The most beautiful system of the sun, planets, and comets, could only proceed from the counsel and dominion of an intelligent and powerful Being."

In more recent times, Albert Einstein, the best known scientist of the 20th century, did not have a personal God. But he always asserted the impossibility of a non-created universe. He felt that God "reveals Himself in the harmony of all that exists". Talking about the Creation of the world, he once remarked to a young physicist, "I want to know how God created this world. I am not interested in this or that phenomenon, in the spectrum of this or that element. I want to know His thoughts, the rest are details."

But to return to the question of the layman. I am reminded of an incident from the life of Emperor Akbar, perhaps the greatest of the Mughal rulers. As we know, Akbar had in his court nine jewels– brilliant men of wisdom, wit, art, music, and literature. The king's favourite among them all was the inimitable, witty and wise Birbal. He was the emperor's counsellor– his guide and confidante. Whenever Akbar *Badshah* was in a quandary, it was to Birbal that he turned. Birbal always had a practical solution for all the emperor's problems.

Needless to say, Akbar was a man of intense faith. He believed in the supreme justice and the power of Allah. One day, a group of agnostic scholars came to his court. They argued with him that there was no God, that his people were looting him in the Name of Allah. They pleaded with him to give up distribution of alms and endowments in the name of charity, for he was simply throwing away the funds of the Royal Treasury. "Where is God, your Majesty?" they asked him pointedly. "Can we see Him? Can you, the *Badshah,* see Him?"

This put Akbar in a dilemma. Unlike a few other kings I could mention, Akbar was always tolerant and liberal in his attitude. He always allowed for diversity of opinions in his court. Not that he was ever in doubt of God's existence, but he had to offer a convincing explanation to the visitors. He had to justify the considerable sum that was being spent on religious activities.

Immediately Birbal came to his emperor's rescue. He got up, picked up a riding whip lying nearby, and went straight to the leader of agnostic group assembled in the court. He began whipping their leader.

Everyone was shocked by this behaviour. At first, they were too stunned to react. Had Birbal gone crazy to whip a visitor to the royal court in the presence of the great Emperor Akbar? As for the agnostic leader who had to bear the brunt of Birbal's blows, he simply could not take it anymore. He began to cry. "It hurts, it pains me! O, I can't bear the pain. Please stop, please! I cannot bear the pain."

Unfazed, Birbal continued to whip him. "Pain?" he asked, as he continued whipping. "You speak of pain? You are uttering a lie! Where is this pain you speak of? Can you see it? Can you show it to me? Can you show it to the emperor and his court?"

"*Jahanpanah,* this man is mad!" screamed the leader of the agnostics. "How can anyone see pain?"

"So you can't see pain, is that so?" said Birbal. "Then how do you say there is pain?"

"Yes! Oh yes! There is intense pain. But it cannot be seen."

Birbal put away the whip. "Just as you can't see pain, but you know it is there, in the same way, you cannot see God, but He is there. Because God is invisible to the naked eye, it does not mean He does not exist."

The agnostics were routed. Birbal's explanation put everyone at ease. The agnostics and the non-believers were ashamed of their aggressive behaviour. Akbar was a mightily relieved man!

My dear friends, saints and sages can at best only describe the attributes of God; they cannot make Him visible. To see Him, to realise Him, you need to put in your own effort; you have to work for it.

Five steps to let God into your life

1. Take refuge in God

Surrender the thread of your life in God's safe hands. Feel the presence of God every moment of your life. Feel that there is a powerful, Divine energy with you and within you. You are not alone; you have a constant companion, and there is no problem which the two of you together cannot solve. Affirm it through a prayer or a hymn. It may be 'Thou who failest not, abide with me!' or 'You be my Divine guide' or 'Lead kindly Light!'

Just say any prayer which comes to you spontaneously. You may pray verbally in the beginning; later on the prayer will become an emotional experience and part of your being. But do not fail to affirm this at least thrice every hour: "I am not alone, God is with me".

Begin your day with this affirmation and your life will change magically.

2. Keep your Daily Appointment with God

At a fixed time and at a fixed place, meet God for fifteen to twenty minutes. Begin with five minutes, then increase the time to twenty minutes. Connect with God and see miracles happening in your daily life. Once you get connected with God, you will be able to communicate with Him; you will be able to experience Him. You will be able to hear the Divine voice and receive His Divine guidance!

To have His experience, you have to kindle the fire of yearning within. This yearning has to be intense and intoxicating, like the longing of one soul for another; like the anguish of separated lovers; like the burning of live coals; like the obsession of a mad man. Walking, waiting, sitting, fill your time with this intense love for the Lord! When true love is awakened, God will respond in many ways. You will be transformed; you will rise above the mundane. Your problems will take a back seat.

Let us also practise silence every day, preferably at the same time and the same place– for this is our daily appointment with our own selves, our true Self, the real Self, the Self Supreme that, for want of a better word, we call God. In silence, let us pray, meditate, repeat the Name Divine, do our spiritual thinking, engage ourselves in a loving and intimate conversation with God.

God is our one true, abiding Friend, the Friend of all friends. And God is available to us at all times. We do not have to go to a particular place to be able to contact God, for God is everywhere. All we have to do is to close our eyes, shut out the world, open our heart, call Him, and there He is in front of us. In the beginning, we will not be able to see Him. Let us be sure that He sees us. Nor will we be able to hear Him speak. Let us be sure that He hears us. A day will come when we, too, will see Him and hear Him speak.

3. Make your life and work an offering to God

Realise that you were made for a unique purpose which you alone can fulfil. Therefore, adopt a positive attitude towards life. The right attitude makes the character strong, and gives a special meaning to your life. Let me share a story with you.

There were three labourers. They were breaking huge stones for a temple to be built. A passerby asked them, "What are you doing?"

The first labourer said, "Can't you see, I am breaking stones?"

The second one frowned, "Do I have an option? I have to break the stones to feed my family."

The third one smiled and with humility replied, "This is my offering to the temple."

Adopt a positive attitude towards work, effort, and results. Dedicate your actions to God.

Whatever you do– it may be a lowly act such as sweeping a room or a noble deed such as saving a life– do it wholly for the love of God. "Whatever you eat, whatever austerity you practise, whatever you give in charity, whatever you do, do it, O Arjuna, as an offering unto Me," says the Lord in the Gita. Can there be a simpler way of communing with God than this, that we offer unto Him every little thing we do, every thought we think, every word we utter, every aspiration we breathe? This is the right way to let God into your life, to practise the presence of God.

4. Believe that nothing is impossible with God

Trust God; entrust all your problems to Him and He will surely provide the right direction. We are told time and again, 'Ask and you shall receive' or 'Knock and the door will open'. We have only to cry out to Him; we have to connect with Him and beseech Him to solve our problems and to mitigate our suffering. He will surely answer our call; He will provide the solution.

I am sure all of you have heard of Napoleon Hill, the inspirational writer. He tells us in his book, *Think and Grow Rich,* "One of the main weaknesses of mankind is the average man's familiarity with the word 'impossible'. He knows all the rules which will not work. He knows all the things which cannot be done."

Napoleon Hill has been hailed as the "Founder of the Science of Success" by millions of readers whom he has inspired with his motivational books. His motto was: "Whatever your mind can conceive and believe, it can achieve".

What exactly is the secret of achievement offered to readers of *Think and Grow Rich*? To tell you the truth, it is not really offered to us directly. It is not even explicitly identified. Hill felt that discovering the secret for themselves would provide readers with the most benefit. Therefore, he presented the idea, 'Define a Major Purpose' as a challenge to his readers in order to make them ask themselves, "In what do I truly believe?" For according to him, 98% of people had no firm beliefs, and this alone put true success firmly out of their reach.

If we wish to make the impossible possible, let us believe in God! Let us make the effort to know God, and develop contact with Him! All around us is the sorry spectacle of restless men rushing in headlong speed, moving mechanically from one task to another, achieving nothing, not knowing where they are going. To such people, I appeal: Learn to be still! Place your trust in God– with whom all things are possible!

5. Rise above self

Sadhu Vaswani was once asked, "What is your religion?" His reply was truly significant. He said, "I know of no religion higher than the religion of unity and love, service and sacrifice." His memorable words still ring in my ears: "Did you see him on the road? Did you leave him with the load?"

Reach out to people in need of help. Go out and you will find many who are in need of comfort, sympathy, and healing. Reach out to nature. Water plants and trees, feed birds and insects. Reach out to the universe. And you will be amazed to know how many things need your love and attention.

Once, a young college girl was travelling by bus. A handicapped boy got in. He had no place to sit. The college girl offered him her seat, but the boy refused saying, "You have occupied the seat first. I have no right to it." Realising the boy's predicament, the girl said, "Please sit down. Anyway, I have to get down at the next stop." At the next bus stop, the girl got down and took the next bus to her destination.

I often say to my friends: Happiness has no permanent address; but it dwells in the hearts of those who live for others.

Look out for opportunities to help others. In the process, your miseries will melt away and you will be able to face the challenges of life with equanimity!

One final thought...

Let me say to you, faith and grace are gifts of God. They are given freely and spontaneously to those who believe in God. All we can do is keep the door of our hearts open, and entreat God to enter therein. "When wilt Thou enter the home of my heart?" should be our constant prayer.

"Where is the dwelling of God?" asked the Rabbi of Kotzk of a number of learned men who visited him. They laughed at him and said, "What are you asking? God is omnipresent. He is everywhere." The Rabbi then gave his answer and said. "God dwells wherever man lets Him in!"

May I, with folded hands, ask every one of you, Let Him in! Let Him in! Let Him in!

Life

Human life is a rare and precious gift from God. We should live this life in such a way that our body and mind are cultivated in the best possible manner; that pure thoughts may come to us, sweet words are spoken by us, noble actions are performed, and right results are obtained, all leading to the ultimate goal– Liberation!

The meaning of life

If someone were to ask you, "What does life mean to you?" What would be your response?

When asked this question, most of us close our eyes for a brief moment and plunge into thought. We are unable to answer right away, and after a vague, random sentence or two, we honestly reply with a sigh, "Actually, I don't know."

Life, for some, is like a constant battle that they are fighting. For other disheartened souls, life is like an empty dream. Then there are some suffering ones who regard life as an unending tragedy.

Life means different things to different people. Happy people will view life very differently from those who are unhappy. By the same token, busy, active, working people will view life differently from reflective, contemplative or meditative people.

Some people think that life is meant to be lived for others, while others presume that life must be lived on their own terms. For some, life is an enigma, a painful mystery. But as they grapple with pain and suffering, even they come to realise that though life may seem cruel and unfair, life actually goes on... it works!

Sometimes, it is the disparity between themselves and others that gravely upsets people. They tend to look at life through their own narrow viewpoint, and assume that because others do not share those views, they are crazy and insane.

Some of us are horrified by the hatred and the violence around us. Rashly, we jump to the conclusion that life is cruel and meaningless.

But there are some questions we have to ask ourselves and introspect to get the right answers. We are born here on earth and life is to be lived in a fitting way. Wouldn't you agree?

Are you getting the best out of your bargain with life? Have you indeed made the most of your life? Are you living your precious human life meaningfully, consciously, purposefully?

We cannot evade these questions, if we wish to live a life that is valuable and worth living! I know that the answers to those questions are not easy! But you will agree with me that we need to think about them, at least occasionally.

A completely different perspective

If I were to ask you what the most beautiful thing in your life is, what would your answer be?

Let me guess: Friendship? Love? Laughter? Family? Books? Music? Knowledge and learning? Nature? Fresh air and open spaces…?

The list would be endless, would it not? It would vary from individual to individual.

This only shows that the magnificent kaleidoscope of life is made up of innumerable, beautiful, cherished facets. The glory and wonder, the joy and laughter, the munificence and colour of life are amazing and awe inspiring.

The supreme gift each one of us has received is life itself. The love and support of our family; the laughter and companionship we share with our friends; the beauty and serenity of nature– the blue skies, the chirping of birds, the swaying green grass, the gentle breeze…

The most beautiful thing about life is that you are alive! So make the most of every moment, every breath of this magnificent life!

Introspection on life

We all want to make the most of life. We long for happiness, peace, and fulfilment in everything we do. But do we know the purpose of this life, the goal of this life?

Have you ever asked yourself as you snuggle into bed and drift into sleep: What have I done with my day today? Have I moved closer to God? Have I brought happiness to anyone? Have I spoken kind words?

I know several businessmen who will not leave their offices before the day's accounts are tallied and closed to their satisfaction. They insist that pending bills and unsettled transactions should not be carried forward to the next day. But how many of us tally our daily accounts in the book of life?

What are we doing with our precious life?

If truth were to be told, we live a life of inertia! We leave our accounts unsettled, untallied. So many of us today are just drifting through life. We do not know where we are going; we do not even know what we want out of life. We work like machines, going through the same routine day after day. We forget that each of us is unique.

Several years ago, a cartoon appeared in an American newspaper. It showed Martians, (the inhabitants of Mars) looking at people on earth. One Martian asks another, "What are those people doing on earth?" The other replies, "They are moving." "Where are they moving?" persists the first one. "They do not know where they are moving. They are just moving," is the reply.

We are just moving like ants in an ant-farm; we are just drifting. But if we wish to succeed, we must realise the purpose of our life; we must fix our goal! We should be able to describe our goal vividly. We should fix it in our imagination. And we should have an unswerving focus on the goal all the time!

Life is precious

Let me tell you the story of a poor farmer, who inherited a small plot of land from his father. It was a tiny field, a stony tract of land. The farmer set out to plough the land, and found that the plough was obstructed by shiny, red stones. Grumbling, he threw away as many stones as he could, and continued his ploughing.

The field was ploughed and sown with crop, but still, the stones continued to lie around. The farmer would throw them at the birds or use them in his catapult to scare the birds away.

One day, as he was late in returning home, his wife brought his lunch to the field. Her eyes fell upon one of the shiny red stones, and she picked it up saying, "This stone is so beautiful! I shall take it home and give it to our daughter to play with."

"Take as many of these as you like," said the farmer. "There were dozens of them lying around, and I have thrown away many of them." Though his wife searched for them, she could not find another like the one she had picked up. So she took the stone home and gave it to her little girl.

A few days later, a wealthy jeweller was passing by their house when he caught sight of the girl playing with the stone. He stopped short in his tracks, took the stone from the child, and examined it closely. Amazed, he said to the child, "Can I see your father?"

"Where did you get this stone from?" the jeweller asked the farmer anxiously. "It is one of the rarest and most precious gems in the world! If you give me a few more like this, I shall give you a fortune in exchange! We don't find such large gems any more. You have probably hit upon an ancient buried treasure."

Can you imagine the farmer's reaction? He had thrown away all his treasure, not knowing its true worth!

Every moment, every breath of this life is precious, like the valuable gems that the farmer threw away in his ignorance.

Why is this human birth so precious?

The answer is simple. It is only through the human birth that we can attain liberation. It is only through the human birth that we can rid ourselves of the burden of karma and break from the bond of birth-life-death-rebirth. This is why it is said that even in the heavenly world, or *swarga loka,* noble souls who are in enjoyment of the bliss that results from their good deeds, still yearn for this human birth. The purpose of the human birth is to work towards a higher life, the life beautiful. Sadly, many of us fritter away this life in worthless pursuits, little realising the value of that which we throw away so carelessly!

I urge you, I earnestly beseech you, be aware that every breath of life is precious! Spend every moment in the consciousness that life is a gift from God. It is only through the human birth that we can achieve self-realisation and return to God, to abide forever in *moksha,* our ultimate liberation.

What do you think is the purpose of life?

Let me tell you what my Beloved Gurudev has taught me in this regard. The purpose of man's life is to grow in purity and perfection. Blessed are the pure in heart, for they shall see God! He who has a vision of God in the heart within, beholds God wherever he turns, in every atom of an atom. He discovers that although God dwells within man, men know it not and therefore, are unhappy. He says to himself, I shall be a servant of all who suffer and are in pain! The purpose of life is that it may be poured out as a sacrifice on the altar of suffering Creation.

Life is a gift of God, and this human life is the greatest blessing that God can bestow on any of His creatures! Life and all its bounties is also a trust given to us, to be used in the service of those who are less fortunate than ourselves.

When we have lived our life in this awareness, when we have loved all of God's Creation and striven to serve them, we are on the way to Salvation!

How can we change our life to make it wonderful?

Life can be changed. Life must be changed. Just think thoughts of joy, love and peace, of purity and prosperity, and your environment will shape itself in accordance with your persistent thinking. Let me offer you a few practical tips to make your life truly wonderful:

1. Realise what you are in essence.

2. Count your blessings.

3. Become a thankful person.

4. Keep the gate closed on the past.

5. Make today count.

6. Trust in the goodness and caring power of God and hand your life over to Him to take charge.

Golden rules of life

- Do unto others as you would have others do unto you.

- Each person must do his or her own duty. Today people claim their rights, but I ask you, what about your duties? In the Bhagavad Gita, the word for duty is *swadharma*. This word is repeated several times in the Gita, but nowhere is there a mention of the word 'right'. If we all do our duty, then our rights will automatically be taken care of. The cosmic drama will be successful only if each of us plays his own role. If I do my duty in the right way, the portals of perfection will be open to me.

- Do your duty and a little more. Humanity is one family. Therefore help as many as you can, as much as you can.

In closing…Maximise your life!

- Change your attitude and renew your perspective.
- Change your thinking– transform your life.
- Take time to relax– refresh your spirit.
- Live in the present.
- Appreciate this moment.
- Cultivate loving awareness.
- Remember, you have the innate ability to reinvent your life.
- Be grateful for the simple gifts of God that are all around you.
- Make each moment count.
- Realise the power of life and the presence of God in your life.

Love

Have you ever asked yourself: What is the secret of a happy, peace-filled, rewarding, fulfilling life?

Gurudev Sadhu Vaswani tells us, "God will not ask whether you have learnt Sanskrit or Latin, Greek or Hebrew. God will ask you, have you studied the word of four letters– L O V E– Love. God will ask whether you have grown in the spirit of meditation, beauty, love. God will ask you, have you learnt the lesson of love? Have you realised its power, its *shakti*? Have you grown in love?"

Love is the light that illuminates the dark ways of life. Love is heavenly. Love is beautiful. To grow in the life of the Spirit, we must learn the art of selfless love. And let me tell you dear friends, this is an art that you can learn very easily. Learn the art of speaking gently, lovingly, and sweetly. Learn to offer a helping hand to everyone who needs it. Learn to be humble and treat others with respect. Look upon all Creation as One Family, with God as the loving Father of us all– and you will have mastered the art of true love!

Today, people talk of hard skills, soft skills, communication skills, and technical skills. May I say to you, life skills are more important than professional skills! Love is far more essential to a successful life than vocational degrees. For love purifies your life and makes it sweet and meaningful.

What is love?

True love is a feeling that touches the mind, heart, and soul. It is perhaps the highest feeling that any human being is capable of, for I believe that love is of God; in fact I believe that love is not just an attribute of God– Love is God and God is Love! This is why I urge my young friends not to fall in love– but rise in true love!

I am afraid many of us have a rather shallow and superficial conception of love. We look upon love as something romantic– a thing of the heart. We regard it as something intangible, ephemeral, something which we cannot even find words to describe.

Native American Indians look upon love as a kind of wisdom. They believe that love is the first wisdom given to us, and we derive all else from that knowledge. The famous writer Carlyle echoed the same idea when he wrote: "A loving heart is the beginning of all knowledge."

Love is not attachment

As the song tells us, it is love that makes the world go round; it is love that gives meaning to life; it is love that makes our life beautiful!

In the fleeting duration of our life upon this earth, we bestow our love upon many people– and many things as well! I know a sister who loves her pet dog almost as much as she loves her children! I know a family which went into mourning when their pet dog died. There is a millionaire who loves his race horse so much that whenever he has a little time to spare, he rushes to the stud farm where the horse stays, under the care of its special trainer. There are teenagers who claim that their cellphone or iPad is a part of their own body, and that they cannot bear to be parted from these adored gadgets. One young man who met me asserted that he loved his new motorbike more than his current girlfriend!

All of us love our parents; some of us may be our mother or father's favourite child, and develop a special love for them; some people I know are closer to their friends than their family members.

Throughout our lives, we continue to love people, even though the love keeps changing, and the people we love too, move in and out of our lives. When young people discover love for the opposite sex and find the love of their life, everyone else in their heart has to take a back seat, while the beloved occupies the position of prominence! A fortunate few marry the partner of their choice; many women claim that when the girlfriend becomes the wife, the man's love for her wanes! As for men, they claim that their wives adore them and worship the ground they walk on– until the first child is born. Then the mother's attention shifts to her first born, and everyone else recedes into the background!

The point is that the objects of our love keep changing. At first, it is the mother, then the father, the siblings, then the spouse, and finally the children. This kind of love is a strong attachment. I do not wish to take away its merit, but I must point out that this love is earthly. This love brings as much pleasure as pain. There are people who cannot live without an attachment. If they lose their dear ones, they adopt pets. When they lose their pets, they feel miserable. Attachment is the cause of all sorrow.

God needs your love!

On the material plane we ask people, "How much have you studied?" "What are the academic degrees you have acquired?" "How much wealth have you amassed?" or "What is your salary?" These are all questions relating to worldly, material considerations.

The man who is wealthy and affluent, enjoys a high status in society, but in the heavenly world, all these luxuries are of no significance. There, the only question asked is, "How much do you love God? How much love do you have for God's broken images, the poor and the needy?" God does not want to know about your bank balance, your qualifications, your designation, your caste or your creed. He asks you about love.

Many of you are householders, and I am sure you must be carrying out your daily routine, conscientiously. I am sure you do your duties willingly. But, do not forget that in doing so, love is also important. Whatever you do, do it with a feeling of love.

Many rich people labour under the delusion that they can bribe their way to salvation and purchase God's favours with their money. They donate money to charitable causes; they contribute lavishly to *yajnas* and *poojas*; they even sponsor the building of temples, and they are confident that God has been won over by their lavish spending. NO. God cannot be bought with money. God can be won only by a loving heart. God can be sought by deep yearning in the heart, by calling out to Him time and again, I have need of You. O Lord! I cannot live without You!

The man who calls out thus, in true longing and love, will surely have a vision of God. For God needs our love and the yearning of the soul for Him.

What is the way of love?

The way of love is selflessness. It is the way of sacrifice. Love has no place for ego or selfishness. Love is an ever expanding positive energy. It was Dr. Rabindranath Tagore who said, "Love is an endless mystery, for it has nothing else to explain it." I cannot define or explain love to you! You have to feel it in your heart; you have to experience its healing, purifying powers, for it blesses both those who love, and those who are loved. One of the most admired women of the modern age, Helen Keller, said, "The best and most beautiful things in the world cannot be seen or even touched– they must be felt with the heart."

Have you ever prayed to God, to show you the way of love? Have you asked Him to bless you and shower you with that beautiful emotion called love?

Do not pray for material goods. Do not ask for petty favours. Ask for something which is more valuable, everlasting, and blessed. God in His infinite mercy and kindness, will bless you with love that is pure and self-energising.

If you wish to walk the way of love, if you wish to know God and understand Him, you must love Him more and more.

The more you love Him, the more you will know Him.

Love all!

There's no selectivity and exclusion in love. We cannot pick and choose what and whom to love and what not to love!

How can we claim our love for God if we do not love our fellow human beings? How can we call ourselves human beings if we watch our brothers and sisters suffering and struggling?

I have always asserted that Hinduism is not a religion, but a way of life. And the Hindu way of life embraces the whole of God's Creation in its entirety! For *Vedanta* teaches us that there is but One Life in all! The One Life sleeps in the mineral and the stone, stirs in the vegetable and plant, dreams in the animal and wakes up in the man. Creation is One Family, therefore let us not forget, that birds and animals too, are our younger brothers and sisters! It is our duty to guard them and protect them!

Our hearts need to be saturated with love, for love is the light which will illumine our life. For this, developed brains are not needed; we need enlightened hearts that can behold the vision of fellowship, unity and brotherhood. Love is what we need to build a new life of the Spirit, a new humanity, a new world of brotherhood and peace. We must eliminate the dark forces of greed, selfishness, prejudice and mistrust– and cultivate the power of love which is also the power of joy and peace!

We all want peace– peace of mind, peace in the family, peace in the community around us, peace between countries, peace in the world, peace with our environment. As I said, there is scarcely a soul upon earth who does not yearn for peace. But how many of us are prepared to pay the price?

I will tell you what I think is the price we must pay: We must love one another. I will go one step further: We must love one another or perish!

We must love one another; we must pray for each other; we must be prepared to sacrifice for each other; we must put aside selfishness and narrow national interests and work for the goal of world unity. To walk the way of love and peace, we must love our neighbours. We must not stop with that, we must love our enemies too. There is no challenge that love cannot conquer, no hurdle that love cannot overcome, and no disappointment that love cannot face. Love is invincible.

What love is and what love is not

Love is not possession. Love is not attachment. Love is above hate, envy and jealousy. Love comes without any strings attached to it. Love is unconditional. Love is divine. Love is pure energy. Love is a flood of sublime thoughts.

Above all, true love must not be confounded with physical sensation or sexual attraction. Thus we have the Sufi distinction between *ishq-e-mizazi* and *ishq-e-haqiqi*– the former is love generated by external beauty; the latter refers to real love, unconditional love, that is, the love of God. The Christians refined the Latin term *agape*, to mean love of God, love for all humanity. *Agape* is unconditional love' love that is undemanding, unconditional and all-giving; this is in contrast to *eros*, physical love that depends on an expectation, an 'if' clause; and *philos,* friendship or personal love that depends on the clause of cause or reason. *Eros* says "I will love you if you…."; *philos* says, "I love you because…"; *agape* says, "I love you unconditionally!" There are no 'ifs', 'buts', and 'because' in *agape*.

Love is within you!

Love is not out there somewhere. It is with you, within you. The more you offer love to the world and the people in it, the more it will come back to you! Indeed, it was a wise man who asserted, "Love grows by giving. The love we give away is the only love we keep. The only way to retain love is to give it away."

I have always been a great believer in the strength and sustaining power of true love– love which transcends the physical and the material, love that is divine and universal, and moves out to all people, to all of Creation!

In love, I believe, is the solution to all the problems of life; if life is a battle, love is its victory; if life is a story, love is its theme; if life is music, love is its melody; and if life is a flower, love is its fragrance!

The world's greatest need today is love-in-action! This love manifests itself in sympathy, service, and sacrifice. If you wish to show true love, you must pour your life out in sympathy, service, and sacrifice, to all humanity.

Someone asked me, "How can I know and feel the kind of love you speak of?" And my answer was, "You will know it when you become love!"

Practical suggestions to grow in the spirit of true love

1. People often talk of 'falling' in love; you must rise in love– in love with God, and in love with your fellow human beings, as also with brother birds and beasts.

    Therefore, establish a firm and loving relationship with God, first and foremost. Make God your father or mother, your friend or brother. Let everything you do strengthen this relationship with God.

    When you have established such a relationship, you will find it natural to offer the love of your heart to everything and everyone around you.

2. Speak softly, speak gently, speak with loving kindness. Treat everyone with love and respect. Greet God in everyone you meet.

3. Do not see the faults of others. When you find fault with others and criticise them harshly, you are drawing negative forces to yourself!

4. Love your family, love your friends and neighbours; but love those who hate you and criticise you as well! Breathe out love to those who ill-treat you and speak harshly to you! For every blow you receive, give back a blessing. This is not an impossible, impractical precept I'm preaching to you. It is a sound, wholesome approach to life that will bring lasting peace and happiness to you!

5. Whatever you do, whatever you say, whatever you think, whatever you give– do it for the pure love of God! When you live life as an act of love and devotion to God, you will find that you can never do anything which will displease God! Your life will become the life beautiful, the life of love and purity.

6. The law of love is the law of service and sacrifice. Therefore, go out of your way to help others. And rejoice in everything that the Will of God brings to you.

One final thought…

Love blesses the one who offers it and the one who receives it. Love can keep you healthy and happy, and help you face the problems of daily life in the right spirit!

Let me repeat: Love is not an attribute of God, Love is God!

Love is never blind. For love sees not only with the eyes, but the mind, the heart, and the spirit. Love goes about with wide open eyes, looking for opportunities to be of service to those in need.

We are told that a holy man was pained to see suffering and misery, wherever he turned. In deep despair, he cried out to God, "O Lord! They call you the God of Love and Mercy. How can you bear to see so much suffering and yet do nothing about it?"

From the depth of his consciousness, he heard God's voice tell him: "I did do something. I created you!"

God has created us and poured love into our hearts so that we may alleviate the pain and suffering we see around us.

Let us not curse the darkness. Let us kindle the light of love in our hearts!

Make the Right Choice

You can choose to be what you wish to be!

Your life, your future, your dreams, your destiny are in your own safe and capable hands. Your destiny is not shaped by any erratic chance, or by the unknown or unseen. The choices that you make define your destiny. To shape your life and your destiny, all you need to do is to make the right choices and bring about the positive transformation you seek. For this, you have been given the gift of free will. The form this free will takes is dependent on your choice of thoughts.

Yes! You have the power, the *shakti* within you, that can transform your life. You have the ability to uncover the potential in yourself to rewrite the story of your life, to take charge of your own life, to discover the joy that is your birthright, to live life like a prince or princess– for you are a child of God, who is the King of kings!

God endowed each and every one of us with free will, allowing each of us the freedom to change our destiny at every step, in every round of life. In other words, each one of us has the freedom of choice to act– to choose right or wrong. At every step of life, we can make the effort to improve our condition. Through our actions, we can actually succeed in changing our own karma and thus altering our own destiny. The choices that we make can be based on love or fear, and the results will reflect our intentions!

We are making a choice every living moment...

We are confronted by the necessity of making right choices almost every waking moment of our lives. What do we choose– rash driving or sober speed? Anger or forgiveness? Indulgence or restraint? Falsehood or truth? Screaming and shouting, or patient explanations? Corrupt practices or upright behaviour? And in the broader context, *dharma* or *adharma*? Righteousness or wrongdoing?

On the face of it, the choice is simple and straightforward, but putting it into practice is challenging for some of us. But practise it we must, if we are to avoid the pitfalls, the negative outcomes that *preya* will inevitably lead us to.

Preya and *shreya*

In the opening of the *Kathopanishad*, Lord Yama explains to the young *brahmin* lad,

Make the Right Choice

Nachiketas, that man is always confronted by two choices: the pleasant– the pleasurable– or the righteous– the good but difficult. The former leads us to worldly pleasures; the latter leads us Godward. You have to choose between the two paths– the easy, tempting, alluring worldly path which will lead you to unhappiness; or the difficult, thorny, and painful spiritual path, which will eventually lead you to Ultimate Bliss! It will lead you to the Realm of Light!

"The senses," Yama tells Nachiketas, "always choose *preya,* the pleasurable path that leads only to death and ruin."

Is this not true? When we run after the pleasures of this world, our happiness can only be fleeting, momentary. We think we are drinking deep, drinking life to the dregs, but in reality, we are just indulging the senses. Excessive indulgence in pleasures can only lead to pain and disillusion, and we end up at death's door, spiritually bankrupt.

Do we have an alternative? Yes indeed, Yama assures Nachiketas. We can avoid the pleasurable path called *preya* and choose the path of *shreya*– the tough and thorny path that begins in the awareness that we are not the bodies we wear and that there is more to us than the senses and the mind– we are immortal souls and our Home is in the Eternal!

The choice is ours. We have to choose between *preya* and *shreya*. But a question arises: **How many of us can distinguish between *preya* and *shreya*?**

Preya offers us instant pleasure and gratification, but its consequences are far-reaching and almost always negative. *Shreya,* on the other hand, involves controlling the senses and their desires; it entails self-discipline, self-control, and denying oneself the gratification that the lower impulses crave. The rewards of such self-denial are wholly beneficial and positive in the long run.

There is a young lady I know who often proclaims, "If the reward for choosing *shreya* is in heaven, forget it, I'm not interested." She refers, of course, to the tough choices she has had to make, and rues the fact that she has had to deny herself soft and easy options. She is right– she will have to wait for those rewards.

However, it must be pointed out that sometimes *preya* can also lead to instant ruin! Take the case of a young man riding an expensive, powerful, fast bike that his rich father has just gifted him; choosing *preya* in his case means riding recklessly, pushing the powerful and sophisticated machine to its limit, unmindful of speed limits and other traffic on the road.

Choosing *shreya* means keeping to traffic rules and regulations, resisting the temptation to ride fast and furious, as the expression goes. Sober and boring, as some of his friends would say, mockingly.

How many cases of highway deaths and injuries have we heard of in recent times, about young men who chose speed and thrill over safety and sobriety?

Happiness is a choice

Choice is not aggression; choice is not a monstrous assertion of one's will; choice is, more often than not, taking an informed decision! Our choices determine our joys and sorrows, long before we actually experience them. Sometimes, it is just choosing the right response, the right attitude to face circumstances! Not unoften, the right response to a certain situation may be the good old virtue of patience.

Dr. Viktor Frankl, author of the book *Man's Search for Meaning*, was an eminent psychiatrist and practising counsellor in Vienna, before he was captured by the Nazis and put in a concentration camp. His wife, his children, and his parents were all killed in the Holocaust.

The Gestapo made him strip. He stood there totally naked. As they cut away his wedding band, Viktor said to himself, "You can take away my wife, you can take away my children, you can strip me of my clothes and my freedom, but there is one thing no person can ever take away from me– and that is my freedom to choose how I will react to what happens to me!"

Even under the most difficult of circumstances, happiness is a choice which transforms our tragedies into triumph.

Make your choice– and act upon it!

Making a decision is one thing, acting to put that decision into practice is a different matter altogether! Have you heard the riddle about the three frogs on a log? One of them made a decision to jump. How many do you think were left?

The unexpected answer is: there were still three frogs on a log, because one of them only made a decision, but he took no action!

Making decisions is a big step, but it is only half the battle. The essential thing is to make the choice and act upon it!

I often narrate to my friends the story of the twin brothers, one of whom was a regular participant at the *satsang* of his guru. His twin chose differently; he preferred to spend his evenings at clubs, drinking and playing cards. Every day the latter felt a pang when he saw his brother return home after *satsang* and *seva*. Every day he promised himself, "Tomorrow, I shall surely go to the *satsang*." Sadly, that tomorrow never came! Death took him away before he made his choice of *shreya*!

Here is a list of choices we can make every day

- Choose God!
- Choose faith– faith in yourself and faith in humanity, faith in the universe around you.
- Choose to be positive.
- Choose to be kind.
- Choose to be confident.
- Choose to face every situation with courage.
- Choose to forgive and forget.
- Choose to dream.
- Choose to believe in the good that all of us are capable of.
- Choose to be happy.
- Choose to make others happy.
- Choose to stay away from negative people.
- Choose to laugh, especially at yourself.

Choose right thinking

Every thought that arises in your mind repeats itself, and forms a pattern. The pattern conditions us and compels us to act on the thought. Thoughts then become actions; actions turn into habits. Habits then dictate our lifestyle and character. Hence, we must take care of our thoughts. Create your own destiny, by deliberately generating positive thoughts. Make them into positive habits, and create positive vibrations for the future.

A man may cheat his business partner or a weak opponent; he may commit a sin in the darkness of the night and think that no one has seen him or observed him. But he has sown the evil seed in his life for which he will reap the equally evil fruit. Without doubt, that person will have to eat his own evil fruit. He cannot pass on the results of his karma to someone else. He himself has to pay for his actions. This is why we are advised to be alert and attentive, to be aware of the activity of the mind. Do not cheat anyone; do not deprive anyone of their honour or credit. Do not criticise or condemn anyone. Remember that the universe is open; your own thoughts will bring you justice and accordingly, you will receive the fruits of your own actions!

Practical suggestions to move on the path of *shreya*

1. Take care of your thoughts; every thought that you think is a seed you sow in the field of your life. Therefore, have good thoughts, God-thoughts. As the wise saying goes, "What you think, you become."

    Think positive! Let me suggest a simple therapy to you: for the next 24 hours, starting now, you must resolve to think and speak positively, optimistically, hopefully about everything. No matter what your concerns relate to– your family, your work, your personal relationships, your health or your future– let your thoughts be positive or nothing!

2. Learn to rejoice in whatever God's Will brings to you. Accept every incident and accident as God's Will. In the measure in which we accept His Will, in that measure we are guided to make the right choice.

    There was a man who suffered from cancer. His wife and children, his near and dear ones were shaken. His friends were deeply concerned, but this young man did not despair. He was firm in his faith and said, "I have cancer, but cancer does not have me." With his courage, he soon emerged victorious, amazing the doctors with his rapid recovery.

    Every experience in life can make you bitter or better. The choice is yours.

3. Cultivate the attitude of gratitude. I read of a man who for one morning every month pretends to be blind. He wakes without opening his eyes, fumbles his way to his kitchen to make coffee, then heads off to the bathroom to shower and brush his teeth. He eats a bowl of cold cereal, dresses himself, and doesn't open his eyes until he gets behind the wheel of his car to go to work. He does this so he can live in gratitude of the many gifts in his life, least among them, the gift of sight.

    A man once told me the motto of his life is, "Think and Thank". When we think of all God's favours, we naturally become thankful.

4. Offer all that you do to the Lord. This is the true *yajna*, or offering that Sri Krishna recommends to us in the Gita. Whatever you think, whatever you do, whatever you eat, whatever you say or do, make it an offering unto Him! When you begin to practise this ideal in deeds of daily life, you will never think or say or do anything that is unworthy of the Lord.

5. Serve as many as you can, on as many occasions as you can, in as many ways as you can, and as long as you can. We are here to serve each other. It is the spirit of service that connects us with others.

6. Live in the moment. The past is gone forever. You cannot bring it back. The future you cannot avoid. Your present is always unrestrained. When things get hectic, try to be centred. It is only in this moment that we are our perfect selves.

7. Choose happiness! As each new day dawns, we face a choice– we can choose to be happy, healthy, helpful, and positive that day. Or we can choose to be dull, depressed, miserable, selfish, and negative. The moment we awake, we begin to make choices.

We can choose what we like! It is through the choices we make that we learn to become responsible for the results that incur. If we make the right choices, we will grow in health, happiness, and vitality. If our choices are faulty, we pay a heavy price for them; we suffer from disease, loss of energy, loss of vitality, loss of creativity and loss of enthusiasm. In this manner, we try not to repeat our mistakes, by learning and attempting to make better and more beneficial choices in the future.

Choose right! Choose God!

Mantras for Peace of Mind

A mantra is a sacred utterance; it is especially associated with India's great ancient scripture– the Vedas– which are a collection of hymns and sacred utterances that have survived for millennia through oral transmission. Thus, a mantra is linked with oral utterance; its special powers are in the depth of its meaning as much as in the sound vibrations it produces in oral recital. Many people believe that there is a power associated with the mantra which can bring about a spiritual transformation.

Mantras are brief, compact and powerful spiritual formulae through which we evoke from within us the deepest and the best. They enable us to transcend negative emotions and become rooted in our essential Self.

How did mantras originate?

Our ancient *Vedic* mantras were not composed or written by any particular sage or scholar. Mantras are not simply syllables or words, but melodic phrases created by mystic sounds, usually mathematically structured meters that were revealed to rishis or seers while in deep states of meditation. These mantras have been handed down from guru to disciple for thousands of years. Our gurus have taught us that mantras can discipline our entire consciousness and open the gates to higher awareness.

What is *japa*?

Japa is constant repetition of a mantra or the Name Divine, with concentration, devotion and deep faith. This form of dedicated repetition has a cleansing and purifying effect on our *antah karan*, or inner instrument. Therefore does Kabir tell us that *naam japa* made his heart so pure that the Lord started chanting his name and following him! In other words, *japa* had brought him close to divinity, to his true Self!

Japa calms the mind and aids concentration. It is said that after intense, continuous practice, the repetition goes on in one's mind without conscious effort, even during work and sleep, as a sort of constant spiritual awareness.

Japa inspires, awakens, and enhances the practice of *Bhakti Yoga*. Through the mystic power that is inherent in the Name or the mantra, it also gives rise to divine energy, grace, and *shakti*. Like the purifying power of fire, *japa* also has the capacity to burn all the karmic residues of our past sins and negative karmas, leaving us in a state of higher consciousness that is close to true bliss, or *Sat Chit Ananda*.

Three distinct types of mantra *japa*

1. ***Saguna* mantras** are those mantras addressed to God 'with form or attribute'. Many of them address a specific deity or aspect of the Divine, such as Krishna, Rama, Shiva or Devi. For example, *Om Namo Bhagavate Vasudevaya*.

2. ***Nirguna* mantras** have no form or attribute and are based on the formless Divine. Examples are '*Om*' and '*Soham*'– I am He.

3. ***Bija*, or seed mantras** are single-syllable sounds whose verbal meaning is not available to us without initiation. They work through the power and energy of sound-vibrations and are closely related to the *chakras*– energy centers– within the body.

Japa also takes three forms: chanted aloud, whispered in a low voice, or uttered in the silence of the heart within. Whichever form of *japa* we practise, the benefits we reap will be many: peace of mind, tranquillity, increased concentration, positive energy levels and freedom from fear and anxiety.

Mantras are for all of us

Many people think that mantra *japa*, or silent chanting is meant only for *abhyasis* and *sadhakas* (those taking up a spiritual discipline). But the truth is that we do not have to confine *japa* or repetition of the Name Divine to a special ritual, bound by rules and regulations. As we become habituated to *japa*, it becomes such a natural part of our life, that it is no longer a restricted or exclusive activity meant for certain places and certain times. It comes as naturally to us as breathing, and does not even interfere with our daily duties and activities. Whether you are driving, walking, cooking, cleaning or attending to your work, *japa* goes on in your mind, uninterrupted. But this state of habitual *japa* can be attained only after long and sustained practice of intensive repetition. Therefore, I often ask my friends, "If, while praying, we can think of worldly matters, why can't we think of God when we are attending to worldly matters?"

Significance of mantras for the common man

Repeating mantras is equivalent to calling on God or communicating with Him directly.

It is not a prayer which is being addressed to any power outside of us, but instead touches a chord within our deepest Self. By repeating the mantras we are merging ourselves with the source of all strength, joy and love.

Initially the effect of the mantra is experienced on the surface level. Constant repetition creates new grooves within the subconscious, giving rise to a continuous flow of the mantra even in one's sleep. No longer is there any need to repeat it consciously. The mantra goes on unendingly within your very depths.

Repeat the mantra relentlessly, till it unites with your consciousness and you become firmly established in it, with your heart flooded by its Light. At this stage we are filled with an inexplicable sense of safety and security.

What are the benefits of chanting these sacred mantras?

Though there are too many to enumerate, let me touch very briefly on just a few:

1. First and foremost, are the rare and precious gifts of peace of mind, calmness and tranquillity, and freedom from needless tension and anxiety.

2. The secure feeling of linking up with a Power that is higher than us; the mature understanding that we have our place in the vast cosmic order that is controlled like a Divine clockwork.

3. The power to conquer negative thinking and lower-sense desires.

4. The generation of a new spiritual energy that can neutralise past *samskaras* or tendencies and clear the mind of accumulated *vaasanas* or desires which drag us down through the endless cycle of birth-death-rebirth.

5. Constant chanting/repetition/remembrance of the mantra takes you closer to God– and this feeling cannot be described in words; it has to be experienced!

6. Each mantra, properly chanted with devotion and faith, helps us achieve the fourfold goals of this human life– *dharma, artha, kama,* and *moksha.*

Naam smaran, mantra *japa, kirtan* and *dhyana* are at the very foundation of *abhyasa.* Together, they quieten the agitated mind, cleaning it of all its impurities, leaving us calm and serene to enter into meditation.

Marriage

Marriage is not just an institution, it is a sacrament, a sacred union. It was after centuries of experience that the wise ones of ancient times formulated the rules of marriage.

The word for the married state in our ancient Sanskrit language is *grihasta ashrama*. Marriage is an *ashrama*– a place of discipline, not a pleasure hunting ground. Marriage is not a license. It is at once a discipline and a responsibility. In marriage, two persons– a man and a woman– offer the whole of their mind, body, and feelings to each other. They do not live for self alone: they live for each other.

The purpose of marriage

Men and women were created by God so that they could form one complete whole. So it is that God endowed men with certain qualities and women with complementary qualities. By themselves, neither man nor woman are complete. Men have strength, determination, energy, vigour, guts. Women have great sensibility, spiritual aspirations, a spirit of sympathy, service and sacrifice. Men rely on their intellect. Women have intuition. Rudyard Kipling said, "A woman's guess is much more accurate than a man's certainty." By themselves, man and woman are both incomplete. Each needs the other. Each has to learn much from the other.

Marriage is also fundamental to civilised society, for it promotes communities, develops lineage and links the past with the future, by encouraging parents and children to perpetuate family traditions with *shraddha*, or devotion.

Hindu *shastras* emphasise the value of *grihasta ashrama* as fundamental to the well-being of society. Members of the other three *ashramas* (*brahmacharya, vanaprastha,* and *sannyasa*) depend on the *grihasta*– householder– for sustenance and support. They need the *grihasta's* help to carry out their duties. As for the *grihasta,* he is permitted to earn his living by the right means in order to support his family, raise his children, and perform acts of charity and compassion that assist others in the three *ashramas*.

Saints and sages refer to the life of the *grihasta* as *jivayajna*– a life-long saga of service and sacrifice for family and society.

Another Sanskrit term for marriage is *vivaha*, which literally means "what supports or carries". The *vivaha* ceremony thus creates a union which supports and sustains a man and woman throughout their married life in the pursuit of *dharma*– righteousness.

A successful marriage

Success in marriage is much more than finding the right person. I find myself rather amused when I hear young people talk about finding Mr. Right or Miss Right and the 'chemistry' that will ignite a spark when they come across this 'right' person.

Love must not be confounded with physical sensation or sexual attraction. These are not enough to make a marriage successful. This is why I urge my young friends not to *fall* in love– but to *rise* in true love!

A wise man said, "In marriage, *being* the right person is far more important than finding the right person!"

Some people believe that making money is the best way to ensure a successful marriage. Both men and women fall prey to this fallacy– for it is indeed a false belief to imagine that money can ensure happiness in marriage. Nor can parity in status, education or wealth lead to a successful marriage. It requires love, commitment, understanding, patience, and forgiveness to make a marriage successful. Both partners must enter into the sanctified relationship understanding its great potential and its deep significance, knowing that they have chosen to live together, to bring out the best in each other and to make each other as happy as possible.

Every successful, happy marriage is a miracle of love

I know dozens of men and women who are alive today, who have been rescued from near-certain death by the miraculous power of love. Despite the troubled times we live in, it is still very common to come across people who have succeeded in making their marriage work– 'silver' medallists who have completed 25 years, 'goldies' who have crossed the 50-year mark. They are a living testimony to the remarkable fact that marital love can grow, endure and triumph against all odds.

Love and respect are essential in marriage

Human relationships flounder when mutual respect is lacking. Marriages fail when companionship and understanding are absent in the partners. Therefore, I urge husbands to respect their wives, and wives to respect their husbands. Give one another the freedom to be themselves, to express themselves, and assert their unique identity! When there is complete understanding, respect and affection, all marriages become 'love-marriages' in the true sense of the phrase.

In a happy and successful marriage, the husband and wife must seek to bring out the best in each other. After all, they have been brought together in the sacred bonds of marriage according to His Divine plan. They should therefore help each other grow, evolve, and unfold their highest potential. If this is highlighted as the goal of marriage, love and harmony will prevail in the home. When this is lost sight of, love soon turns into disillusion, and the partners fail to get the best out of their marriage.

Happily married

Let me pass on to you ten practical suggestions. I sometimes refer to them as the ten commandments of marriage. The best way to make marriage last is to put it first.

1. The very first commandment is, avoid the next quarrel. If one of you is in a mood to quarrel, the other one should be patient. His or her turn will come at the right time, but both should not lose their temper at the same time.

2. The second commandment of marriage is, be a good listener. Listen to what the other person has to say. We like to talk but are not prepared to listen. Let us be good listeners.

3. The third commandment of marriage is, appreciate your spouse. Everyone loves to be appreciated. Do not find fault with your spouse when you are in the midst of other people. When we appreciate others, we help to draw out the best in them.

4. The fourth commandment is, keep your love fresh! Successful marriage is falling in love, again and again, with the same person. After marriage, spouses take each other for granted.

5. The fifth commandment is, do not expect perfection from each other. No man or woman is ever perfect. It was Jesus who said, "Call me not perfect. Alone the Father in heaven is perfect!" Marriage involves two imperfect human beings joining together. Accept your spouse for what he or she is, not for what he or she would be, could be, or should be.

6. The sixth commandment is, be a good forgiver. To make marriage a success, to make it a source of happiness and harmony, you have to forgive much. It is the prerogative of marriage to give and give and give– and forgive– and never be tired of giving and forgiving. Never bring up a mistake of the past.

7. The seventh commandment of marriage is, you must be patient, loving, understanding, kind and true to each other.

8. The eighth commandment is, develop a healthy sense of humour. If two people have to live with each other, they must develop a healthy sense of humour. They must learn to laugh and make each other laugh.

9. The ninth commandment is, if ever there is a misunderstanding, do not hide your feelings. Do not hesitate in discussing whatever is in your heart, freely and without fear.

10. The tenth and the most important commandment is, every day, you must find time to sit together and praise the Lord and thank Him for having brought the two of you together.

Materialism

This is a material world we live in, but we must never lose sight of the fact that we are essentially spiritual beings; our real Self is the immortal *atman*, which is above and beyond all material desires!

Materialism is attachment to worldly wealth. It is the tendency to consider material possessions and physical comfort as more important than spiritual values.

The choice is ours!

These are the options before each one of us– to aspire for spiritual wealth or to chase after the material world. You have two options– be of the world, be worldly; or be of the Spirit, and turn your back upon worldly desires. The choice is yours, either to enjoy the luxuries of the world or to make friends with the One who ever abides, who faileth not. You can go out into the world, and struggle hard for name, fame, position, power, wealth, and status. Or you can detach from the world and invite the Almighty to fill your heart with Divine love.

You have to choose between the two paths– the easy, tempting, alluring, worldly path which may give you power and wealth, but which will lead you to unhappiness and discontent; or the difficult, thorny and painful spiritual path, the path of yearning and intense aspiration, which will lead you to Ultimate Bliss! For as sure as the sun rises in the East, it will lead you to the Realm of Light!

God– or the world

Sadhu Vaswani sang in his immortal *Nuri* song:

Two cannot dwell in one heart,
The World and God.
O jignasu! Abandon your attachment
To the world.
Awake, Arise! Give place for only One
In your heart.

This verse encapsulates a great lesson. There is place only for One in your heart. As the saying goes, you cannot ride two horses– that of the world and that of God. Therefore, the Bible tells us: You cannot serve two masters– Mammon and God.

One thing is for sure, you cannot divide your heart into two. You cannot partition it, and say, "Okay, one side I will reserve for the luxuries of the world, and on the other side, I will make room for the Almighty, the Illumined One." Lord Jesus, more than two thousand years ago, had said the same thing, "You cannot serve two masters at the same time!" Hence, choose your master, for the choice is yours.

Success is not measured by material things alone

Many of us are apt to equate happiness and success with money, material wealth, and possessions. This is sheer ignorance. We imagine that celebrity film stars and rich industrialists must be the most contented and happy, carefree people in the world. Alas! This is far from the truth. These so-called billionaires and trillionaires live with permanent stress, insecurities, and anxieties that would drive ordinary mortals to depression and frustration!

You cannot be happy just because you own the best stocks and bonds; you cannot be at peace because you own a fleet of yachts or private jets. Jesus uttered nothing but the truth when he said that it is easier for a camel to enter the eye of a needle than for a rich man to enter the gates of heaven!

Socrates was one of those rare breed of men who refused to be trapped by the lure of material possessions. He taught that if men were truly wise, they would not be obsessed with wealth. Determined to practise what he preached, he did not even wear shoes.

However, Socrates loved to visit the marketplace and gaze contentedly at the vast abundance of all that was on display. When someone asked him what drew him to the marketplace, his reply was, "I love to go there and discover how many things I am perfectly happy without."

I wonder what our modern advertising professionals and marketing executives would have to say to that! These people are constantly persuading us to try this, buy that or use the other so that we can be happy. Millions are spent on advertising budgets which assault our eyes and ears talking about the latest products without which we just cannot be happy– if they are to be believed, that is!

If happiness and peace could be bought from stores, all of us would be out shopping!

What do you possess?

When Prophet Muhammad (peace be upon him) was talking to a group of his disciples, he asked each one of them to tell him what they possessed.

The first one, Hazrat Usman, replied, "I have a wife and children, some wealth, and quite a few worldly possessions, as is natural for a man in my position."

The others too, answered on similar lines, until it was the turn of Hazrat Ali. Ali declared, "Master, my only possessions are God and the Prophet. Save these, I have nothing!"

Prophet Muhammad said to the others, "Ali knows the truth, for worldly possessions matter very little. We cannot take them with us to the world beyond. Attachment to them leads only to pain and suffering."

"This is the lot of those who love the world. But true devotees of God have withdrawn their attachment completely from the world. They are always engaged in contemplation of the Beloved. They have transcended the region of births and deaths."

What can money buy for you?

Sadhu Vaswani cautioned us against the allurements of this material world. He said, "He who runs after worldly pleasures is no different from a thirsty man trying to quench his parched throat with the salt water of the ocean! Excessive salt water will only damage the intestines; it may even result in death." Our condition is no better. We try desperately to satisfy our desires, but our desires keep on multiplying and there is no end in sight to extinguish the ever-burning fires of *trishna*!

We will all do well to remember that it is futile to run after material things. Even if we manage to accumulate wealth, we must bear in mind that it does not really belong to us. Can we take it along with us when we leave this earth? Will it 'buy' us accommodation in heaven? How pointless then, to think that our wealth belongs to us! We are merely trustees of worldly wealth that is placed in our hands. Everything belongs to Him, the Creator. The best use to which we can put our wealth is to spend it all judiciously, in the service of the poor and the broken ones.

Do not get entangled in materialism

There was a king who received great comfort and solace from the wise words of a holy man. Grateful beyond words, he wanted to express his appreciation, and offered him an expensive gift– of a pair of golden slippers.

The holy man smiled. He wanted to make the king understand that worldly gifts were unsuitable to a man of God. "O king," he said, "If I accept this gift, you must also give me fine clothes to match these golden slippers."

"And so I will," promised the king readily. "You will have royal robes studded with gems and precious stones."

"But your Highness," said the holy man, "Would it not appear ridiculous if I wore royal robes and golden slippers and move on my own feet from place to place?"

"That can be easily settled," said the king. "I will give you the best Arabian mare from my stable, for you to ride on."

"Hmm," said the holy man thoughtfully. "Would it not be strange for a man to have all this– and lack a beautiful abode, a lovely wife, and servants?"

"All this, I shall arrange for you to have," the king assured him.

"But then sire," said the holy man, "If I should have a son, and if he should chance to die, will you bear my grief and weep instead of me?"

"How could I do that for you?" said the king, startled out of his fit of generosity. "You must bear your own grief, you must weep for yourself."

"Then, O king," said the *sanyasi*, "I will not take the golden slippers, the golden robes, the Arabian mare, the beautiful house and servants, or the lovely wife! I do not wish to be led into pain and misery."

The king understood the message. He realised that material things, identification with the physical, can never lead to true joy. What we need, more than material wealth, is the wealth of the Spirit– for it offers us the freedom of liberation from *maya!*

Sadly, many of us remain trapped in the entanglements of the world. This is true of every *sansaari jeeva*– he is intoxicated with the pleasures, possessions, and powers of this world, with worldly love and longing– for 'I', 'me', and 'mine'. He must detoxify himself of this *maya* and enter into another kind of intoxication– he must lose himself, nay, drown himself in the intoxication of God's love.

Is this possible for us?

What is wrong with earning money? What is wrong in accumulating wealth for the security of our loved ones, you might ask. Nothing– if we are able to be content with what we possess. But unfortunately, we do not stop there. We look at others, we compare ourselves with them, and we are unsatisfied if we have less. We are haunted by the greed for more, more, and more!

Many young men and women ask me, "When we live in the world, how can we ignore it? Is it possible for us to turn our back upon life?" Yes. We live in the world, and we should have a zest for living. Life is God's greatest gift to us, and we should not be dead to this great gift. Treasure your life! Cherish this beautiful world and all of God's Creation! Therefore, love everyone. Love everything around you. Give the love of your beautiful heart to one and all. But do not allow yourself to be mired in materialism! Do not be excessively attached to the world. Love– Yes; attachment– No! Love without attachment– let this be the guiding star of your life. If you are attached to worldly things, your very attachment will sooner or later drag you into the dark pool of turbulence and passion.

The fatal pull of materialism

Make no mistake! Material pleasures can exercise their fatal attraction on many of us!

First and foremost, there is the desire for sense-gratification. This is what Sri Ramakrishna referred to when he spoke of *kamini*, the personification of sense-indulgence, as one whom we must guard against.

We are told that the devil once called for a meeting of all its associates. It was a stock-taking session to determine which of them could wreak the greatest havoc on mankind.

Anger, jealousy, greed, and envy were present, among others. Each one boasted of his numerous victims. Soon, a heated argument ensued as to who, among them, could cause the most damage.

Impurity won, hands down. Conferring the dubious distinction upon him, the devil remarked, "He is the one with the sharpest sword, the deadliest weapon. All he has to do is to sow a single thought of impurity in the mind, and that will take care of the rest."

When lust, desire, greed, and craving dominate our minds, how can we embark upon any spiritual practice?

Secondly, there is the desire for wealth, for material possessions. When we concentrate our efforts and attention on making money, we often lose the ability to concentrate on anything else. We all know the story of King Midas. He thought he had all that he could ever wish for, when everything that he touched turned to gold. He learned the hard way that gold could not appease his hunger!

Thirdly, there is the desire for power, position and fame. Alas! Some of us stoop very low to gain power, position, and authority. After all, why are graft, corruption, and bribery so rampant in the world today? Why are flattery, falsehood, and hypocrisy so prevalent among the mighty and the powerful? Such practices only point to the lowest elements in human nature. They taint our minds and hearts and impede our spiritual progress– the only progress that matters.

Let us but ask ourselves: What is it that we seek through wealth, power, and sense-indulgence? Where will they lead us eventually? Of what avail is earthly greatness and worldly wealth when we know that the call can come any time for us– and we shall be reduced to an urn full of dust and ashes!

Break free from the clutches of materialism

1. When you take a pause and look at the world around you, you discover its beauty and joy afresh! Darkness can make you appreciate the beauty of candlelight and moon light. It is also a fact that an excess of artificial light creates headache and stress. So get out of your AC offices and homes. Feel the warmth of the morning sunshine and the gentle breeze!

2. Sometimes, we allow ourselves to be trapped by our routine. We allow ourselves to fall into a rut of our own making, and think that we cannot get out. "This is my life," we think; or, "This is my job… I have no options." We become tired, depressed, and cease to pay attention to our own feelings and inner aspirations. We are not listening to our hearts…

Materialism

Some years ago, there was a talk in corporate circles of something called a 'downshift'. That is, a slowing down of the pace of life– an alternative lifestyle sought by busy young executives who suddenly realised that they did not want to spend the rest of their lives just making money. Thus, strange 'downshifts' came to pass.

A thirty-year-old couple who were high powered financial executives discovered the joys of cooking together. They gave up their lucrative jobs in a London bank and opened a cozy cafeteria in a seaside town. They laughed, played, and worked together; they cooked and served tasty meals; they chatted with their customers and charmed everyone with their 'personal touch'. They never ever looked back on their profitable careers.

A wealthy man from France took a vacation in a Himalayan resort. The peace, tranquillity and the clean mountain air so appealed to him that he decided to live and work there as a ski instructor.

A research scientist from an American university happened to hear an Indian spiritual teacher talking about meditation and silent prayer. The scientist felt his inner being transformed. He accepted the teacher as his guru and became a devoted volunteer in his *ashrama*.

These people listened to their inner voices. They were not carried away by the dazzle of money and by their jet setting executive lifestyles. They thought about what they wanted out of life. They asked themselves what they would like to do, what they would love doing, and they followed the dictates of their heart. Money, power, position were all secondary.

3. You do not have to quit your job to make a change. Think of the activities you enjoy. Do you like writing? Then begin to write short stories, poems, and articles. Do you enjoy singing? Join a music group and take lessons in classical instrumental/vocal/western music. Do you enjoy theatre? Join a drama group. If you love animals, volunteer to serve with Blue Cross, SPCA or a local animal shelter. Do you love reading? Offer to read for the visually disabled or to the inmates of a home for the aged. Do you love babies? Volunteer to help out at an orphanage. Do you love going to the temple? Offer to assist the devotees who throng the local temple during the peak hours. Do what you love. Find joy in activities that appeal to your heart, and not merely to the head.

4. Exercise your soul! Turn to nature to nurture you. Learn to spend at least a little time every day in outdoor activities– it can be something as simple as walking, or just sitting on a garden bench. Being in touch with the healing forces of nature helps to restore calm, peace,

and a sense of harmony to your life.

Many of us are trapped in the blaring noise, the glaring lights, and the mechanical routine of a demanding society. We are surrounded by the buzzing of alarms, the ringing of telephones, the clatter of the keyboard, the loud volume of the TV, the high decibels from speakers, horns, engines, cars, buses and trucks. The glare of the TV screen and artificial lighting is constantly hurting our eyes. We get up like mechanised robots and go about our daily routine listlessly.

Alas, very few of us take time to sit quietly and commune with nature. I know people in Mumbai and Chennai who do not go to the seaside even once a year. I know many Bangaloreans who have never taken a walk in the city's famous Cubbon Park. I know people in Pune who have never explored the green and lovely hill tracks which surround the city.

When you turn to nature, you rediscover yourself. When you turn your back to the noise and commotion of the city life, you are able to capture the beautiful silence of the soul within you.

Mind Matters

More precious than gold and silver, greater than the greatest wealth, greater than any asset, is the mind. It is a priceless gift that God has bestowed on human beings. In your mind, you have a 24-hour friend. You may be alone, helpless or in distress, but your mind is ever ready to help you and guide you to overcome any situation. It is your precious friend, an invaluable asset. Therefore, you must use it in the right way. Do not let the mind be your master. Let it be your servant in the service of God and suffering humanity.

Significant are the words of the Upanishad: "The mind alone is the cause of man's bondage. The mind is, also an instrument of man's liberation."

The brain has been called a "fabulous mechanism". It is the power behind our mind! The brain is about the size of half a grape-fruit but is truly a most wonderful organ. It is capable of recording 800 memories per second for 75 years without exhausting itself. It is a storehouse of between ten billion and one hundred billion pieces of information. Even the most powerful computers in the world have memories that hold only a few million items of accessible information. The human brain retains everything that it takes in and never forgets anything. Even though we don't recall all the information received, everything is on a permanent file in our brain.

A few years ago I read this: if a computer were to be built to match the brain's potential, it would occupy space comparable to the size of one of the tallest buildings in the world– the Empire State Building– and need one billion watts of electrical power to run. The cost would work out to an astronomical figure.

It is a real wonder, that the mind is such a powerful instrument in our lives!

The mind is one of God's most amazing gifts to man. Scientists tell us that we use only one-fiftieth of the brain power available to us. We must train our minds and use its tremendous power for our own good and the good of others.

How exactly does intuition or sixth sense as we call it, work?

Intuition is the gift of knowing things, understanding things which the mind does not know or understand. Our knowledge is based on what the senses tell us and on what the mind decides. But that may not be the whole truth. The senses very often betray us. The mind often jumps to wrong conclusions. It is then that intuition takes over. Intuition knows, intuition understands the truth of our situation, as it really is. In intuition, women excel over men. Men have tuition but they don't have intuition. They have sight but they don't have insight.

Shampooing the mind

Shampooing means cleansing. We need to cleanse our minds, we need to unclutter our minds ever so often. Our minds are full of wrong thinking, wrong ideas. The minds of so many of us are negative. We must cleanse them of their negativity. To do this, we must dig into our consciousness and cleanse ourselves of all those rotten thoughts that hold us captive today– thoughts of impurity, selfishness, greed, lust and hatred.

Our minds should be clean and uncluttered. It is only then that we can hope to be happy. With all those negative, harmful thoughts within us, how can we be at peace with ourselves? When I was young, whenever unwanted thoughts would enter my mind, even if I was sitting in a classroom and the teacher was lecturing, I would immediately slap myself. My classmates would ask me what the matter was. I would say it was a mosquito. I was talking about an internal mosquito. Therefore, whenever you find a negative or an undesirable thought waking up in the mind within you, slap yourself immediately.

Sadhu Vaswani, as a young boy, used to keep a pin with himself. Whenever he found an unwelcome thought waking up within him, he would just pierce the pin into his flesh until the body felt so much pain that the mind would cry out, "Forgive me, forgive me! I will not think such a thought again."

Another excellent way of shampooing the mind is to think good thoughts, God-thoughts or chant the Name Divine silently in the heart.

What is the difference between the soul and the mind?

The mind is an instrument of cognition, of knowing things, comprehending the material world. The soul is a ray of God, that which you essentially are. The mind is an instrument with which we learn and grasp things. The soul is immortal, the mind is mortal. The mind is discursive, the soul is synergic. The soul integrates everything, but the mind analyses.

We need the help of the mind in doing our work on the physical plane– that is why we have brought with ourselves this instrument. Out of God emanate many rays, every ray is a soul. This is what makes all of us one. The soul is universal. The mind is individual, the mind individualises, differentiates and separates, but the soul unites.

Inner beauty

Inner beauty, I believe, is beauty of thought, aspirations, prayers. If our thoughts are pure, if our aspirations are pure and beautiful, and desires likewise pure and beautiful, we are beautiful within.

Every impure impulse, impure thought, impure emotion that stirs within us, spoils our interior beauty. Therefore, we must turn to prayer. Keep on praying again and again if you want to grow beautiful within.

All these years, our minds have been wandering, doing nothing, gathering nothing. Instead of letting the mind wander after useless and irrelevant things, pick up a beautiful thought of a great one. It may be a *sloka* from the Bhagavad Gita or a line from the *Sant Bani*, the *Gurbani* or the Bible. Let us keep on repeating the great thought and try to enter into the depths of the meanings of the words we repeat. This will help considerably in controlling the wandering of the mind.

What causes the wandering and turbulence of the mind?

The three qualities at play in nature– *tamas*, *rajas*, and *sattva*– are also at play in the mind. *Tamas* is total lethargy and ignorance. *Rajas* is the opposite extreme– too much activity and restlessness. *Sattva*, the desirable state, is tranquillity– when both sides are well-balanced. When we achieve this state of focussed activity and complete mental relaxation, we achieve stillness of the mind. When we are in a state of imbalance, that is when the mind is disturbed, and loses its equilibrium.

The root cause of this wandering of the mind and soul is alienation from the Divine Will, separateness from the source of all life. We keep ourselves apart from God, the Creator of this universe. How can the lotus bloom without water? How can the *rajnigandha* spread its fragrance without moonlight? How can man ever be happy without God?

Selfish thoughts are at the core of forces that disturb the mind. Selfish thoughts pave the way for stress, worry, anxiety, disappointment and fear. These thoughts need not be suppressed– they should be replaced with positive, selfless ones.

Let me share with you a beautiful prayer in the words of my Gurudev Sadhu Vaswani:

Far away from you, I have wandered.
Show me the way, shower your grace on me.
Wherever I am, wherever I may be, whatever I may do,
In every thought, in every word, keep me close to your heart!

Why is it necessary to control the mind?

Many people often ask me why it is necessary to control the mind. "What's the use of going blank?" They want to know, "Is it necessary for me to become without feeling like a stone? Shouldn't I care and feel for people? Shouldn't I be conscious of my responsibilities to others?"

Certainly, you must feel for others, and feel for yourself. It is not recommended that you stop thinking or feeling, when you learn to control the mind. When you have conquered the mind, when you have achieved inner tranquillity, you will begin to create new, beautiful, positive thoughts and feelings. Once this is achieved, even if negative thoughts arise in the mind, they cannot cause ripples in your inner calm and peace. This is why spiritually awakened men do not suffer from fear, worry, anxiety or restlessness.

"The mind is its own place," wrote Milton, "and in itself, can create a Heaven of Hell, a Hell of Heaven." How true! The mind can create strife and conflict; it can also create peace. If we are to live a life of peace and freedom from fear, we must discover peace within ourselves. We must be still within the mind.

It is no easy task to calm the mind. A mind that is wandering and restless is like a disturbed lake; waves are constantly rising on its surface, and it is unable to reflect the stillness of the sky. When we control our thoughts, we still the mind, and it becomes capable of beautiful, elevating reflections– reflections of the Divine Light within us.

There is one thing we can all do to stop the wandering mind in its tracks, to train the mind in *ekagrita* or one-pointed focus: it is to develop love for God. As we all know, when we love something or someone deeply, our mind constantly gravitates towards that person. We have to apply the same principle to mind control; we have to cultivate love for God in our hearts. I truly believe that inner peace and stillness is not possible until we awaken love in our hearts, the utmost love for God.

Let your mind be a friend!

It is essential that we cultivate the subconscious mind so that its tremendous power can be harnessed for our spiritual growth.

1. Always entertain positive thoughts. Never harbour thoughts of jealousy, hatred or lust.

2. Do not react emotionally to things that happen.

3. Never make any negative suggestions in regard to what you want to be. Thus, for instance, never say, *I have a bad memory*. This will only lead to loss of memory. Rather say, *my memory is improving*.

4. Let love and forgiveness be the law of your life. Many types of illnesses are caused by intense hatred and resentment.

5. Read books, and if at all you must watch TV, watch programmes that inspire and uplift you rather than those that feature violence, sex, crime and other acts of viciousness. This is especially important in the case of young people.

Man came to the earth as a pilgrim, but has become a wanderer. Even in our spiritual quest, we wander from creed to creed, from one school of thought to another, and are filled with unrest. We move to temples and churches and places of pilgrimage, and meet with disappointment. For, not until we turn within, will we find that which we are seeking. Truth is within! Wisdom is within! The source of all strength is within! Therefore turn within!

Mother Earth

The Earth Spirit is benign to all; it is benevolent to all living creatures– animals, birds, insects and human beings. It sustains all forests, waters, fields, mountains, and rivers, and provides for all for their needs. My Gurudev would often urge us: Be like the earth, be humble as the earth, be ever forgiving, and be ever giving. Ceaselessly it absorbs the negative energies we generate and converts it into positive energy. That is why it is said: Keep touching the earth, it will purify you. In fact, the Indian tradition of *Sashtang Namaskar* as in a temple, bending on our knees and bowing down as in a *Gurudwara*, or sitting on our heels in prayer as in a mosque, are variations of touching the earth.

The earth has the magical power of transformation. As the saying goes: Give earth garbage and it transforms it into flowers. Earth is a great forgiver. You can hack it, dig and burn it, and yet it does not punish. On the contrary, earth gives back corn, vegetables, and fruits. Our earth is sacred, and every grain of sand, every drop of water, every wisp of wind that blows over it is sacred. For this self-sustainer, self-re-creator is the manifestation of the Divine. The perfect symbiosis of the tangible and the non-tangible, every particle of nature is not only about Science and Geology and Geography, but about Spirituality and the manifestation of the Divine in all Creation!

Earth is a Divine Mother

Reverence for the earth opens a new door to life on earth. Guru Nanak tells us: "*Pawan guru, paani pita, mata dharat mahat!*" It means: Air is the guru, water is the father, and earth is the mother. Wind and water are like the guru, as they purify the person. Water cleanses and wind blows away the accumulated filth. Earth is the mother because it is ever giving, ever forgiving, ever loving.

In my old fashioned, artless way, I have referred to her as "Mother Earth". But I doubt if we have the right to call ourselves her children anymore! We are actually a vital component of God's good earth, and it is our sacred obligation to preserve and protect this planet that God has given to us as a habitat. Alas, we live upon earth as if there is no tomorrow– as if we care nothing for unborn generations who will continue to live here long after we are gone!

As the crown of God's Creation, we should have been guardians, protectors, wardens of Planet Earth. Instead, we have exploited her shamelessly, selfishly and O, so foolishly.

Is this the way we treat our Mother?

"Verily, the whole world is the body of God," says the *Vishnu Purana*. When our scriptures talk of 33 million gods, they refer to every aspect of Creation which reflects and emanates God's glory! Are not the oceans, seas, rivers, mountains and forests, the fields of rice and wheat and corn, the trees and plants and flowers and all the creatures that breathe the breath of life, embodiments of *Purushottama,* the Lord Supreme? Therefore, the *Atharva Veda* reminds us: "Earth is my Mother; Her son am I; and Heaven my Father: May He fill us with plenty…"

The *Vedic* hymn also describes the Earth as *Vasudha,* for she harbours great natural wealth; she is *Hiranya Vaksha,* for there are vast gold and rich mineral reserves in her bosom; she is *Visvambara,* for she links us with the rest of the universe; and she is to all Hindus, *Bhumata,* or Mother Earth. We attribute qualities of patience, forbearance, tolerance and compassion to this Universal Mother who sustains and supports us and all other forms of life, while we trample upon her, desecrate her, and exploit her ruthlessly! I often hear environmental activists talk of the plunder of forests and hills and even of the rape of the earth– these may be disturbing words, but we cannot deny an element of harsh truth in them!

The sanctity of nature

The Upanishads tells us: *Isha Vasyam Idam Sarvam.* All that is, is a vesture of the Lord. The rivers, the hills, the woods, trees, plants, flowers and grass, the blue skies, the sun, the moon and the stars, the people, the places– all that you see around you, is the vesture of the Lord. Lift the veil, and you will behold God in everything you see. God watches you every moment, wherever you turn.

How wonderful is it that the Lord is to be seen and felt in every aspect of His magnificent Creation! We perceive the beauty of the created universe every moment that our eyes are open– but alas, we do not behold Him, for our eyes are veiled by *ajnana,* ignorance.

We fail to realise that He is with us, He is in all that we see, and that He is watching us, watching over us all the time! When man attains this state of profound awareness, he no longer looks upon the created universe as *maya,* or illusion. To him, the entire world is God's *leela* – the play of His Divine Will. In his heart arises the fervent prayer:

Jidhar dekhta hoon, udhar tu hi tu hai
Ki har shai mein jalwa, tera hubahoo hai

Beloved, I see you wherever I turn!

Sri Ramakrishna would often laugh at Englishmen, who loved to spend time in woods and gardens, exclaiming, "How beautiful! How beautiful!" He pointed out how these great admirers of nature failed to look beyond the manifest beauty to the un-manifest– the Divine beauty and power of the Creator.

Alas, we live in oblivion of the Creator, when all the beauty of nature around us fails to awaken our awareness of His presence. Therefore, let the beauty of Mother Nature serve as a reminder of the Lord and His countless blessings upon us. Nature and all of humanity constantly affirms His beauty and His Divine presence to us. Blessed is the man who beholds the Lord in everything he sees, and in everyone he meets!

Let nature be our teacher

I remember, one day we were in a garden, sitting at the Lotus Feet of our Master, when he pointed to some beautiful flowers and said to us, "Look at these flowers! How beautifully they bloom! But they do it silently. Even so must you serve silently. These flowers spread their fragrance in silence. Even so must you serve in silence."

Then, pointing to the sun he said, "The sun, even as it shines, sends life-giving warmth and light to the earth. But it shines silently! And remember, there are millions, billions, perhaps trillions upon trillions of creatures whose very existence depends upon the sun– but the sun shines silently. Even thus must you serve silently!"

Nature does not practise unfair discrimination either. The same sunshine that lights up your day shines alike on the peasant and the pavement dweller. The gentle breeze that caresses the locks of the child in your arms, soothes the work-weary labourer and the frail senior citizen reclining in his chair. The rain pours on the mansion and the hutments. The sea does not 'put on' special shows for the affluent and prosperous holiday crowd. The well-heeled trekker and the humble sadhu feel uplifted by the majesty of the mountains. The dark, lovely and deep woods attract the simple seeker as well as the trained photographer and the avid bird watcher.

Heal the earth!

Today the earth needs healing. The forests are being destroyed, the mountains are being denuded and eroded. Water has become scarce; rivers have sunk. Rivers like Saraswati and many tributaries of the sacred Sindhu are lost forever. All this is happening today, but centuries ago, it has been narrated in the *Vishnu Purana,* where we have a conversation between the Earth and Lord Vishnu. Like a true selfless mother, Mother Earth appeals to Lord Vishnu. "O Lord, I am unhappy. I am unable to bear the sorrow anymore. My children are suffering, the entire humanity is passing through troubled times. Humanity is crying out to you, devotees are calling you. I am unable to bear the violence, the crying, the suffering, and anguish of human beings. O Lord! Please come to our help, because I am unable to bear the burden. Please come and redeem humanity. My Lord! Come and protect Your devotees!"

Will Lord Vishnu appear again as *Varaha* to rescue the earth from our depredations? Or will He send down the cataclysmic deluge to drown us with our Mother Earth and put an end to our violence and atrocities?

At peace with nature

We must make peace with Mother Nature. We must cultivate a symbolic relation with her–or we will hurtle down the abyss of self-destruction.

Here is the beautiful opening *sloka* of the *Shanti Suktam* from the *Atharva Veda:*

May peace prevail in the skies
May peace prevail on earth
May peace prevail in vast space
May peace prevail in the flowing river, and in plants and trees!

Mothers

A mother is the foundation as well as the centre of family life. It is my opinion that child bearing, giving birth, nurturing and mothering are not just biological functions given to a woman. I am convinced that there is something unique in their mental, emotional and psychological make up that renders women fit for these special functions. It may be true that in a dark, ignorant age, these were thought to be weaknesses, even severe limitations placed on women, making them inferior. However, it is only the mother who makes those loving sacrifices that bring joy and harmony to marriage and family life.

The mother's role is that of a homemaker– this is her ultimate career. All other careers exist just for one purpose– to uphold this ultimate career.

When all is said and done, it is the mother and the mother alone who is a far superior citizen than the soldier who fights for his country.

Mothers shape future generations by tenderly rearing children, and making them useful citizens. If only we are aware of their pivotal role, the honour and vital position they hold in society, we will realise that they are the supreme assets of national life. The mother's value is higher than that of a successful statesman, businessman, artist or scientist.

When does a mother's nurturing begin?

In the Hindu way of life, love and care for the child begins even when it is in the womb. Hindus strongly believe that the mother's state of mind, her emotional environment, and her spiritual attitude during her pregnancy will influence the child in the womb. The mother-to-be must be surrounded by peace, calm, serenity and beauty; she must hear and speak holy words and prayers; and she must think pure and noble thoughts– so that she may bring forth a child with the same qualities.

Hindu mothers are also enjoined to eat *sattvic* foods during pregnancy. They are discouraged from attending needless social gatherings such as parties and receptions, and instead urged to attend *satsangs,* visit temples, and participate in *bhajan, kirtan* and *naam japa*. All these rules are simply meant to ensure that the child receives the most positive influences and vibrations while he is in the womb. These instructions also help remind the mother that the little baby she is moulding within her, is also an immortal soul– and her every word, thought and action will affect him.

Why are mothers special?

The mother is the greatest influence in her child's life– especially during the formative years, when the child is in the impressionable, moulding stage. It is at her feet, in her hands, that the child's character is shaped. The mother's life becomes a shining example which the child emulates. She can infuse in the children love for their cultural heritage, traditions and values, so that the children will always know where their roots are.

A mother's importance should never be undermined. She is the first one and the chief custodian to introduce culture and ethics to her child.

Andrew Jackson, the seventh President of the United States of America, was brought up by his widowed mother, who worked as a housekeeper to her rich relatives to give her sons a good education. This brave, selfless woman was a source of great inspiration to Andrew in his boyhood. Here are her golden words of advice to her son, who became an orphan when he was just fourteen years old:

"In this world, you must make your own way. To make your own way, you must have friends. You can make friends by being honest, and keep them by being steadfast. But, they will expect as much from you as they give to you."

"To forget an obligation or be ungrateful is a base crime. Men guilty of it sooner or later must suffer the penalty. In personal conduct, always be polite but never fawning. None will respect you more than you respect yourself."

"Avoid quarrels without yielding to imposition, but sustain your manhood always. Don't try to remedy assault, battery and defamation through the law."

"Never wound the feelings of others. Never brook wanton outrage upon your own feelings. Calmly vindicate your feelings or defend your honour. If angry at first, wait till your wrath cools before you proceed."

It is through the mother that a sense of confidence and self-esteem is instilled in the child. She is the source through which the child can fulfil his dreams. A mother can assume multiple roles and fill the gaps in a child's life, but no one can take her place. It is only a mother who can be full of hope even when she is worried, can maintain her equilibrium in the midst of chaos, and can remain solid as a rock during an emotional crisis. The natural state of a mother is that of selflessness. When she wants to scream and cry, she wails it with a smile. She stands up against any injustice and strives in every way to protect her children and keep them safe.

A mother's firmness, sweetness, fortitude, courage, patience and goodness are potent powers. Mothers are appreciated for being good listeners, and for not saying 'I told you so'. A mother is not just a person to lean on, but one who makes leaning on unnecessary. We often forget how much a mother gives and is willing to give.

'Mother' is the word akin to God, which is on the lips and in the hearts of children. Mothers are in partnership with God in giving life and providing a guiding light. They are the initiators in getting their children to know God, fear God, worship God and love God.

Mothers help us to face the world with dignity and confidence. A mother is the silken string that firmly holds the family together.

The French sculptor, Bartholdi gave 20 years of devoted effort towards sculpting the Statue of Liberty. When the time came to carve the face, Bartholdi, after examining several outstanding heroes, chose as a model for the colossal masterpiece– his own mother. Yes, a generation of true mothers can change the face of society.

One final thought…

It is said that when God was in the midst of Creation, he decided to create woman– who would be the bearer of life in the world. And he said to her: I hereby endow you with the following:

- Wisdom to recognise truth
- Courage to deflect all adversity
- Strength to move mountains
- Tenderness to take the earth to your heart
- Enthusiasm to inspire the world
- Hope for the earth which gave you birth
- Playfulness, so you can dance with your children
- Laughter that will echo through the valleys
- Tears to soothe the sorrows of life
- Hands that can work or caress
- Intuition to become what you were meant to be!

Need I say more about the value of a mother?

Mukti: The Goal of Life

What can I say to you about this ultimate goal– liberation, *moksha*, *nirvana*, at-one-ment with the Divine? It is the final freedom that truly releases us from this endless cycle of birth, death and rebirth; it is that haven of emancipation that helps us walk free from the rising, threatening, drowning waves of the ocean which our sages called *sansaar sagar*. Only *moksha* can ensure that we are freed from the bonds of persistent karma; only *moksha* can free us from the *samskaras*, the *vaasanas*, the material conditioning of birth after birth of human life that keep causing us to be born again and again.

Liberation is also self-realisation– the exhilarating, blissful experience of attaining our true identity as aspects of the Divine. It is the bliss of knowing the one truth really worth knowing, the absolute and ultimate truth, that our real home is in the Eternal; it is our right to return there once and for all, permanently, for our dear Father awaits our arrival with deep love and longing!

True liberation can only be achieved when the mind, remaining detached, does not long for or desire anything, does not grieve about or regret the loss of anything, does not reject or refuse anything, nor attempt to cling on to anything.

Tateh kim? What then?

What is the goal of life? Good education, a successful career, marriage, producing off spring and then placing the children on the same wheels, like repeated animal experiments? Is that all there is to life? Make money, get married, beget children, take care of their education– and beyond that, nothing?

"*Tateh kim? Tateh kim?*" asked Adi Shankara, centuries ago. What then? Is making money the be-all and end-all of life?

I believe every one of us realises at one stage or another, that life on this earth is transient, and that the journey of the soul must continue even after we have ceased to be on this physical plane. Even those of us who refuse to acknowledge God and dismiss the concept of the soul are mystified and intrigued by what awaits them after death. *Tateh kim?* Everyone agrees that a new chapter begins at the point of death.

What happens to us in the interim between death and rebirth? Are all souls condemned to be born again and again– caught in the cycle of birth, death and rebirth?

According to *Vedanta* wisdom, there are four possibilities open to the soul after death:

1. For one who has attained enlightenment during this life, there is total liberation from the cycle of birth and death. Such a one attains *sadyah mukti*, or instantaneous liberation and is not born again.

2. For one who has not attained liberation, but achieved purity of mind and devotion to Brahman, there is a force which pushes the soul beyond the pull of this world and towards liberation. This is *krama mukti*– gradual or sequential liberation. In this process, the soul is led along a path of Light and so attains an increasing expansion in consciousness until liberation is attained.

3. For one who has tried to live a virtuous life, but is not ready for liberation, there is a finite period of existence on the astral plane, where the astral body experiences pleasurable conditions. This is known as *swarga*. It is not liberation, but a relative experience of pleasure. This finite period is brought to an end when the soul's good karma is exhausted, and the soul is reborn into a new life.

4. For one who has accumulated no good karma at all, there is the painful fourth alternative– a period of intense suffering. But this period also comes to a close when the sinful karma is exhausted, and the soul is reborn in a new embodiment.

The four goals of life

Hinduism outlines four *purusharthas*, or goals of life: *artha, kama, dharma* and *moksha*– or, to settle for a simple translation, wealth, desire, duty and liberation. The best part of these goals is that you do not have to select any one. You can legitimately choose and pursue all four, as you evolve spiritually. It may also happen that as you achieve each goal, your consciousness may rise until you decide that ultimately, there is only one goal that matters: liberation from the bonds of karma, liberation from the continuous cycle of birth-death-rebirth.

It was a wise philosopher who said, "Life is like a house. Without *dharma*, the house has no foundation. Without *artha*, it has no walls. Without *kama*, it has no furnishings. Without *moksha*, it has no roof." In other words, all these values– *dharma, artha* and *kama* are but means to an end.

The ultimate goal of human life is *moksha* or liberation– and this requires untiring, unfailing, persistent self-effort from us. *Moksha* is not just a *purushartha* (personal goal or objective); it is *paramartha* (the ultimate goal of life). The Gita tells us that when we overcome the qualities of *tamas* and *rajas,* and grow in *sattva*– detachment and dedication to God– we are on the way to liberation. Liberation is not determined by destiny; liberation cannot be predicted by astrology or palmistry. Liberation is achieved only through self-effort and the grace of God or the guru.

How can we become aware of the purpose of this human birth?

The basic premise in Hindu thought is that there was a Divine intention, a purpose for which God ordained the Creation of the cosmos and this universe in which we live. Everything in this universe works according to a Divine plan; there is no chaos or disorder in the Divine scheme of things. Man is but a small speck, a minor component in this scheme, but he too has a purpose to fulfil in his life. That purpose is to walk the way of perfection, towards the ultimate goal of human life, which is liberation and union with the Divine Spirit.

If, as you say, the purpose for which God gave us this human birth is to seek *moksha,* union with Him, why is this liberation so difficult for us ordinary mortals?

According to the Hindu philosophy, it is only through the merits of good karma that a creature enters the human form– and this human birth is bestowed on us so that we may seek liberation, break away from the bonds of worldliness, and escape from the wheel of fire that is the circle of birth-life-death-rebirth. And yet, this human incarnation brings with it deadly enemies within!

There is a story about a blind man who found himself locked up in a hall which had 84 doors. The blind man wanted to come out of the hall. He was informed that 83 doors were closed, only one door was open. It was for him to find the open door and come out. He kept on touching the wall as he walked step by step. He came to the first door and found it closed. He moved further to the second door, to the third, and so on. He found that they were closed. Just as he arrived at the open door, there was an itching sensation on his hands, so he took them off the wall to scratch them. In the process, he passed by the open door, missing it completely.

This is our condition. We all are blind. We have had to pass through countless *janmas* (births), and now we have taken birth as human beings. This human birth can actually lead us to that open door. But, alas! Each one of us feels some itch, some desire or the other. Those deadly thieves are after us and our spiritual treasure. Some of us feel the itch to gamble; some of us are consumed by lust; some succumb to greed; some are drawn to pleasure, some to power. While satisfying our itch, this golden opportunity of the human birth slips through our fingers.

Work towards your own liberation

Many of us are apt to imagine that liberation from the bonds of karma, freedom from the cycle of birth and death, is not attainable for the likes of us. This is a defeatist, pessimistic attitude. Why wait for successive births, when liberation is possible for us sooner? If you do not liberate yourself in this lifetime, when will you do it? When we set our sights firmly on the goal, we accelerate the pace of our own spiritual evolution. This is achieved through *bhakti* (devotion), *seva*(service) and *sadhana* (practise of austerities like meditation). The most effective *sadhana* is *guru seva* and *guru bhakti*! The true purpose of our life is liberation and self-realisation– and we become aware of this only when we attain the feet of the guru. It is the guru who reveals to us our true identity– the *atman* within us.

Once we have handed ourselves over to the guru in full faith, he will see to all else– indeed, it will be his responsibility to ensure that we attain the goal of this human life!

Liberation is for all of us!

To cherish a desire for liberation; to crave for escape from the cycle of birth and death and rebirth; to desire to see the Truth and to discover one's true identity– believe me when I say, these are invaluable assets for any 'ordinary' mortals, as we often refer to ourselves! We do not have to renounce the world, nor do we have to become ascetics. But we must become pure in thought, word and deed; we must acquire detachment; we must free ourselves from excessive desires; we must cultivate love and longing for the Lord. To my mind, anyone who becomes aware that there is more to this life than physical existence, is well on his way to the Truth and thus to 'enlightenment'. If he is able to accept the conditions that life imposes on him in a spirit of equanimity; if he remains in a state of balance and *samattva*; if he accepts all that happens to him in a spirit of surrender to the Lord; if he sends out love and blessings to all people, indeed to all creatures that breathe the breath of life; if he is able to rise above grudges and resentments; if he realises the karmic burden he is carrying and decides that he will try to 'settle his accounts' once and for all– such an individual is, to my mind, a *jivan mukta* in the making. He looks upon this life as a means of spiritual upliftment!

Let me quote to you these beautiful lines from the *Ashtavakra Gita*:

"If one thinks of oneself as free, one is free, and if one thinks of oneself as bound, one is bound. This saying is true, 'Thinking makes it so'. Your real nature is as the one perfect, free, and action-less consciousness, the all-pervading witness– unattached to anything, desireless and at peace. It is from illusion that you seem to be involved in *sansaar*."

Walking the way to liberation

The way is shown to us by none other than Him whom we seek to attain, the Lord at whose Lotus Feet we will all find ultimate bliss! I refer to the Gita, where Sri Krishna teaches us how we may reach the goal of life. In fact, he tells us of three ways to attain liberation.

Scholars divide the eighteen chapters of the Gita into three sections: the first six chapters, the *karma kanda*, teach us the ideal of right, selfless action. We are taught that the performance of one's own duty– *swadharma*– is of paramount importance. Chapters 7-12, the *bhakti kanda*, teach us how we may transform karma or action into worship of the Lord. When we do our duty in a spirit of joy and love, we grow in devotion, in pure love for Sri Krishna. In the third and final section called the *jnana kanda*, the Lord takes us further. This section includes the intellect in action and devotion so that total surrender to the Will of the Lord is made possible.

Sri Krishna also relates various techniques to achieve self-realisation:

- On Me alone fix your mind; let your understanding dwell in Me.

- If you are not able to fix your thoughts steadily on Me, try to reach me through the practice of concentration and meditation.

- If you are unable to do this, even by performing actions for My sake you shall attain perfection.

- If you are unable to do even this, then taking refuge in Me, renounce attachment to the fruits of all actions.

The marvellous thing about the Gita is that it tells us to choose the path that appeals to us, the one that suits us best. This is in tune with the liberalism, pragmatism, and freedom from dogma that characterises *sanatana dharma* at its best. What matters is the spiritual discipline that enables one to reach the goal– not its technique or methodology. In fact, Sri Krishna assures us that none of us can go astray if we follow any one of the paths: In whatever way people approach Me, on that way I meet them.

One final thought...

Do you still feel diffident about seeking and attaining liberation? You need not despair, for the Lord offers you the short, straight and simple way to attain the goal of life:

Fix thy mind on Me; be devoted to Me; sacrifice to Me; prostrate thyself before Me. So shalt thou come to Me. I pledge thee My troth; thou art dear to Me.

XVIII-65

And, even more emphatically:

Abandoning all rites and writ duties, come unto Me alone for refuge. Grieve not! I shall liberate thee from all sins.

XVIII-66

Divine grace, liberation, *moksha, mukti,* can be obtained through unconditional surrender to the Lord.

As for me, I believe that the purpose of this life is to grow in purity and perfection. Perfection is not to be dismissed as an impossible dream! Like excellence, the pursuit of perfection is itself a worthy goal. This pursuit is made possible by the fact that God, who is the essence of all perfection, dwells within each one of us. When we become aware of this fact at the conscious level, half the journey is completed!

Name Divine

I sometimes think of the Name Divine as a locked door. If only we can open it, we too, may live in the abiding presence of the Beloved. The way to open it is the Way of Love.

Think of God in any form that draws you. He is the Formless One, but for the sake of His devotees, He has worn many forms and visited the earth-plane again and again. Call Him by any name that appeals to you. He is the Nameless One, though the sages have called Him by many Names. Do not quarrel over forms or names. You stick to the one that draws you, let others stick to the one that draws them. All forms and names ultimately lead to the One who is beyond form and formlessness. "On whatever path men approach Me," says the Lord in the Gita, "On that I go to meet them– for all the paths are Mine, verily Mine!"

Sitting in silence, let us repeat the Name Divine, meditate on some aspect of the Divine Reality or on an incident in the life of a Man of God. Choose any Name that appeals to you: repeat it again and again. Repeat the Name– yes, but not merely with the tongue. Engrave the Name upon your heart and repeat it with every breath of your being. Repeat it with tears in the eyes. Repeat it until you can repeat it no longer, until you disappear from yourself, your "ego" is dissolved, and you sit in the presence of the Eternal Beloved.

Why is it beneficial to chant the Name Divine?

Guru Nanak in his sacred verse tells us, *"Wada sahib, ooncha thaon, oonche upar ooncha nao."* The Name of God is the Alpha, the highest. There is nothing higher than that. Fortunate is the man who understands the divinity of the word 'Rama'. Such a man lives in the world but never ever forgets the Name Divine. The chanting of the sacred word goes on within his heart. The Name of 'Ram' is so sacred that by chanting it man can overcome his lower self. He can raise his energy from the lower *chakras* to the higher *chakras*. Chanting the Name Divine gives him spiritual strength.

Impure thoughts and sinful impulses wake up in the mind, again and again. Never yield to them, but sing the Name of God– not in a mechanical way, but with deep feeling and emotion. Pour into the unclean mind, the purifying *Gangajal* of the Name Divine. Whenever an unclean thought comes to you, immediately, in that very instant, say to yourself, "I was made for greater, nobler, loftier things. I shall not be a bundle of unclean, impure desires," and start repeating the pure Name of God.

The Name of God is like the waters of the Ganga. The River Ganga is like a mother– *Ganga Ma*! It purifies those that bathe in it. As you emerge from the waters of the River Ganga, of the Name Divine, you will feel cleansed, washed, purified. The Name of God is at once pure and cleansing. It purifies those that sing it with deep love and longing of the heart.

When should we chant the Name Divine?

Any time, any place is suitable to chant the Name Divine! It is the surest way to overcome the pervading sense of separateness from God with which contemporary life is infused. It is the best way to move closer to the goal of life and to make God real in our life. When we chant the Name Divine, we invite Him to be with us for 24 hours a day. To chant *Rama*, *Krishna* or *Hari* is to tell God, "O Lord, be Thou near to me always."

Let me urge you, in your daily life, whether you are cooking, cleaning, teaching, learning, managing your business or working in an office, remember Him constantly. You can make Him a part of your life, even if you are a householder, bound to the *grihasta ashrama* with its manifold duties and cares. Do your duty, dedicate all your work to God and chant the Name Divine. By chanting the Name Divine, the mind is purified, and the yearning for God surfaces; then we realise that we have wandered far from our real dwelling. Then it is that we cry out, "Dear Lord, take me back to my true home!"

In the rush of life and its mundane activities, we tend to forget the Divine Presence around us. We do not make God real in our life. As a result, we go astray; we become insecure; we are afraid; we worry; we fear the worst. It is our ignorance that causes us to imagine that God has abandoned us. The fact is that it is we who have abandoned Him, kept Him away from our lives. Let us bring Him back into our life by calling out to Him with love and devotion. We have to remember Him every moment of our life, we have to bond with God and experience His presence. Then indeed, all will be well, and all manner of things will be well, to quote the well-known song.

Chanting the Name Divine keeps us in constant awareness that we are not alone; God is always with us! God is protecting us, God is leading us, God is guiding us, God is watching us, God is watching over us– then why should we worry? Why should we fear anything? We must make awareness of God's presence a constant habit. Unlike all other habits, it should become integral to our daily living. And this is done by the simple act of *Naam Smaran*.

Keep chanting the Name Divine. Make this a habit. Let chanting the Name Divine be a spontaneous, natural process, which fills the mind, whenever it is empty. Keep the mind occupied in the most natural way. Just as you walk or sit or do any routine work almost 'automatically', so too, in the same way, chant the Name Divine. After constant repetition, the Name Divine will become a part of your life and nature.

How should we chant the Name Divine?

A dervish once remarked, "Today, people chant the Name Divine out of habit. They do so mechanically. Chanting the Name Divine should be filled with yearning. It should be a cry from the soul and not a mere utterance. Today people are ignorant, they are not aware of the potency of incantation. They merely utter words with their lips without putting their hearts and their aspirations into them. Of what value are such words? Chanting should be of deep yearning, it should be out of thirst for the Lord! Such chanting is blessed!"

Once we asked Gurudev Sadhu Vaswani, how we should chant.

Gurudev Sadhu Vaswani gave us the example of a drowning man: imagine this man, caught up in the waves of a stormy ocean; strong waves beat him down, and he is struggling to keep afloat. He is told that chanting the Name Divine alone can save him. How would he chant, under the circumstances? He would chant with such faith and fervour, as if his life depended on it, wouldn't he? Even thus, we should chant the Name Divine, in faith and longing.

Every one of us is being drowned 'by the dark waters of the world' in this *Kaliyuga*. If you want to be saved, if you want to cross the turbulent ocean safely, then chant the Name Divine with intense yearning!

The Name Divine is a treasure

There are so many beautiful thoughts, every one of them more precious than gems and jewels, that we read in the Sikh scriptures. Here is one such nugget from the *Sukhmani Sahib*: "Those who reflect on the Name Divine, are counted among the wealthiest on earth."

Mira was aware of this great truth; therefore she sang, *"Payo ji maine Ram ratan dhan payo..."* I have attained the greatest of treasures, she proclaimed; it is the wealth of the Name Divine; it is the treasure that cannot be looted by thieves; it is the wealth that grows and multiplies when it is spent…

How many of us care for this treasure today? How many of us bow down to those whose wealth is the Name Divine?

Why is chanting the Name important to us in *Kaliyuga*?

Five hundred years ago, Sri Chaitanya Mahaprabhu and his followers would go out in groups, chanting the Name Divine. *Hari bol, Hari bol...* singing in ecstasy, beating drums and *dholaks,* totally lost in the intoxication of the Name. They would go out into the streets, drawing people to join them in the incantation of the Name Divine.

Chaitanya Mahaprabhu taught us that *Krishna Nama Sankirtan*, the constant chanting of the Lord's Name, is the supreme way to uphold faith in this age. Chanting the Name Divine is a powerful healing force! It destroys sins and purifies the hearts through *bhakti*; it ensures universal peace. In today's difficult times, recitation is the easiest way to realise the goal of life. Chant, chant the Name Divine, sip its sweetness, chant with sincere emotion, chant with deep devotion, chant and chant!

Sikhism too, believes that one should meditate on God as much as possible in *Kaliyuga*.

Now, the Dark Age of Kaliyuga *has come.*
Plant the Naam, *the Name of the One Lord.*
It is not the season to plant other seeds.
Do not wander lost in doubt and delusion.

I call *kirtan* the shortest, quickest route to God! *Kirtan* is a simple *sadhana* for all of us. Singing the Name Divine is the surest, easiest way to become completely harmonised with the Lord! It achieves the impossible, by keeping all our senses under control! In *satsang*, the *kirtan* we sing with those around us goes on as a steady flow. Our hands are either folded together in tribute or gently clapping in rhythm with the singing. Our eyes are either closed, lost in *kirtan*, gazing at the radiant face of the guru, or focussing on the image of our *ishta devata*. During *kirtan* the tongue tastes the nectar of the Name Divine; the smell of incense and *agarbattis* fill the air. It is verily a feast divine for all the senses!

A western scholar of Hindu beliefs and practices actually describes this as *Kirtan Yoga*! It is easy, simple and practical; all of us can practise it effortlessly!

Singing the Name Divine in the company of other devotees is particularly beneficial. It cleanses and heals body, mind, and soul. It clears your aura. It paves the way for the life beautiful! Therefore, let us all chant and sing the Name Divine– not mechanically, but with love and devotion!

There are two types of *kirtan*. One, in which you simply chant the Name Divine; the other in describing and singing His glories. The first type of *kirtan* is what you do for a few minutes in *satsang*. *Kirtan* should not be limited by time. It should not be bound by minutes and hours. *Kirtan* should be continuous; it should bring joy and ecstasy with the group chant. *Kirtan* is spiritually elevating! When carried on for a long time, it spreads its beautiful, peaceful vibrations and uplifts the soul!

The second type of *kirtan* is singing the glories of the Lord, such as describing the *leela* of Krishna in Brindaban! His miraculous birth, His *raas leela* with the *gopis*, His games with cow herds, His tantalising ways! Singing the glories of the Lord or even thinking about Him is a form of *kirtan!*

For *kirtan*, only one thing is absolutely essential: devotion for the Lord and yearning for His Lotus Feet. Devotion comes with faith. Devotion or *bhakti* is an emotional upsurge. It powers us from within. It comes with a certain conviction. The chant by itself or singing by itself does not purify you. It is your *bhava*, your emotion, which will release the subtle forces of cleansing that will purify your inner instrument and elevate your soul to sublime heights of *bhakti*. Ultimately it is your intense devotion which will kindle the yearning for the Lord. This is the beginning of true transformation. This is when you see the spark of Divine Light, which dispels the darkness of the *Kaliyuga* that is enveloping you on the outside.

Kirtan is truly a *Sahaj Marg*– it is an easy path. You can do *kirtan* anywhere, anytime of the day. You can think of the life of great ones, anywhere and anytime of the day. The beautiful thoughts about the Radiant Ones will purify your inner self and a day will come when you will behold the golden Light within!

New Age

I am often asked: "What is your vision of the New Age?"

My answer and my vision are very simple! Mine is a vision of a world without war, a world without want. A world in which every human being can live a life of dignity, with all the necessities of life provided, and can hold his head high. A world in which peace prevails among nations and harmony among the peoples of the earth. A world in which the right to live is guaranteed to every creature that breathes the breath of life.

Mine is the vision of a world in which this truth is recognised– that life and all its bounties, all that we are and all that we have– our time and talents, knowledge and wisdom, experience and influence, prestige and power, wealth and strength, indeed, life itself– is a loan given to us, to be passed on to those whose need is greater than ours!

I am convinced that we are standing on the threshold of a new age of love and peace that will see all nations and all people united by the bonds of brotherhood.

Life as a movement onward

I believe a new age is dawning, a new cycle in history which has started. The nations, races and peoples of the world must unite together to march onward, forward, Godward!

Godward, I say. For God and religion cannot, and must not be kept out of this vision. Religion must not be set aside, even though people tend to discredit religion these days. As for me, I repeat my firm belief that it is not religion that has failed us, it is we who have failed religion. It is we who have failed religion, because we only speak of religion, we do not bear witness to it in deeds of daily living. We do not bear witness to the teachings of the great prophets. It is life that is needed, not words! I may recite prayers, chant hymns and sing songs of praise. I may read unending passages from the scriptures, I may go to the temple, the church or the mosque seven days a week, but if I do not bear witness to the great ideals of my religion in deeds of daily living, am I any better than a gramophone or a tape recorder? I may even write wonderful commentaries on the Bhagavad Gita, the Upanishads or any other world scriptures, but if I do not reflect the teachings of these scriptures in my actions and words, am I better than a desktop printer?

What the New Age needs

The world does not need gramophones, tape recorders or printing machines. True life is needed; true religion is needed in terms of vitality, energy, right action. "Blessed are the peacemakers," said Jesus. The world today needs peacemakers– not those who merely talk of peace, but those who carry peace within their hearts and transmit it to everyone around them. It is such people who can save the world, which, today, is madly rushing from danger to destruction. Blessed are the peacemakers. May they heed the words of Jesus, "Be not hearers of the Word, be doers of the Word." They will be the saviours of our sinking civilisation!

One world, one vision, one hope

No matter what our backgrounds, cultures, beliefs, faiths, and histories, we are involved in the future of the world together. Our future peace, prosperity and security depend not only on ourselves or on our own nation, but on the success and well-being of all nations! Unless everyone achieves the desired goals, there can be no lasting peace and security. Every missed opportunity, every failed goal, could be a root cause of global insecurity.

When we achieve the goal of universal peace, as well as the more specific developmental goals, we will be eliminating the 20th century concept of 'first', 'second' and 'third' world countries. There will be just a single 21st century world in which all of us will have shared hopes and shared responsibilities.

One world; one vision. This is the hope that sustains enlightened thinkers and progressive organisations. It is not just a dream any more– it has already become an economic and commercial reality with the world becoming a global village.

But the unity of the world cannot stop at just the commercial level. We have to move onward, forward. After all, we share one world; we live on the same planet. Is it not our responsibility to make this world a better place to live in, for ourselves and our children, and our generations unborn?

We need one another

One is the world– and the only one we have. Isn't it time we took care of it and its resources? And shouldn't we begin by taking care of one another? How can we take care of one another if we are constantly quarrelling, constantly bickering and waging wars with one another?

It was a very wise soul who said, "The world can only be as good as the people in it." So let us resolve to be good– to become better, so that this world can benefit with our efforts.

True, we need to change, we need to develop, we need to make progress. But the change must be for the better, not for the worse. The progress and development must be for everybody's benefit, not for the privileged few alone.

We need hearts, not votes

Ultimately, politics brushes only the surface of life, and cannot touch men's hearts. On the other hand, religion goes to the very root, and transforms the lives of individuals, their thinking, their morals, their conduct and character. Politics is the product of the mind and the intellect– and these are often instruments of division. True religion is born of intuition and higher understanding– and these are essentially unitive. This is why I affirm that we need a new unitive vision of the spirit. We must turn our attention from machines and money to the soul of humanity.

The British historian Toynbee, surveying the situation of civilisation in the 20th century, pointed out that the world's hope is not in love of money and power, but in the spiritual qualities of justice, tolerance, sympathy and self-offering to the Eternal.

Onward, forward, Godward!

Sadhu Vaswani taught us that the various creeds and religions of humanity are but different ways of attaining one goal. Different religions are but branches of one religion– the Religion of the Spirit. No matter how widely they may differ in their externals, they are all born out of one common and universal spiritual need– the need to unite the entire world in a spiritual brotherhood of man. For this is the vision that should inspire us, the vision that will move us onward, forward, Godward!

My personal hope: The new *Satya Yuga*

The *Srimad Bhagavata Purana* tells us: When the Supreme Lord has appeared on earth as Kalki, the maintainer of religion, *Satya Yuga* will begin, and human society will bring forth progeny in the mode of goodness…

May I say to you, we can create our own *Satya Yuga*, here and now! We can do this by adhering firmly to *satya* or truth, in thought, word and deed! There is no religion higher than truth.

The way ahead

The task that lies ahead of us is breathtaking in its utter simplicity and awe-inspiring in its critical significance.

The task is to build a new world– a world without wars, a world without want, a world in which peace and joy will be every man, woman, and child's birthright. The task is to create peace– or perish. The choice is ours.

The future must belong to a new civilisation where man will be a truly evolved super-being, who sees every human being as his equal, his friend, his brother, his sister.

Who will build this brave, new world? To them, let me say: Build your own lives first, in peace and non-violence!

To the youth– the inheritors of the earth– I say: Let there be an unquenchable thirst, and an insatiable hunger in your hearts for peace. Let there be a divine unrest in your spirit so that you will not be content with gold and riches, power and position. Let there be a spiritual yearning in your lives, so that the cult of comforts does not make you old before your time.

May you realise the message of Swami Vivekananda and Sadhu Vaswani, that simplicity is strength and all imitation is weakness. May this quality of simplicity flower into service and sacrifice.

The power of our sympathy, simplicity, service, and sacrifice will then surely build a new civilisation, a new world, a divine humanity!

A new dawn is at hand…

All around us, today, is a ring of darkness. But darkness cannot stay forever. When I look into the future, it is so bright, it dazzles my eyes. It is up to each one of us to make this future a reality.

Let each one of us kindle a little light– a little lamp of kindness, courage, and compassion. Let us plant trees for future generations: trees under whose shade we may never sit. Let us do little acts of kindness. Is not kindness better than knowledge, more important than wisdom?

Let us be a little more kind than necessary. Be kind, for who knows the next person you meet may carry a hurt in his heart. Let us do what little we can to help make the world a better place to live in. The greatest mistake is made by him who does nothing because he can do only a little!

A new age is knocking at our doors.

When shall we let it in?

New You

As midnight strikes on December 31, year after year, we all have the habit of wishing one another, "Happy New Year!" I think it would be quite safe to say that each one of you utters these words at least five hundred times between January 1 and January 3. 'Happy New Year' is indeed a beautiful greeting. I have no quarrel with it whatsoever, but I think there is another greeting that outshines it, and that is, "Happy New You!" I wish you a happy new you! I wish for myself, a happy new ME! Would it not be wonderful if we could rejuvenate, revitalise, renew ourselves every year, so that we become brand new!

Birth after birth, through many lives, we have worn the same old thoughts, habits and attitudes of selfishness and greed, hatred and strife, mistrust and hostility, lust and greed, anger and jealousy. If we are to enjoy a new life, a new experience, a new being, we must discard our old self, the tattered garment that we have worn for too long. For long have we clung on to thoughts of negativity, of lack and want, of disease and pain, of fear and failure.

Greeting cards and New Year gifts cannot make us new. They tell me that we now have digital cards that are animated and play music when they are opened. Regrettably, these cards cannot make us truly happy and peaceful. We need to wish each other a Happy New You, instead of Happy New Year. Every second, every nanosecond that comes to us from the spotless hands of God is brand new. Every breath that we draw is an instant of eternity that is fresh and unsoiled. It is we who have to become new, to make each second, each minute of our life happy, healthy, prosperous and harmonious. It is we who need to be renewed and revitalised, so that our lives can become new! We need to change our attitude, the way we act and react, the way we think and the way we respond to others. We even need to change the way we think about ourselves!

The princess's wedding

Gurudev Sadhu Vaswani once narrated to us a beautiful story about a wise and benevolent king, who thought of a very unusual way of celebrating his daughter, the princess's wedding. He decided that each and every one of his subjects would be invited to the grand wedding feast. The wedding invitations would not to be restricted to the wealthy, affluent and powerful. "All my people are equal to me; all my people shall be made the chief guests, the royal guests of honour at my daughter's wedding," he asserted. He sent his messengers to every village, every street, every house in the kingdom, to issue special invitations for his daughter's wedding and the royal banquet to follow. The wedding would be held in the open, enormous palace gardens, so that thousands upon thousands of his special guests could be accommodated, and a sumptuous banquet served to all of them.

There was one condition that the king imposed: all the guests who attended the wedding should adorn themselves in new clothes; they had to cast away their old clothes and wear brand new garments. This demand was not unrealistic, nor would it cause them any trouble; the palace servants would provide new clothes for all the guests; each and every guest would simply have to dispose of his old clothes and dress in the brand new clothes before entering the palace gardens to attend the royal wedding!

How wonderful it would be, if we could also be guests at such a wedding! How wonderful it would be, if we could cast away our old garments of frustration, resentment, anger, envy and jealousy, and make ourselves new with fresh, brand new garments, garments of light that cast no shadow, garments of radiance that would make us worthy participants in the festival of life that God holds for us every day!

When I talk about making yourself anew, I do not mean changing your outer appearance or looks! I do not want you to go and get yourself a new haircut, tattoo your arms, sport new earrings, colour your hair, or wear a new perfume! The story of the king and the new garments is a deeply symbolic parable which holds a lesson that all of us need to learn. The story beseeches us to reinvent ourselves, to shake off accumulated negativities of the past and assume a new self, a self that is higher, a self of purity and prayer, sympathy, service, selflessness and simplicity!

Renew yourself! Reinvent yourself!

Change, but make sure you change for the better! If you are wondering how to change, here is a simple suggestion: write down everything that you do NOT like about yourself. Are you short tempered? Do you blame others for all that goes wrong? Are you suspicious? Do you envy others? Do you always imagine the worst about others? Put down all those negative traits and then try to change for the better. Cast off those old shabby garments of negativity, and make yourself new!

Get rid of your excess baggage

If you wish to become new, you must learn to wipe out, delete, and forget many incidents of the past! No man can become a master of himself until he learns the art of forgetting. Whatever you may have done in the past, whatever disappointments, frustrations you might have gone through, whatever mistakes of omission or commission you may have done, do not carry them into the future! All of this is too much heavy baggage to carry with you. It will only wear you down!

At the end of every day, every week, every month, every season, every year, drop all the excess baggage of the past and look towards a bright future with a light heart. The word forget is so suggestive; take the *t* out of forget, and you get *forge*: to forget is to forge ahead. Indeed, the true art of living for those who dwell constantly in the past, is the art of forgetting!

Get rid of the old! Be ready for the new!

Begin with what you have

You have decided to change for the better; to make a new you. Do not wait for the world to change; do not wait for others to alter; do not wait for conditions to transform around you. Begin where you are, begin with what you have.

Let me share with you a story which was narrated by a lay preacher called Russel Conwell, who lived in America in the 19th century. They say that he was once asked to make a speech at a reunion of his friends, who were Civil War veterans. He agreed, and delivered a speech as requested. That speech proved to be so memorable, that he was asked to repeat it at other gatherings and forums, until he had repeated that speech, or other versions of the same, at least six thousand times! This sermon is now known as the 'Acre of Diamonds Sermon'.

The story is very simple. A villager lived with his family on his one-acre farm near a river. All that he had, all that he and his family needed, came to him from the one-acre farm. He lived a life of happiness and contentment until one day, he met a traveller from a far-off land, who sought his hospitality for the night. The visitor told the farmer that he was on his way to prospect for diamonds, so that he could make a fortune. As for our farmer, he had never even heard of diamonds; he had never ever seen a diamond, nor did he know what a diamond was or what it was worth. The visitor explained that diamonds were the most precious substance in the world. He continued, "Long ago when the world was formed, there was a congealing molten mass, and even today in the centre of the earth, this molten mass can be found. When the mass is found close to the surface, we mine it. I tell you, diamonds are precious beyond compare! If you had a diamond the size of your thumb, you could buy this whole valley. If you had a diamond the size of your fist, you could own this whole province. And if you owned a diamond mine, you could place each one of your children on thrones, from the influence of your fabulous wealth."

That night, the farmer went to bed, discontented, unhappy and feeling poor and deprived, for the first time in his life! The story goes on to tell us that he sold his farm, put his family under the care of relatives, and went out prospecting for diamonds. He travelled all the way across Asia Minor to Spain and then crossed over to Africa, but he never found what he was looking for. He never ever returned home to his family.

That was not the end of the story. The farm had been bought by a young villager, who worked hard tilling the soil, to feed his family and earn a living. One day, he found a hard shining rock by the side of the river, in his field. He liked the unusual glitter and hardness of the rock, and kept it on his table as a showpiece. History repeated itself; the same old visitor came to the same old farm, seeking shelter for the night. He saw the rock on the table and his eyes lit up. He was an honest man, and said to the young farmer, "I tell you, that rock you have there is a diamond! It is worth a fortune! Where did you find it?" The farmer explained that he had found it near the river, on his own field. The next morning, he and the visitor went to the selfsame spot where the rock had been found, and started digging. I am sure you can guess what they found: a small diamond mine, in that very acre of land that had been sold away by the disgruntled farmer a few years back! The poor farmer had lived and died and never realised, that he had once owned a whole acre of diamonds.

The diamonds had been there for millions of years, on that very plot of land; but the unhappy farmer had set out in quest of them without realising what he had. So I tell you, begin with what you have; do not go out chasing after non-existent rainbows or diamond mines!

Expect the best for yourself– and get it!

You have decided to become new, so expect the best for yourself. Picture yourself transformed, and your life changed for the better. For this, my friends, is an inviolable law of life– whatever you expect will come to you. As I have said time and again, your thoughts have magnetic power! Thoughts are tremendous forces. Every thought you think draws to itself what you think about. Think success, prosperity, joy and peace, and success, joy, prosperity and peace will come to you! Change your thinking and create a new you!

Every morning, we awaken from sleep with certain expectations. Some of us literally spring up from bed with the thought, "I know that today is going to be a wonderful day!" Others open their eyes to the new day with a depressing thought, "Oh no! I know this is going to be one of those awful days when everything will go wrong!" You are determining how your day will unfold with your own thought forces!

Your expectations can become powerful currents of energy, creating the conditions you desire and dream of, if they are allied to prayer, belief and faith. Therefore, choose to expect nothing but the best! Develop a strong sense of focus on all that is positive. Do not let your mind oscillate between anxiety and fear; repeat to yourself the reassuring mantra: All is for the best in this best of all possible worlds! Tell yourself, in the words of Robert Browning: God is in His heaven, and all is well with the world!

Sow good seeds in the field of your life!

Give the world the best that you are capable of and the best will come back to you!

The best that I can give to the world are good thoughts, good words, good actions. As I said, when I offer the best that I can to this world, the best will come back to me! Therefore, sow good seeds in the field of your life!

Most important of all– make God real in your life!

If you wish to make a new beginning, become a new you, and start a fresh new chapter in the book of your life, invite God into your life! If you have always been in contact with God, renew your contact with Him. If you have neglected your special relationship with Him, bring Him back into your life. If you have lived in forgetfulness, it is still not too late– invite Him back into your life.

What does it mean to make God real in your life? It is not a stranger that you are trying to 'cultivate' all of a sudden! God is not a remote figure, living up there somewhere in a dim and distant heaven! Closer is He to you than your own heartbeats, and as much a part of your being as the air you breathe in! The trouble is, that some of us take Him for granted, even as we take our heartbeats and our breath for granted! Techniques like *pranayama* and meditation make us more aware, more conscious of our breathing. So too, can prayer and silent contact with God, make us aware of His constant presence in our lives.

God is protecting us, God is leading us, God is guiding us, God is watching us, God is watching over us; then why should we worry? Why should we fear anything? We must make awareness of God's presence, a constant habit. Unlike all other habits, it should become integral to our daily living.

Let me tell you, this is not a one-minute exercise; it is a constant exercise of consciousness. You cannot close your eyes for sixty seconds and say, "There! That's done. I have invited God back into my life," and continue with your old ways and habits.

When you get up in the morning, tell God, "You are not far from me, You are with me. O God, I was fast asleep throughout the night, it is You, who have taken care of me. Today is a new dawn, a new day and I know that You will take care of me and help me become new!"

In the rush of life and its mundane activities, we tend to forget the Divine presence around us. We do not make God real in our life. As a result, we go astray; we become insecure; we are afraid; we fear the worst. It is our ignorance that causes us to imagine that God has abandoned us. The fact is that it is we who have abandoned Him, kept Him away from our lives. We have to be firm in our faith. We have to remember Him every moment of our life. We have to bond with God and experience His presence. Then indeed, all will be well, and all manner of things will be well.

Thoughts to create a New You!

Happy New You!
May all be well with you, today, tomorrow and a thousand years hence!
May you walk with God today and trust Him for the morrow!
Be the Architect of your own destiny!
May you always be happy– and make everyone around you happy!
Be of good cheer, for God is with you– the Friend of friends!
Be at peace with yourself, with the world, and with nature!
Make the most of the new day, the New Year and all the new opportunities it is about to offer you!
Think good thoughts, speak kind words and do good deeds!

May you be God's gift to your family, friends and neighbours!
May your highest aspirations come true this year, and every New Year!
May the joyous tune of gratitude ever be on your lips– Thank you God! Thank you God! Thank you God!
God is with you; God is watching you; God is watching over you!
God is! So why be anxious?
Peace be with you!

Sarve Bhavantu Sukhinah
Sarve Santu Niraamayaah
Sarve Bhadraani Pashyantu
Maakaschit Dukkha Bhaag-Bhavet
Om Shanti! Shanti! Shanti!

May all beings be happy,
May all be healthy,
May people have the well-being of all in mind,
May nobody suffer in any way.

Old Age

Old age is in the mind. You are as old or as young as you think yourself to be. If your mind is always ready to undertake new experiments in the great laboratory of life, you will remain young in spirit– forever! After all, youth is determined by the spirit, not by your age.

It is in the nature of all matter to change with time. Wood, rock, stone, soil– you name it– everything disintegrates with time. The body is no exception. But what is ageing to the body, can be maturing of the mind and evolution of the soul! And we know, age cannot affect the spirit within you.

Youth is not a matter of age; youth is not a matter of years; youth is a state of mind. If your mind continues to be fresh, if your mind is always open and ever receptive to new ideas, you will continue to remain young forever! It is only when we lose faith in the belief that something wonderful will happen, that we begin to feel old.

Keep your mind fresh! Keep your mind open! Keep your mind receptive to new ideas!

Looking forward to old age

There is a friend of mine in the U.S., who recently celebrated her 90th birthday. In a letter that she wrote to me, she said, "I am celebrating my 90th birthday, and I am looking forward to being old!"

She always thought of old age as being ten years ahead of her! She wrote, "When I was eighty, I thought I would be old at ninety; now I think I will be old when I am hundred!"

Her words made me recall these beautiful lines from a poem by Robert Browning:

Grow old along with me;
The best is yet to be!

It is attitude that counts!

Let me tell you about another American lady, who is described by all her friends as a delightful, charming person who is always positive. At 94, she continues to remain friendly, cheerful and full of high spirits. They asked her, "What is the secret of your happy life?"

She replied, "The secret is a very simple one. It is my enthusiasm for life. And because I always think positive, I am positive!"

The moment you lose your enthusiasm, you begin to feel old. The source to the fountain of youth is youthful thoughts. The key to youthfulness is the innovativeness and creativity which we inculcate into our lives and share with those around us.

'Problems' of old age

It is said that old age affects our memory, but I think it is disuse rather than old age that affects our faculties! Our mental powers become rusted when we stop using them, exercising them adequately.

Old age does make us weak and frail; it impairs our strength, but at whatever stage of life we may be in, we must exert our strength to the maximum extent possible. We don't have to go out and play tennis or football. But we must move about as much as we can! If we have lived a life of temperance and moderation, we will surely be reasonably healthy in old age too!

It is thought that there can be no pleasures in old age. However, I would say that old age actually saves us from the dangers of excessive indulgence in pleasures! Moreover, the autumn years bring their own pleasurable experiences! Cicero talks of "the learned leisure of a virtuous old age".

Many people are often filled with undue anxiety at the thought of old age, as they feel death is drawing close. But death can come to us at any moment, at any age of life! Many young people do not wake up to see a new day. And if young people have the prospect of a long life before them, old people have already enjoyed it in actual experience!

How to age well

Let me offer a few suggestions to help elders stay mentally and physically fit:

1. Be as physically active as possible. Walking and stretching are good exercises for fit and healthy elders. For the not so able, even passive exercises and above-the-neck exercises

are beneficial. Make sure your exercise routine includes balancing acts like Tai Chi and Yoga.

2. Word games, puzzles and Sudoku are excellent stimulants for the brain. You can also try games like counting red objects in the vicinity, or green objects when you are out on your walk or drive.

3. As and when you can, break your routine and vary your activities. You might try taking a different route on your daily walk, or changing a staple item in your diet.

4. You can enjoy *sattvic* food, but ensure that you do not overindulge in salt, sugar and fats.

5. Make time for periods of quiet restfulness and a meditation session every day.

6. Don't try to cling on to youthful appearance! Accept wrinkles and grey hair with dignity. Contentment, happiness, kindness, gratitude, staying connected to others, interest in the world around you– all this can make you beautiful from the inside!

7. Keep in touch with family and friends! Don't use them to air your complaints, but express an interest in their activities and concerns.

8. Learn something new every day! Every new day is the harbinger of a new beginning. Hence, we are reborn with each day. Just as iron rusts from disuse and water loses its purity from stagnation, similarly one's vitality is sapped through inactivity. Therefore, it is imperative to keep busy and engrossed with something new. It may be embracing the latest technology or reading a new book.

9. Laugh out often, with frequent and deep belly laughs. The laughter lines on your face will not age you. It is the absence of laughter in your life which will make you grow old.

Aging may be inevitable, but to grow old gracefully is a choice.

Optimism and Pessimism

Optimism is defined as "an inclination to put the most favourable construction upon actions and events or to anticipate their best possible outcome". It is thought to be the philosophical opposite of pessimism. Pessimism, derived from the Latin root, *pessimus*, meaning the worst, is a state of mind which makes our perception of life negative, especially with regard to future events. Optimists generally believe that people and events are inherently good, so that most situations work out for the best in the end. Pessimism, on the other hand, is sometimes thought to be a negative self-fulfilling prophecy– if an individual feels that something is bad, it is likely to get worse! Oscar Wilde described a pessimist as, "One who, when he has the choice of two evils, chooses both."

There is a choice!

We have a choice in life– the choice between optimism and pessimism. A true optimist is indefatigable in his hopes. He will find a ray of hope, a hint of solution in every difficult situation. The optimist is fortunate because his outlook on life will always be positive and constructive. He is of the outlook that if a door may have closed, the window is still open!

An optimist realises that he cannot control everything that happens to him, but he can control his response to what happens to him. This lesson should be taught to students in schools and colleges, for it gives courage to cope with every situation. Optimism has roots in the goodness of God. It is anchored on faith and courage.

When I was in school, our teacher emphasised the importance of improving our handwriting. He often asked us to write out phrases and sentences. One of them was, "Every cloud has a silver lining". The dark nimbus clouds also have a silver lining somwhere; behind the clouds the sun shines and its rays light up the edges of dark clouds.

Two contrasting attitudes

Have you heard these beautiful lines which I love to repeat:

Two men looked out from prison bars;
One saw mud, the other stars.

Is it not true that when you look at someone with a closed mind, they seem to be limited?

When you perceive someone as being selfish, they turn out to be selfish? And when you look at someone in a friendly and positive way, you find love and beauty everywhere?

There is a common puzzle or conundrum, which is used to illustrate two contrasting attitudes: does one regard a glass of water, filled to half its capacity, as half full or as half empty? Most definitely, optimists would reply, "Half full," and pessimists would respond, "Half empty".

A mayor who was very proud of his city was asked how the recession had affected it. He boldly answered, "We don't have a recession here, but I admit we are having the worst boom in many years."

Be an optimist

An optimist is a man who has immeasurable enthusiasm, unbounded determination, unbelievable faith, indestructible confidence, is too big to worry, too noble for anger, and gives everyone a smile.

The concept of optimism is often linked with the name of Gottfried Wilhelm Leibniz, who held that we live in the best of all possible worlds, for he believed that God created a physical universe that follows the laws of physics, and was therefore perfect.

Personal optimism is said to be correlated to a healthy sense of self-esteem, which includes psychological well-being as well as physical and mental health. Optimism has also been correlated with better immune systems in healthy people who have been subjected to stress.

A distinguished academician, Martin Seligman criticises psychologists for focusing too much on causes of pessimism and not enough on optimism. Through his research, he found that in the last three decades of the 20th century, medical journals published 46,000 psychological papers related to depression and only 400 on inner peace and joy. In other words, even medical experts are obsessed with pessimism!

Pessimism is curable; all it takes is a strong dose of faith and hope. But optimism is incurable– and it is also contagious!

Why dont you become a 'carrier' of optimism?

Parents and Children

Parents are often overwhelmed by a sense of awe, mystery and deep love, when a new born comes into their lives. There is a blessed sense of relief, a light-headedness of wonder that makes one almost dizzy, and pure ecstasy on seeing the little one for the first time! And the thought arises in the mind of everyone who beholds a new-born– I am witnessing the miracle of God's Creation!

I say to all parents: your children are your greatest treasures. Do not get so busy gathering silver and gold, that you neglect your richest treasure! Your children need your time, attention and love– for without love and attention, no child can grow up in the right way. They need your love, your friendship, your care, your guidance and discipline. They need your loving attention so that they have the assurance that they are not alone, that there is someone who loves them dearly, someone whom they can turn to at any time of the day or night.

Are you giving your children the time they need?

Today, parents are busy doing countless things. In 'upper class' families the father is a jet-setting executive, hopping across continents, playing golf at weekends, constantly talking on the cell phone at the dining table. As for the mother, she is a glittering socialite, arranging kitty parties, visiting her beauticians for extended sessions, and spending the evenings at charity dinners, parties, concerts and ballets.

Many 'middle-class' parents fare no better. Juggling a double-shift between their jobs and home, working mothers talk of spending "quality-time" with their children– a euphemism for 'very little time'. As for the poor, they are struggling to feed the family, and they dare not talk of such luxuries as "quality-time".

"Of course we lead a busy and active life," these parents will say. "But this does not mean that our children are neglected. They are provided with every comfort we can offer them. We have appointed servants to take care of their every need. And they know we love them!"

Let me say to all parents– your children need *your* love, above all else. The nature of the soul is love– and without love, no child can grow up in the right way. You must give them your time! You must try to sow in their plastic minds seeds of character, without which life can have no meaning or value. You must help them to grow in the love and fear of God.

Parents as role models and mentors

Today, many parents complain that their children do not respect and obey them. I would say to them, "Don't stop with complaints. Try a little introspection to see where things are going wrong."

Parents are not only their children's first and foremost teachers, they are also their children's role models and mentors. If you want your child to be exceptional, you must also become exemplary role models. As we all know, children are great imitators. They are extremely observant, attentive and sharp. Thus, it is essential that we set a good example before them. Examples speak louder than words!

Discipline blended with love

Without discipline, no art can be learnt– definitely not the art of living. The best discipline is self-discipline. Unless parents have self-discipline and self-control, they cannot expect their children to be disciplined.

Discipline is necessary; discipline is vital. However, discipline must not be confounded with suppression or oppression. Harsh "Dos and Don't's" will not give rise to the results we desire. We must treat our children like the intelligent beings that they are. We must teach them about the values that are essential to them. We must lay emphasis on the gift of human life and explain to them that discipline is needed to reach life's goals.

All discipline must be blended with love, so that the child is assured that it is for his own benefit, and not in obedience to blind, arbitrary 'rules'. I do not believe in the old-fashioned saying, "Children should be seen and not heard." I think the sound of children's laughter and their tinkling voices are among the most melodious sounds on earth.

Physical punishment

Many parents do not seem to have the correct notion of 'discipline'. Some of them resort to hitting, slapping, and pulling the ears. Others employ psychological punishment by refusing to talk to the child or even look at him. Yet others issue threats and dire warnings. Some resort to constant nagging and verbal abuse. All this will only frustrate your child and make him defiant.

Discipline is necessary, especially when children are in the learning stage and their parents are their first and foremost teachers. But love and discipline should go together. It is not enough to be teaching parents; you must also be caring, loving, understanding parents!

Every child is a unique individual!

Parents must realise that children are not your 'toys' or 'personal achievements'; nor are they your future insurance. They are souls whom God has entrusted to your care. You are not expected to pamper or indulge them mindlessly. Rather, you must blend firmness with affection, discipline with love, to give them a secure and healthy environment where they might grow to absorb the deeper values of life. If you thrust your child into the mould of your making, he will turn out to be the proverbial square peg in the round hole.

Comparison and criticism are not conducive to a child's wholesome development. Instead, adopt the spirit of understanding and appreciation. Become acquainted with your child's strengths and weaknesses; recognise his limitations; appreciate his talents and unique gifts; encourage him to realise his full potential.

Talk to your child; get to know him well; understand his dreams, fears, and aspirations. Consult him about his plans for the future. Allow him to grow and evolve in accordance with his own spirit!

Do not pamper your children

Today, even many middle-class parents imagine that spending as much money as they can afford on their children, indulging their every whim and fancy, spoiling them with lavish gifts and pampering them is the equivalent of showering love and attention on them.

They are sadly mistaken!

As for rich parents, they are often very particular that their children should grow in the awareness that they are very special, very well off, and belong to the exclusive upper strata of society. There is talk of *khandan*, of family prestige, and of habits and activities that suit an upper-class lifestyle.

Children need not be taught how to spend money on themselves. It is far more important to teach them how to be economical, how to put their wealth to a more compassionate, selfless use, and how to share whatever they have with others.

I would therefore urge affluent parents to avoid unnecessary extravagance, pomp and opulence. Instead, children should be taught the value of self-sacrifice.

The family that prays together, stays together

The home, I believe, is the door to the Kingdom of God. Therefore, every day, all the members of the family– from the youngest to the oldest– should spend a little time in prayer together. Let there be a little, exclusive family *satsang*– even if it is for no more than ten to fifteen minutes. I assure you– this will give a new tone, a new life, a new spirit to your home!

To enhance the faith and piety of the children, it is essential that we narrate to them stories of God, the *avataras*, of saints and spiritual leaders. This will make them aware of the great power, the Divine *shakti* that moves the entire universe. Encourage your children to turn to God in prayer, for all that they need.

Teach your children to surrender themselves to the grace of God and the guru. Let them realise that God and the guru are always at hand to protect them, guard them, and prevent them from yielding to evil and temptation. Teach them to remember their God and guru first thing, when they awaken, and last thing, before they fall asleep.

Teach your children too, that the secret to joy and peace is making God real in their lives, through the practice of daily prayer!

Raising children in the right way

- Make your children your top priority at all times! There is a difference between children and adults. Children live in the now; they are free from anxieties of the past and fear of the future. If a child is in need of something or wants an answer to a question, never say to him, "I shall fulfil your need or answer your question tomorrow or at my leisure."

- Every child is a human being, with a heart and soul. Never let him feel unwanted, and never forget that the child is an individual, with his own personality and innate talents. Understand him and encourage the creative principle within him to express itself freely. Guide him in a healthy, constructive way by bringing out the best that is in him. Do not impose your will on him and say, "I am a doctor, so my son should become a doctor!"

- Do not discriminate between children. Don't play favourites with the eldest or youngest. Children are very sensitive.

- Keep your child very close to yourself, until he is at least three years of age. He needs your affectionate touch. It is a great blunder to hand over little children to *ayahs* or baby-sitters.

- It sometimes becomes very necessary to scold children. Whenever you do so, avoid being emotional. Let your words on such occasions be like whips of love. Explain the fault clearly to the child, and allow him to speak out, if he has anything to say.

- Even at a young age, children should be trained to attend to household chores. Let them cultivate reverence for manual work.

- Let children grow in the spirit of selflessness by training them to share food with the starving ones. Before you eat your food, set apart a share for a hungry one– a man, a bird, or an animal. Example is always a better teacher than precept.

- The home is a door to the Kingdom of God, the kingdom of true happiness. Inculcate faith and devotion in your children. Teach them to love and revere God and the guru. Teach them to turn to God and the guru, whenever they need anything, or have a problem to solve. As a family, spend a few minutes in prayer with the children every day!

- At a prominent place in your home, keep a big, beautiful picture of your *ishta devata* or your guru: whenever you or the children leave the house or enter it, make it a habit to bow down to the picture and offer a small prayer.

One final thought…

Parenting is not only one of the greatest pleasures of your life– it is also an onerous responsibility, involving psychology, ethics, human resource management, spirituality, morals and religion. Whatever I have outlined above is not to be taken as a rigid set of rules, but it can help your own parenting style towards your child.

Your children look up to you for a sense of security, identity and belonging. The world we live in is changing so fast, that they are exposed to powerful, sometimes negative influences from outside. The only weapon you have to fight these negative influences is your love– therefore make your children feel loved, cherished and secure! Express your love in as many ways as you can, as often as you can. Let your discipline and control become expressions of your love and concern– rather than being merely negative feedback and criticism. Give them your unstinted praise and appreciation when they deserve it. Treat them as young adults and responsible members of the family unit. You will find that your children bloom and flower into mature, sensible adults under your loving care!

Patience

There are many virtues which can be cultivated by means of other virtues. For example, love leads you on to compassion; compassion leads you on to selflessness and service of the suffering ones; faith gives you hope; truth gives you honesty and integrity. But you need a lot of patience to learn the wonderful virtue of patience!

The synonyms for the word patience in the English language are even more revealing: composure, stability, self-possession, submissiveness, sufferance, endurance, fortitude, stoicism, all of which imply qualities of calmness and persistent courage in trying circumstances. Patience also denotes uncomplaining bearing of pain, misfortune, annoyance, or delay. And finally, 'patience' also refers to determination, persistence, assiduity.

Patience is not just a virtue, it is a compendium of several good qualities.

Patience in daily life is an ability or willingness to suppress restlessness or irritation when confronted with delay, such as a good teacher who has patience with a slow learner. Patience is also used to refer to quiet, steady perseverance; even-tempered care; and also diligence– we praise people who work with patience.

Alas, we spend much of our time and energy trying to control things which are out of our hands. The futile effort leaves us frustrated, impatient and embittered. We need to develop the virtues of patience and acceptance– not as passive, helpless victims, but as wise and understanding human beings.

If a man has not learnt to be patient, he has learnt very little.

Tolerance, understanding, acceptance– the world has great need of these today. Above all, we need to be patient with ourselves!

Let nature be our teacher

Nature becomes our best teacher when we are learning to be patient. If only we observe Mother Nature, if only we would appreciate her splendid panorama in all its wondrous magic, we would decipher that nature does not hurry, it is never in haste, and everything happens in its due course. Look at the sun, it religiously rises in the morning and sets in the evening. This has gone on for centuries, and it will continue to do so for centuries to come.

The sun keeps shining, giving its light to the earth and sustaining all the creatures on it. The sun never changes its course; it never fails in its task of affording light and warmth to us.

Likewise, the trees stand firm in sunshine and rain. The trees do not complain. In fact, they bless us by providing us with shade, fuel, wood and fruit. A tree is invaluable to man. Yet we pay no attention to its presence, nor do we acknowledge the many benefits we receive from it.

Patience is essential for seekers

Let me add, patience is a great virtue; patience is essential for every aspirant who wishes to make progress on the spiritual path. This path, as we all know, is difficult and has many obstacles. Without patience, we would never be able to tread this path.

When we read the life of Sri Dattatreya, we learn that the earth taught him the qualities of patience, forbearance and doing good to others.

From the moment we get up from sleep, we stand upon the earth, we tread upon it, we stamp upon it, and we jump upon it and trample upon it. The earth puts up with it all– it puts up with billions upon billions of people like us and continues to support us. The trees that grow upon the earth share this quality with their earth mother. They provide shelter and fruits to everyone– even to those who throw stones at them.

Let us not give up our effort on the spiritual path. Let us not lose courage, but cultivate the virtue of patience, and face the challenges of life with equanimity and fortitude. Let us continue with our *sadhana* and with our prayers.

The true seeker learns to cultivate endurance, compassion and selflessness from the earth.

Life teaches us patience

Patience teaches us to accept life gracefully and not sink into the morass of complaints and self-pity. Very often I have heard people complain that they work very hard, but do not receive adequate reward or recognition for their efforts. Once I met a man who was perhaps going through the same experience. He said that whenever he felt his efforts were unappreciated, he would go to an area where labourers were laying new roads. Here, he would watch the labourers breaking stones, tirelessly. These men keep hammering the stones in order to break them into rubble. They keep on at this back-breaking work ceaselessly. They continue with the drudgery of breaking stones day in and day out for a pittance, which is often barely enough to feed their large families. Their patience and untiring, uncomplaining effort, is something that spiritual seekers would do well to emulate.

We all need patience

Even for those of us who do not aspire to spiritual progress, patience is vital in our daily dealings. With patience, one can solve one's own problems and help others as well. Patience brings rhythm and harmony into our chaotic lives. And as we have discussed above, Mother Nature too follows the law of patience in her ceaseless cycles and steady rhythm.

In this world of haste and waste, stress and tension, trials and tribulations, patience assumes great worth. Patience is necessary to avoid dissipating our energies. Patience makes life smooth and stress-free. The great scientist, Isaac Newton said, "If I have ever made any valuable discoveries, it has been owing more to patient attention, than to any other talent."

Patience is also the antidote to the two principal vices– restlessness and wandering mind– which give rise to several other weaknesses such as impatience and laziness.

So let me urge you, do not lose patience easily, but be strong willed. Cultivate the strength within. Do not become irritated by minor, irrelevant incidents, and do not waste your energies on futile discussions and debates. Let there be no war of words that drain you of all energy. Keep your mind under control and focus on more valuable and constructive thoughts.

Patience is not passivity

Patience is not a passive virtue, as some people think. Patience, as experts are now beginning to understand, is a 'proactive choice' and a vital way of perseverance that keeps you moving towards your goal. The lives of the great ones bear ample testimony to this.

When Lord Zarathustra first had his vision of Truth and began to preach his message to the people, he was met with scorn and derision. Not once did he get an eager, receptive audience, willing to listen to him. The people were just not ready to receive from the Prophet the revelation meant for them and the rest of mankind. He was countered with jeers and howls wherever he went; they even pelted stones at him, inflicting wounds on his pure, sacred body. He bore in gentle and loving patience the pain and the scorn heaped upon him.

On his lips was the smile of mercy and in his heart was the prayer: "O Ahura Mazda! Have mercy on them and lead them out of darkness of the Evil One, into the Light of Thy Truth!"

As we know, the scoffers and disbelievers could not stop Zarathustra from his ordained path. His followers grew in number, and they gave the master their undying loyalty and commitment. To this day, the Parsis in India retain his qualities of patience and gentleness!

Patience is the best antidote to suffering

Patience is the alchemist that turns every blow into a blessing, every burden into a benediction. As the pilgrim moves on the spiritual path, he is tried and tested, just as gold is tested by being thrown into the crucible. Significant are the words of Hudayafa al-Yaman, "When God loves a servant, He proves him by suffering." If the servant is patient, he will not avoid suffering, but instead will greet it with a smile, knowing that all that comes from God is good.

The man of patience thrives on suffering– the more he suffers, the more his soul shines. The great Sufi teacher and mystic, Jalaluddin Rumi, unfolds a very beautiful picture in his *Masnavi,* an extensive poem. He writes, "There is an animal called the porcupine. It is made stout and big by blows of the stick. The more you cudgel it, the more it thrives. The soul of a true believer is, verily, a porcupine. The more it is chastised, the more it thrives… So it is that God's chosen ones have to bear a greater share of suffering than other worldly men." Suffering gives strength to their souls, and patience blunts the sharp edge of suffering!

Listening requires patience

Communication experts tell us that among the younger generation, listening is perhaps the most neglected of skills. Evidence shows that many people have problems with listening. This is not because they are deaf or hard of hearing; it is just that they are rather inefficient as listeners, because they are too impatient to pay attention to what others are saying. We miss much of what is said and forget much of what we hear. Experts say we retain only 25% of what we hear after 2 days!

Experts also point out that impatience is one of the worst barriers to listening. Nowadays, you can hear people talking aloud altogether, at the same time. This happens in meetings, discussions and even on TV chat shows! People have no patience to let the other person finish what he has to say. They want to interrupt, add their own comments or narrate their own experiences. Such competition indicates a lack of maturity. We must cultivate patience and courtesy, at least to the extent of allowing the other speaker to finish whatever he has to say.

Patience at the workplace

Many people today lose patience with their employers and quit their jobs– only to regret the rash decision later, when they find it difficult to obtain a new position. A little patience and tolerance could have saved them from the insecurity of unemployment. I always tell my friends that they must abide in patience, until the way before them is clear.

Managers and employers too, expect too much from their subordinates and lose their temper and patience when their expectations are not fulfilled. They shift the blame on to the other team members, losing valuable, experienced, trusted, loyal employees due to their rash, impulsive and impatient behaviour.

Are you one of those people who is dissatisfied with your work environment?

Remember, you are the right person in the right place, learning the right lesson at the right time. When you have learnt it, out of the very depths of life will sound the words: "Move on!" And the conditions around you will change, and you will find yourself in a new environment!

All it takes is patience.

How to learn the virtue of patience

My friends say to me that this is the age of instant solutions, instant foods, and instant cash: no one has the patience to wait, let alone cultivate the virtue of patience! I must point out to them, that the best things in life are achieved only after you have put in hard work and waited patiently for your efforts to bear the fruit! There are situations in everyday life that tax our patience. In all of them, a handful of patience is worth a bushel of brains– as a Dutch proverb tells us.

Patience can and must be cultivated by all of us, and I would like to offer you some practical suggestions for the same:

1. Avoid doing things in haste. "Multi-tasking" is a much valued attribute today; but in earlier, more relaxed times, we believed in the saying: "One thing at a time, and that

done well, is a very good rule, as many can tell." Make a list of tasks to be completed, and go about each one systematically, taking the help of others if it is available.

2. Change your attitude to life and people, so that you may overcome stress and irritation. When your attitude is constructive and helpful, you automatically become more patient and understanding with people around you.

3. In this as in other things, acceptance is crucial to peace and harmony. Realise that there are some things in your life which are not under your control, and that you cannot change everything and everyone around you to suit your way of functioning.

4. Learn to relax consciously in stressful situations. Deep breathing is an instant de-stressor. In the long run, meditation also helps you to become stable, calm and patient.

5. When a situation becomes impossible for you to handle, learn to let go. Let go, let go, let God.

6. Remember, good things may not always come to people who wait, but very few good things in life come straightaway to any one!

7. Get your priorities straight. Ultimately, peace and goodwill are far more important than instant gratification of your desires. Take time to live! Take time to offer kindness and understanding to people around you, and create harmony in your environment by being kind, tolerant, patient and understanding!

Have patience with life; have patience with this world; have patience with everything and everyone. But above all, have patience with yourself!

Prayer

Essentially, prayer is an act of communing with God or the Divine. Prayer is fundamental to all religions. Prayer is waiting upon God, in love and longing.

Prayer is not at all a complex matter. In fact, prayer is very, very simple. Prayer is like speaking to a friend. Suppose your friend were to come to you. It would be so natural for you to discuss with him your dreams and desires, your anxieties and worries, your aspirations and achievements, your problems and perplexities, and ask him to help you. Do the same with God. He is the Friend of all friends. When all other friends fade away, He is the one friend who will remain. All you need to do is call out to Him in love and faith. He is available to us 24 hours of the day and night, seven days a week, 365 days a year. He is ever ready to help us.

Prayer is an enormous source of power. The word prayer is derived from the Latin root, *precarius* which means, "obtained by entreaty". All prayer is a supplication to the Lord.

Talking to God– and listening to God

Prayer begins with talking to God. Later, a stage comes when we are silent and He speaks to us. True prayer arises more from the heart than from the tongue. Until we have listened to the voice of God, we have not proceeded far on the path of prayer. Prayer should flow spontaneously, out of a love-filled heart. One look of the eye, one exclamation, may be more acceptable to the Lord than hundreds of fixed prayers offered in a mechanical way, day after day. Feeling is needed; emotion is needed, for more important than words, is the vibration of love which they carry.

In the beginning, we do not hear His voice; but let us be sure that He hears us! We may not see Him; but He sees us. And ultimately a stage comes in the life of every seeker when he sees God and hears His voice. For God can be seen; He can be touched and felt; His voice can be heard. He is more real than all things which we perceive with the senses. But to be able to see Him and hear Him, effort is needed– effort to awaken deep longing, yearning for God.

Where is the best place to pray?

You must believe firstly, that God is all around. You do not have to go to a particular place to pray. It is always good to go to temples, mosques and churches. But it is not only in these shrines that you can contact God. He is right in front of you, wherever you may be. All you have to do is to close your eyes, shut out the world, open your heart and call Him with deep love and longing– and there He is, with you!

When is the best time to pray?

My spontaneous response to that question would be: here and now!

I would say that the best time to pray is the early hour of the morning, when there is a descent of holy vibrations from above. However, some people prefer the quiet hours of the evening, when they feel relaxed after the demanding work of the day is done. Many people have no choice and snatch any opportunity they can to pray– sometimes, even on their way to work, on a bus or a train.

Time, therefore, need not be a constraint. We must just pray, whenever we can, as and when we can.

Do we need to offer set prayers?

No, it is not necessary for us to offer set, established prayers.

So often, prayers are read from books; they are worthwhile in as much as they draw our attention to God. However, mere mechanical repetition is only the first step.

God does not care for the form, the shape, or the vocabulary of our prayer. It is the feeling with which we pray that counts.

You do not have to be learned to be able to pray. You do not have to be well versed in Sanskrit or Latin or Persian. Indeed, being highly educated, far from being a help, becomes a hindrance in the way of prayer. Sri Ramakrishna was illiterate; he could not even sign his name. Yet he prayed, for hours together. He prayed as one who stood in the presence of God, speaking to God as a child would speak to his mother.

How may our prayers be answered?

To put it simply, there are four ways in which God answers our prayers. Many of us are apt to complain that our prayers have not been answered at all. This is not true.

EVERY PRAYER IS ANSWERED! The trouble with us is, we fail to recognise the answer.

As I said, God answers our prayer in four ways:

1. The first is "Yes." We ask for something; we pray to God, and He says, "Yes, my child. Here it is; I give you what you asked for."

2. The second is "No." For a good reason, God tells us, "No my child, I will not grant your prayer."

3. The third is "Wait." When God tells us to wait, there is great wisdom in it; it is as if God is telling us that the time is not ripe for us to receive what we want. So he tells us, "Wait. The time is not yet."

4. The fourth is, "Here is something better." We have asked for one thing, but He grants us something else and says, "Here is something different, something better that I want to give you."

When the answer is in the affirmative, when God says "Yes", we feel very happy. We praise God, we thank Him; we call Him a loving God, a wonderful God, and our faith in Him becomes stronger. But the other three answers– "No", "Wait", and "Here is something better"– it is these three that test our faith.

When God says no, the man of true faith believes that there is a meaning of mercy even in the negative answer. He says to himself, "If God does not want to give me this, it must be for my own good." It was a wise man who said, "I have lived long enough to thank God for not having answered many of my prayers."

Three modes of prayer

Whatever the nature of your prayer– asking, affirmation, denial, praise, intercession or surrender– there are three ways in which you can offer your prayer:

1. Vocal Prayer is a loud repetition of a preset prayer or your prayer in actual spoken words. There are several such prayers given to us in the scriptures of all religions. Vocal Prayer helps us to focus our minds on God, and is a good beginning for the seeker who wishes to follow the path Godward.

2. Mental Prayer is a prayer uttered in the mind, through thoughts. This involves feeling the presence of God within you, and being able to concentrate on it. Having uttered a silent, mental prayer, one must hold oneself in stillness and silence until one feels God's peace descending within. This can be a beautiful spiritual experience.

3. Spiritual Prayer is perhaps the highest form of prayer. It leads us to that rare moment when we feel we are at One with God. Some people are blessed with a Vision in such a state. Yet others undergo a mystical experience, which is impossible to describe in words. It awakens the soul to Cosmic awareness, and enables the *sadhaka* to taste momentarily, *Sat Chit Ananda*– true bliss.

It does not matter which form or type of prayer you choose. God understands your needs, and He is always there for you. Prayer may not change your situation– but it is sure to change you. Outwardly, things may continue to be the same– but if you are changed, outward things will cease to matter!

Without setting aside time for prayer, we can accomplish nothing. We come up with so many excuses for shortage of time, which prevents us from praying. Our inability to pray is blamed upon the tyranny of time. "Where is the time to pray?" is the eternal lament of many.

On the contrary, it is when we have so much to do, that we must set aside more time than usual to pray, for prayer, in fact saves time. As prayer is essential to our lives, we can use our time to no better advantage. It is through prayer alone that we can tap into limitless and infinite resources of God. There is no better means than prayer to reach out to the Infinite.

Problems – Solve Them!

The word problem has an interesting origin. It is derived from the Greek word *proballein*, which means to put forth (from *pro* 'before' + *ballein* 'to throw'). Problems are thus objects thrown before us as in a game! We can catch them, deflect them, or throw them away!

Problems and challenges are not a dead end; they are only a bend in the road. Problems are not stumbling blocks; they are stepping stones to a better, richer, more radiant life. Not unoften, problems become the door through which God enters our lives. We have surrounded ourselves with hard shells which keep God away from us. Problems crack the shell, allowing God to easily enter our lives.

Are you facing a problem or challenge? Do you want the circumstances around you to change completely in order to suit you? Do you get frustrated and desperate when things don't go your way?

Do not try to change what is not in your control! Instead, try altering your perspective on life. Change the way you look at your problems; modify your way of thinking. Try to adopt a different attitude; take a different line of action.

Try focusing on a solution, instead of focusing on the problem.

A small exercise for you

Choose an incident from the life of a saint, a martyr, or a great personality. Jesus Christ, Gautama Buddha, Imam Hussain, the martyr of Karbala, Guru Tegh Bahadur, Sri Ramakrishna, Mahatma Gandhi are some of the names that spring readily to mind. None of these great souls had an easy time, none of their paths were strewn with flowers. They faced the kind of problems and challenges that might have left us crushed and defeated. Ponder on the magnanimity of their Spirit; marvel at the strength of their souls which enabled them to surmount all those extraordinary challenges and forge their way forward, Godward.

Derive strength, hope and inspiration from the lives of these great ones!

Scrap the negativity

It is said that Alexander Kuzmin, mayor of the city of Megion in Western Siberia, told his officials that they must stop using phrases such as "I don't know" and "It's lunch time", when citizens approached them with problems. Mr. Kuzmin felt that city officials should help improve people's lives and solve their problems, not make excuses!

"Bring me solutions, not problems", is a phrase that former British Prime Minister Margaret Thatcher was well known for using.

Simplicity is the key!

A friend once said to me that there is actually a website called "Solutions, not problems", operated by a consultancy service provider!

One of Japan's biggest cosmetic companies faced a management mishap, leading to the memorable case of 'the empty soap carton'. The company received a complaint that a consumer had bought a premium brand of soap, but upon opening the box, found it to be empty. Immediately the authorities isolated the problem to the assembly line, which transported all the packaged boxes of soap to the delivery department. For some reason, one soap box went through the assembly line empty. Management asked its engineers to solve the problem.

Highly qualified engineers worked hard to devise an X-ray machine with high-resolution monitors which would be manned by two people to screen all the soap boxes that passed through the line to ensure they were not empty.

No doubt, they worked hard and they worked fast, but they spent an astronomical amount to do so.

On the contrary, when an ordinary assembly line worker in a small company was posed with the same problem, he did not get into such complications as X-ray machines and monitors; he came up with a simpler solution. He bought a strong industrial, electric fan and faced it towards the assembly line. He switched the fan on, and as each soap box passed the fan, it simply blew the empty boxes out of the line.

It would benefit us to remember that not all problems require complicated solutions; in fact, some solutions are really simple. Therefore, let us learn to focus on solutions, not on problems!

Problems at work

One of the major causes of stress at work is that we are overwhelmed by the problems we face– work-related problems, relationship problems, problematic schedules and impossible deadlines.

All we need to do when we feel overwhelmed by stress is to remember that every problem has a solution!

I always say that problems are wonderful presents thrown at us by providence– only, we fail to realise that they are actually gifts, because they come wrapped up in a soiled package!

A problem is like a pebble. If you hold it close to your eye, it seems magnified, and it blocks your entire vision. If you hold it at arm's length, you can see its shape, its colour and its size. If you drop it at your feet, you can effortlessly walk over it!

Sometimes, we need to utilise lateral thinking while solving problems; we must learn to think 'out of the box' as we say! Let me tell you of a case that exemplifies using alternative ways of tackling problems.

We are told that when NASA began to send astronauts into space, they faced an unexpected problem: the pens that were available to them at that time wouldn't work at zero gravity– ink would not flow down to the writing surface. They spent all of 12 million U.S. dollars and took a decade to solve this problem. They developed a pen that worked at zero gravity, upside down, underwater, in practically any surface including crystal and in a temperature range from below freezing to over 300° C.

As for the Russians, they found a simpler solution: they used a pencil.

A sense of humour can help

Humour has its own indispensable role in helping you to solve your problems and succeed in life. I have often been asked, "Which do you think is the most important of the five senses?" My reply has always been, "None of the five, but the sixth one, the sense of humour." With your sense of humour, you can confront the most difficult of situations and can come out unscathed.

There was a student who was always smiling and cheerful. Wishing to cut him down to size the professor asked him, "What is there to smile about? Can you, for example, think of a solution to end unemployment?"

"Yes, Sir!" replied the student, cheerful as ever. "I'd put all the men on one island and all the women on another."

"Pray, how would that help?" sneered the professor.

"Well, they would all be busy building boats!" the young man announced.

A sense of humour can lift your spirits, put a twinkle in your eye, and a smile on your lips. In this mood you can take on the world.

Change your thinking!

When people say to themselves again and again, 'I am unhappy', 'I am miserable', 'People are against me', 'Conditions are against me', 'I am overwhelmed by my problems' and so on, they are gripped by a misery of their own making from which there can be no release except through their own effort. They imagine that they are injured beyond repair, and they simply cannot rise above their problems.

Instead, they must affirm to themselves, 'I was born to be happy', 'Happiness is my birthright', 'God created me to be happy'. As their conscious and unconscious thinking changes, conditions and people will also miraculously change. Thought by thought, step by step, as their minds change, the world will also change, and they will find satisfactory solutions to all their problems.

Turning problems into opportunities...

There is an old saying: There are no problems– only opportunities. Change the way you see your problems. Instead of regarding your problem as a difficulty or hindrance, see it as an opportunity.

Too often we focus on problems that we do not hear good fortune knocking at our door. When you are fixated on your problems, when you only think of what is wrong, you will only see problems and fail to catch opportunity by the forelock.

To turn things around, start by understanding your problems. Think of solutions, and you will attract solutions and opportunities. Locate the root of the problem and then think about how you can overcome it. Rephrase the problem– it might make it much easier to solve it. Even if you don't come up with any answers immediately, when you accept that you will find a solution, you will begin to experience a shift. You will move from feeling helpless to gaining confidence and a "can-do" attitude.

Seek solutions through prayer!

We should form the habit of praying and seeking solutions through prayer. We should appeal to the Cosmic Power to come to our aid and help us in sorting out problems and puzzles of life.

Remember, whatever seems impossible for man, is always possible for Him. Hence, ask of Him, He who is the Universal Giver.

When faced with problems, man is desperate to extricate himself from it. A well-known writer in the U.S.A. was once offered $1,000 by a man who was facing many problems. He said to the writer, "You solve people's problems. I will give you $1,000 if you solve my problems. Take care of my problems once and for all so that I do not have to face any more."

At this, the writer told him, "Go to a spot, a few furlongs away, where there are about a hundred thousand people who have no problems at all."

"No problems at all?" the man said in astonishment. "Show me the place. Maybe, I can rent space there."

The writer said, "That place is the graveyard. About a hundred thousand people have been buried there, and they have no problems whatsoever." The writer continued, "So long as there is life, there will be problems. Once your name appears in the obituary column of a daily newspaper, you will be absolved of all problems."

Difficulties arise in our lives, to teach us a lesson. They come to us so that we may evolve and rise above mundane happenings. Facing vicissitudes and challenges of life, will help us to grow in the inner Spirit of life.

Life has its fair share of problems…

Marriage, relationships, family quarrels, misunderstandings, trouble at work, children and their education, health, finances, career…there is no area of life without its attendant hurdles.

We need to build our moral strength and work out our own problem-solving strategies to cope with the obstacles that life throws at us.

Here are a few techniques to help you:

1. Hand your life and its problems to God. God can solve complications that seem unsolvable to you!

2. Stop trying to escape from reality. Face and embrace the facts so that you grow in awareness of the truth about life and people.

3. Cultivate the spirit of acceptance. The Buddha taught that the secret of life is to want what you have and not want what you don't have.

4. Take time to resolve problematic situations. As the story of the tortoise and the hare tells us, slow and steady wins the race. By being rash, we hinder our own chances of success. In rashness and haste, we are likely to make mistakes and pay for them later. We may choose a quick way out, but it may not necessarily be the best way. The old proverb tells us: the slower you go, the sooner you get there. A slow, disciplined, considered approach leads to lasting change and improvement.

5. Practise gratitude. It is easy to point out our troubles rather than count our blessings, but this only shuts us away from all the good that God has so generously bestowed on us! Be aware that your very life is a great gift! A change in perspective can make all the difference. Recognising the good and receiving it with gratitude is a remedy for mental and emotional well-being. This attitude of gratitude shows us how we can make use of the good we have been given and even use it to cope with the problems and difficulties that arise.

Prosperity

Prosperity is not just having a lot of money. It is an attitude, a mindset that thinks in terms of abundance, instead of lack and want. When the realisation dawns that there is nothing you lack, then the whole world belongs to you.

True prosperity is more than material abundance. A man may have plenty of money, but if he has no faith, he is destitute. The constituents of true prosperity are: (1) self-knowledge; (2) health and strength; (3) qualities of character; (4) fellowship with nature and (5) wealth of the world.

It is by no means bad to have money. We do not need to feel guilty about possessing wealth. In fact, one of the best things we can do is use our wealth judiciously and generously, on ourselves and our loved ones, as well as on deserving causes and our underprivileged brothers and sisters. The most charitable countries in the world are also those which enjoy a high level of prosperity and a good standard of living.

Prosperity does not lie in having an abundance of possessions, but in having fewer wants. The richest man is not he who owns the most, but he who is content with what he has. Wealth has never provided universal happiness. Often, the more a man possesses, the more he desires. Instead of filling a void, money tends to create it.

Abraham Lincoln had no great admiration for mere financial success. "Financial success," he once said, "is purely metallic. The man who gains it has four metallic attributes: gold on his palm, silver on his tongue, brass on his face, and iron in his heart."

Sadhu Vaswani's "Gospel of Wealth"

Sadhu Vaswani taught us that wealth must be earned, not simply obtained, or 'legally' possessed. The earning of wealth draws out your powers, teaches you concentration, helps a planned existence and is a contribution to the welfare at once, of your personality and society.

He would emphasise the notion that poverty is NOT morally and spiritually superior to prosperity; and that a vital nation and its thinking people should not repudiate wealth, but seek to convert it into national, social and individual prosperity.

My 'Formula for Prosperity' is rooted in the fundamental assumption that money is not in itself evil, that true wealth is valuable, and that the ideal of prosperity encompasses a sense of abundance and well-being that transcends mere wealth and money.

Are you wealthy? Do you aspire to greater wealth? Then, let me say to you: you do not have to feel guilty about your wealth, or ashamed of your genuine aspirations. But you must remember that the best thing you can do with your wealth is to convert it into personal, social and national well-being.

True prosperity

True prosperity belongs to him who has touched the Source of prosperity, whom for want of a better word, we call God. The needs of such a person are provided for even before they arise!

I believe that we bring our wealth with us when we are born into this world; it is determined by our karma. That which we have 'earned' shall be ours; not a penny more, not a penny less! But there is another kind of wealth on which no one can put a limit. It is for us to acquire, ad infinitum! This is the wealth of self realisation, the wealth of the *atman*!

Is money 'bad'? Is poverty 'good'?

There is nothing wrong with man possessing riches. Things begin to go wrong when the riches possess man.

Money in itself is neither good nor evil. It is up to us to put money to good or bad use. No one can deny that all of us need money for our survival in this world. But we can make money by honest means, put it to good use, and make ourselves and others happy by spending it wisely and well.

Equally, poverty in itself is not virtuous! Poverty has its charm for those who value self-denial. Yet the fact remains that it is not possible to live a really fulfilled life until we are able to satisfy our legitimate needs and also the needs of those who depend on us.

A Formula for Prosperity

Prosperity = $\mathcal{F}$n (Hard Work, Integrity, God's grace, and Philanthropy)

My formula emphasises honesty, hard work, integrity, discipline, dedication and God's grace.

When these virtues join forces in creating wealth, that wealth is truly earned– it will last with you, and it will bring benefits and blessings upon you and the good causes you spend it on.

Four aspects of prosperity

1. Material Prosperity

There is nothing wrong with earning money. There is nothing wrong in investing your money wisely for the security of your loved ones. All I say to my friends is– do not equate material possessions with happiness! Do not equate your 'success' with possessions! The truth is that life can be easy and smooth, if we do not have to worry about money. Alas, very few of us are really content with what we have; very few of us can truly say, "I don't need any more money."

Cultivating the right attitude towards material wealth:

- Do not feel guilty about making or wanting money, but always ensure that you adopt the right and honest methods to earn your money.

- Visualise your own success in acquiring wealth. Believe in yourself and achieve your goal!

- As Norman Vincent Peale tells us: "If you want to get more out of life, put more into life!" In other words, be prepared to work hard for your wealth.

- Do not resent the wealthy for their luxuries. Do not fall a prey to envy. The key to your wealth is your own attitude! Pay the price of what you want– and get it, win it honourably.

- Rely on God's grace to help you in your endeavours. Ask God's help to achieve your best potential.

- Do not exploit, deny, deprive or cheat others to gain your wealth. Grow rich– but help others grow rich too, and when you begin to acquire more, give some of it away in loving service of those who are not as fortunate as you!

- Cultivate positive thoughts about wealth: Many of us hold negative ideas about money– guilt, envy, fear, frustration and so on. Do not allow these negative emotions to affect you. Rather, use your visualising power to think positively about wealth and being wealthy.

- Build up a clear vision of what wealth means to you– and what you would like to do with your wealth.

2. Physical Well-being

"Health is wealth", is an age old adage. Life and its great gifts cannot be enjoyed until and unless one has a healthy body and an alert mind. Happiness, prosperity, and good health usually go together. We cannot experience true prosperity unless we cultivate mental, physical, and spiritual well-being. Unfortunately for many of us, we take our good health for granted when the going is good.

The foundation of a healthy body is a loving, content, peaceful mind. We must let nothing agitate or disturb our inner calm. You cannot consider yourself as a fit candidate for prosperity if you neglect your mind and body. An unhealthy, unfit body is a severe and strenuous burden to carry about in life.

3. Emotional Well-being:

Count your blessings! You will be filled with hope, optimism, and faith that will help you face the challenges of life! The great rishis of ancient India knew how valuable emotional well-being is for true prosperity. Therefore, at the end of every *Vedic* prayer, we hear the sacred chant– *Om Shanti, Shanti, Shanti!*

Peace in the heart within– emotional well-being– is vital to a sense of true prosperity. Possession of material riches without the presence of inner peace is equivalent to dying of thirst while bathing in the river.

Peace is our birthright! *Ananda*, bliss, the peace that passeth, nay, surpasseth understanding, is our birthright! We are God's children– and God is the Source of unending, eternal bliss! If only we could cultivate this faith– that whatever happens to us is in accordance with the Divine plan, that there is some hidden 'good' in it for us– we would not lose our equilibrium as often as we do!

There is an ancient story that tells us about a wise old man who was about to pass away. Knowing that he was on his deathbed, he called his four sons together and said to them, "I do not have a great deal of money, so I pass on to you four golden rules of a peaceful life. If you build your life on these rules, you will be blessed with that which is the best of gifts– a peaceful and blissful mind."

The sons were eager to benefit from their father's wisdom, and begged him to give them the four golden rules of a peaceful life. These were:

1. Seek not to please men: seek only to please God.
2. Take serious things lightly and light things seriously.
3. Laugh as much as you can.
4. Cultivate the spirit of acceptance.

4. Spiritual Fulfillment

When you grow in the awareness of the spirit, you identify yourself with the Everlasting. You begin to say to yourself, "I am not this body. I am the *atman*, the deathless spirit. My spirit is of the universe. My essence is of God." This realisation releases a tremendous energy of the spirit within you, that can transform your life and your personality completely!

Becoming aware of the Divine within you, you begin to recognise and respect the divinity in others, and your consciousness expands; you become more understanding, more tolerant, more loving and forgiving, more magnanimous– in short, more divine than human! You discover the joy of spiritual fulfilment, which is far, far greater than material wealth.

Never gain the world at the expense of losing your soul. The material wealth you possess can be stolen, but the treasure of the soul can never be taken away from you.

We are told of a wealthy industrialist, who leaped from the 9th floor of a hotel in Chicago. He left behind a note, "I am worth ten million dollars as per the judgement of men; but I am so poor in spirit that I can no longer live."

Is material wealth and worldly happiness an impediment on the path of spirituality? The answer is, when you begin to tread the path of spiritual awareness, then you will find that you do not really aspire to material possessions. You leave it to the Lord. It is for God to give you whatever He likes. God is our Master– and let me assure you, He is a very benevolent Master!

Spiritual awareness helps you to surrender the thread of your life in His safe, benevolent hands– and you will find miracles happening in your daily life!

Within each one of us are immense energies of the Eternal, tremendous powers of the spirit. If only we can unlock even a fraction of these powers, we will find that there is nothing that we will not be able to achieve.

Relationships

A loving relationship is one of the most valuable assets a human being can be blessed with.

We ensure that our money, our precious metals, our movable and immovable assets are secure and well protected. But I wonder how far we value something that is our greatest asset in this worldly life, namely human relationships.

As human beings, there are quite a lot of people and things that we relate to. We cherish Mother Nature and the environment we live in; we develop a special attachment to certain locations like our favourite parks, beaches or mountains; we have special nooks and quiet places within and outside our homes; there are also certain times of the day that are special to us. In fact, we have a vital working relationship with so many of these treasured spots and times– our peaceful morning walk, our quiet ten minutes on the terrace or the balcony, our comfortable stretch on that cosy rocking chair…

But human relationships are special! They need to be nourished, sustained, and carefully cultivated so that they do not wither away due to our neglect. If there is one thing we take for granted in life, apart from the air we breathe, it is those very relationships that make our life meaningful! We choose our favourite relationships carefully enough to begin with– but having made them, we choose to allow most of them to thrive on benign neglect!

Every relationship is unique and special. Parents, spouses, children, family, friends, neighbours, colleagues, superiors, subordinates, employers or employees– every relationship needs to be nurtured with love, understanding, and patience.

Relationships are not confined to family alone, though to most of us, families must always come first. I would like you to think of the larger family today– of friends, friends-in-the-making, colleagues at work, neighbours, and the hundreds of people whose lives you touch in one way or the other…

The interconnectedness of human beings

This is one of the most beautiful things in life. Let me give you the beautiful words of the original sermon by poet John Donne: "No man is an island, entire of itself; every man is a piece of the continent, a part of the main; if a clod be washed away by the sea, Europe is the less, as well as if a promontory were, as well as any manner of thy friends or of thine own were; any man's death diminishes me, because I am involved in mankind. And therefore never send to know for whom the bell tolls; it tolls for thee…"

Today, nearly six hundred years after the sermon was delivered, people hold it up as an exemplary warning against isolationism and indifference. No one suffers alone, the poet argues emphatically; and being aware of another's pain and suffering only makes us stronger and more sensitive, more caring!

Stop criticising: Start appreciating!

Pause and think for a minute: How have you chosen to treat your relationships with the people who matter most in your life?

True love enhances; it does not degrade or devalue. True love builds up the self-respect of the loved one and does not diminish it in any way. If you truly love someone, how can you belittle that person?

In any relationship, we should not idealise the other. In time we will find that they have feet of clay, and are unable to live to our expectations. Instead, we must accept others as they are; we should water and nurture any growing relationship with sincerity and genuineness.

Relationships are for cherishing, not for criticising, fault-finding, and playing the blame game. The best way to nourish relationships is by making an effort to understand people, putting yourself in their shoes, empathising with them, and appreciating their presence in your life…

Today, most people view relationships negatively. Think of the familiar complaints you hear in every direction… My parents don't understand me/ My children don't appreciate what I do for them/ My husband can't spare time for me/ My wife doesn't realise the stress I face every day/ My staff is no good/ My superior is very harsh… and so on and so forth…

For a change, shall we choose the following positive assertions just for today?

- I am lucky to have parents who are so supportive…
- My children make my life worthwhile…
- Life is beautiful because of my friends…
- I'm glad to be working and happy to be part of a team…
- Where would I be without all of them who make my life what it is?

- I value all the people in my life… the domestic helpers, the office assistants, the shopkeepers who serve me, the civic workers who keep the city, the traffic, and the systems moving… Where would I be without their unseen presence?

Let us choose here and now, to understand and appreciate the people in our lives; let us learn to listen; let us learn to put ourselves in the other person's shoes before we find faults or criticise them.

Egocentric love demands that the other person should live, act, and do everything for your benefit alone! I'm afraid that it is demeaning and degrading to regard a friend or a partner or a child as someone who can be possessed and controlled.

Relationships are like a fist full of sand in your hand. If held loosely on the open palm of your hand, the sand will remain. The moment you close your fist to hold it tight, the sand begins to trickle out through your fingers.

When relationships are maintained loosely, with respect and freedom, they sustain. But when they are held on too tightly and possessively, the relationship and the bonding begin to unravel, and then slip away and are lost.

Let us cherish our elders!

If you are fortunate enough to have family elders, grandparents, learn to love and cherish them! Recent research carried out by psychologists at Emory University tells us that children who know first-hand about their family history (having heard about their parents and their families from their grandparents, including details of where they came from, where they went to school, how the family made or lost its fortune, how the uncles and aunts grew up, etc.) always proved to be more resilient and positive than children brought up in islation. This kind of family knowledge builds what psychologists call "the intergenerational self", or the sense of belonging to something larger than the individual self!

Sadly, old age homes in 21st century India are full of senior citizens who have not only given the best years of their life to their children– but also bestowed their life-savings, pensions, and provident fund on their offspring in the fond hope that they will be loved and cared for in their old age– only to be 'dumped' in such homes when the children no longer need them!

The fundamental values of our society are being eroded with the fragmentation of families and the rejection of old people– and 'unwanted' children. For, at the other end of the spectrum, our orphanages are also overflowing with abandoned children– especially girl children, who, it seems, are children of a lesser God! Why else would their own mothers abandon them on rubbish heaps and street corners?

Do our hearts beat within us? Are we human beings with a heart, mind, and soul? Can this happen in a civilised society which boasts of an ancient culture?

Cherish the women in your life!

We no longer value a woman who lives for her husband or her children. But we must insist that there is more to a woman than family and relationships. I think no woman would willingly sacrifice her relationships for the sake of achieving career goals or professional success! For that matter, no man would wish to do that either. Ideally, we would want to have it all: professional success, personal fulfilment, and rewarding relationships within and outside the family!

The old proverb stating that there is a woman behind every successful man has now become gender-sensitive, and we acknowledge that there is an understanding man, indeed an understanding family, including a sweet natured and helpful mother-in-law (mother-in-love, as I like to call her), behind every successful woman! All our most successful women would agree that they would not have reached where they were, without the love and support of their family.

The wife of a successful executive or businessman puts aside her selfish or personal claims upon his time; she takes on his responsibilities at home and gives him the space to succeed. Equally, an understanding husband encourages his wife's aspirations and special talents, and creates an environment where she can succeed. If ego intervenes in such relationships, everyone loses!

Healing and restoring relationships

We have said that human beings are not perfect! The plane of action, is also the plane of friction. Somewhere, somehow, we snap; we lose our temper; we lose our sense of balance; we blame each other, often unfairly. And then, before we even realise it, a misunderstanding becomes a major rift, a minor difference of opinion becomes an irreconcilable break… A relationship nurtured carefully for years, seems to break apart…

When tensions are rising and troubles are mounting, it is people who are close to us that bear the brunt of our stress. We are often courteous, polite, and kind to perfect strangers, but rude and brusque to our own spouses and parents. Isn't that sad?

The first step here is to tell ourselves firmly: I am NOT the victim! The other person is NOT the offender!

We need to rid ourselves of persecution complexes; we need to come out of the victim-trap and develop emotional maturity. We will then find that our perception alters, our reactions are more measured, and our attitude becomes enlightened.

Truly it has been said, life is too short to be small. Let us not be small-minded. Let us be generous with praise, appreciation, and encouragement. Let us avoid anger, irritation, and fault-finding altogether! Let us be swift to love and lavish in our kindness.

We often think of our friends, spouses, and parents as "pillars of strength" which are always there for our solid support. I urge you to occasionally think of them as precious plants that need loving and constant tending!

Keep ego out of your relationships!

A well-known relationship expert remarks that the ego has no relationship skills! The ego tries to manipulate people by adopting various negative techniques like aggression, resistance, withdrawal, and intolerance. Our hearts, on the other hand, rely on intuitive techniques like understanding, forgiveness, patience and trust, to nourish our relationships and take them forward. When our understanding hearts win the battle over the ego, relationships flourish; when ego takes over, relationships lose out.

How does ego manifest itself in ruining relationships?

- We expect too much from others, and are not prepared to give as much as we take.

- We cultivate a sense of entitlement; we imagine that others are there to do what we need and make life easy for us.

- We lap up praise and appreciation, but we are not prepared to appreciate others.

- We become critical, even judgmental to the point of severity and harshness. We set impossibly high standards for others, which do not apply to us.

- We cease to cultivate that wonderful 'attitude of gratitude' that makes lives meaningful.

- We forget what it is to forgive with an understanding heart.

- We live under the illusion that we do not have to apologise under any circumstances.

There are other extremes to which low self-esteem or a negative ego can take us: we may become passive or withdraw altogether; we may become depressed and frustrated; worst of all, we may erase our true nature while trying hard to be the kind of person we imagine other people expect us to be. All this is not selfless; it is self-destructive.

Life reflects your attitude…

A stranger arrived at the gates of a city, which he was visiting for the first time. An old woman sitting on the roadside greeted him, "Welcome to our city."

"What kind of people live here?" the stranger asked her.

"What kind of people live in your home town?" the old woman asked him with a smile.

"Oh, they were terrible," swore the stranger. "They were mean, nasty, malicious and selfish. They were impossible to live with."

"You will find people here are pretty much the same," the old woman said to him.

A little later, another stranger arrived at the city gates, and was welcomed by the old woman.

"What kind of people live in this city?" the second traveller asked.

"How did you find them in your home town?" the woman asked him.

"They were a wonderful lot– hard working, friendly, and easy to get along with."

"You will find the people here likewise," the old woman assured him.

Approach people with love and understanding– and you will find the same reflected in their approach to you.

Religion

What is religion? Most of us understand religion in simple terms: as belief in and worship of a superhuman controlling power, whom we refer to as a personal God or Gods. Thus we use as synonyms of religion, the words faith, belief, or denomination. Sociologists and anthropologists describe religion as "a collection of cultural systems, belief systems, and worldviews that relate humanity to spirituality and moral values".

To define religion is to delimit religion! Narrow and rigid definitions tend to exclude many faiths which are devoutly held by people. For example, a theistic definition would exclude Buddhism, which is a non-theistic faith. Many definitions equate religion with one form or another of Christianity. This would label two-thirds of the world's population as non-religious!

Definitions and distinctions can be left to the experts. I am more concerned with what religion means to all of us in terms of our life and actions, in terms of deeds of daily life.

Gurudev Sadhu Vaswani had a simple suggestion for all of us. He was, indeed, a rare saint. He was a saint of silence, a saint of few words. Those few words were potent with wisdom. One of the teachings he gave us was this– Religion: let us talk of it less, practise more!

These words are inscribed on a large hoarding just outside the Mission Headquarters in Pune. *Religion: let us talk of it less, practise more!* Through these simple words he conveyed the whole philosophy of living, because religion is a way of life.

Life, not words

Men today are beginning to lose faith in religion, because religion has been separated from life. Religion will come into its own, when men learn to live in amity and peace with their fellow men. Civilisation is sinking, for there is lack of unity in our lives. Civilisation may be saved if life is built in the vision of the One-in-all.

May I tell you, our practice of religion is superficial. We attach great meaning to the words, written or spoken. We give importance to reading books. Yes, I admit they do have their value. They have their value in giving you the external knowledge.

Religion is not reading or reciting scriptures; religion is not performance of elaborate rituals and *poojas*; religion is not giving or hearing discourses. Nor is it preaching of the scriptures, singing devotional songs, or mechanical incantation of holy words! What is important is your *bhav*, your feelings, your emotions, your surrender to the Lord!

May I also add, external practices do not constitute religion. Singing *bhajans* and clapping hands is not religion. These are but outward forms of expression. The essence of faith lies within! The essence of religion is spirituality. And spirituality is best expressed through the service of love.

Religion is not to be studied. It is to be lived, it is to be experienced. We can experience religion, practise and uphold *dharma*, by cultivating good thoughts and by doing good deeds. We have to bear witness to religion. God does not want words, he wants our good actions. Religion means doing our duties, shouldering our responsibilities, and service to society and humanity at large.

On one occasion, Jesus admonished his disciples and said to them, "Here you call me Lord, but in the Kingdom of Heaven I shall say I know you not." He also told his disciples, "You must not be *hearers* of the Word, but *doers* of the Word."

It is life that is needed– not creeds, not dogmas, not labels or loud professions of faith.

Compassion is the root of religion!

Daya dharam ka mool hai… sang a saint of India. Indeed, compassion brings with it kindness, it brings love, it brings fellowship, and it brings service. A man whose heart is filled with compassion is a friend of all; he is kind and loving to all, not only to human beings, but also to birds, animals and insects.

Today, I am sad to say, our hearts have become hard as stone. But once hearts are lit with devotion and love, the rigid crust falls off. When the heart is filled with love it becomes soft, it acquires the capacity to sympathise and empathise with those in sorrow and suffering and those in distress.

Saint Narsi Mehta had composed a beautiful song in Gujarati. It was a great favourite of Mahatma Gandhi, and was sung as an early morning prayer in Gandhiji's *ashrama*.

The song begins with the beautiful line which all of us are familiar with: "*Vaishnav jan to tene kahiye, jay peerh paraayee jaaney rey!*"

It means: *He is a true Vaishnava, a true devotee of the Lord, who can feel the pain and suffering of another.*

A man who has compassion in his heart is spiritual. He may not go to *satsang*. He may not practise or even believe in rituals. But if he practises kindness in his daily life, he is truly a devotee of the Lord, a superior being.

Religion is a way of purification

Religion is a way of self-growth and self-realisation. Every religion has its distinct essence. Islam emphasises brotherhood; Buddhism preaches compassion; Hinduism exalts the supremacy of the *atman,* the Soul– I am that: *Tat twam asi*; Christianity gives the message of love and forgiveness. The goal of all these religions is to purify and develop the higher self.

All paths lead to the One!

In the fourth chapter of the Bhagavad Gita, we find a beautiful *sloka:*

However men approach me, even so do I greet them; for the path men take from any side is Mine, O Arjuna!

(IV – 11)

Speaking to his dear devoted disciple Arjuna, the Lord says, "At the end of each path do I stand. All ways are My ways. All men everywhere walk to Me!"

Gurudev Sadhu Vaswani's comments on this *sloka* are truly memorable: "His Path, indeed, is the One Path: there is no other. He is the One Bridge that spans the sea of sorrow, the Bridge of Light. The Bridge has diverse colours, and each is called by a different name. The Bridge has different sections or stages. *Jnana, bhakti, karma* are some of the names used by men to indicate what helps them to cross: but the path for all is still His path."

All paths lead us to God. Therefore, fights, feuds, arguments, discussions, debates and differences in the name of religion are futile. You can follow the path that draws you; let another follow the path that draws him; yet another can take the path that he chooses– ultimately, all of you will arrive at the same destination.

Rumi, the great Sufi mystic tells us, "Every prophet and every saint hath a way, but it leads to God: all the ways are really one."

Truer words were never spoken! In the Kingdom of God, the Kingdom of Heaven, there are no Hindus, Christians or Muslims. In the Kingdom of God, we will not be judged according to our labels or the creeds we believe in, but according to the life that we have lived.

Beautiful indeed are the words penned by Sadhu Vaswani:

In all religions, the Light is Thine,
In all scriptures, the Inspiration is Thine
In all the saints, the Picture is Thine ...

"The Creation of God," he said, "is bound by golden chains to the Feet of the One God, the One Divine Father of us all." At His Feet are we all one– men of different religions and no religion. For no one is alien in the Kingdom of God. All scriptures embody spiritual wisdom. Therefore, sectarian strife and quarrels in the name of religion are due to lack of knowledge, lack of understanding and want of sympathy. So it is that quarrels, discords and hatred have entered the sphere of religion. Religion, which was meant to be a bond of union, has become a source of dissention. Little wonder then, that young men and women today, are turning away from true religion.

Sadhu Vaswani did not stop with words. His life bore witness to the profound truth of the Oneness of all religions. The religions of the world are not contradictory or antagonistic, he taught us. All religions are true, for all lead to the one Goal: and the Goal is God.

God is Love

A man came to Sadhu Vaswani and said to him, "You say God is Love; God is Mercy. Why is it that your God stands by and watches while there is so much violence and suffering in the world?"

Sadhu Vaswani pointed to a tablecloth, which he had just removed to be put for wash. At the back of the cloth was a mishmash of crisscrossed stitches, with knots and ties and tangles. It all looked so untidy. But when the cloth was turned right side up, the man saw on it, beautifully embroidered, the words, God is Love. "It is we who turn religion inside out," the Master explained. "God is Love; God is Mercy when we see life right."

Today, in the name of religion, we have fights and feuds, sectarian strife, hatred and violence. But let us not forget that religion came to unite, to reconcile, to create harmony among men. **It is not religion which has failed us, it is we who have failed religion!**

Therefore, Sadhu Vaswani constantly urged us, "Let us talk of religion less, practise more!" We need to follow his wise counsel now, more than ever before; we need to put into practice the great truths and ideals of religion in our daily life. And if we really take the trouble to study the great religions of the world, we will come to know that they emphasise the ideals of love, peace, service, piety, prayer and brotherhood.

Why is there rivalry in religion?

I humbly submit to you, that rivalry in religion is meaningless. There can be no rivalry among true religions.

There are some who believe that they have the one full and final revelation of the truth, and those who stand outside the circle of their own faith must necessarily be in error. There are some who approach religious issues without the spirit of sympathy; they fix their attention on what they regard as the aberrations and extravagances of a particular religion and say, "This religion is a monstrosity!" Saddest of all, we have people who hurt and kill in the name of religion. They are ignorant of the fact that they are killing their own brothers and sisters!

Religion should help us to move towards peace and bliss, both inner and outer. It should help us to cultivate spiritual qualities and be better human beings.

Your religion is your mother!

Our religion, the faith we are born into, is like a mother to each one of us, and all religions are sisters. If Hinduism is my mother, Christianity is my aunt. I often say, "If Krishna is my father, Christ is my uncle!"

All mothers may not be equal in virtue or intelligence, but it is natural for everyone to regard his own mother as the best in the world. Each one honestly believes that his religion is the best. Among my friends are people belonging to different religions, and we have found that there is a basic unity among all religions. This basic unity, not the differences, must be emphasised, if we are to have peace in the world.

If I regard my religion as the best and consider other religions as inferior to mine, there will surely be quarrels and strife among the people of the earth. Behind the desire to convert is the belief that my religion is superior to that of the person whom I seek to convert.

Religion

This is what leads to discord and strife. Everyone regards his own mother as the best, but that does not prevent him from learning something from his aunts. Nor on that account, would he expect or ask others to give up their mothers and adopt his own.

You do not choose the family in which you are born, nor even the religion to which you belong. The choice is made by God and is for your highest good.

Respond- Don't Retaliate

We all wish to live a life of peace and joy. If you want to experience all-pervading peace, there is one discipline that you must practise in your life: to speak sweetly, act kindly, and to refrain from retaliation.

Even if someone insults you or humiliates you, do not retaliate in anger. Just by bringing someone down, you cannot raise yourself up.

It is a sad fact of life, that if someone hurls at us one harsh word or a single insult, we return ten harsh words and multiple insults in retaliation. We snub and put people down effortlessly with acid remarks and sharp phrases. We actually feel proud and triumphant when our harsh words shock and hurt the other person. But this triumph turns to bitter ashes in no time. How can we love ourselves for being unkind and abusive? If we wish to be at peace within and without, we should refrain from retaliation; we should return silence instead of trading insults. Even better, we should return sweet words for ruthless reproaches. We lose out on our own inner peace when we hit back at others. On the other hand, we trumph over our own base emotions when we remain courteous and refuse to retaliate!

The blame game

Hakim Luqman has given a wonderful prescription for health and happiness: *Kam Khao, Gam Khao*. Eat less, and conquer your anger. By remaining silent and refusing to retaliate, we are enhancing our inner store of positive energy. But by lashing out, we only unleash negative energies within us. Ego clashes are everyday occurrences in our lives. We play the blame game, holding all others responsible for our mistakes. Pass the blame on to others! The blame game is played mostly in self-defense. Often, we become extra cruel in order to teach the other person a 'lesson'. We strike back and consider it our strength. The fact is that winning the blame game puts us on what is called an ego trip. The blame game is indeed a no-win situation, for the problem is not solved, or even understood. Everyone is only interested in passing the buck; no one wants to find a way out of the difficulty.

Speak gently!

May I share with you these beautiful lines which I love to reflect on:

Mitha bolan
Niv chalan
Hathun bhi kuch de
Rab tina de paas
Vo jangal kyun dhoondhe.

In translation, this beautiful verse means:

Speak gently,
Walk humbly,
Give something in charity.
Then you need not to the forest go
For the Lord is with you already!

If you do these things dutifully, then there is no need for you to undertake *tapasya* or penance. There is no need for you to go to a *tapoban* in quest of God. For God, the source of joy and happiness, will come in quest of you– and meet you!

A veritable roadmap for the life beautiful is given to us in those three injunctions: (1) Speak sweetly; (2) Walk humbly; and (3) Give something in charity with your own hands.

Time and again, I have appealed to my friends and fellow *satsangis,* with folded hands: speak sweetly. Let me share with you these lines which I read somewhere:

Speak gently! It is better by far
To rule by love than fear;
Speak gently! Let no harsh word mar
The good that we may do here.

Rude behaviour is ignoble. Harsh words cause deeper wounds than sticks and stones. The poet-saint, Thiruvalluvar, tells us: *Burnt flesh and skin heal sooner or later, but the wounds inflicted by a harsh tongue never, ever heal.* Why should we be guilty of inflicting such wounds? Therefore, let us resolve to speak gently, softly, sweetly.

The *tapasya* of the tongue

Each one of us is responsible for our own actions; we are accountable for all that happens to us. As Lord Krishna tells us in the Gita, man can be his own best friend or his own worst enemy. Our own actions are responsible for the reactions of others. When we harbour evil thoughts towards others or utter harsh words to others, the same negative energy reverts back and hits us. By retaliating or deliberately insulting someone, we sow the seeds for the reactions of others. It is the Universal Law of Nature that whatever you send out comes back to you. If you send out negative energy, it reverts to you like an echo, sooner rather than later.

A saint was once asked, "Please tell us Guruji, how did you attain such a peaceful state of mind?"

He thought for a while and then replied, "I have practised only one self-discipline, one *sadhana,* and that is the *tapasya* of the tongue. I have controlled the impulse to speak unnecessarily. Many a time, when I was tempted to speak, I have controlled myself and remained silent."

Such is the mark of saints. They are calm and peaceful, composed and balanced in all states and conditions of life. Their humility makes them the beloved of the Lord.

The Lord has no need of the proud, the learned, the wise, the wealthy and the powerful. He always chooses the lowly and the humble, who have no bloated egos. He accepts those who with His grace, have completely overcome their ego.

The witness of the great ones…

One day a man went to the Buddha and said, "You have destroyed the essence of our religion. You are an atheist. What do you think of yourself? Are you hankering after power and status? You are a betrayer of your faith and you call yourself a sadhu? I have nothing but contempt for you!"

Gautama Buddha heard him out patiently. At last he smiled and said, "Dear brother, if someone gives you a gift and you refuse to accept it, then to whom will the gift belong?"

The man replied with a sneer of contempt, "It is just like you to ask such a foolish question! The gift will of course belong to the man who brought it in the first place."

Gautama Buddha smiled and said, "In that case, the heap of abuses that you have brought for me must remain with you. For I choose not to accept them." Hearing this, the man was stunned into silence.

Prophet Muhammed (peace be upon him) always carried a sword. He had inscribed on it certain maxims. The first maxim was, "If anyone hurts you, if anyone harms you, forgive that person immediately. Forgive before you are asked for forgiveness." The second maxim was, "If anyone has done you wrong, do good to him." The third maxim was, "Always speak the truth, even if you have to pay a heavy price for it."

We would do well to write down all the three maxims on a piece of paper and read them every day. Gradually, we will internalise these valuable truths and translate them into deeds of daily life.

Forgive and forget!

A scientist was doing research on meteorology. Every morning and evening he noted down the barometer readings on a sheet of paper. He did this for many years. The papers filled with the accumulated data of several years were piled up on his table. He had a reliable servant who did not disturb him or move the papers on his tables. The servant for some reason had to leave for his home town; in his absence, he offered the services of a woman who would work as a substitute. The new maid was unaware of the scientist's research work. The very next day after his morning walk, when the scientist returned to his room to note down the outside temperature and compare it with earlier temperatures, he was shocked to see his table cleared and his research papers missing. He called the new maid in and asked her, "Where are the papers that were placed on this table? Have you kept them somewhere else?"

The maid replied, "Sir, the pile of papers was old and dusty. The pages had turned yellow. I therefore gathered them and burnt them."

Can you imagine what the scientist felt at that time? All the painstaking research work of twenty long years had turned into ashes. The amount of time and effort that had gone into the work was enormous. Even then the scientist remained calm. He did not lose his head. He did not retaliate; he did not resort to calling names or heaping abuse on the maid. He lived with the faith that whatever happens, happens for the best. He felt that there must be some hidden meaning in what had happened. He did not so much as utter a single harsh word to the maid. He forgave her even before she could ask for forgiveness.

Each outburst of anger is like the eruption of a volcano, and the words we utter in anger are like the hot lava that flows from the burning volcano, destroying every living thing in its way. By retaliating with bitterness and harsh words, we are only harming ourselves.

There is always a better option to harsh words

India's epics and *puranas* are a veritable treasure trove of the highest spiritual values. Our culture embodies the values of reverence, obedience, and sacrifice. Thus, when Sri Rama is ordered by Queen Kaikeyi to renounce his throne and go into exile for fourteen years, he does not retaliate or refuse; he obeys her instantly, without the least trace of ill-will or resentment. To be good to those who are good to us is easy; it is also normal human behaviour. But to be good to those who are bad to us is a great human virtue. By refusing to retaliate in anger, by refraining from tit-for-tat, we are washed and cleansed, we become purer.

Once, I was an invigilator at an examination. While supervising the candidates, I noticed that one of them was looking into his palm, now and then. I went closer to him. When he opened the palm, I could see several formulae written on it. I told the boy, "Brother, if you do not get enough help from these formulae, you can ask me." The boy was stunned; he never expected this kind of reaction. In fact he thought that if he were caught he would be punished.

Years later when this boy had become the Director of a company, he came to meet me. He said, "Whatever I am today is because of you. Your reaction at the examination taught me a great lesson. It has taught me the value of integrity. I am ever thankful to you for your teaching by example on that unforgettable day."

I said to him, "God was kind to you. He guided me to be kind to you. Or else, I would have rusticated you for cheating during the examination. You would have been debarred from studies for three years." Some teachers have a wrong notion that to discipline a student they have to reprove him with harsh words and punish him. Their argument is this: if they punish one student, the rest of them will get the message alright. But it is not so. You can discipline and transform students through loving kindness.

Sri Krishna in all!

In India, we have the beautiful tradition of greeting everyone we meet with folded hands and the reverential greeting: *Namaste*! It is the God within the human form that we salute thus. If Lord Krishna Himself resides in the people we meet, how can we talk harshly to Him? Should we not be soft, gentle, reverential, and sweet to the Lord? Each one of us is the image of Lord Krishna. We should speak to each other reverently, gently, and sweetly. Even if you disagree with others, and want to refute their arguments, you can do so with humility in your heart. You may disagree to comply with their requests, but you can do all this without hurting anyone, without creating discord, without using harsh words. You can negotiate with the most stubborn and egoistic individuals, using your personal charm and gentle words. This behaviour will come to you naturally, if you realise that Sri Krishna is within every one. Automatically your attitude will change and you will be reverent, considerate, and gentle with others. You need not disclose to the other person that he is an image of Sri Krishna, for that may merely inflate his ego. But you should remind yourself, that Sri Krishna is seated within the hearts of all.

The sweetest thing in the world

A king once put a question to the noblemen sitting in his *darbar:* What is the sweetest thing on earth? He said to his courtiers, "I do not want a text book answer. Your answer should come from your own experience." One of the lords seated there, answered, "The sweetest thing in this world is honey." The second lord said, "The sweetest thing is unrefined sugar-candy." The third person answered, "The sweetest thing is sugar." The fourth was, "*halwa.*" Thus many such answers were given.

The king then posed a second question, "Which is the bitterest thing in the world?" "Poison," replied someone. The king immediately chided the person, "Have you ever taken poison? Have you ever experienced its effect? I said, the answers should come from your own experience. A person who has taken poison, cannot be alive."

There were many answers such as *karela* (bitter gourd), copper sulphate, and so on. At last, one man gave an answer which pleased the king greatly. He said, "Your majesty, the answer to both your questions is one and the same: it is the human tongue. Man can have a sweet tongue or a sharp tongue. A sweet tongue is soothing; it is like a balm. It is the sweetest thing. A sharp tongue hurts and harms. It is the bitterest thing in the world." The king was very pleased with the answer and rewarded the man for the same.

The sweetest and the bitterest, the gentlest and harshest thing in this world is 'the tongue'. Time and again, the volunteers at the Sadhu Vaswani Mission serve *gulab jamuns, jilebi* and ice cream, so that all of us may develop a 'sweet' tongue. If you are one of those who love these sweet desserts, do enjoy them, but ensure they help you to develop sweet, gentle speech.

Reverence for All Life

The Law of Reverence is fundamental to the Hindu way of life.

The Law of Reverence is the Law of *Shraddha*. The essence of the Vedas, or what we call *Vedanta*, is one of the abiding principles of Hindusim. *Vedanta* teaches us that there is but One Life in all! The One Life permeates the entire universe and all of Creation. The One Life sleeps in the mineral and the stone, stirs in the vegetable and the plant, dreams in birds and animals, it wakes up in man. Therefore, let us respect, revere life in all forms.

Reverence, I always say, is of three aspects: Reverence for what is above us, reverence for what is around us, and reverence for what is beneath us.

It was the poet Tennyson who penned those memorable lines, which I love to quote again and again:

Let knowledge grow from more to more,
But more of reverence in us dwell!

If there is one quality which is sadly lacking in our lives today, it is the beautiful virtue of reverence.

Start with the child!

My Beloved Master, Sadhu Vaswani, emphasised that this beautiful concept of reverence for all life should be inculcated in children through the right type of education, and imbibed by them through all their school activities: sports, games, literary activities, scientific experiments, and all curricular and extra-curricular activities.

Vidya dadati vinayam– so our scriptures teach us. True knowledge, true scholarship, is humility. Education must be rooted in all forms of fundamental reverence– reverence for the teacher, and on the part of the teacher, respect and love for the pupils. Such was the spirit that prevailed in our ancient *ashramas*. How I wish we could rekindle this beautiful attitude today! Only in such an atmosphere of mutual respect and reverence can true ideals and high values be imparted.

Why reverence for the world around us is essential

The same *shakti* that is present within you, is manifested in the workings of this vast universe. The One Life animates all Creation– and that life energy comes from God, who is the Creator of the entire universe and the Bestower of all that we have. When we link ourselves to the power and energy of the universe, our own finite power and energy are multiplied manifold.

Think of yourself opening the windows of your room early in the morning, and breathing in deeply the fresh, cool, invigorating morning air.

Think of all those who rise early to take a pre-dawn walk on the beach, in a park, or in an open space, often ending with *surya namaskar.*

Think of a tired teacher or researcher, putting her work away for a few minutes, to look up at the clean blue sky and refresh her eyes and her mind.

Think of the business magnates in Mumbai who snatch precious minutes from their hectic schedules to go jogging on the promenade at Nariman Point or at the Bandstand in Bandra.

Think of the busy New Yorker who juggles his routine to be able to spend a few minutes at Central Park.

All these people have one thing in common: they are recharging their spirits by contact with the refreshing energy of the universe.

Unlike the human mind, the universe does not emit negative energies. Sunshine or rain, calm or storm, morning or night, the universe is always a storehouse of marvellous positive energy.

We have often heard people saying, "I've been cooped up in my office all day, and I have a headache," or "I've been pouring over my accounts for hours, and I'm exhausted." Have you ever heard people complaining, "I've just come back from a walk and I feel drained out" or "I have taken a stroll in the park and I am suffering from a headache?"

The positive forces of nature, the life-giving energy of this universe is meant to restore us to emotional and physical balance, and revive our flagging spirits. We must tap this energy if we wish to achieve the best that we are capable of. Therefore I say, reverence for nature is essential. Reverence for nature will help us live healthy lives which bear witness to the Spirit of the One Life in all.

Today, I am told, 'Environmental Science' has become a compulsory subject for the graduates of all disciplines in a few Indian universities. But I feel that theory is not enough. Our students must be taught to revere, and be one with the spirit of nature!

Man, they say, is the Crown of God's Creation. Therefore, let our children be taught to take on the role of guardians, protectors, and wardens of nature!

Reverence for all races and religions

We must encourage our young people to respect all races and religions. The world today is being torn apart by religious fundamentalism and religious fanaticism. Our youth must learn that true religion is not institutional, that true religion will never condone violence and hatred.

We must teach the younger generation to have reverence and respect for Indian ideals. At the same time, we should also teach them that the truly great ones are not a monopoly of India, but have appeared in all countries and all climes; they have enriched the lives of all races, and inspired and illumined all religions.

Therefore, let us teach them to love and revere Sri Rama and Sri Krishna, Allah and Isa, Mahavira, Buddha, Zoroaster, and Guru Nanak. Let them be taught of Rishi Veda Vyasa, Rishi Vashishta, Prophet Muhammad, St. Francis, Guru Gobind Singh, Baha'u'llah, Sri Ramakrishna, and Mahatma Gandhi.

The inner revolution, the cultivation of the Spirit in our youth, must come from reverence for the great ones of the East and West, and their teachings.

Reverence for suffering humanity

Our education must give us the best knowledge– specialisation in key disciplines, practical application, and leadership skills. But we must also be taught to love, revere, and pour out our compassion on the creatures of God, who suffer and groan in pain.

Sometime ago, one of India's distinguished and valiant daughters, Kiran Bedi, I.P.S., visited our Sadhu Vaswani Mission to address a special gathering of teachers that we had organised in connection with the Platinum Jubilee of our MIRA Education Movement. Asked about the kind of educational reforms we needed in India, she asserted boldly that community service of the deprived and downtrodden should be given equal, if not more importance than theoretical education in our colleges and universities.

Sadhu Vaswani would have rejoiced in spirit, to hear her repeat the ideal that he cherished dearly– service of the poor, service to society. He urged his students to serve not only the poor and needy, the sick and the suffering ones, but also to serve the criminals and sinners. To this day, students and youth groups from the Sadhu Vaswani Institutions visit inmates of the local jail on *Raksha Bandhan* Day, and tie *rakhis* on the wrists of their brothers, the prisoners. They visit the prison during Diwali to distribute sweets and new clothes.

Sadhu Vaswani said to us, "To every one of you, I say: Take Sri Krishna at His word! Does He not say that the dearest Name for Him is *Daridra Narayana*– the Lord of the poor and needy ones? So see Him in the poor, and seeing Him, make your knowledge an instrument of service, your education an offering, a *yajna* to the Lord!"

Reverence for brother birds and animals!

Reverence for what is below us is vital. Therefore, we should emphasise the need to put an end to all forms of exploitation. We must realise once and for all, that all our transactions, all our relationships, all our activities, should be based on the principle of justice.

Of course, even corporates and multinationals today are raising their voices against all other forms of exploitation. So I might be forgiven for voicing my support for birds and animals– those dumb, defenseless creatures, which, as Sadhu Vaswani taught us, are our younger brothers and sisters in the One Family of Creation.

Gurudev Sadhu Vaswani said to us, "Holy, holy, holy is every creature. Touch ye these children of the Lord with reverence and love! Harm them not! But serve them in deep humility! These birds and beasts, these animals, these creatures– all are children of Krishna, the forms the Lord hath put on!"

Reverence for God and the Universal Spirit

The Bhagavad Gita, the song of the Lord, is essentially a Song of Life. It shows how a man (the *jiva*), who lives a life of separation, may be united with the Source. Man has been separated from the Eternal in whom is his Home, hence his restlessness. Travelling across millennia comes the word of the Lord:

> *This be my word Supreme to Thee, O Arjuna!*
> *Let go the rites and writ duties:*
> *Come to Me for single refuge!*
> *Bring thy heart to Me!*
> *Fix thy thoughts on Me!*
> *Serve Me! Worship Me!*
> *Cling in faith and love and reverence to Me!*
> *So shalt thou come to Me!*
> *And I shall free thee*
> *From the bondage of sin!*

The Lord Himself tells us to come to Him in love and reverence.

I think the greatest affliction of modern civilisation is that we are moving away from God, and the awareness that we are His children.

Very many years ago, a young man came to meet Gurudev Sadhu Vaswani. He was utterly desolate and downcast, and he said to the Master, "I am just thirty years old, and I am a total failure! I have lost my job. My ancestral property is mortgaged. My wife has left me, and I am unable to support my old mother. I am utterly frustrated with life. What shall I do?"

Sadhu Vaswani said to him, "You are not a failure! You are not poor and broken! You are like the prodigal son who has drifted away from his rich father and does not know how infinitely rich he is."

The young man was bemused. "Excuse me," he stammered. "Who is this rich father you are speaking of? My own father passed away five years ago, and he only left behind debts which I am yet to pay off!"

Sadhu Vaswani smiled and said to him, "I am speaking of our Heavenly Father. He is the Father of us all. And He is the source of all supply. He is the source of all that you and I will ever need or desire. He is the source of prosperity, plenty, and peace. He is the source of happiness and harmony. He is the source of love and joy, strength and wisdom, power andsecurity. All you need to do is turn to Him in love and reverence, and you will lack nothing!"

All we have to do is turn to Him with absolute reverence, and all our needs will be fulfilled!

The 'Book of Noble Conduct'

St. Serapion of Egypt was a learned one who bore witness to the great precept of the religion of service in deeds of daily living. Like most 'scholars' of those days, he was very, very poor. His education and learning had not been used to advance his status and wealth in society. His most valuable raiment was a long coat of very coarse cloth, which he often pawned, and once sold outright to help the poor and needy. At times, he would even pawn himself– commit himself to prolonged manual labour for a certain period of time, working for a rich man– so that he could obtain money to feed the poor.

One of his close friends was shocked to see him in tattered clothes on one occasion. "What is the matter?" he remonstrated. "Why are you so famished and unclothed?"

"The answer to that question is to be realised– not interrogated," was the saint's reply. "I cannot bear to see helpless ones suffer. My 'Book of Noble Conduct' tells me that I must sell off all my belongings to serve the poor and the needy."

"May I see this 'Book of Noble Conduct' which you regard so highly?" enquired the friend.

"That book has also been sold off to help my needy friends," the saint replied briskly. "It was sold for a noble purpose– and it will pay doubly, because the person who obtains it will be transformed by the spirit of service, and do all he can to help the desolate and destitute."

He was a great man imbued with reverence for all humanity!

Risk: Learning to Take a Chance!

"No pain, no gain," says an old fashioned proverb. "Nothing ventured, nothing gained," is another wise saying. It is only because the early *Homo-sapiens* took calculated risks, that you and I live in the advanced civilisation of the 21st century! If your life is absolutely free of failures, chances are that you have not taken risks, and thus lost the opportunity of learning many valuable lessons in life. Therefore, we are told: "The person who risks nothing, does nothing, has nothing, is nothing, and becomes nothing. He may avoid suffering and sorrow, but he simply cannot learn and feel and change and grow and love and live."

When I suggest that you learn to take risks, I do not refer to gambling, or hazarding your hard-earned money on racing or any such irresponsible and rash act! There are numerous definitions of risk available in dictionaries, but what I refer to specifically is an action where there is both the probability of making a good profit as well as the possibility of incurring a loss– a chance taken in the hope of a favourable outcome.

Today's business environment is full of terms associated with risk, such as: risk management, risk assessment, credit risk, risk analysis, currency risk, market risk, high risk, and even value at risk! This only goes to prove that the ability to take calculated risks is an essential aspect of successful business management.

What are the benefits of risks?

Distinct from success or failure, when you take risks with faith in God and confidence in yourself, you learn the truth about yourself. You learn to do what you think you cannot do; you learn to do what is difficult for you to do; you learn to take initiative; you learn to take responsibility for your own actions. As the French humanist Andre Gide tells us, "Man cannot discover new oceans unless he has the courage to lose sight of the shore."

The 'thrill' of risk

Risk taking must not be confused with thrill-seeking. By this, I mean reckless behaviour, which leads to many disastrous accidents and avoidable mishaps. Psychologists call this compulsive novelty-seeking behaviour. It is mostly adolescents who indulge in such behaviour to attract attention and enhance their low self-esteem. Ironically enough, it is in the 'developed' countries of the world that such thrill-seeking games abound. Statistics tell us that a disproportionate share of thriller sensation-seeking personality types are found in the United States, where 'extreme games' such as hang gliding, paragliding, and dirt cycling are popular.

Nothing ventured, nothing gained!

The kind of risk taking I encourage is different. I refer to situations where we are afraid to venture, because we fear that we may not do well. If we limit ourselves to situations which are sure to bring us success, we will never know what we are capable of achieving. We will simply end up limiting our own opportunities drastically.

What kind of risks should we take?

Each of us has our own preferences! There can be no right and wrong, black or white, this or that when it comes to taking a chance. All we need is the courage to take responsibility for our own decisions and the determination to live with the consequences of our choice. We have to assess our chances and we have to choose what we think is right.

Taking calculated risks...

Clinical psychologists tell us that we must appreciate the value of taking risks, and also teach our children about well-planned, systematic risk taking which can help them become high achievers. According to them, there are six steps to systematic risk taking:

1. Understanding the benefits of risk-taking, which include increasing one's confidence, the ability to take on a challenge, reinforcing a sense of control over one's life, developing skills for coping with anxieties and overcoming fears, and providing practice in important decision making.

2. Initial self-assessment of risk-taking categories. This is the ability to distinguish between intellectual risks, social risks, emotional risks, physical risks, and spiritual risks. Some risks may be easier for us to take on than others.

3. Identifying personal needs– we need to understand and prioritise our own risk levels in different categories. A gifted learner, for example, can take the intellectual risk of appearing for a tough, high-level examination; an athlete might stretch himself to the extreme limit, in order to break a world record; an ardent lover, might take the emotional risk of declaring

his love boldly to his beloved. It all depends on how strongly we feel the need to achieve a particular goal.

4. Choosing the kind of risk that we feel will bring us great satisfaction. This will make the risk more palatable and easy to manage for us.

5. Taking the risk– that is, actually going ahead to take a chance in the interest of our own success.

6. Processing the risk experience. Most of the beneficial effects appear not as a result of merely taking risks, but as a result of processing the risk. The processing that follows risk-taking activities stimulates the expression of feelings, and also helps us to clarify our strengths and weaknesses. This can be invaluable for our future growth.

Why are people afraid to take risks?

As children, we hardly stop to think of risks; we just go ahead and do as we please. But as we grow older, we restrict ourselves. We draw a circle around ourselves and are reluctant to step out of the self-imposed boundaries. We begin to think of the consequences, we fear the repercussions, we even worry about what people might say.

Many worry that a risk might ruin their fortunes or land them in trouble. The chances of a risk not working out along expected lines fills them with dread.

It is this all or nothing, do or die attitude that people prefer to play it safe. They fail to anticipate the larger sense of adventure, the possibilities that lie open to them, and the new world that they can explore by taking a chance, trying a hand at something new. In short, they fail to see the magnificence of the dark, deep, lovely woods, as they concentrate on only one tree!

Avoid extremes!

Which is better– to be a reckless doer or a fearful non-doer? The best option is to avoid both extremes. Experts tell us that we must stop thinking of risks as just do-or-die situations. Instead, we must start thinking of risks as a journey of exploration. It is not about a one-shot success or failure; it is about exploring different aspects of our life and personality.

Isn't it better to be safe than to be sorry?

Ask yourself: was Columbus just taking a risk when he set out to explore the new world beyond the Atlantic Ocean? It was a chance accident that he discovered the Americas. Experts revisiting history tell us that nearly 500 years before Columbus set out on his voyage of discovery, a Viking expedition may have been the first Europeans ever to have touched North American soil! We learn too, that 'exploration' was not an adventure or risk, but a family business for the expedition's leader, Leif Erikson!

Similarly, entrepreneurs do not take risks when they explore options to diversify or expand their business. Companies do not take risks, either; they simply choose to explore an alternative way of conducting their business. They choose to do things contrary to the norm.

If they did not take those risks, they would just stagnate or become obsolete.

If the great scientists and inventors did not dare to think differently from others, if they had stuck to the beaten tracks and not risked their reputations and positions to experiment with new things, where would we be today! We would not have airplanes, automobiles or space programmes; we would be without antibiotics and lifesaving drugs; nothing ventured, nothing gained!

The joy of being 'alive'!

An enterprising researcher and consultant had one question, which he put to each and every one of his clients: When, at what times in your life, have you felt most alive? Without exception, each one of them referred to situations in which they stretched themselves well beyond their normal limits to achieve something they had never done before. For instance, when someone with extreme fear of drowning, overcame that fear and learnt to swim.

They all pushed themselves out of their restricted 'comfort zones' to take calculated risks. During these moments, they were not afraid of the consequences. Rather, they focussed more positively on the great satisfaction that the outcome would provide them. However, when they related these experiences later, they did not emphasise these outcomes; they dwelt with great pleasure on the process of the actual risk-taking.

The researcher concludes that the real prize of risk taking is not in your daring or in the desired outcome; it lies in who or what you become in the process of risk taking.

You emerge confident, engaged, alive. What makes you feel fulfilled is the approach to life, which is open-hearted, exploratory, and willing to learn new things!

My 'take' on risks!

To my mind, learning to take a calculated risk is akin to a leap of faith– it liberates us from fear, helps us engage with life constructively, and accomplish the best we are capable of.

Stepping out of narrow, self-imposed comfort zones; facing challenges; taking tough decisions; innovation and experiments; breaking new ground; building up confidence; accepting our mistakes; learning from our failures– these are the traits of great leaders, and they grow and evolve in stature by taking risks.

As we always hear, the ship is perfectly safe when it stays in the harbour. But that, alas, is not what ships are meant for!

One final thought...

Here are the beautiful lines penned by Rabindranath Tagore:

The song that I came to sing remains unsung to this day.
 Have spent my days in stringing and in unstringing my instrument.
The time has not come true, the words have not been rightly set…

The problem with stringing and unstringing the instrument over and over again is that sometimes the opportunity to sing our song suddenly, unexpectedly, and irretrievably is gone!

We must sing the song which we have come to sing. Each one of us has come to this earth-plane to sing a particular song, a wonderful song that no one else can sing, except us. We are unable to sing that song because we are not prepared to take risks. Learn to take risks, so that the beautiful song of your life may be sung to the best of your ability.

Sadhana

In its basic form, the Sanskrit word *sadhana* is "the means of accomplishing something". To be more specific, it refers to a spiritual practice prescribed by ancient Indian religions, especially Hinduism and Buddhism. In short, *sadhana* is a spiritual discipline which is essential for all seekers of truth. But, every seeker after truth is different in temperament, in personality, in mental and spiritual strength. Therefore, there are several *sadhanas* available to the seeker on the path to self-realisation, perfection, or liberation.

Which *sadhana* can I choose?

There are literally hundreds of *sadhanas* or means that one can undertake in pursuit of spiritual growth. We can take to prayer, which is one of the simplest and easiest; we can take to *pooja*, or organised ritual worship; we can choose meditation, which is nothing but a journey inward; we can choose *Japa Yoga*, which is intensely focussed chanting of a sacred mantra. There are tougher austerities too, like fasting, penance, *tapasya*, and so on.

Let me share with you the secret of *sadhana* at its simplest. It is to remember God– not once a day, not occasionally, not when you have a little free time– but to live and move in His presence, and feel His Divine energy flowing through you!

Practice makes perfect

Many years ago, as a young boy scout taking music lessons, I realised that if I wished to sing in tune, I needed to practise with my teacher. I had to do my *riyaaz* with him so that my singing would become harmonious. Practice is what makes one a good artist, a good sculptor, a good musician.

This applies to life as well; we have to undertake *sadhana* under the guru's guidance so that we may not slip back into old and worn out habits. This is why we need the guru as our guide and guardian, at every step, in every stage of life. Only an evolved soul, a friend of God, one who has seen God and known God, who lives and moves and has his being in God– only he can help us on the path of *shreya*. And so, Sadhu Vaswani writes:

Can you leap without feet?
Can you smile without lips?
Can you rest without sleep?
Nor can you find the way– The True way– without the Guru.

If there is one person who can always keep us connected to the higher self, it is none other than the guru!

The three-S *sadhana*

Gurudev Sadhu Vaswani, who has been the inspiration, the guide, the guardian and the leading light of my life, offered us a simple, straightforward *sadhana* which each and everyone could practise effortlessly: the three-S *sadhana* of Silence, *Sangha* (fellowship), and Service. He urged us to practise silence every day. He emphasised the spiritual fellowship that was available to us at the *satsang*. Above all, he urged that our life, our wealth, our talent and our time were all but a loan given to us by the Almighty, to be poured out in selfless service to those less fortunate than ourselves.

Silence, *sangha*, and service! If only we could follow these simple *sadhanas*, we would indeed find our lives transformed!

How does *sadhana* help us?

Why should we practise *sadhana*? What will it achieve for us? What will we get out of it? These are questions that many people ask themselves when they hear about *sadhana*, and its necessity for the seeker.

If these questions arise in your mind too, I can offer you a simple answer: there is a simple input-output ratio that operates in *sadhana*. You will get as much out of it as you put into it! Put in sincerity, dedication, commitment, faith, and perseverance, and you will achieve your goal. Indeed, you will achieve much more than you expect, with the grace of God.

Simple steps for *sadhana*

1. Every day, wake up with the thought that you are a child of God, and that God loves you dearly. He has bestowed on you the greatest gift– the gift of this human birth.

2. Learn to love yourself just as God loves you. Remember, the others around you also share the same spark of divinity that dwells in you. Therefore, learn to love others, for all Creation– the birds of the air, the animals on the land, the fish in the waters, the tiniest creatures that breathe the breath of life, those which stand rooted, those which walk, those which crawl and swim– are His children, and therefore, your brothers and sisters in the

One Family of Creation.

3. Develop your own set of devotional practices to make your life beautiful and meaningful– whether it be meditation, reading from the sacred scriptures, the *bani* of saints, or just reciting your favourite prayers.

4. Spend some time in silence, in a quiet space, every day.

5. Fill your heart with gratitude for all the bounty that God has bestowed on you. Do not forget the sun, the moon, the rain, the stars, the sky, the flowers and the breeze. If all the prayers you ever uttered consisted of the words, "Thank You God!" you have said the best prayer possible! Gratitude enables you to see God in all that you behold. Remember, you cannot always change external circumstances. But it is entirely within your power to change your attitude to what happens around you. Quit the habit of criticism, fault-finding and constant complaints. Practise the spirit of loving and grateful acceptance.

This is *sadhana* at its best!

Satsang

Satsang is a place of hope and serenity; it is a place of positive vibrations, which protects us from the negativity of the world. The temptations of the world are many and these allurements are powerful. Anytime, they can drag us into the whirlpool of pleasure, pelf and worry. Let me tell you, when we go to the *satsang* we are sure to earn our own reward! We can imbibe the teachings of the holy ones, ponder over the sacred words of the scriptures, and internalise spiritual values.

The very word *satsang* means fellowship of truth. Truth, as we know, is a difficult virtue to assimilate. Truth is ever vigilant and like a sentinel stands, brandishing its iron weapon, preventing any unauthorised entry into its domain. For inside the domain of truth, there is only truth, there is One Name, One Shyam, One Rama and One Love. Once you enter this domain you cannot come out. *Satsang* of the true type offers you a glimpse of this realm; it enriches, empowers and beautifies the inner self.

Positive effects of *satsang* and its relevance today

A friend once expressed his surprise to me, at the fact that people continue to be drawn to the *satsang*, "in this day and age" as he put it. The fact is, people need *satsang* today, more than their parents and grandparents did in bygone times!

This is not just my personal opinion. Many *satsangis* tell me that *satsang* gives them a sense of stability, a positive frame of mind, a certain sense of mental well-being and peace of mind. They say that *satsang* links them with a higher energy and in that positive, joyful atmosphere they feel happy and rejuvenated. Whether they hear discourses, recite prayers, read from the *bani* of great ones, or participate in singing the Name Divine, they feel elevated. At such times, their minds are free from worldly cares and anxieties. There awakens a desire within them– the desire to follow in the footsteps of the truly great ones. They yearn to imbibe the ideals of saints and sages, and make their lives more meaningful, more worthwhile. For a short time at least, they forget mundane worries and get immersed in the pure waters of the Spirit. Emotions rise above the senses, and in their hearts they cry out, "O Lord! This is bliss. O Lord! You have given me this beautiful gift of life. Till now I have wasted it. But from now onwards, I will strive to achieve the goal of this human birth!"

Many people who attend the *satsang* also feel that it cleanses and purifies their thoughts by its sacred environment and holy vibrations. They are able to discard negative emotions like envy, jealousy, avarice, resentment, and anger, which trouble all of us at times. It further helps them by awakening in them the higher impulses that human beings aspire to, such as charity, compassion, and philanthropy. And when they yield to these noble impulses, they find that they achieve a sense of harmony and joy that surpasses all worldly satisfaction! In short, they assure me, *satsang* generates a sense of peace and tranquillity, which helps them to evolve into a higher state of living and thinking.

Who are we to say that *satsangs* are irrelevant these days?

The Sadhu Vaswani *Satsang*

People often wonder about what exactly goes on in a *satsang*. What are the disciplines prescribed? What is the message of the discourses?

Let me tell you a little about the Sadhu Vaswani *Satsang*. The discourses in our *satsang* are universal in approach. The main teaching given is this: the gift of the human birth, so freely bestowed on all of us, is invaluable. Saints and sages of all faiths and all ages have emphasised that human life is God's greatest gift to us. But it is a gift that is meant to fulfil a purpose. It is a rare and valuable gift, not meant to be wasted on earthly pleasures. It should be used to achieve the ultimate goal– liberation through service of the Lord and the suffering children of the Lord.

One of the disciplines we practise in the *satsang* is to sit in silence, meditate, and go within the self. For we believe, that in the practice of silence we get answers to the most profound questions that vex our minds. In silence, we perceive our true selves.

Satsang is nothing but the safest and easiest spiritual route that we can take. It cleanses and purifies our hearts and minds. This cleansing of mind and heart is done through the chanting of the Name Divine; associating with men of God, as well as with like-minded aspirants who share our quest for liberation; through *kirtan, bhajan,* and recitations from the sacred scriptures; through listening to discourses that enlighten us. Just as we clean our body with soap and water, similarly we can purify our mind and heart by washing them in the pure waters of the Spirit, the *amrit dhara*, that flows perennially in the *satsang*.

What are the three treasures that we receive from *satsang*?

The first treasure is that we learn meditation. Sitting at the lotus feet of a holy one, we learn to meditate. Meditation stills our restless mind. The treasure of meditation and concentration is found only by those *satsangis* who go there with true devotion. It is said, through concentrtion, you will experience bliss. First we learn concentration, and then we move to meditation, which takes us to higher regions of awareness and bliss!

The second treasure which we receive is *naam kirtan*, chanting the Name Divine. By chanting the Name Divine, by immersing ourselves in the holy waters of the spirit, we wash away our worries and tensions. By chanting the Name Divine, our *antah karan*– inner instrument gets purified; our senses become integrated and focussed, and we feel energised.

The third treasure which we receive from *satsang* is prayer. Prayer is integral to the *satsang*. It is contact with the Unseen, a link to the Universal Self. Prayer helps us to build a relationship with the Invisible. Prayer is a rare treasure and he who knows to pray is truly blessed.

How can we earn the true treasure of *satsang*?

A few practical suggestions will show the way:

1. Seek the company of people who go to *satsang*. Association with them will give you the impulse to enter the world of *satsang*, a world of spiritual quietude and prayer.

2. Set apart some time every day to refrain from worldly activities and focus on the inner world within you. Enter into nurturing activities like meditation, recitation from the scriptures, etc.

3. Keep yourself away from all unproductive talk, gossip and controversies. Do not criticise others, nor entertain gossip about them.

4. Do not miss your daily appointment with God. Fix a time for your meditation. Resolve that you will meditate for 15 minutes or half an hour or an hour. During this period you can chant the Name Divine, you can commune with God, meditate on some inspirational teachings, or pick up a sentence from some spiritual literature on compassion, oneness, or other virtuous topics, and reflect on it.

One final thought...

Living in the world as we do, our minds cannot remain steady without the protecting influence of *satsang*– fellowship with the pure and holy.

Saints and sages, rishis and holy men have shown us many paths leading to happiness. But the path which is open to each one of us is very easy, and it is the path of *satsang*. *Satsang* does not mean passivity; it does not mean just being physically present in the *satsang* hall. *Satsang* means true fellowship with everyone. True *satsang* means being immersed in *bhakti*. True *satsang* means love for all. True *satsang* means earning blessings by being His instrument of service to others. When you go to *satsang*, you earn your own reward: you imbibe the teachings imparted by the holy ones; you ponder over the sacred words of the scriptures; you internalise the spiritual values taught and you automatically begin to make the effort to bear witness to the teachings of the great ones in your daily life.

Service

Service, it has been rightly said, is the rent we have to pay for being tenants of this body. Every morning, as we wake up, we must ask ourselves these questions: What can I do to help? What can I do to make a difference? For indeed, each one of us can and must make a difference. There are so many tasks to be accomplished by us– there are hungry ones to be fed; there are naked ones to be clothed; there are elders to be cared for; there are children to be taught. There is so much work to be done! And every one of us– from the youngest to the oldest– can make a difference.

I would define service as doing the Will of God. It is true that the world has many "doers". But in this critical period of chaos and disorder, the tortured soul of humanity cries out for Will-doers– those who do the Will of God. The one who would truly serve, must be a Will-doer. Then will his action, blended with *bhakti* (devotion), be radiant with *jnana* (knowledge).

We can make a difference

"There is not much that I can do on my own," is what many of us think. We are mistaken. The tragedy for many of us is not that our aim is too high and we miss it– but rather that our aim is too low and reach it!

We tend to believe that the little that we can do, counts for nothing, against the vast canvas of the world's misery and suffering. But just as little drops of water together make the mighty ocean, so too, little acts of kindness and compassion can and will make a difference.

All we need is a caring spirit

When I go to big cities like Mumbai, Delhi, Kolkata, and Chennai, I find that people seemed to have stopped caring. They have become insensitive, indifferent to the needs of those around them. Their attitude to the hardships they see around them is defined by the words: "It's none of our business."

Surely, it *is* our business! Mankind is our business. The Vedas give us the wonderful concept of *Vasudaiva Kutumbakam*– humanity is one family. In this one family of humanity, every man is my brother, every woman is my sister. It is my duty to do all I can to help them to the best of my ability, to the best of my capacity. I must do all I can, to help as many as I can, in as many ways as I can, on as many occasions as I can, to lift the load on the rough road of life. I often say to people: the opposite of love is not hatred; the opposite of love is apathy, indifference to the needs of those around us.

Service– A panacea for all ills

Would you like to be happy, healthy, contented and at peace with the world? Would you have the real joy of life? Then, my advice to you is– go out and offer loving service to the Lord. And remember, the best and noblest of all actions which you can offer to the Lord is service of his comfortless, sorrowing and struggling children! Happiness does move in a circle. The happiness that moves out from us, flows back into us.

The gifts of caring, affection, appreciation and love are sometimes the most precious gifts you can share with another; for you are giving of yourself.

Five rules of service

The very first rule of service is, serve silently!

Do not serve for show or publicity. Let the right hand not know what your left hand gives away. I am afraid that today, we serve with cries and clamour. We seem to have confounded service with show and noise. People 'serve' for various motives– some to acquire name and fame; some even serve for money; some do it to obtain power and position in society; some build temples for recognition; some erect monuments that they may be remembered after death. It is only the man who serves silently who is truly blessed.

The true strength of a nation is not in popularity and publicity. The true strength of a country, the true strength of a community, the true strength of a society, is in those who serve silently!

The second principle of service is, serve humbly!

Serve with humility– this is no easy task. Many of us are apt to imagine that the act of giving– of our time, money, effort or resources– is an act of superiority. We feel that we are conferring a great favour– doing *meherbani*, as they say in Hindi– on those whom we seek to serve. I think it should be the other way round. We should be grateful to those who give us the opportunity to be of service to them.

We have received countless blessings from God, so many favours from the marvellous universe we live in. We owe a debt of gratitude for these innumerable blessings bestowed upon us. We will be able to pay back the debt, only if we go out and serve the less fortunate ones– the aged, the infirm, the handicapped, the unwanted, the unloved, the hopeless and the homeless ones. We should be deeply grateful to them, for they are giving us the opportunity to serve them, to give back at least a fraction of all that we have received from the Lord.

The third rule of service is, serve lovingly!

Love is what the world needs most today. Love does not merely make the world go round– it is what makes the ride worthwhile, as Franklin Jones has said. And true love is love-in-action; for love that does not express itself in action, does not exist at all!

There are very many wealthy people who speak harsh words to the people they serve. They may give a poor man money and tell him, "Don't show your dirty face to me again!" or they may lose their temper and yell, "Don't be so lazy! Don't expect me to prop you up all the time!"

This is not true service! The people we seek to serve are not apart from us– they are a part of us. This sense of identification is very essential for true service. When you serve others, you must identify with them. This is the secret of the Life Beautiful– which is loving sympathy that goes out to all. There is no separation between us and the suffering ones we seek to serve.

The fourth principle of service is, serve unconditionally!

Service should not become interference. If you wish to reform the world, begin with yourself. A true server realises that he must mend his own life, before he begins to set others right.

Many people take to service with an ulterior motive; their service comes with strings attached. They expect the beneficiaries of their generosity to follow their ideology and their beliefs, or subscribe to their way of thinking. It is said that some service organisations even try to convert people to their religion, in lieu of services rendered. This is surely inimical to the spirit of true service, which, at its best must be spontaneous and unconditional. Jesus would never countenance our service as an offering to him if we insisted on serving only Christians. Krishna would not accept our service if we offered it only to Hindus. Service should be a labour of love, and love knows no barriers of caste, creed, race or religion.

The man of true service serves without judgement. He never ever asks if the others deserve his charity or compassion. The service that benefits society and ennobles the individual is service without strings attached. It does not arise out of pity, duty, guilt or desire. It is not performed with calculation. It comes spontaneously. It blesses both the giver and receiver.

The fifth rule of service is, if you would serve aright, cultivate the soul!

Cultivate the soul! Therefore, know that you are only a tool, an instrument. God is the One Worker. Therefore, do not confound the means with the end. Renouncing all egoism and selfishness, become instruments of the eternal *shakti* that shapes the lives of individuals and nations.

The essence of *Vedanta* may be summed up in the one concept: All Life is One. If such oneness is accepted, the question arises, who is serving whom? For the pious and the devout, all work is an offering to God. All work is His work. You and I are only instruments of God.

Service is a spiritual discipline

Service helps us to expand our vision beyond our narrow, restricted world. For how can we be truly happy, when our brothers and sisters suffer? How can we be so insensitive that we do not respond to their suffering? Service makes us evolve spiritually, and helps us realise in deeds of daily life, the great truth of the Brotherhood of man. Such service helps us towards God-realisation; it awakens the Divine within us.

Shakti: The Power Within You

Gurudev Sadhu Vaswani often said to us, "You are not a weakling as some of you imagine yourselves to be. In you is a hidden *shakti,* an energy that is of Eternity."

The word *shakti* is derived from the Sanskrit root, "to be able". It is translated as "power" or "energy". In Hindu belief, it is the active power or manifest energy of Lord Shiva that pervades all of existence. Scholars tell us that in its most refined aspect, it is *Parashakti,* or pure consciousness. This pristine, divine energy unfolds as *ichha shakti* (the power of desire, will, love), *kriya shakti* (the power of action) and *jnana shakti* (the power of wisdom, knowing), represented as the three prongs of Shiva's *trishula,* or trident. A divine spark of this supreme energy lies within each one of us, and is ours to tap.

It has been said that the energy of the mind is the essence of life, but the energy of the mind is only one half of the story. The energy of the spirit is far more potent, far more powerful.

Our ancient rishis have also taught us about this tremendous power, or *shakti* within us. Once this *shakti* is awakened, there is nothing that we cannot achieve. All we need to do is to unearth this spiritual strength.

During the troubled days following the traumatic Partition of India, Sadhu Vaswani urged the refugees from Sind to be strong within. He exhorted them to be self-sufficient and refrain from begging for government help. Again and again, he repeated magic words which became a mantra of positive thinking for all of us: "Within you lies a hidden *shakti;* awaken that *shakti* and all will be well with you." I remember, too, his unforgettable call to the shattered community, "Believe and achieve!"

Shakti is not the power of the occult!

In the past, many westerners regarded India as an 'exotic' nation of the 'Orient'– but both those adjectives had the wrong connotations for them. Fed on a diet of 'exotic' fiction, they regarded India as a land of snake charmers, half-crazed ascetics, pseudo-yogis who layon beds of nails, ate glass and iron scraps, and men who levitated while in *padmasana.*

Many of us who are proud to regard the India of the 21st century as the superpower of the future, and the knowledge capital of the emerging IT industry, will no doubt be put off by such blatant prejudice. But I assure you, such prejudices did exist in the past, with or without reason.

Let me also add another unpalatable fact: such feats as I have described above, were equated with *yogic* powers and *siddhis*. They were actually attributed to the Hindu way of life and our concept of the *shakti* within!

When I urge you to release the *shakti* within you, I do not refer to such occult powers. The kind of *shakti* that I wish to make you aware of, has nothing to do with these occult powers.

All the great spiritual teachers of humanity have effectively discouraged their disciples from practising occult powers. In truth, *siddhis* often become a distraction, a diversion from the path of spiritual growth. Therefore, we are urged to keep away from these occult powers.

One of Sri Ramakrishna's disciples came to him and said, "Master, I have acquired the power of reading people's minds. Merely by looking at a person, I can tell you what is going on in his mind."

"Shame on you!" said Sri Ramakrishna to him. "Of what use is it to dig into such filth? Give up this horrible practice, and walk on the straight and narrow path that leads you to your Divine Mother!"

The straight and narrow path that leads us to our own Divine Mother is the path of faith! This is the way we must follow to discover the Divine power that is vested in all of us!

The true seeker must understand once and for all not to confuse the occult and the exotic with genuine spiritual *shakti*. It is essential to remember that the truth we seek is within ourselves, and that this power has nothing to do with trying to impress others!

The Divine power is within us!

In the *Bhagavad Gita*, Sri Krishna tells Arjuna, "O Arjuna, I reside in every heart." In each one of us is the Divine Spirit. Just imagine, the Almighty, the Power Supreme dwells within us. Each one of us is a potent Krishna. Yet, we live like weaklings. At the slightest difficulty, before the smallest obstacle, we retreat, we give way and break down. We succumb to pressures and problems, we get caught in a vicious circle of desires. It is sad, that despite the great *shakti* of Krishna within us, we despair and fall into melancholy.

We go through life, without ever unfolding this *shakti,* without using it for our own betterment. Little do we realise that this hidden power can transform our lives. There is a powerhouse within us and still we live in a state of permanent power failure!

How can we tap into this *shakti*?

Relax, let go of your worries and tensions, and let your mind rest in God. True relaxation is resting– resting in God– until God's *shakti* flows into you and fills your entire being. For this to happen, it is necessary to enter into silence from time to time. "The very first word in the Scripture of Life," my beloved Master, Sadhu Vaswani said, "is silence!" Sit quietly at the Lotus Feet of the Lord and gaze at His beauteous face. In that gaze, lose yourself, until you discover the Light within you. Learn to be still. So many of us rush about, multitasking, 'performing' like prize athletes! Let us learn to be still. In stillness, God's strength will flow into us, making us fitter for use when the time comes to act.

The true strength of life is the strength of stillness. The world worships the strength of action, but so much of the world's action is cruel, aggressive, and tainted with sordid selfishness. True strength belongs to him who has learned to rest in God. Such a one becomes the very picture of peace.

Concentration and focus are essential to access this *shakti*

One of the main teachings of Sadhu Vaswani is, "Open the lotus of your heart." To open the lotus of the heart we need intense devotion for the Lord. We need to integrate the mind. We need to concentrate and focus the mind.

Ramana Maharishi was a great soul. His devotees called him *Bhagwan*. But Ramana Maharishi lived a human life. One day, a disciple from overseas came to visit him. He asked Ramana Maharishi, "O, Holy Man of God, what is the difference between you and us? What is that *shakti* in you that we do not have, that draws people to you? Disciples from all over the world come to pay their respects to you. But no one even gives us a glance. What is the reason?"

Ramana Maharishi picked up a pencil and said, "The difference between you and me is, I am the point of this pencil which can write and you are the other end of the pencil which needs to be sharpened to be able to write. I have focussed all my *shakti* on the one point, but your thoughts are scattered and you wander endlessly."

The trouble with most of us is that our minds are restless. Just think over it. From morning till night, our minds run in so many directions. If we were to focus all our energies on a single point, we would scale great heights. Nothing is impossible for the man of concentration. Glimpse within and you will witness an invaluable treasure.

Practical suggestions to kindle the source of this *shakti*

- The first thing we must do in order to awaken this kind of *shakti* is to turn the mind inward, towards this powerhouse within us. The more willing we are to tap this energy within us, the more power will flow through us. We need an arousal of consciousness. Instead of constantly worrying about what may happen and what we may not achieve, let us look within, to tap these hidden powers that are ours by right!

- We must develop faith in ourselves. Truly has it been said, "Nothing splendid has ever been achieved except by those who dared to believe that something inside of them was superior to circumstance."

- We must remember that there can be no true gain without pain. The energy within us must be channelised into meaningful, constructive action. Let us earn our own merit; let us achieve our heart's desires with effort and hard work. What we achieve through our own effort, can never be snatched away from us.

- We must not succumb to the illusion that we are weaklings. To explain this ancient concept through a modern metaphor, I give you the words of a recent writer: "We are all such a waste of our potential, like three-way lamps using one-way bulbs."

- Awaken the spiritual power within you! This is the true meaning of self-reliance. Your spiritual energy has to develop from within. It is you yourself who must grow and evolve in spiritual strength in order to make a success of your life on earth and in the dimension beyond.

Therefore, let us awaken the *shakti* within. Let us grow in spiritual strength and be blessed.

Silence

Silence is twofold: there is outer silence, which is absence of noise, freedom from the shouts and tumults of daily life. And then there is interior silence: it is freedom from the pull of desires, cessation of mental acrobatics, stilling of the play of conflicting forces in the mind within. This silence is the true wealth of the Spirit. It is the peace that passeth, surpasseth understanding.

There are millions of us who do not know what it is to go into silence, even briefly! We may be all alone, in perfect solitude; but the clamour of our thoughts and feelings drown the inner voice. Getting to know oneself, understanding our true nature and realising what we really want out of life is a long, exploratory process. It does not happen in a flash. It is the practice of silence that can open the doors to the inner recesses of our hearts which we have neglected to take charge of, in the hustle and bustle of life. Our excuse is that we have no time!

Why do we need silence?

Even as particles of dust cling to our clothes, so too, particles of noise cling to our hearts. To clean our clothes, we wash them with soap and water. Even so, to cleanse our souls, we need to take a dip in the waters of silence.

It is a medically proven fact that silence heals us. It helps us avoid stress and tension. It cleanses us, it strengthens us. We feel exhausted, again and again, because we are not in contact with the Source of strength and inspiration which is within us. Our interior life is starved.

We live in a world of appearances– they are as shadows, having no substance, no reality. To shadows we cling for strength and sustenance. At best, they can excite and stimulate us for some time. They cannot give us the strength we need to face the battle of life, to master the cravings of the flesh, the savage appetites which fling us, again and again, into storms of passion and pride.

Strength is needed. Therefore, we must practise silence every day.

Just as people in cities turn to parks and woods and hills to refresh themselves, you too must enter into the haven of silence within you. And silence reveals. Silence will bring you face-to-face with yourself.

Silence heals

In spiritual terms, silence is of greater value. We live in a world of entanglements and allurements. The sharp arrows of cravings, animal appetite, of passion and pride, of ignorance, hatred and greed, wound our souls again and again. Our souls bear the scars of many wounds. They need to be healed, and silence is the great healer for our spiritual afflictions.

Spend some time in silence everyday! Begin with fifteen minutes, then gradually increase the period to at least one hour. At first, the practice may appear to be meaningless, a sheer waste of time. But if you persist in it, silence will become alive and the Word of God will speak to you. And you will realise that practising silence is, perhaps, the most worthwhile activity of the day.

The great Christian mystic, Thomas Merton, says that silence is a beautiful and ever-flowing river, in which you must take dips again and again. Silence purifies the mind, heals the heart, and reaches the very depths of the soul within!

God can be seen, God can be felt, God can be touched, God can be heard– in the depths of silence. We can truly experience Him, for He is more real than all the objects of this material world. It is in these depths that the beauteous face of God is revealed to us, and the radiant music of his voice can be heard in the stillness of the mind. God dwells in silence. He teaches through silence. And in silence He clears the doubts of many. So it is that the knowers of the secret do not speak.

Wondrous are the fruits of silence. He who tastes them is always at rest. He proceeds from one work to another, gently, slowly, quietly, taking time to rest and pray in between.

Those who do not know of the wonders of silence are fond of talking, and those who are dull and unwise love to argue!

Let silence be the law of your life!

Simplicity

Nothing is greater than simplicity; indeed to be simple is to be great.

Simplicity is not a way of life favoured by many of us in this materialistic generation. Yet the great founders of world faiths– messiahs and prophets like Buddha, Jesus Christ, Prophet Mohammed and Guru Nanak– lived lives of utter simplicity. The rishis of ancient India, Christian saints who built up the great monastic orders, and the Sufi saints of the East and West, lived in simplicity. Mira and Avvaiyar turned their back on luxuries and wealth and chose to live lives of austerity. On the contrary, our present trends, preoccupations, and even the current 'mental climate' do not agree with simplicity as a way of living. We have conveniently relegated simplicity to be a foible of saints and the odd eccentric geniuses, and have decided that it need not be practised by the rest of us.

Alas! We have moved away from the ideal of simplicity! This entails simplicity in living, simplicity in thought, word and deed, and even simplicity in our approach to problem-solving. In fact, our society has become 'gross', with over-emphasis on food, luxuries, and a richly excessive material environment. Everything we value has a price tag attached to it; the more expensive it is, the happier we are to acquire and possess it. We value people and things in terms of money power alone. What is the bank balance of this man? What car is he driving? Where does he live? What kind of clothes is he wearing? We are constantly estimating people's material worth. With such an obsession for the materialistic aspects, how can we even begin to follow the path that can lead us to God? We are caught up in gross materialism, we have neither the time nor the inclination to search for the Truth, let alone to find the 'Ultimate'!

Our obsession with material possessions...

Many of us are apt to equate happiness and success with money, material wealth and possessions. I blame this erroneous equation on our acquisitive culture. It is one of the reasons why we have moved away from the ideal of simplicity. People cannot be happy just because they live in mansions or penthouse apartments. They cannot achieve peace and inner harmony just because they drive expensive cars. They cannot be considered 'successful' just because they are millionaires.

Alas, many of us regard these opulent luxuries and other outer 'symbols' as indicators of our happiness and success. These material resources are not as valuable as our inner, personal resources.

If we forfeit artificiality and intellect, and return to the real, essential life by practising awareness, we will surely be reckoned as wise.

Perhaps we are complicating our lives unnecessarily, maybe even unintentionally, with excessive acquisitions and unnecessary possessions. But worst of all, we tend to ignore, forget or take for granted things that should really matter to us! We cherish, hoard, and crave all the things that money can buy; we forget all those precious things that have no price.

How many luxuries do we need?

Today, we live in an age of conspicuous consumption– we acquire goods not out of necessity, but out of the desire to 'show off' our wealth and status. The distinguished economist Thorstein Veblen, who first studied this phenomenon, predicted that the price of ostentatious goods would go upwards, while people would simply reject low-priced options. We are witnessing the Veblen effect even now!

May I tell you, I cannot help but think that this is primarily because we have become obsessed with making money! Our secondary concerns are our social status, acquisitions and possessions, and what 'others' think of us. Thus, we are reduced to what Kabir described as grains caught between the two constantly moving surfaces of the grinding stones, crushed by our own actions and feelings!

Why we should all cultivate the virtue of simplicity

Quakers, members of the Christian Society of Friends, set a wonderful example for all of us. They believe that a person's spiritual life and character are far more important than the quantity of goods he possesses or his monetary worth. They also believe that one should use one's resources, including money and time, deliberately and consciously in ways that are most likely to make life truly better for oneself and others. Their 'testimony to simplicity' includes the practice of being more concerned with one's inner condition than one's outward appearance, and with other people more than oneself.

Are these not principles worthy of our emulation? Simplicity and modesty in attire never ever go out of fashion. Excessive use of jewellery and ornaments not only appears to be exhibitionistic, it also raises issues of safety.

Life is not really complex. It is we who complicate it. Modern knowledge has grown incredibly multifarious and torturous. Sooner or later, to bring back its equilibrium, it must return to simplicity.

Nowadays, we come across so many people who speak not just to communicate or to express themselves, but to display their scholarship or even their polished accents! They pronounce their opinions more to impress others rather than to express their views. There are others who use words to terrorise, threaten, coerce, or browbeat those around them!

Beyond expression, there is also the simplicity of faith and acceptance– the firm belief that all that happens to us, happens according to the Will of God. Excessive questions in the vein of "Why me?" or "What have I done to deserve this?" can be replaced by simpler responses: "How can I deal with this situation?" or "What are the lessons I must learn from this incident?"

The crass culture of consumption…

Today, it is fashionable to talk of a globalised world. We call the world a global village, but there is no beauty, no simplicity, no original thinking in this global marketplace. I only see a cult of comfort, a cult of shallow cleverness, a cult of narrow selfishness, a cult of decadence. In the wise words of Sadhu Vaswani: "Dear friends, dear young men and women who are the builders of a new world, let us not be reduced to mere consumers! Let us abjure mindless spending and meaningless acquisitions! Let us choose the life beautiful which is also the life of simplicity!"

"The world is too much with us," wrote the poet Wordsworth. Truer words were never spoken! Caught in the mad rush for possessions, power and material acquisitions, we become prime targets for stress.

Keep it simple!

Keep it simple! This is the mantra which can help you live a purer, more peaceful and happy life, and reduce your stress and tension. Keep it simple! Possessions and acquisitions may seem marvellous, but after a while, you do not own them– they own you.

One day, Sadhu Vaswani and I were visiting a village. Suddenly a swarm of locusts flew by and destroyed the entire harvest. Gurudev Sadhu Vaswani looked at the earth and said,

"Today, the swarm of locusts have destroyed the crops and ruined the earth; but I am sure by the grace of God the earth will rejuvenate and once again it will be green with the crop."

Friends, desires are like the swarm of locusts; they destroy the 'field of our being'. We have to be careful and alert, so that desires do not crush our energies and reduce us to zombies.

Henry David Thoreau and his mantra of simplicity

As a young writer, Henry David Thoreau had felt stifled and miserable in the city of Concord, where he lived. He was a Harvard graduate, and began his professional career as a teacher. But he wanted to lead a peaceful life, to devote his life to study, to thinking and writing. He found the society around him uncongenial for such an aspiration. Everywhere around him, men were only in pursuit of one thing– material gain. People were only interested in amassing property and possessions, enslaving themselves to 'things' and 'goods' that really meant nothing to Thoreau.

Thoreau realised that the world's greatest thinkers and philosophers of the past had lived lives of Spartan simplicity. He decided to take a leaf from their books. He decided to leave Concord and live alone in the woods, isolated from all the artificial trappings of so-called civilisation; he would concentrate on improving his soul's estate.

In March of 1845, Thoreau set out for Walden Woods with a borrowed axe. He started building a cabin for himself on the edge of Walden Pond, on a tract of land belonging to Ralph Waldo Emerson, his mentor. On July 4th, the cabin was completed, and a vegetable garden was planted. Carrying with him his flute, a few note books, pens, and a copy of Homer, Thoreau moved into the cabin in the woods, to launch his experiment in simple living and high thinking.

"He chose to be rich by making his wants few," remarked his friend Emerson.

Thoreau was just 28 years old when he began his remarkable experiment. He was not a misanthropist, nor a hermit. He had many friends in Concord, but he wished to escape from the artifices of civilisation and live a free and simple life.

"The mass of men lead lives of quiet desperation," he wrote. "Most of the luxuries, and many of the so-called comforts of life, are not only not indispensable, but positive hindrances to the elevation of mankind."

He lived in Walden Woods for a little more than two years. Having completed his trial period successfully, he returned to conventional, social life. From his notes made in the woods, he produced *Walden*, the masterpiece which made him famous, and inspired Mahatma Gandhi.

"I went to the woods because I wished to live deliberately, to front only the essential facts of life, and see if I could not learn what it had to teach, and not, when I came to die, to discover that I had not lived…"

The record of experiment in serene, simple living, *Walden*, is as relevant now as it was 150 years ago.

"Our life is frittered away by detail… Simplify, simplify," said Thoreau. "Simplify your life."

Simplicity of life and elevation of purpose. Simplicity! Thoreau urged his reaers again and again, "Don't burden yourself with possessions. Keep your needs and wants simple, and enjoy what you have. Simplify! Don't fritter away your life on non-esentials. Don't enslave yourself for luxuries you can do without."

His message of simplicity is crucial to us now!

Sindhi Community

The international community of Sindhis has every reason to be proud of itself. Highly civilised, cultured, enterprising, hardworking, hospitable, generous, philanthropic in thought, word, and deed, full of the spirit of faith and courage, they are indeed a model community.

Today, any 'group' or 'community' is judged by quantitative values such as per capita income, net worth and assets. The Sindhis have excelled in trade and business, in whichever part of the world they have chosen to settle. Indeed, the Sindhis are a community blessed abundantly by Goddess Lakshmi!

Sons and daughters of Sind! We are indeed proud of you, your hard work, your determination, your fortitude and perseverance. Like the proverbial Phoenix, you have risen from the ashes of Partition, with a new form, a new life, a new spirit.

The true spirit of Sind

I give you the words of my Beloved Master, Sadhu Vaswani:

"There are so many, who can believe only one thing at a time. I am so made as to rejoice in the many and behold the beauty of the One in the many. Hence, my natural affinity to many religions; in them all, I see revelations of the One Spirit. And deep in my heart is the conviction that I am a servant of all Prophets."

In these words lives the true spirit of Sind– the land that opened its heart and its doors to many faiths and cultures down the ages– Greek, Persian, Arab, Scythian, Afghan, Moghul and British– apart from the original culture of the Sindhu civilisation and the culture of *Akhanda Bharat*. The 'open window' also became an inviting entrance to aggressors and invaders.

Most people agree that Hindu Sindhis all over the world are secular, liberal and cosmopolitan in their outlook. They are tolerant, broad-minded, and respect other faiths. Above all, they are not bound by dogmas or rituals. But the important thing for Sindhis today is to remember their roots, their origins, while celebrating their unique, eclectic culture. They must not lose sight of their unique identity.

What makes Sindhis unique

One unique– and positive– feature of this amalgamation of cultures in Sind is that the Sindhis have no untouchable castes among them. There are the *Amils*, whose ancestors were civil servants, or worked for the administration; and the *Bhaibands*, whose ancestors were businessmen, bankers, and traders. This is in contrast to almost all other Hindu communities in India. This emphasises the distinctive non-sectarian, liberal and tolerant aspect of the Sindhi community. If it was considered a 'negative' feature by conservatives in the past, it is admired and appreciated by people today.

We must also remember that Sikhism left its own strong influence on Sindhi Society. Many Sindhi Hindus are ardent devotees of Guru Nanak. Like Buddhism, Sikhism was also unorthodox in its approach, emphasising the original Hindu spirit of tolerance.

The rich and lyrical Sindhi language

Sindhi is one of the world's ancient languages. The fact that Sindhi has been written in the Arabic script over the last few centuries, has led to the mistaken notion that it is a Persian-Arabic language. Rev. M.A. Shirt, one of the earliest Sindhi scholars from Hyderabad, was of the opinion that as far as its grammatical construction is concerned, Sindhi is "the purest daughter of Sanskrit".

The Sindhi language, with its rich and vast vocabulary, gave us the treasure-house of the immortal Sufi poet-saints, Shah, Sachal, Sa'mi, Bedil and Bekas. In more recent times, Sadhu Vaswani, the saint of modern India, has left us with his immortal *Nuri Granth* which fills us with spiritual ecstasy, rapture and deep devotion.

International scholars and linguists are unanimous in their view that Sindhi is a sweet and melodious language. Today, Sindhi is spoken by 18.5 million people in Pakistan and nearly 3 million people in India. Sindhi Hindus have carried the language to all parts of the world, after Partition.

Once written in Devnagiri, a modified Arabic script was introduced for the language by the British East India Company. After Partition, the government of India brought back the Devnagiri script, alongside the modified Arabic, for writing Sindhi.

The rich oral traditions of the Sindhi language

Do you know that Sindhi has 25 names for a single animal– the camel; or that it has 12 names for water; that there are words like *sika, ukir, taat* which have no equivalence in any other language? If Sind was susceptible to various invasions, this also gave it the advantage of assimilation of several Middle Eastern and Central Asian cultures. The beautiful blend of multiple languages and dialects into the mainstream Sindhi language, has given this language a rare richness, incomparable with any in the world.

The Sindhi language is the only language in the world which has precise kinship terms. For instance, *Maasaat* and *Saut*. Even Hindi does not have definite terms. *Maasaat* in Hindi is *Mausera bhai* and *Saut* is *Chachera bhai*. Sindhi words are specific in defining social relationships. This aspect of Sindhi language proves its depth, and its social culture. It alludes to our strong emotional bonds, our healthy social organisation, and our loving and caring behaviour.

In fact, there is a proverb for every situation, every condition, and every event in Sindhi. A mother, on a wintry morning, while baking *loli* or *koki*, would tell children, '*Jayko karay ghee, so na kare mau na pee-u*'– meaning, what *ghee* can provide us with, even our parents cannot (thus, emphasising the nutritive value of *ghee* at breakfast time). Whenever anyone showed signs of anger, mothers would say to their children, '*Thado gharo, chhaanva mein vihare*'– meaning, if you are cool, you will always find the shade– so relevant in the hot summers of Sind. If anyone was unhappy, mothers would say, '*Dhukh sukhan ji sunh*'– meaning, sorrow beautifies happiness. Another common proverb is '*Jedha utha teda loda*'– meaning, the higher you go, the more problems will occur. One proverb, born out of the lessons of history and used in every household is– '*Jedan lagay vaa-u, odhan dije puth*'. Loosely translated it means, 'Do not confront' or 'Do not walk into the storm.'

Sindhi language, identity and culture

Experts tell us that language reflects culture: perception and thought are not separate from language. Rather, language defines cultural concepts and stimulates perception and thought. Thus, culture and language are inter-twined. Therefore, we are warned, culture may not survive language loss.

By shifting from their mother tongue Sindhi, to dominant languages like Hindi or English, Sindhis are endangering their language and their culture. Fewer and fewer speakers use

Sindhi; children do not learn Sindhi as their mother-tongue. This leads to an inevitable loss of cultural knowledge, and the loss of the great heritage of language and literature. Only native speakers and writers of a language can keep it alive. Therefore, Sindhis must become at least passive bilinguals, if not proficient speakers of their mother tongue.

In order to preserve a language successfully, it has to be spoken in the home/family environment. Every Sindhi must therefore:

- Preserve cultural knowledge through language

- Maintain access to Sindhi through reading, writing, recital and singing

- Promote efforts to revitalise Sindhi in the home, and in the community

Sindhi is one of the great languages of the world, with a long history and rich literary traditions. It is up to the younger generation to preserve, protect, and propagate the language.

Seven-point programme for the Sindhis

1. Take care of your health!

Sindhis need to be more health-conscious. We are so absorbed in our work that we tend to neglect the body! There is an Arabian proverb which tells us: He who has health, has hope; and he who has hope, has everything. A commonplace saying in English warns us: When wealth is lost, little is lost; but when health is lost, everything is lost!

The so-called 'lifestyle' of the younger generation gives me great cause for worry. It seems to me, that young and middle-aged people have failed to maintain a healthy work-leisure balance. Ambitious, career minded executives insist on working fourteen hours a day, and cannot 'switch off' even when they get home to their families. Businessmen work twenty four hours a day, seven days a week– or so it seems to me. I am reminded of an English poem I read long ago:

He spent his health to get his wealth,
Then, with might and mien
He turned around to spend his wealth
To get his health again!

2. Help one another!

Kindness is the one great quality that distinguishes well bred people. Such people are kind at all times, on all occasions. They are kind in thought, word, and deed. Kindness, like charity, must begin at home. We must learn to help one another. If we find a member of our community in trouble, let us go out of our way to help him. If we find one who is going down, we must try our best to lift him up. In the measure in which we lift others up, we, too, are lifted up!

3. Let us unite!

I have repeatedly said, the Sindhi people have wonderful qualities. But I cannot help thinking that we lack unity! "The multitude, which is not brought to act as a unity, is confusion," said Pascal, the great philosopher. When the Sindhis begin to speak with one voice, the world will take heed of us!

Unity is strength; separation is weakness. Therefore, Sindhis must stand united, and speak with a united voice.

4. Be simple!

Today, the Sindhis are one of the most affluent communities in the world. Richly have they deserved their success– for it has come to them without any political backing, without any special protection, reservation or privilege, without state grants or subsidies. Our people have worked hard and with wisdom to earn this success, and the world respects them for the same!

The Sindhis are indeed, a gifted people. What they lack is simplicity! We do not have to assume poverty in order to practise the great virtue of simplicity. In fact, I think simplicity is the most becoming ornament for the wealthy! All our great ones have been utterly simple in dress, diet and daily living. Let us remember, too, the words of Emerson: "To be simple is to be great."

5. Pay attention to your children!

Once, Sadhu Vaswani was addressing a meeting of wealthy bankers. Many of them were 'millionaires' of those days. The Master had the courage and moral force to tell them frankly: "You are busy gathering silver and gold; but you must not neglect your richest treasure– your children!"

Let us give time and attention to our children! Let us be careful to see that they receive the right type of training and atmosphere in the home, and the right type of education in the school and college. Let us make sure we make the right choices for our children!

6. Let us keep our language alive!

Today, we are a scattered community. The linguistic division of India did not make provision for a Sindhi homeland; in fact, it was rather late, when Sindhi was finally recognised as an official Indian language under the constitution.

Those were losses, events beyond our control. But what is in our power to do, we must not neglect to do. If our community is to survive, we must keep our language alive!

Your children may be living in Spain, Dubai, Singapore, Indonesia or America; they may be multilingual, learning French, English and German at school, speaking Hindi, Marathi or Gujarati fluently. Do they know to read and write and speak in their own mother tongue?

If your answer to that question is no, you have failed to pass on one of your richest assets to your children!

7. Cultivate character!

A community grows strong in the measure in which its members develop qualities of character– integrity, honesty, simplicity, sincerity, purity and prayer, sympathy, service and sacrifice. Is not character the very foundation of a beautiful life?

Self-discipline is a quality that we all Sindhis must cultivate. The Gita tells us that we must do our duty alike in success and misfortune; we must not be swayed by excesses. This is evenness, this is true discipline.

Let the motto of every Sindhi's life be, in the words of Sadhu Vaswani: "Truth, though she take me to the scaffold; Truth, though she lead me through the fire!"

Let the day soon dawn when every Sindhi can, with a sense of fulfillment, utter the words: "I AM A SINDHI!"

Spirituality

Spirituality begins with the quest to know the self, and this quest is endless in itself.

The meaning of life has been one of the fundamental issues in philosophy, theology and religion. Since the dawn of civilisation, men of thought have grappled with such questions as: Who am I? Where do I come from? Where am I going? What is the purpose for which I am born? How may I fulfill that purpose?

Spirituality is in many ways a quest to find answers to these questions.

Science and spirituality

Science is the discovery of nature's laws, while spirituality is the discovery of the Self. In the final analysis, both are discoveries; both are an experience of "awareness". Our rishis had this "awareness"; they gained spiritual knowledge through intuition. It is significant that they referred to spirituality as *atma vidya*.

Spirituality makes us raise the fundamental question: What is man? Or, to put it more personally, what am I? It is precisely this self-knowledge that we must seek, in order to find complete fulfilment.

The ultimate aim of true education, we know, is to attain self-knowledge, to pursue the path of self-discovery. Of what use is any form of knowledge, vocational, professional or technical, if we lack knowledge of the self?

Science and spirituality are two faces of the same coin– one deals with the material, the other with the Spirit. One works with the visible, the other with the invisible. One is concerned with the outer, the other with the inner.

Inevitably one supports the other. I believe, science without spirituality is lame, and spirituality without science is blind. Both must go hand in hand. Science on its own cannot present a full and complete picture. Science only deals with the measurable, but spirituality steps further towards the immeasurable. More and more scientists now share this common view of a close relationship between science and spirituality, because the ultimate question of matter and Creation cannot be understood unless the consciousness is factored in.

Albert Einstein has said, "Everyone who is seriously involved in the pursuit of science becomes convinced that a Spirit is manifest in the laws of the universe."

Science involves the mind, and spirituality is entwined with the heart. Science with the heart will be the religion of the future. Science endeavours to uncover the abstract principles underlying nature. Spirituality enables us to do this in a proper way.

Spirituality as a quest for God

Most spiritual traditions teach us that knowing the true Self is equivalent of actually knowing God. For God is immanent in all Creation; He is the Indweller in every soul. Therefore, knowledge of the Self is knowledge of the Indweller, the *antaryami* who resides within all of us. In other words, spirituality, or the quest to discover the nature of one's own highest consciousness, is in essence, the quest to discover God.

Spirituality as a self-discipline

There is a practical aspect to spirituality that I wish to emphasise. It is said that God 'pierced' our five senses so that they are constantly tuned to the outer reality, and therefore, cannot grapple with what is within us. But the senses can be controlled, so that the mind and consciousness can be focussed within. In this sense, spirituality too is a discipline– essentially, self-discipline.

Spirituality is not asceticism

We are born into the world of nature, but our second birth is into the world of the Spirit.

I am often asked whether spiritual aspirants are forced to lead a dual life. There is a perception of a conflict between spirituality and the world. What should an aspirant do?

We are not human beings who undergo a spiritual experience. Instead, in reality, we are spiritual beings who are going through a human experience.

The Divine is not something that is far away and above us. It is everywhere in heaven and on earth, it is within us, right here in this body. Each one of us is a living, moving shrine of the Divine.

Spirituality is normal; it is our true nature, even though we refer to it as extraordinary. Spirituality is simply a means of arousing one's Spirit.

How can we connect with the soul? How can we promote our spiritual well-being?

- Make God a reality in your life. Make Him a friend, a partner, a guide, a guardian, a parent, and invite Him to watch over all that you do.

- Spend a little time in prayer, in introspection and in silent communion with God.

- Realise the value of the present moment– the here and the now. Realise that this moment is God's greatest gift to you.

- Do not live for yourself alone– for that will make life small and selfish. Learn to live for others– and you will find that life blooms like a beautiful flower!

- Do not wait for old age to begin to practise your spirituality! The happiest people are those who fuse, integrate spirituality into their daily life.

True spirituality is not a matter of indoctrination. It cannot be inspired by compulsion. You are free to enquire into its principles; you must be convinced of their truth, before you accept them. The laws of life are inviolable; they need no defenders, no patrons, no protectors. Each one of us must reach the Highest by his own free choice. This is the great truth taught to us in the ancient scriptures of India.

Let us choose to assert our spirituality!

Stop Complaining!

Complaints stem from a sense of unhappiness and dissatisfaction with life. Istead of complaining, we should respond to dissatisfaction with a positive attitude. Complaining constantly will only worsen matters. When we repeatedly complain, we become difficult and unpleasant to deal with, compelling others to keep their distance from us! Thus, we cut off the source of help and support that we feel we need so desperately!

Many of us pass through certain phases of life, "rough patches", as they are called, when everything seems to go wrong. In such circumstances, people tend to become negative; it is our duty to offer them help and support. Moreover, we must inspire them to cultivate faith and repose their trust in God.

People complain constantly…

There are some people who complain incessantly! It seems that complaining has become a way of life with them, that they simply cannot stop grumbling! Their complaints have nothing to do with pessimism or optimism, pain or suffering; complaining has simply become second nature to them! The traffic is too bad; the telephone lines are congested; the weather is too hot or too cold; people are rude or indifferent; servants are lazy and inefficient; the subordinates are insubordinate! I could go on and on: nobody understands me; nobody appreciates me; nobody knows what I am going through; nobody cares; nobody helps; nobody knows…

Of course, one feels sorry for such despondent people. However, when they are offered a remedy for their misery, they refuse to take it! You suggest to them, "Why don't you try to be what others are not; you must try and appreciate others; you must care; you must understand; you must help others…"

They will glare at you as if you have suddenly switched over to speaking Latin or Greek! They simply cannot register what you are trying to say to them! They want only to be at the receiving end of care, compassion, understanding, help, appreciation and sympathy. They do not want to give away any of those beautiful feelings to others!

Selfish people are born complainers. Nothing will ever convince them that many others are far worse off than they are. Nothing will persuade them that they have a lot to be grateful for. They prefer the martyr's syndrome: I am the most misunderstood, unappreciated creature in the entire world!

Complaining has become a habit with us!

All of us complain at some time or the other. We feel exasperated at waiting interminably in a traffic jam or in a doctor's waiting room; we become angry when flight schedules are disrupted and our carefully laid travel plans fall apart. We react with indignation when government officers treat us with disrespect and callousness. This is but natural; in such situations, complaining becomes a way of letting off steam. But trouble starts when we make complaining a habit, and think that it is the best way to deal with life and its problems! Compulsive complainers make it their way of reacting to life! No matter what happens, they complain, they cry, they express their unhappiness volubly, they protest, they feel extremely sorry for themselves, they leave very little room for anyone else to step in and do anything for them!

Complaining can become a vice difficult to relinquish. It is like those little children who acquire the habit of sucking their thumbs, and thereafter cannot give it up when they are scolded or pulled up! Sadly, many of them actually begin to feel better when they complain persistently. Let me hasten to add, this is an entirely illusory feeling. They have managed to make others miserable with their constant whining; they believe they have unburdened themselves of all their negativity, and are entirely satisfied with their session. But the trouble is, their problems are no nearer to being solved!

Things go wrong with constant complainers!

People who complain constantly do not wish to take responsibility for themselves and their actions. Ask them why their goals are not accomplished, and they will come up with a list of excuses. What they do not realise is that their energy and intellect are so focussed on finding faults in their situations and in others, that they cannot concentrate on achieving their goals. They do not realise how tedious and futile their constant complaints are. They have effectively undermined their own power and efficiency, and retain control only by complaining.

Constant complainers also suffer from a false sense of superiority because they find faults with everyone except themselves. They are convinced that others love listening to their complaints; they do not realise that they are actually driving their friends away, and will soon have only themselves left as their sole audience!

Take a look at some of their complaints:

1. I am overworked and it is the fault of my boss. (What about your time management?)

2. I am late, and it is the fault of the public transport system. (Why don't you try leaving home early?)

3. My targets have not been met and it is the fault of my subordinates. (Why don't you lead from the front?)

4. My job is the most difficult and unpleasant. (Why don't you make way for someone who can handle it?)

5. I have been overlooked for promotion because the system is corrupt. (Have you looked at your own performance record?)

There is a way out!

I mentioned that all of us complain at one time or another– dynamic complainers find a way to solve their problems; they give vent to their negativity through complaints and then go on to find a way out of their difficulties. Chronic complainers are far from dynamic; they are in fact defeatists who are more interested in making excuses and shifting the blame onto others. They are happy and satisfied in just complaining; they do not want to lose control over their pet excuses.

Let us stop focussing on all that is wrong and focus instead on all that is right; let us stop wailing about what we don't have and instead be grateful for what we have; let us take the time to appreciate people for what they are and what they can do, instead of focussing on their defects. When we complain and criticise constantly, we are drawing negativities into our lives. Each time we utter something negative about life, we actually begin to believe it more and more, and make it come true in our lives. Our imagined ills become our reality. Needless to say, the reverse is also true. When we believe things are going good, they become better, actually. When we visualise success and talk about all that is positive, success actually begins to take shape for us.

Let us stop complaining, start thanking, appreciating and feeling good about ourselves!

Practical suggestions

1. Learn to value people. A successful business values its people as its assets, rather than as

'staff' or 'workforce'. A respected, well-treated employee is a satisfied employee who will work even harder to enhance his self-respect and prove his worth to an appreciative employer. "People are our number one assets" is not just a cliché. People are, in fact, the life blood of an organisation. The best brains and the best talents in an organisation need to be nurtured in an environment that allows them to grow personally and professionally. A good manager keeps them focussed, motivated and happy. What kind of a manager are you? What kind of a manager would you like to have as your boss?

2. Realise that no one is perfect. It was a wise man who said, "Only in grammar can you be more than perfect." And an Italian proverb warns us wryly, "He that will have a perfect brother must resign himself to remain brother-less." And here is a brilliant piece of inductive reasoning: "I am a nobody. Nobody is perfect. Therefore, I am perfect!"

The spirit of tolerance and acceptance is essential to a happy life and a peaceful mind. The world we live in is far from perfect; we ourselves are not paragons of perfection, and the same goes for the people around us. As they say, it is a crazy, mixed-up world– but we must recognise ourselves as part of all this imperfection, and accept life as it is.

What does it mean to be compassionate and gentle, kind, loving, and patient? It is surely to accept people with their imperfections and weaknesses, and still continue to appreciate their worth! If they are imperfect, why, so are we!

3. Look for merits, not defects. The secret of successful relationships is to be found in an understanding heart– preferably, your own!

The secret of a harmonious and peaceful life is: focus on people's merits and strengths– not on their weaknesses and defects. If you wish to be happy, you can begin by thinking, "Everybody has something good in him; there is something that I can learn from every human being."

4. Take the lead in appreciation! Human relationships thrive on caring, sharing and mutual appreciation. We rely on our loved ones, our friends, and those closest to us, for moral support and encouragement.

No one knows who wrote or said these lines originally, but all of us have read these lines and been inspired by them: "I shall pass through this world but once. Any good, therefore, that I can do, or any kindness that I can show to any human being, let me do it now.

Let me not defer nor neglect it, for I shall not pass this way again."

Is it not true that all of us feel happy when we are appreciated? In this, as in other things, what we send out comes back to us. For life is like a boomerang: what we are, what we do, comes back to us. When we give our best to the world, when we send out warmth, love, and appreciation– it all comes back to us.

5. Recognise that we need one another! Have you ever stopped to think what a great debt of gratitude you owe to others? How can we ever begin to repay these debts? We can start by acknowledging the contributions that others have made for our benefit, and by doing what little we can for others, in our own way.

   The farmer grows the food that is put on my table; the tradesmen deliver the groceries and articles that make my daily routine smooth. What can I do for them? I may not be able to go and help the farmer in his field or the grocer in his shop, but I can pay my taxes honestly, I can deal with all tradesmen kindly and generously, I can do my bit to make this world better in some way or the other. If all else is impossible for me, I can at least spread a little sunshine with my smile and good cheer!

   We gain from others when we realise that as human beings, we are all interdependent. We learn from others when we realise that we need their help, and seek the same with humility. At such times, we come to learn how little we know, and how we cannot get on without others. However, we would miss these valuable insights, if our pride and ego stood in our way.

6. Give people what they deserve– and a little more! Let us treat people as we would like to be treated by them. Who are we to judge another's worth? What if God were to apply the same scales to us as we apply to others? In this aspect, let us err on the side of generosity, compassion and kindness, so that God may look at us with mercy rather than justice.

   "Treat people as if they were what they ought to be, and you help them to become what they are capable of being," writes the great German author, Goethe. Do you treat people well because they are good looking, wear expensive clothes and jewels, or arrive in an expensive car? You are not exhibiting a desirable personality trait!

   Give others the best treatment that you are capable of– it may not say much about them, but it reveals the truth about you.

Do not judge others harshly, lest God should do the same to you!

7. Offer thanks to God every moment of your life! There is a meaning of mercy in all that happens to us– for God is all love and all wisdom. He is too loving to punish us. He is too wise to make a mistake. Therefore if something comes to me that is contrary to my personal will, I must accept it as the Will of God. As Gurudev Sadhu Vaswani taught us, "Every disappointment is His appointment."

Acceptance with due gratitude is also a subtle law, which puts you on the path of self-growth. "O God, whatever You do and whatever happens, has a purpose and a meaning. Your scheme of things is perfect. I accept your Will." This should be your attitude in life; whether you succeed or fail, ever remain grateful to God!

It is not enough to speak of gratitude or enact deeds of gratitude– we must live gratitude by practising acceptance of God's Will in all conditions, in all incidents and accidents of life.

Let us stop complaining, and start thanking!

Stress- Beat It!

Stress is a much-used, much misused term. Experts on stress management tell us that stress is "the wear and tear on your body caused by life's events." It is the sum total of the body's physical, mental, and chemical reactions to circumstances which cause fear, irritation, worry, anxiety and excitement.

Stress originates from a French word which means constriction or delimitation. It is true that stressful situations seem to squeeze us, and limit our emotions and reactions. Stress therefore, is regarded as a potential killer. It saps one's energy and undermines one's well-being.

Stress is purely subjective. What is a stressful situation for one man, may be child's play for another. For instance, if a person is asked to say a few words to a large gathering, he may panic and completely lose his nerve. A fluent public speaker, on the other hand, would regard it as an opportunity, and end up speaking eloquently!

There are hundreds of stress-causing experiences, or stressors, in our everyday lives. These stressors can create positive stress or negative distress. Our body and its systems are conditioned to cope with stressors and function well up to a certain level. When the limit is exceeded, we become victims of stress.

Too little stress makes life dull, boring, irritable and apathetic. Too much stress overwhelms a man, leading to many of the modern lifestyle ailments such as hypertension, heart attacks, nervous breakdown, malfunctioning of the colon, pain in the neck, asthma, constipation, duodenal ulcers, migraine and certain forms of epilepsy. Stress and tension also cause insomnia or sleeplessness.

Causes of stress

Man's lifestyle in the modern age is one of the main causes of stress. Somehow, modern life and stress seem to go together. The way we work, talk, and function every day, contributes to the building up of stress. People rush about all the time, as though they are carrying the burden of the entire world upon their shoulders. People fritter away their time, accumulating what they think they need– only to realise that they don't need it at all. They resemble squirrels in a cage– running, running all the time– but getting nowhere.

We seem to be in a hurry all the time! It is not only when we are on our feet that we are hurrying; when we are seated, at rest, our minds are rushing somewhere or the other. We may be waiting outside an office, waiting for an appointment with a doctor, waiting for an interview call– but our thoughts are scurrying. This mental race is one of the main causes of tension.

Another cause of stress is irritation. We give in again and again to irritation. We may not always express it– but the irritation inside unnecessarily burns up our emotional energy, which can otherwise be used constructively.

Yet another cause of stress is that we are overwhelmed by the problems we face. We give in to frustration and feel we cannot cope with life!

Mental fatigue and exhaustion is another reason we react negatively to stress situations. We often underestimate the demands of intellectual or mental work when compared to hard, physical labour. Psychiatrists say that people who work with their brains need more sleep and rest than manual workers. When mental fatigue sets in, we cannot think clearly or react reasonably.

Practical suggestions to overcome stress

1. **Adopt a positive attitude to life.** This cannot be done in a day, but you must begin now! Many people say, "I'll change my attitude one of these days." One of these days is none of these days! Affirm to yourself, "Right now, from this moment, I shall adopt a positive attitude."

2. **Do not anticipate trouble**. So many people give in to this habit. "Oh, what will happen to me? What will be my condition if this were to happen?" In the process of fretting, they lose much of the joy of living.

3. **Live in the present!** I tell people again and again: you should not make yourself miserable by thinking of the past or of the future. The past is a cancelled cheque. The future is a promissory note. The present is the only cash in hand. Use it wisely and well. Make the most of it!

4. **Do not hold a grudge against anyone in the heart within you.** When you do so, it only disturbs your peace of mind. Hatred is self-punishment. Very often, our ill-will and resentment cannot touch the other person– but we ourselves become poisoned by

our negative feelings. Has someone wronged you? Has someone cheated you? Has someone maligned you? Has someone taken undue advantage of you? Has someone spread scandals against you? Forgive them, before forgiveness is asked.

5. **Cultivate the spirit of gratitude.** There are a thousand blessings that God has bestowed upon us. We are rarely conscious of these– we only complain about what we lack. This adds to the stress and tension of our lives.

So many of us say, "I don't know why God is doing this to me. I don't deserve it." How many of us ever say, "Such a wonderful thing happened to me today. I don't know how it came to pass– for I don't deserve it?"

Whenever people come to me in a state of tension and depression, I tell them to count their blessings. Not just count them in the mind, but actually write them down and make a list of them. When you actually start making a list, you will surely find that you have a lot to be grateful for!

It is hard to feel stressed or tense, when your heart over flows with gratitude!

6. **Simplify your life!** "The world is too much with us," wrote the poet Wordsworth. Truer words were never spoken! Caught in the mad competition for possessions, power and material acquisitions, we become prime targets for stress. Modern technology has blessed us with countless gadgets, yet they do not seem to make us happy! They only add to the stress and tension of our lives!

Some people talk into three telephones at a time– while another cell phone sings aloud from their shirt-pocket. I have seen young men and women walk down parks and green lanes with ear phones from their stereos around their head– lost to the world of beauty around them.

7. **Develop a healthy sense of humour.** Humour is perhaps the best antidote to stress. When you laugh out loud, you will find your body, mind, and heart relaxing!

Try to be with people who bring laughter into your lives, and learn to laugh at yourself– you will find that stress and tension melt away.

8. **Develop faith, cultivate faith**. One cure for stress is trust. We lay our trust on banks which

fail, on bonds whose values fluctuate, on friends who betray us, on earthly power and dominion, on worldly goods which are perishable. We try to build our security on things that are insecure themselves. We must lay our trust in God. We do not know what the future holds, but if we trust the One who holds the future, we will be free from stress.

9. **Practise the technique of relaxation.** You must relax at least twice every day– relax your body, relax your limbs, relax your muscles. There are several techniques to help you achieve relaxation of body and mind. You can pick up any one which suits you– but you must make sure you practise it regularly!

10. **Go out of your way to help others.** There is no stress buster stronger than this– go out of your way and help others. Forget your petty self, your empirical self. It is this petty self that is the home of tension. Kindness is one of the greatest remedies of stress. Kindness is the balm that softens and smoothes the rough patches of life. It is the healing touch that can take away the pain and misery of human existence, and when you send out kindness to others, you will find it returns to you manifold.

Success

I would define success as the ability to be happy and make others happy; the ability to love and be loved; the ability to remain in peaceful harmony with oneself, with those around you, and with God's cosmic laws. I believe that true success is in some way or the other, related to inner happiness and peace of mind. It has been rightly said that if you lose your wealth, you lose but little. If you lose your health, you lose something. But, if you have lost your peace of mind, you have lost everything!

Success is not what people take it to be

Every one of us wants to be successful. Though we move along different pathways of life, we are all in search of success. However, there are only a few who know of the elements of success, the factors that contribute to building up success.

Today, success is being confounded with making money, with amassing millions and billions. John D. Rockfeller was a multi-millionaire, for whom success was not accompanied by happiness. He was the richest man in the world and yet all his millions could not make him happy.

Some people equate success with power and position. Many of us tend to equate success with visible material acquisitions. There is no happiness in wealth, but there is considerable wealth in the experience of happiness.

Outer things, external achievements, are not the yard sticks for success. Power, prestige, position, social influence, higher degrees awarded by universities– all these are outer things. They only touch the fringe of life, they do not enter the depths within. A man may have all this, and yet he may be intellectually barren, he may be emotionally unbalanced, and spiritually sterile. Would you call such a man successful?

Success, we think, is getting whatever we want; but our wants keep on increasing. To be truly happy, we only need to count our blessings!

Why do we have failures at all?

Many people think: why did God not create a world in which there was only success– what a wonderful world it would be!

But when you come to think of it, it is failures that give meaning to success. Wherever you have success, there is bound to be failure. The two go together. It is failure that draws out the best that is within us. It is failure that unfolds, unlocks our hidden powers. In the measure in which we face failures in the right spirit, in that measure that the tremendous power that lies locked up within us is unfolded.

How can we turn failure into success?

Failure has a place in life. It is very necessary. But even as success is not permanent, failure is not permanent. Do not forget that failures are not final. You fail only when you accept failure as final. Always think of failures as stepping-stones to success, not stopping stones. Every failure is a source of building your moral muscles.

If you wish to turn failure into success, the conscious and the subconscious must cooperate with each other. Whatever you believe in your heart, the subconscious reinforces that belief. If you believe that you cannot achieve something, if you believe that you cannot do something, if you believe that you cannot have something, the subconscious will take up your belief. Its job is only to see that it proves your beliefs. Whatever you believe in, your subconscious will create conditions, so that your beliefs are proved correct.

To turn failure into success, you must have a strong belief of success! If you consciously paint a picture of yourself as a successful person, success will definitely come to you. But if you are convinced that you are a failure– even if you are placed in the best of circumstances, with the best of resources– you will fail! Such is the law. If you think of scarcity, scarcity will befall you. If you imagine abundance, abundance will flow into your life.

How may we achieve the success that we seek?

The first secret of success is: Work not for wages, work for the love of God.

Work for the love of suffering humanity, work for the love of work itself. Work then becomes a source of joy and delight.

Today, wherever I go, I find people who are assigned any work always asking, "What do I get for this? What is there in it for me?" People work only for wages today, for some returns. They have forgotten what it is to work with joy, to make their work a source of delight. This is why work has become a cause of so much boredom and frustration.

The second secret of success is: Do your duty and a little more!

People who do their duty and a little more, are not looking for rewards or recognition. But people who do less than what they ought to, do not realise how and where they lose out.

Today, the emphasis has shifted from duties to rights. Every one of us is claiming his or her rights. Women want their rights. Yes sisters, you shall have your rights, but what about your duties? Men clamour for their rights. Yes brothers, you must have your rights, but what about your duties? If only each of us carried out our duties conscientiously, sincerely, earnestly, and faithfully, there would be no need for anyone to fight for their rights!

Three simple words spell the third secret of success: Believe and achieve!

Believe in yourself, believe in the work you have undertaken. Believe that you will succeed in your work. If you do not believe in yourself, how can you hope to succeed? Success is the sum of small efforts– repeated day in and day out tirelessly.

Within each and every one of us is a tremendous potential to overcome obstacles and achieve success, to face difficulties and overcome them. There is just one thing we have to do to tap this vast potential, this tremendous power– we must believe in ourselves.

The fourth secret of success is: Fix your goal!

You are unique. God made you for a special purpose. Discover that special purpose. Make it your goal and once you have fixed that goal, you must always keep your eyes fixed on that goal. It has been said that winners make goals, while losers make excuses!

The fifth secret of success is: Help others!

Help others willingly! Help others with love and kindness! By providing assistance to others, we ensure our own success. It is sharing which gives a jump-start to success. Therefore it is only by giving that one can attain success. Look for someone who is grappling with a problem and help him solve it or someone who is hurt and injured and assist in their healing. The simple four-word formula for success is– Make Yourself More Helpful!

The sixth secret of success is: Prepare a plan.

Every day, as you get up in the morning, you must plan on what you wish to do that day.

Remember, time is the most precious of all possessions and we waste our precious time in idle pursuits, doing nothing! The wise have always emphasised that an intelligent plan is a vital step to success. For the man who plans well, knows where he is going, knows what progress he is making, and has a pretty good idea when he will arrive, success is bound to follow!

One final thought...

If you really want to succeed in life, you must contact the source of success– God. God is the source of all success.

Let us learn to rely more and more on God to succeed in life. God invites us to hand our problems over to Him. Do we have a better option than the best?

Suffering

Suffering, sorrow, grief, hardship, loneliness, and pain are given to us to make us strong in Spirit, to endow us with moral courage, or what I call muscles of the Spirit. Difficulties give us courage and strengthen our will-power. They put us through a process of cleansing and purification.

Each one of has to go through the experience of suffering; hence, we must learn to accept suffering as a part of growing. Learn to value suffering, because there can be no self-growth without suffering.

It was said of Jesus, when he suffered intense pain and agony on the cross: "He came to save others; how is it that he cannot save himself?"

This remark was obviously made in ignorance, for suffering is a gift consciously chosen and willingly accepted by saviours and saints, helpers and healers of humanity.

As Gurudev Sadhu Vaswani puts it so beautifully, "Suffering is the benediction which God pours upon His beloved children to whom He would reveal the meaning of His infinite mercy, to whom He would reveal Himself, His wisdom and His love!"

We know that Sri Ramakrishna Paramhansa, during his final days, was afflicted with acute pain and suffering due to cancer of the throat. Despite the severe pain and discomfort in talking, he constantly spoke to his devotees of God and spirituality. He could eat very little, but his joy and radiance were infectious. During these days of affliction, some of his devotees, unable to see his suffering due to the advanced stage of the cancer, begged him to cure himself through the power of prayer. The saint agreed to do this, smiling gently. Sometime later, he sent word for Swami Vivekananda and told him that he had indeed asked Mother Kali to help him overcome his inability to swallow food. He said to his dear devoted disciple, that the Divine Mother drew his attention to all the people in the *ashrama* and the outside world, and asked him if he was not eating through all their mouths!

The truth is that Sri Ramakrishna's consciousness was no longer tethered to the shell of his own physical body. He had transcended the physical aspect of pain and suffering.

Why does God put us through the test of pain and suffering? Isn't that harsh, strict, and unkind?

On the other hand, it is only God's kindness and His concern for us that places these tests before us, so that we understand ourselves, grow in self-realisation, and develop spiritual strength. In other words, it is for our own spiritual well-being. Taking these spiritual tests will enable us to grow in wisdom, understanding, and faith.

Behind every suffering that afflicts us, is the shadow of God Himself. God wears the cloak of suffering and comes to us to cleanse our life. Those who know this truth, welcome suffering. Those who do not know this truth complain. They reject the very idea of suffering being valuable for spiritual progress! They scoff at teachers who tell them that suffering and pain purify the body and the soul. It is very similar to the process by which your washing machine soaks, churns, rolls about, rinses and wrings your clothes dry to cleanse them!

There is a little known story about Kunti, told to us in our ancient books. Once, Sri Krishna granted Kunti a boon to ask for whatever she wanted. What she wanted was indeed strange! She said to the Lord, "Lord, give me a little suffering all the time. For I have come to realise that in pleasures and enjoyments, You are often forgotten. But in pain and suffering, You are always remembered."

Kunti was right. Today, many of us enjoy the luxuries of life, we take pleasure in the many comforts we have. When everything goes right, we forget God, we feel we can manage our lives perfectly well without His help. We may remember the Lord in passing, as we mutter a few prayers mechanically, but we are alright without Him! We get on with our lives. We are too busy, too involved, too wrapped up in our worldly activities to remember Him!

But the moment things start going wrong, the moment difficulties strike, we turn to God with alacrity. We call out to Him to come to our aid. As Sant Kabir points out, we do not need God when the going is good. We need Him only in suffering, we remember Him in difficulties, we remember Him when we are in trouble.

What is the cause of our suffering? Taking the question one step further, what is the purpose of all the suffering we go through?

Suffering, I think, is of two types– the first is unnecessary suffering, which we create for ourselves through wrong thinking and wrong feeling. The second type of suffering comes to us from God; it comes to the best of men, the noblest of souls. It came to Krishna and Christ, to Buddha and Zoroaster, to Moses and Prophet Mohammed, to Nanak and Kabir, to

Ramakrishna Paramhansa and Sadhu Vaswani. This type of suffering does not come alone; it brings with itself the strength, which endures, and the comfort which lends sweetness to the suffering.

The suffering which man brings on himself, is hard and unbearable. Most of us will realise that this is how we felt when we have passed through trials. When we do not respond to life's incidents and accidents in the right attitude, it can break our spirit and throw us in an abyss of gloom. But if we are able to cast all thoughts of self aside, and behold the loving hand of God in every condition and circumstance of life, we have a positive answer to the question: why did this have to happen?

We realise that everything that happens, happens for our good. Everything that comes to pass is the result of God's infinite goodness and unfailing love for us! Therefore, I often recite this prayer:

Thou know'st everything, Beloved,
Let Thy Will always be done!
In joy and sorrow, my Beloved,
Let Thy Will always be done!

When we take things personally, selfishly, when we feel that we are the victims of God's unfair, unjust ways, even a little pain becomes hard to bear. But when we accept pain and suffering as God's Will for us, He takes up our burden, and the yoke becomes easy to bear!

May I give you the words of the German mystic, Meister Eckhart: "Believe me, if there was a man who was willing to suffer on account of God and God alone, then though he fell a sudden prey to all the collective sufferings of the world, it would not trouble nor cow him down, for God would be the bearer of his burden."

Suffering is a gift from God

Gurudev Sadhu Vaswani has given us a profound message in one of his poems which is like a prayer:

In all circumstances and under all conditions, in sorrow and suffering, remember that God knows best. Whatever He does is for our benefit. What may seem to us, to be an obstacle, a difficulty, or just misfortune, has been sent to us with a definite purpose. Whatever happens to us, whatever befalls us, has a hidden meaning, which we are often unable to see or comprehend.

How may we know whether we are suffering for the sake of God or for our own wrong doings?

When we suffer for our own sake, even a little of it becomes hard to bear. When we suffer for the sake of God, He shoulders the burden and we feel a weight lifted from our chest.

Is it true that suffering gives saints their healing power? Is this what makes the men of God redeemers of their race?

Yes, it is true that saints receive arrows of pain as gifts from the All-Giver! In sunshine and in rain alike, they rejoice, give gratitude to God, and sing His holy Name. Every great one of humanity has had to bear his cross. Krishna and Buddha and Jesus walked through the valley of the shadow of death. Who are we to say, "We must escape sorrow, anguish, and pain?" We, too, must bear our cross, bear and bleed.

And when we bleed, let us remember that the Will of God is working through us; through suffering and pain, God's Will is purifying us, preparing us for the vision of the one Lord of life, light and love, in all that is around us, above us, below us, within us.

Overcoming physical pain

If we want to be unaware of the pain which the body feels, we have to dissociate ourselves from our bodies. The greatest tragedy of man, his greatest illusion, is his identification with the body. I am not this body. This body is only a garment I have worn in this present earth incarnation. I have put on and put off many such bodies through this endless adventure of existence, through which I have passed.

In the measure in which you are able to dissociate yourself from the body, in that measure you will find that pain of the body will affect you to a lesser degree. Epictetus was a wise man, one whom I would call a *brahma jnani*. One day, he had a bad fall and his leg broke. His friends gathered around him and said to him, "Epictetus, we are so sad to hear that your bone is broken." He laughed and replied, "My bone? I have no bones. It is only the bone of the leg of my body that is broken."

Just imagine such a dissociation! If only we could achieve this, we would not feel physical pain.

Suffering comes in a special package

It is most important for us to note that whenever suffering comes to us, God always gives us the strength and wisdom to bear the suffering. Sorrow and wisdom, suffering and endurance– these are just two sides of the same coin. Look at the coin– one side is suffering; on the other side is the wisdom and the strength to bear that suffering. Never, ever does God send suffering to us, unaccompanied by the strength and wisdom to cope with it. This is why we continue to live, this is how mankind has survived personal and public calamities, and still continues to survive and flourish. The very fact that we are all alive and breathing is a testimony to this great truth– that we invariably conquer suffering with God-given strength and wisdom.

What is the best way to handle such difficult situations?

Our journey through life has been perfectly planned by Infinite Love and Infinite Wisdom. There can be no mistake. Every experience that comes to us is just the right experience occurring at the right time to train us in the right way. So let us accept all that comes and never attempt to circumvent anything.

Again and again, we try to run away from what appears to us as an unpleasant experience, and try to avoid what we regard as difficult situations. We may succeed in keeping them away for a while, but we can never avoid them all the time, for they are, indeed, essential to our growth. God means us to face them in order to develop our moral and spiritual muscles. If we avoid an unpleasant experience, it will return to us in due course with redoubled force, and we shall be compelled to take up the challenge until we have learnt the lesson it has come to teach us.

Therefore, the best way to face difficult situations is to accept them and cooperate with their inner purpose, all the while fixing our mind and heart on Him, who has planned for each one of us the glorious liberty that belongs to His children of the Spirit.

There is so much suffering in this life that many people begin to question God's existence…

These are persistent questions that still haunt some of us: Who is God? Where does He dwell? How can we prove that He is?

Suffering

It is not just deniers and atheists who have raised these questions. Philosophers, saintly souls, and wise men who realised God in their lifetime have also been troubled by these persistent doubts.

People who go through mental turmoil and suffering also find it difficult to believe in the existence of God.

Let me tell you about Dr. Annie Besant, the founder of the famous Theosophical Society of India. When she was a young woman, she worked on the editorial staff of a prestigious magazine called *The New Review*. She was an intellectual woman, given to mature reflection and logical thinking.

Her daughter fell seriously ill soon after birth, with a severe attack of whooping cough. The baby was running high fever, and as the temperature rose, the infant developed convulsions. Annie Besant was distraught at the sight of her little child going through these violent fits. She could not bear to think of her innocent baby being put through such suffering.

"They say God is all mercy and love," she said to herself. "Is this the kind of mercy and love He shows my child? What has this tender, innocent babe done to deserve such suffering?"

She virtually gave up all faith and belief in God after this happened. She became an agnostic. She probed preachers and religious teachers. No one could answer her questions satisfactorily. "Where is God's love and compassion? Why is this child, who hasn't even hurt a fly, subject to such suffering?"

One day, she came across a book by Madame H.P. Blavatsky, entitled *The Secret Doctrine*. The editor had sent it to Annie Besant to be reviewed. As Annie Besant began to read the book, a new understanding dawned on her, and she was deeply impressed by its contents. One of the chapters in the book was entitled *Karma and Reincarnation*. She read it again and again, and began to view life through a new perspective. She seemed to have found, at last, answers to the questions she had been asking. Here was the only satisfactory explanation for her innocent child's suffering: it was nothing but the result of the karma of the child's previous births!

Enlightenment came to her as in a flash of lightning. She understood that the present life was not the first life, the only life lived by her, or her child. She had lived many, many, other lives before she had entered this body– likewise, her infant. It was due to the child's actions in those earlier births, that it was going through certain consequences in this birth. The infant had done something earlier, the fruit of which it was now faced with. The whole thing was crystal clear; the mystery was unravelled. She began to understand things, which were earlier inexplicable.

Because of this understanding, Annie Besant left her country, left behind her friends and family to come to India. She regarded India as the great land of the rishis, sages and saints, who offered the most profound and satisfactory solution to life's problems. She came to live in Chennai, and founded the famous Theosophical Society of India. Many of us may not know that *Theosophy* actually means "wisdom concerning God" or more literally, "God wisdom"as translated directly from the original Greek. Annie Besant once said, "Mysticism is the realisation of God, of the Universal Self. It is attained either as a realisation of God outsidethe mystic, or within himself. In the first case, it is usually reached from within a religion, by exceptionally intense love and devotion, accompanied by purity of life, for only the pure in heart shall see God."

What we need above all else today, is the rediscovery of the great truth that God is– that He is real and that we need to renew our faith in Him.

A few tips to tackle suffering and pain in the best way

1. We must divert our mind from the fact of suffering. If our attention is focused on suffering, it tends to get multiplied manifold.

2. In times of pain and suffering, we must learn to count our blessings. For those of us who are pessimistic enough to imagine that there are no blessings to count, there is a simple exercise. We can take a piece of paper and list all the things in our life which we cannot do without.

3. We must learn to dissociate ourselves from the body, the mind, and the ego. This is not easy, but it is the first step towards self-realisation. It is the mind that creates all our suffering; once we transcend the mind, there is no suffering at all– only peace and joy.

4. In all conditions and circumstances of life, we must continue to thank the Lord. We must make it a habit to praise the Lord at every step, in every round of life. Even in the midst of fear and frustration, worry and anxiety, depression and disappointment, let the words, "Thank you God! Thank you God! Thank you God!" be upon our lips constantly.

We will find that we are filled with an amazing sense of peace.

5. Do not try to run away from trouble and pain. They are essential to our growth. God means us to face them and acquire strength and wisdom.

6. Accept the Will of the Lord and fix your minds and hearts on God. Realise that God is always by our side, watching us, guiding us, guarding us, and protecting us.

Sufism and Sind

Sufism is dear to the heart of the Sindhi Community. If you were to ask some scholars what is the true religion of Sind, many of them would tell you without hesitation, Sufism. Shah Abdul Latif says, "*Náe nén nihár, to mein dero dosta jo.*" Translated into English this means, "Look inside you, the friend lives there". Of course the 'friend' here is God, by whatever name you choose to call Him– Krishna, Christ, Allah, *Bhagwan* or Buddha.

Sufism is said to have been born in Persia. Scholars regard the Sufi way of life as a harmonious blend of "Greek neo-platonism, Indian Buddhism, Zorastrianism, Magan and Nestorian beliefs". Some believe that Sufism was born as a way of life in South Asia, when Islam mixed with the Hindu, Sikh, and Buddhist cultures in Sind. Sufism has also been influenced by pre-Islamic and non-Islamic schools of mysticism and philosophy.

Why Sufism is so dear to me...

Whatever I know of Sufism came to me from my Gurudev, Sadhu Vaswani. Gurudev was always in his element when he spoke of or wrote concerning the great Sufi mystics. It was asthough he was one of them. His own life was one of detachment and dedication, self-denial, service and silent sacrifice. "Who are you?" he was asked. And he answered, "I am a Sufi. I adore the Lord as blessed beauty, as immortal love. Love is the sacrament of my life. For in love, shines the very light of God."

Who is a Sufi? How did Sufism originate?

I was at a sacred *dargah* a few years ago, and on a tablet at the entrance, were carved these thought-provoking words: *Be silent and behold the Beloved!* To me this captures the essence of a Sufi! A true Sufi speaks but little. A true Sufi ever remains silent. He is silent, and in silence, he beholds the Beloved!

A Sufi is a humanist first, a humanist with the qualities of a saint. Sufism is a blend of the finest values of *Vedantic* and Islamic cultures.

What is the meaning of the word *Sufi*? According to some, it is derived from the Arabic word *Sufi* which means wool. The earliest Sufis were ascetics who wore coarse garments of wool– a symbol of voluntary poverty and renunciation of the world and its pleasures.

There are some who associate the word *Sufi* with the word *safa* which means pure. The great Sufi mystic Rumi was once asked, "What makes the Sufi?" He answered without hesitation, "Purity of the heart, not the patched mantle!" The true Sufi is a man of purity, inner purity of the heart. For, without purification, there is no illumination: and without illumination there can be no unification with God– which is the ultimate goal of the Sufi's quest. According to some, the word Sufi is linked with *ahl al-suffa* which means "people of the bench". They were the men who, in the days of the Prophet, sat by day and slept by night on the benches outside the mosque, where the Prophet worshipped. They were men of non-possession, who kept away from the world. They ate what was given to them and wore simple, coarse garments.

There are others who associate the word *Sufi* with the Greek word *Sophia* which means wisdom. For the true Sufi is a seeker of wisdom, a seeker after truth.

To which denomination do Sufis belong?

The faith of the Sufis rises above all creeds and denominations and religions. It is a way of life rather than a philosophy, theology, or school of thought. The use of the familiar English suffix "ism" should not make us equate Sufism with a school of thought such as Capitalism or Socialism. The Sufi way of life seeks to set men free from the bondage of creeds and dogmas, of rites and ceremonies, calling men away from all things external to the interior life of the Spirit.

God brought the Sufi Saint Bayazid Bastami to Sind. This is what he learnt in Sind.

Bayazid was known as the "wandering Sufi". In his wanderings, he met the Sindhi *Pir* Abu Ali, on the banks of the sacred River Sindhu. Abu Ali gave him three great dictums of truth on Sufism.

The first dictum: God is One. Call Him by any Name. Allah, Rama, Rahim, Krishna, Christ. He is One. Do not be misguided by bigots or fanatics. The Creator is One. Believe in this principle of Oneness. Do not go astray and be caught in the debates, quarrels and fights over religion. He is One.

The second dictum: The One Creator resides in all. There is no difference between the Creator and His Creation. He is the One in all. Sooner or later, He will awaken the soul and kindle the flame. In this mystical phenomenon, the saint is only a step ahead of a sinner, for the sinner too shall experience the light of love, which is already within him.

The third dictum: Annihilate your ego. Become nothing. Not even zero. For zero too has space in it. Annihilate your ego; annihilate yourself. And behold the vision of the Lord!

Following these three dictums, Bayazid attained his goal. He had the vision of his Beloved.

The Sufi goal and the Sufi path

The goal of life, according to Sufi mystics, is union with God. The very first step on the Sufi path is *tauba*, or repentance. When God or the master looks upon someone in grace, the soul within him is awakened. This is the first stage. The awakened soul turns his back on worldly pleasures and seeks only one thing– union with the One Beloved.

With awakening comes the realisation that the body is a temple of God. It must be kept clean and pure, so that it might become a channel of God's forces in this world of doubt, darkness and death. Therefore, in the second stage, fear has a place in the life of the Sufi. It was Guru Nanak who said, "The heart which loves God, fears Him!" And fear inspires constant watchfulness and vigilance over the heart.

Fear of God leads to detachment– the third stage on the Sufi path. For the love of God, the soul renounces everything that is non-God. After all, we know that the root of all sin and suffering is attachment to worldly things. True detachment is inner detachment from desires.

Then comes the fourth stage– a very important step on the path. It is poverty, the inner poverty of the Spirit. A man may possess the whole world and yet be poor. Another may possess nothing and yet be rich. True poverty is humility of the heart. It is the knowledge of one's own nothingness. *Na hum! Na hum! Tu ho! Tu ho!* I am nothing, O, Lord! Thou alone art!

Poverty, therefore means utter dependence on God, not upon the things of the earth. The truly poor man has cast his cares upon God, and lives free from worry and anxiety. He desires nothing; he wills nothing. His desire and will are merged with the desire and Will of God.

The fifth stage is patience. Patience is the philosopher's stone which turns every blow into a blessing, every burden into a benediction. As the pilgrim moves on the path, he is tried and tested even as gold is tested by fire. Significant are the words of a Sufi mystic: "When God loves a servant, He proves him by suffering." If the pilgrim is patient, he will not try to avoid suffering, but will greet it with a smile, knowing that all that comes from God is good.

SUFISM AND SIND

The sixth is the stage of *tawakkul*, or self-surrender. It is entrusting oneself to God, completely, entirely, utterly. It is passing out of oneself so that nothing of oneself remains: alone the Beloved exists.

Tawakkul does not mean that a person must do no work. It is rightly said in the Bhagavad Gita: "To work, you have the right, but not to the fruit thereof!" This is the spirit of *tawakkul*. Do your work– do it in the best way you can, but do not be bothered about the results or rewards of your work. It was Hatim who said, "It is our business to worship God as He bids us. It is His business to provide us with daily sustenance as He promised us."

The seventh and the last stage is gratitude. The pilgrim on the path has now arrived at a stage where he is grateful to God for whatever comes his way. Whatever be the Lord's Will, is the very best that can ever happen. To quote the words of Jani, "The Sufi has no individual will. His will is obliterated in the Will of God– nay, indeed, his will is the very Will of God." When this happens, he wants nothing; he lives in a state of at-one-ment with God.

Surrender

Many of the world's great religions emphasise the concept of surrender to the Lord's Will, but perhaps none so emphatically as Hinduism. In the immortal promise made to us in the Bhagavad Gita, Sri Krishna tells us:

Renouncing all rites and writ duties come unto Me for single refuge....

Mam ekam saranam vraja...

Saranam– surrender– involves the utter submission of one's will, the subjection of one's thoughts, ideas, and deeds to the teachings of God, your *ishta devata*, a Divine power, or a great teacher whom you have chosen as your guru.

The Hindu philosophy of *Vishishtadvaita*, as propounded by Sri Ramanuja, emphasises the concept of *Saranagati*– total surrender at the Lotus Feet of the Lord. This kind of surrender is not a matter of words uttered by the lips. It is an attitude of the heart. It requires total, absolute, unconditional faith. How many of us are capable of such faith?

True surrender

The spirit of true surrender is born out of humility, faith, and devotion. It is faith that gives the disciple absolute confidence in God and the guru. It is faith which makes him repose all his trust in God and the guru. It is faith that gives him the firm conviction that the guru's words are the highest truth.

The disciple who is blessed with such faith does not argue, does not debate, does not analyse the pros and cons of surrender. He simply surrenders himself at the Feet of God and the guru.

The *sadhana* of surrender...

Surrender is not servitude, surrender is not abject slavery. Surrender involves the highest *sadhana*, the highest discipline. If there is anything we 'give up' in surrender, it is our lower nature, our 'almighty' ego, our selfish interests and desires, our negative ideas, prejudices, preconceived notions and biases. All of these constitute a terrible burden that we carry, and for which there is no place when we undertake our spiritual journey. They constitute an 'excess baggage' which we cannot carry on to a higher plane.

Through surrender, we can shrug off this unnecessary load, and we are left refreshed and regenerated. Therefore, surrender is not a form of weakness or loss. Instead, it instills within us the energy, faith, and courage to follow the spiritual path.

To surrender is to assume command over your lower self. Do not make the mistake of imagining that it is slavish, beneath your dignity, and that you are giving up your freedom to another. If this is your notion, then it would be far better that you do not seek a guru, or even think of taking the ultimate step of self-surrender.

If truth were to be told, many of us are abject slaves of our own desires, vanity, and ego. If you wish to attain victory over the self, surrender to God and the guru is a very necessary, preliminary step. Remember, he who conquers the ego is a true hero. He is truly liberated and free. It is to achieve this victory, this freedom, that a disciple surrenders to His Will. Now decide for yourself, will you be a slave to your lower self of desires and passions? Or would you rather be a devoted aspirant or disciple, and conquer your lower self, making your ego your slave?

Why are people reluctant to surrender?

In modern parlance, the term 'surrender' is given a rather negative connotation, and is associated with defeat and subjugation by a superior power.

We associate surrender with failure and defeat. However, true spiritual surrender can be achieved only by the strong, the bold, and the brave. Surrender signifies indomitable strength.

Perhaps it is due to this misconception that some modern 'aspirants' object to the concept of surrender. To them, surrender seems to imply slavery, servitude and abject submission, especially to a guru. "True, we need a teacher to lead us on the path of spirituality," they concede. "But why should we surrender to someone who is just another human being like us? In what way is he superior that we should surrender to him? Respect– yes. Obedience– yes. Surrender…?"

This is typical of young people today; they value their sense of independence and self-worth. Their way is the way of questioning everything. They do not take orders from anyone; they believe in following their own way, they live and act by their 'own sweet will'.

Surrender is not an idea to be debated or argued about. It must come naturally and spontaneously. Otherwise, it is better not to practise it at all! Just as you cannot have a compulsory volunteer, you cannot have enforced surrender– for the realm of the Spirit is verydifferent from the realm of military discipline.

The value of self-surrender!

The true mark of a seeker is self-surrender. A seeker encounters many difficulties on the path, and many of his efforts are futile. The seeker often reaches a blind alley and that is when he realises he cannot proceed without the grace of his guru. That is when he knows he has to take refuge at the Lotus Feet of God or his master. The seeker prays to God: "O Lord! By myself I am helpless. I need Your grace. Please accept me and protect me. My Lord! You are all powerful. Please hold me. Abide by me, for alone, I cannot walk on this path."

The world, according to the Upanishads, is an act of God in *yajna,* sacrifice. The universe is thus a self-offering of joy. In the Gita, Sri Krishna says to Arjuna: "O Arjuna, whatever you do, whatever you eat, whatever the worship you perform, whatever the alms you give, and the *tapasya* you practise– do it all as an offering unto Me."

"Surrender all to Me!" This is the message of the Gita, in essence!

When you surrender all your actions to the Lord, you feel joy within. When you surrender, you do not expect the fruits of the action, for the very act of surrender releases you from the tension of expectation. And the travel becomes light!

Self-surrender is a gateway to a new life. You cannot be reborn in Spirit except by passing through the portals of *saranagati*.

True renunciation lies in the attitude of the mind. The man of renunciation, having rid 'himself' of 'self' lives for others. His heart flows in a ceaseless stream of sympathy to the poor and the broken ones, to the birds and animals. Without renunciation there can be no spiritual progress. Renunciation does not mean that you go and live in a forest or on the peak of a hill. True renunciation is renunciation of one's own self, renunciation of the ego. You feel true bliss and enjoy true happiness when you live for others and surrender all your actions to God.

Some aspirants demand to know whether they can experience 'increased grace' and 'greater blessings' through surrender.

My answer to them is this: do not surrender with any expectation or desire. When you expect or desire something, you are still stuck with 'I' and 'Mine'.

Yet another query is: why is there no help or grace even after we surrender?

If you have truly surrendered, how can you have complaints and grievances? When you surrender truly, you must be able to abide by the guru and God's Will, and not insist on what you desire.

Complete surrender is, perhaps, not possible for beginners. But the practice of even partial surrender will lead to peace and tranquillity, and eventually, make complete surrender possible.

What is it that we are required to surrender?

Let me quote the words of an aspirant: "Our problem is that we don't want to surrender that which we can surrender, and instead surrender that which we cannot."

Surrender is not giving up your duties and responsibilities. Surrender does not involve withdrawal to a forest for meditation and turning your back on your commitments and *Karma Yoga*. Surrender means giving up one's selfishness, one's individual desires, likes and dislikes for the sake of a higher goal, such as self-realisation.

You must remember one thing: the guru does not force you to surrender. He wants nothing, desires nothing from you personally. He is beyond desire and expectation, utterly without selfish motives. Surrender– the impulse to surrender to one whom you regard as a worthy master– comes from within you.

The culmination of all human endeavours is absolute surrender to the Divine Will. Sri Krishna enunciates this doctrine in the Gita:

Fix thy mind on Me; be devoted to Me; sacrifice to Me; prostrate thyself before Me. So shalt thou come to Me. I pledge thee My troth, for thou art dear to Me! XVIII – 65

Mind, heart, sacrifice, reverence are all required to be directed to Sri Krishna.

Abandoning all duties, come unto Me alone for refuge. Grieve not! I shall liberate thee from all sins! XVIII – 66

Here is indicated the supreme secret which Sri Krishna reveals to his dear disciple Arjuna. The school of Sri Ramanuja regards this as the *charama sloka*– the final verse, the summing up of the Gita.

He who hath surrendered himself hath found the greatest security of life. And he need wander no more. All his cares and burdens are borne by the Lord Himself. How beautiful are the words of the Gita:

They who worship Me
Depending on Me alone,
Thinking of no other–
They are My sole responsibility!
Their burdens are My burdens!
To them I bring full security!

The more we meditate on the Lord's words, the more we shall grow in that true life which is a life of self-surrender. The life of faith is a blessed, carefree life. It is a life free from the shackles of earthly 'experience'. To be truly free is to be born anew, to become a pure child of God. Such a one lives with God and walks with God and speaks to Him and hears Him speak.

What is your idea of surrender?

The one lesson we all need to learn is utter dependence upon God. Everything else will follow. We must turn to God for every little thing we need until one blessed day, we find that we need nothing– our one and only need is God! Then we make the great discovery that all we need is already provided for. Before a need arises, it is already fulfilled. Everything comes to pass at the right time, in the right way. Then one lives like a king. When a king moves out, everything is prepared for him well in advance, he does not have to ask for anything. All his needs are anticipated and provided for.

Ye are kings! Why wander ye starved and clothed in rags, because ye are unaware of your royal parentage?

What are the marks of a man who has surrendered his will to the Will of the Lord?

- He who seeks refuge in the Lord, becomes a servant of the Will Divine.

SURRENDER

- He welcomes not gain, he fears not loss. He desires not pleasure, he runs not away from pain. He seeks not success, nor does he avoid failure. He accepts all that comes to him as a gift from the Lord, who loves him and whom he loves above all else.

- He finds that life is the great guru, the great teacher, the great initiator.

- Every experience enriches his inner life, leads him onward in the march of the true, the good, the beautiful and the holy.

- Every pain makes him perfect, every suffering makes him strong.

He whose refuge is the Lord, lives in constant awareness of God's presence. Such a man is never alone, for his God and his guru are always with him, blessing him, guiding him, protecting him, and leading him on! He hears God's gentle voice. He feels the warm pressure of His hand on his. He hearkens to the voice of his unseen Friend, and he always feels safe and secure even in the face of danger and death.

Teachers

It is well nigh impossible to express the highest truth in words. Therefore, there is nothing really that even the greatest teacher can say. All she can do is simply give of herself. The whole purpose of education is to teach by example. This is why the best teacher is one who suggests, not one who dogmatises. The true teacher puts in the effort to bring herself down to the level of the student, visualising through the eyes of the student, hearing through his ears, and understanding through his mind.

All of us have passed through the hands of several teachers, from nursery to post graduation and beyond. But we remember only a few, while others are completely forgotten! Do you wonder why this is so?

If you have studied under a teacher whom you still remember with love, affection, and reverence, you are truly blessed! And if you are a teacher who has had such an impact on a student that he remembers you for years after his education is completed, then you are truly blessed!

Therefore it is said: An average teacher instructs; a good teacher guides; a great teacher inspires.

They tell me that the age of the 'teacher-less classroom' is here! There is talk of e-learning in a virtual classroom. An interactive computer, they say, can give you all that the teacher can, without a teacher's strict discipline and eccentricities.

With the greatest respect to technological advances, may I offer my humble opinion that this can never be 'education' in its true sense! Instruction may be offered through the virtual classroom; information may be made available through the computer. However, teaching is much more than this. Teaching in its truest sense is communicating– a process in which the personality of the teacher interacts with the personality of the students. You can go to a library and read hundreds of books; you can collect data from the Internet; you can listen to recorded lessons on CDs; but can any of these compensate for the living, moving presence of a good teacher?

Why is teaching regarded as a 'noble profession'?

A teacher is not just another employee, just another professional; hers is not just another career. A teacher has chosen not only a vocation, but an avocation. Students look up to her for having ideals and standards. Her commitments to her chosen profession are very many; she deals with them all in her stride because she has made a choice. A teacher knows that imparting knowledge is the most rewarding and enriching of all human experiences. Teaching moulds the teacher's personality, strengthens her convictions, and teaches her patience, love, and acceptance.

If this is not a noble profession, I don't know what else is!

Why has this noble profession fallen into disrepute in recent times?

Like many other countries, India too passed through a period of student unrest and indiscipline, causing many teachers to feel that theirs was no longer a 'noble profession', that society, institutions, and perhaps even the people did not give them due respect. On the one hand, they did not really belong to the highly-paid category; on the other, they were made to feel that they were just doing a paid job, like clerks or managers or supervisors. Many good teachers suffered from a tremendous loss of morale.

Unfortunately, many inappropriate people who regarded teaching as 'just another job' also got into the profession, leading to compounded confusion and misunderstanding.

If Indian education is to retain its ancient status as *Vidya*, we must treat our teachers with the respect and regard they deserve. And if our teachers wish to be more than mere purveyors of knowledge, if they wish to retain the high stature of gurus, their single-minded goal must be the pursuit of excellence in all that they do.

How can a good teacher strive to make a difference?

A teacher is not a paid employee who does a stipulated job within designated hours. A teacher's objective must not be merely to help her students pass examinations. I believe every teacher can be– and must be– an agent of personal development, individual growth, and social transformation. Each student in the class has, in a sense, entrusted his future in the teacher's hands. This is a great privilege, an honour, and also a tremendous challenge and responsibility.

Teachers owe it to themselves and their students to rise to this challenge.

A teacher may be a great expert in her chosen subject. Such a one is highly valued by students, parents, and institutions. While it is true that 'subject experts' may be remembered with awe, it is teachers who have offered guidance, support, and inspiration who make a lasting contribution to the students' well-being and development.

It is crucial that a teacher realises once and for all that her profession has more potential than that of the politician to shape the future of the nation. In order to change the world, we have to begin with ourselves. It is men and women of inner conviction who can influence the world around them.

Who in your opinion is an ideal teacher?

Whenever I am asked this question, I hear the words of my beloved Master ringing in my ears. He said to us again and again, "The true teacher is a friend!"

The true teacher is a friend. She is a friend of her fellow teachers; she is a friend of her pupils; she is a friend of all Creation; she is a friend of men, women, children, birds and animals; she is a friend of all who suffer and are in pain.

I believe it is in an atmosphere of friendship that a teacher can draw out the best that lies within the mind and heart of the pupil.

Historic personalities are only images, and fictitious characters only live in the imagination, but a teacher is real! A teacher's influence touches the life of the students!

A teacher has the ability to inculcate in the students many ideals, including truth, courage, ethics and morality, patience, honesty, courtesy and good conduct, hard work, kindness, dedication, commitment, and idealism. These values can be instilled in the youth of today only through real, tangible people who are none other than teachers!

How would you describe a good teacher?

In my humble way, I would describe a true teacher as a builder, a sculptor, an artist, and a champion!

The teacher is a builder. I love to repeat the words of my Master, Gurudev Sadhu Vaswani: "New India will not be built in the Rajya Sabha and the Lok Sabha, but in the home and in the school!"

The best and most constructive changes we have made in our educational system were meant to make our education nation-oriented and value-oriented. We have not yet perfected the system, but if it is to succeed in the task of nation-building, it is the teachers who can make it possible.

This places a great challenge as well as a tremendous responsibility on our teachers, but I cannot help thinking that it is also a great privilege! To take up this challenge successfully, to build responsible citizens, and to build a new India, the teachers too, must have ntional goals and Indian values. Only then can they pass these onto their students!

The teacher is a builder, not of bridges and buildings and townships, but a builder of good human beings, a builder of minds, a builder of life.

It is man who needs to be rebuilt. And who will build good human beings but the teacher? It is the teacher's sacred task to build the lives of the students who come to her. In building their students, the teachers are simultaneously building the future of the nations.

The teacher is a sculptor. I emphasise the teacher's role as a sculptor who shapes and moulds the individual into a wholesome personality because a sculptor can wield his chisel to shape a stone into a thing of beauty. I believe the crucial transformation from a selfish individual into a socially responsible citizen can be achieved only through the shaping, moulding power of education. As an individual, a young man or woman is apt to imagine that he or she is at the centre of the universe, and everything and everyone must dance to his or her tune. It is the teacher's duty to humanise such youngsters, to make them realise that life is not just taking, receiving, grasping, gaining, and ordering others. Growth is not just physical expansion or even intellectual development, but spiritual growth, through assimilation of values. This growth can be generated not through textbooks or degrees, but through a true teacher.

The teacher is an artist. If the spiritual unfolding of pupils is the aim of true education, am I not correct in describing the teacher as an artist who must embellish the beauty of their hearts and minds, so that they may bloom forth in full perfection?

Education, as we have discussed, is a matter of inner transformation. Imparting information, passing on theories and techniques, cannot help our students to face the multiple challenges of life. What they need are illumined minds, enlightened intellects, and inspired hearts– these alone can bring peace and joy to students, and enable them to live their lives fully. Being able to draw out these attributes in students requires the skill and talent of an 'artist' of the highest order.

Only someone with creativity can express the life force within; only someone with the creative impulse can draw out and reveal the inner beauty in her students. Creativity is the first mark of the true teacher. Not only is she herself gifted, but the stimulating environment she creates in her class brings out the latent innovative faculties and resources of her students. She must nurture and extend their creativity and potential in every way possible. She must let them find new horizons, let them explore the unknown dimensions of their own personalities, let them discover their wings!

The teacher is a champion. I say to all teachers: Do not underestimate yourself or your influence! You have chosen a noble profession. There can be no two opinions on this, that education is the very foundation of civilisation, human progress, and democracy. And all of you, who belong to this noble profession must, of necessity, be noble and wise and great! You uphold, protect, and propagate the supreme wealth of *Vidya*, and are in a class apart. How could I expect anything less than greatness from you?

By being a part of this noble profession, you have committed yourself to a valuable mission, which is making a profound contribution to the nation and the world. The question should not be, "How much can I achieve?" but rather, "What is it that I cannot achieve, if I set my heart to it?"

Let me urge you, therefore, to hold your head high, fill your heart with hope and optimism, strive with self-confidence, live and work in a manner true to the ideals of your great vocation– and do everything you can for the young aspirants who have entrusted themselves to your care!

A final word to teachers: Our students must not only grow in knowledge, but also in wisdom. It is not just their minds that you have to cultivate, but also their character, and their souls.

Is this not the piteous need of today's world– that we need men and women of wisdom, men and women with *atma shakti*, spiritual strength? And who can fashion such a new force, such an enlightened young generation, but devoted, committed teachers like you?

Therefore I urge you, do not stop with your 'subject'; do not be content with preparing your students for examinations; do not be satisfied with distinctions and first classes from the university; do not think your job is done when your students are 'placed' in jobs with lucrative salaries. The question you must answer is this: have you prepared them for life? Have you promoted ethical attitudes and moral values? Have you cultivated their character? Have you touched their soul?

The spiritual component in education cannot come from without, it already exists in you, the teacher, in the choice you have made to be an educator. Bring this spiritual light to bear upon all that you do, and you will become a true teacher in every sense of that word!

A young man wrote a letter to Thomas Carlyle for his advice. "I wish to be a teacher. Could you please share with me the secret of successful teaching?" Carlyle replied succinctly, "Be what you would have your pupil to be. All other teaching is unblessed mockery."

Temptation- Fight It!

The word temptation is derived from the Latin word *tentare*, which means to prove, to test. Temptation is the touchstone of the soul. Even as gold is tested on the touchstone, even so man's character, the loftiness of his soul, is tested by the temptations he is able to overcome. Conquering temptations can unlock the hidden powers of the Spirit.

I would also describe temptations as the dumbbells of the soul. Just as dumb-bells in the gym strengthen our physical muscles, even so temptations strengthen the muscles of the soul.

When a temple bell is cast in a foundry, the foundry-man does not at once fix it in the temple, but first tests it out with his strong hammer to check for any flaws. In a similar fashion, man is tried and tested with the hammer blows of temptation before he grows in perfection.

Not many of us, however, can withstand such blows of temptation. Many of us are so weak that we easily succumb to temptation. We convince ourselves that it is only this once that we shall yield to temptation, to experience what the forbidden is. Alas! Once we relish the pleasure of temptation, we become ensnared by sin and find it difficult to come out of it. Therefore, beware! Never yield to temptation. But stand up in the strength of your soul and, in the words of Jesus, say to temptation, "Get thee behind me, Satan!"

There are myriad temptations. There is the temptation to gratify the senses; to steal what belongs to another; to drink, smoke, or take drugs; to overeat or to eat forbidden food or food of violence; to send out thoughts of ill-will to others; to speak harsh words or to indulge in untruth; to gossip, to spread scandals against others; to waste time in playing cards or other frivolities; to accept bribes, to indulge in unlawful profiteering, to make money by means fair or foul; to evade the payment of taxes. There are a hundred and one other temptations. To be able to overcome any type of temptation, you must be ready and willing to turn a new leaf. You must decide once and for all that you will never, never, fall into sin again.

Why do we succumb to temptation so easily?

Have you ever looked at a fly sipping honey? At first, it is very careful to see that its legs are free. It sits on the edge of the spoon containing honey, perhaps thinking to itself that after just one wee little taste of honey, it will fly away. But once it tastes the delight of honey, it forgets everything and goes all out for it. When it has had its fill, it finds that its legs are stuck in honey. It cannot fly away and it dies a tragic death in its sweet grave.

Such is the case with man. He is lured into temptation by the expectation of a little pleasure. Once he has tasted pleasure, he is drawn to it, again and again, until he becomes the slave of a habit he cannot overcome. Pleasure leads a man astray.

Why does man commit a forbidden act against his will?

Significant are the words of the great lawgiver, Manu, "Desire is never satisfied by the enjoyment of the objects of desire. It grows from more to more, as does the fire to which fuel is added." And the *Yoga Vasishta* tells us, "We think it is we who enjoy pleasure. But, in truth, it is pleasures that enjoy us. For while pleasure always remains young and vital, it is we who keep growing old and get consumed in the fire of pleasure."

The selfsame question has been considered in the Gita. Arjuna asks Sri Krishna, "Master! Why does a man commit sin against his will? What is the force that drags him, irresistibly to pathways of evil?"

Many of us have had a similar experience. We do not wish to fall into sin. In our saner moments, we wish to avoid sin. Then suddenly, there wakes up within us a storm, and we are led astray.

In answer, the Master says to Arjuna, "You say that man is dragged to the path of sin. That is not so! For man is not a machine. Man is endowed with will-power, the power of determination, the power to make his own choice. Man can never commit sin against his will. Man's will consents, gives the green signal, before man falls into sin. And, Arjuna, you ask me what force makes man commit sin. The force is *kama*, desire, lust. It is the enemy of man. It is man's deadly foe. Beware of it! And, never forget, that desire is insatiable!"

The fire of *kama* cannot be quenched. The more you seek to satisfy it, the more fuel you add to its flame. *Kama* reigns over man's unregenerate senses. His reason is clouded— he cannot discriminate between right and wrong, and there are no depths of degradation to which a man, under the influence of *kama*, will not stoop.

Practical suggestions to overcome temptations

1. We must be ready and willing to wash our hands of temptation right now and here, and be willing to make any sacrifice for it. No price is too heavy to receive entry into the new life. But it must be done NOW! This willingness to become new, to renounce the old life of sinfulness and pride, is very important.

2. We must seek God's mercy and the grace of a guru. We must humble ourselves, we must make a clear confession of everything in the presence of God or a God-man. When our heart becomes contrite and lowly, the way to the Kingdom of Heaven is opened for us.

3. We must not indulge in a lot of retrospection. Let us not then think of our past sins, for whatever we think of, repeatedly, to that we are drawn. Let us think instead of God's mercy, which can wash off the blackest spots from our hearts. Let us keep our eyes fixed on God and His mercy, His goodness, His beauty, His purity and His truth. And we shall grow God-like.

4. Avoid the occasions that lead to temptation! If we cannot remove temptation, we must move away from the temptation! I have heard people tell me that they resolutely lead their diabetic spouses away from the dessert display at dinner parties! I have met people in the U.S.A., who are tempted to gamble, but swear that they will never visit Las Vegas! One way of winning over temptations is to not be defeated, by departing from the place and the situation where defeat is imminent!

5. Never forget that impurity begins in thought. Therefore, we must take care of our thoughts. Thoughts are forces, not to be trifled with. Thoughts are the building blocks of life. If we entertain pure thoughts, we build for ourselves a noble future. If otherwise, we work for our own ruination.

6. The moment an evil desire or thought wakes up within, we should immediately, without the least delay, push it out and punish ourselves. Beloved Gurudev Sadhu Vaswani always carried with himself a pin, and on his body, we found many scratches. When he was a young man, he kept with himself a stick. If an undesirable thought came to him, he would close the doors of his room and beat himself with the stick, until his mind repented and promised to never entertain such a thought or desire.

7. An idle mind is the devil's workshop. If we wish to be free from temptations, we must keep busy all the time. Our mothers were well aware of this truth, and they were

TEMPTATION— FIGHT IT!

especially careful to see that their daughters were kept busy all the time.

8. We must see that the food we eat is *sattvic*, pure, earned by honest means, without doing violence to anyone.

9. Take care of your breathing: breathing has a direct influence upon the mind. Let your breathing be deep and rhythmic. *Prana*, or the life breath, is vital to our physical, mental and moral well-being.

10. Should you yield to temptation, should you happen to fail, put it behind you as quickly as possible! Don't dwell on it. Instead, immediately rise and move on, ever onward, forward, Godward!

Time

Man's greatest tragedy is that he thinks he has plenty of time. The true value of time should be realised. You should seize it and enjoy every moment of it. Precious time should not be frittered away in idleness, laziness, or procrastination. Ordinary folk merely think about how they can spend their time. But the extraordinary and wise ones actually make good use of their time.

Today, it is fashionable to talk of time management. Old fashioned proverbs that we heard in our childhood taught us that time and tide wait for no man. Modern management gurus like Stephen Covey tell us, "Managing your time well makes you successful."

I really do not know about time management! I do not think that time is easy to manage or control. Those who make the worst use of their time by being ineffective and inefficient, are the first ones to complain about the shortness and insufficiency of time. We must respect our time and that of others.

The value of time

We cannot borrow time; we cannot stop or slow down time; we cannot put the clock forward or backward. So how can we manage something which we cannot control?

My answer is simple. Spend your time wisely and well. Do not become a slave to the clock and the calendar or the computer and cellphone alarm. Do not let them govern you. Be aware that every second, every moment of life is precious and do not fritter your time in idle and mindless activities. Because, while it is easy for us to move in time, walk with time, keep pace with time, we must not forget that time never turns back; time never retraces its steps; time does not wander or digress.

Time is the coin of the highest denomination in your life. Therefore, it has great value. Be very careful about how you spend it. At the same time, be aware that others do not come and squander it.

Every one of us is given the same number of hours every day. Rich people cannot buy more hours. Scientists cannot invent more minutes. Clever people cannot stretch time. Misers cannot save time to hoard it and spend it another day. And yet, it has been pointed out, time is always fair and forgiving. No matter how much time you have wasted in the past, you have a full day before you every morning. Your success depends on your using it wisely and well– by planning and setting priorities.

Take care of your moments!

God gives you a gift of 86,400 seconds every day. How do you spend all those precious moments?

Time is the most precious of all possessions. Time is our capital. Every minute, every moment, is priceless. There is a Chinese proverb which says, "An inch of time is an inch of gold. But an inch of gold cannot buy an inch of time." We realise the value of the moment only when the last moment arrives.

Alexander, the world conqueror, was defeated by a tiny insect. He died of malarial fever from a mosquito bite. As he lay dying in his white tent, he asked, "Is there anyone who will give me a healthy breath of his life? In exchange I will give him my whole empire." There was no answer. Alexander is said to have exclaimed, "I wasted millions upon millions of my breaths in carving out an empire, in exchange of which I cannot get a single breath!"

The river of time flows on. The hours quickly change into days, the days into months, and the months into years. Suddenly, one day, the bell rings and the call goes forth: "Vacate the house (of the body)!" The body drops down and man realises that he has lost the golden opportunity of the human birth.

We must be very careful about our time. We must use it creatively and never forget that every moment is just the right time to do a right thing. If we wait for more opportune moments, we may have to wait till eternity. Time is fleeting! If we are to make the most of this life, the time to begin is NOW! Take care of your moments and the years will take care of themselves.

In the classic story *Alice in Wonderland*, one of the wise characters ironically called the Mad Hatter, tells Alice, "If you knew Time as well as I do, you would not talk about wasting *it*. It is *him*! If you only kept on good terms with Time, he would do almost anything you like with the clock."

Are you investing your time wisely?

The other day, I read that an art collector had paid over a hundred million dollars for a painting at an art auction. Experts voiced their opinion that all of it was money well spent, because the 'investment' would repay rich returns in a few years' time; the price would almost double in 10-15 years, or so I was told.

How careful we are about our investments! How diligently do we study the stocks and shares before we choose what we think is right for us! My only question to you is this: are you investing enough time and attention in your children, who represent your real wealth? Are you spending enough time to cherish relationships that are special and mean the most to you? Do you ring up old friends? How often do you visit or make phone calls to your grandparents? How often do adults visit their parents? All these people need your time, your love, and your attention!

It is not your work time or business time I am concerned about; most people are careful enough to ensure that they fulfil all their work related responsibilities adequately, so that their jobs are secure and stable. These days, we have sufficient productivity tools and gadgets to help us deal with our work in an efficient and organised manner. What I am worried about is the time you have at your personal disposal; I want to ensure you spend it as effectively, usefully, and fruitfully as you spend your work time.

Inspiration: Living in the present moment

A Zen master was teaching his disciple how to develop the right attitude to life and to work.

The disciple asked the master, "How shall I develop mental discipline in my search for truth?"

The master replied, "You must exercise yourself."

"How may I exercise myself?"

"You must eat when you are hungry; you must sleep when you are tired."

"But that is what everyone does. Do you mean to say this is sufficient to exercise oneself to acquire discipline?"

"But that is what most people do not do. When they eat they are doing a hundred things. When they sleep they are dreaming of a million things. That is not what I mean by exercise…

Exercise your mind to live in the present moment, whether you are working, eating, or sleeping."

God's good time

The Bible tells us quite simply, "There is a time for everything and a season for every activity under the Heavens." In our old fashioned way, we called it 'in God's good time'. The trick is to recognise that it is God's good time, and therefore, do what we have to do at the right time.

I recall with gratitude a valuable lesson that Gurudev Sadhu Vaswani taught me. One day, he expressed a desire to have some fruits for breakfast. Eager to please him in every way I could, I asked him, "Gurudev, what fruit would you like to eat? Tell me and I will get it for you immediately!"

Sadhu Vaswani looked at me and smiled. "I think I would like to eat a few cherries," he said to me.

"I will get them immediately," I said and rushed off to the market in a tearing hurry. I searched high and low, but there were no cherries to be found for love or money. Every vendor gave me the same reply, "The season for cherries is over. You will not find them now."

Tired, dispirited, and crestfallen, I returned to my Master. "Forgive me Gurudev," I said to him, "Try as I might, I simply could not find any cherries."

Sadhu Vaswani said to me, "There is a season for everything. Once the season is over, we cannot avail of its benefits."

Come April, mangoes make their appearance in India's colourful markets. In May and June we are hardly likely to find any fruit except mangoes on the streets, and in the handcarts and stalls of the fruit vendors. With the onset of July, mangoes start to disappear. In August you will pay a heavy price for the rare mango, and in September, you cannot find mangoes no matter how hard you try. There is a time, a season for everything. If this season gets over, it will not come back again!

You may wait for the next mango or cherry season. But life does not easily give us a second chance. This life has been given to us for our spiritual evolution. And now is the time to begin. If this season is over it will not come back! Whatever is most important to us, must be done now. And the most important thing for all of us is the higher life that we seek. Therefore, we should start working for it now. Now is the time. Now is the right season. There can be no postponement.

What is time management?

Experts define time management as "the art and technique of arranging, organising, scheduling, and budgeting one's time for the purpose of generating more effective work and increasing productivity".

Sounds too complicated, doesn't it?

Time management is not the prerogative of only the business and corporate world. Students, teachers, workers, professionals, mothers, you and I– all of us need to understand the value of time and use it effectively.

It was Edison who said, "Time is really the only capital a human being has, and the only thing he can't afford to lose."

In our age of speed and stress, time is no longer an abstract concept. "Time is money," is the modern mantra. In fact, people would argue that time is more precious, more valuable than money!

Time management is essential for all of us, if we wish to:

- Eliminate hurry, hustle, stress and pressure in our daily work and personal life.

- Escape from the clutches of 'deadlines' that threaten to overrun our lives.

- Create time and space in our lives for all that we really want to do.

- Organise our lives and work in such a way that we really enjoy 'living' in the fullest sense.

- Fix our goals and set our priorities so that we achieve what matters most to us.

- Escape the clutches of procrastination– that notorious 'thief' of time.

- Give of ourselves, freely and fully, to those who matter the most to us– to our spiritual pursuits, our higher aspirations and creative impulses.

There are a few simple steps to make the most of 24 hours:

1. **Early to bed, early to rise.**

    Getting up early in the morning is truly a bonus. Not only does it benefit you, but it also sets the tone and pace of your whole day.

    When this early start is invigorated by your personal appointment with God, you will truly find your day transformed!

    Start early! Spend your earliest working hours in silent prayer or meditation. Give time to your parents / spouse / children.

    Arrive at work before time. Organise your desk. Check your schedule for the day. Hand your day over to God's care– and begin your work.

    You will be amazed by what you can achieve!

2. **Organise your life in day-tight compartments.**

    Draw a circle to represent a 24-hour period. Into this circle, chalk out all the work that you think you can achieve, conveniently, comfortably, without stress.

    Forget all the rest. It will have to wait for tomorrow.

    True, there may be a lot of work that you have to do. But there is a limit to what you can accomplish today. Therefore, put a cap on it!

    When the day is over, plan for the next 24 hours.

3. **Set your priorities.**

    Ask yourself what is important for you and your work. Devote time to those activities.

    It is very important to eliminate non-essentials from your life– activities which are neither important, nor useful.

4. **Don't force yourself to hurry.**

    "The truly wise ones, are never in a rush to do their work," says the poet, Subramanya Bharathi. "With the utmost patience, they work slowly, steadily, like the seed that sprouts into life."

Isn't this an amazing image– the seed that sprouts into new life! You cannot put it on fast-forward mode; nor can you put it in slow motion.

When you hurry, you cannot keep your mind calm and focussed. Modern lifestyle, culture, and work, force us to hurry, hurry, all the time! Of course, we need to be quick and efficient in all that we do– but hurrying is wasteful!

5. **Do one thing at a time.**

Do not fritter away your energies attempting to do too many things– chances are that you will not do justice to anyone of them.

- Do not talk on the phone while you are writing a report.
- Do not read while you are eating.
- Do not text on your cellphone when someone is talking to you.
- Do not talk on the cellphone when you are driving! You are jeopardising your life and others' lives too!

When you do too many things at a time, the vital power of your mind is scattered, and your work will not be the best that you can do!

One final thought...

Sant Kabir says, "What you can do tomorrow, do it today. What you can do today, do it right now. For the holy ones tell us that this human birth is rare and precious."

Any good thing that you wish to do tomorrow, do it today, do not postpone it, do it right now. Our time is limited and we should not spend it foolishly in false pursuits. This life of ours is rare and precious, and not a moment should be wasted.

Your life is yours to live; your time is yours to spend. Hence, make a choice. Do not waste time. You have already lost precious time. You are lagging behind in achieving your goal. Wake up! Arise! Make your choice. Live your life wisely and well!

Truth

Satyaat nasti paro dharma– there is no religion higher than truth. This is the injunction laid upon us by the ancient scriptures of India.

Truth is the very first step that the seeker has to take on the path to salvation. Truth is dear to God, and dear to men of God. It is every guru's fervent wish that his disciples should always bear witness to the truth in their daily life, and that they should always refrain from falsehood.

The power of truth

Satya, truth, is described as one of the cardinal qualities of *daivi sampadi*, or Divine heritage, in Chapter XVI of the Bhagavad Gita. Undoubtedly we will face great difficulties in our quest for truth; but the man of divine qualities overcomes them by his perseverance on the path. Many of us, alas, give up the effort. "It is an impossible ideal to put into practice," we assert. "It is not just unattainable, it is impractical," we lament.

There are many excuses people offer for not adhering to the truth. We are afraid that the truth will hurt us and our chances of advancement and success; we use untruth to cover up our deficiencies. It is only a man of courage who can stand up to the test of truth at all times in his life. We have the much revered concept of *Satyam, Shivam, Sundaram*– the embodiment of truth, goodness and beauty, that is Lord Shiva. Further, the ten *yamas*, or restraints recommended by the ancient scriptures, urge the seeker to refrain from falsehood. Abiding by truth will lead to realisation of the Supreme Soul, the Almighty, and ultimately *Sat Chit Ananda*, or true, eternal bliss.

There is a beautiful incident narrated to us in the Gospels of Sri Ramakrishna. Sri Ramakrishna once said, "The virtue of truthfulness is most important. If a man always speaks the truth and tenaciously holds to truth, he will realise God; for God is Truth. I prayed to the Divine Mother saying: 'Mother, here is knowledge, here is ignorance– take them both and give me pure love for You. Here is purity, here is impurity– take them both and give me pure love for You. Here is good, here is evil– take them both and give me pure love for You.' But I could not say, 'Here is truth, here is untruth.' For if I give up truthfulness in this way," said the master, "how can I keep the truth that I have offered everything to the Mother of the universe?"

Such is the power of the spoken word. The Vedas urge us not merely to speak the truth, but also to speak only that truth which is pleasant, useful, and cannot cause hurt to others.

God is Truth

Our scriptures pay tribute to this fact by referring to God as *satyapriya* (lover of truth) and *satyaswaroopa* (embodiment of truth). Mahatma Gandhi often said, "People say God is Truth. I believe that Truth is God!"

For Gandhi, the logical equivalent or manifestation of God was to be found in truth. Truth is God, he declared. Truth is Rama, Narayana, *Ishwara*, *Khuda*, Allah, and God. He regarded truth as the very foundation of his value system. The pursuit of truth, the attempt to realise truth in one's thoughts and actions, he said, is the substance of the religion of man. "Devotion to truth," he wrote, "is the sole justification for our existence." Little wonder then, that his autobiography was entitled: *The Story of My Experiments with Truth*.

The trap of falsehood

What we do not realise is that one untruth leads on to another; to 'cover up' our earlier deceits, we are forced to utter more lies, thus getting entrapped in a vicious cycle of falsehood. Out of greed, out of personal avarice, out of fear of reproaches and punishments, out of a desire to curry favour with those in office, we speak untruths: and let us not forget, exaggerated compliments, insincere statements, hypocritical utterances— all of them are equivalent to falsehood!

Truth, therefore, has several dimensions. It is a complete moral code by which we must live our lives. I cannot be honest with my family, but dishonest at work; I cannot claim to be truly honest, if I am true to my friends but untrue to my clients and customers; I cannot claim to be 'good' if I donate millions in charity but 'cook up' accounts to make illegal profits!

India: Then and now

It is said that when Alexander the Great came to India, two things impressed him most of all— the purity of the women of India, and the reverence for truth among all Indians. In those days, the Greeks referred to this land as Hindu, possibly derived from the River Sindhu. It was also referred to as *Indu*, meaning bright and pure. I recalled this legend with regret, when a news headline caught my eye: India was among the top ten nations of the world– in corruption and bribery! I shudder to think what Alexander would have said about our land, if he came to India now!

Truth spells courage

The path of truth is not for the weak-willed and cowardly. As Emerson once put it, "God offers to every mind its choice between truth and repose. Take which you please– you can never have both."

Whenever Gurudev Sadhu Vaswani narrated stories affirming truth and courage, he would exclaim, "Truth, though she lead me to the gallows! Truth, though she take me through the fire!"

To travel the path of truth is not only difficult, it needs a tremendous amount of discipline, courage, steadfastness and determination. But the rewards of following this path are spectacular and most important, eternal.

If we want to lead a new and transformed life, we must follow truth. Even if truth harms us, we should not leave the path of truth. It is better to be poorer by walking on the path of truth, than to be richer by wallowing falsehood.

Love is truth and truth is love

There was a French writer and mystic, Simone Weil, of whom I am very fond. She passed away several years ago when she was barely in her thirties. Young in years, she was ripe in the wisdom of life. She was a woman of wonderful insights. Her life was a life of sacrifice. On one occasion she uttered words which I can never forget. She said, "I set out in quest of truth: I fell into the arms of love!" Yes– Truth is Love, and Love is Truth!

Truth is humble

There is the saying, *Satyameva Jayate*– truth triumphs, victory belongs to truth. Hence, some people argue that if they speak the truth, they have the right to do so loudly, firmly, and authoritatively. However, the fact is that truth can be best conveyed in a soft, gentle way. Truth is humble! Therefore, while speaking the truth we should never be arrogant. Truth does not have to be bellowed from the rooftops; its power is in conviction and integrity.

Always speak the truth

We talk of 'white lies' and 'harmless falsehood'. We think a 'little' lie will cause no great harm to anyone. We are mistaken! Today, we utter all kinds of lies, all shades of lies, including white lies and lies to escape wrath and punishment. I doubt if any official or business transaction these days can be concluded without uttering one falsehood or the other.

Our scriptures teach us that there is nothing more sinful than untruthfulness. Because of this, *Bhudevi*, Mother Earth once said, "I can bear the heavy burden of any sinner, but I cannot support a person who is a liar." Consider the severe load that Mother Earth must be carrying today!

Are we truthful? Do we live a truthful and transparent life? If we are truthful, many of us would be forced to concede that our life is full of lies and falsehood. Social psychologists talk about the "games" people play, the "roles" that they assume in their daily life. Under the roles and games we play, our real personality is hidden from the world. We wear a mask of goodness, we dress well and perfume our bodies and pose to be honest and clean.

It is human nature to try and find in others what we lack. We are untruthful. We suspect others of being the same. It is also human nature to conceal one's own faults from one's own self. We are not able to face our own faults. When we are not true to our own self, how can we be true to others, how can we be true to our guru?

God is Truth and if you aspire to move nearer to God, then you should bear witness to the truth in deeds of daily life. Therefore, always speak the truth!

Understanding

Is it not true that the one urgent and piteous need of the world today is understanding? We need understanding among individuals and families, among neighbours and groups, among the nations of the earth. We cannot have global understanding until, first, the hearts of people become understanding hearts, even as we cannot have international peace until, first, there is peace in the hearts of men.

The greatest famine in the world today is the famine of understanding. No two people seem to understand each other. Today, people speak of emotional incompatibility. It is a myth invented by jurists and lawyers to be able to argue in favour of divorce. There are no emotional incompatibilities. There are only misunderstandings and mistakes which can be corrected where there is the will to do so.

King Solomon prayed, "Lord! Thou hast granted me so many things. Grant me one thing more. Grant me an understanding heart." Understanding hearts are needed.

Today, brain power has been developed, technological progress has been made, science is marching on. But the problems that are before civilisation today, will not be solved by the developed brain alone. Understanding, awakened, illumined hearts are needed.

True understanding consists not of discarding one's knowledge but, in fact, rising above it. In order to transcend it, one has to let go of one's set views and beliefs. Knowledge is a solid block which obstructs understanding, while understanding is like water which can easily flow and penetrate.

Developing the will to understand

A young man came to his father, who was a rishi, a sage. The young man said, "Father, I seek knowledge!"

The father said to him, "My child, get thee understanding!"

The son said again, "Father, I seek power!"

Once again, the father said to him, "My child, get thee understanding!"

Knowledge is good and power is good. But without the spirit of understanding, both knowledge and power are perverted into instruments of social chaos and destruction. It is the spirit of understanding that is needed. If we would grow in the spirit of understanding, we need to develop the will to understand. This is very important. The intense desire to understand must be there in our hearts.

A few years ago, I was in Switzerland. There I met a wonderful Frenchman. Our difficulty was communicating with each other. I do not know French, and he knew only a few words of the English language. Even so, we managed to get through to one another, because there was the ardent desire to do so. It is this desire that is very necessary.

This is the very first condition of developing an understanding heart– we must have the will to understand.

Dialogues of the deaf

I spoke of the need of the 'will to understand', as I called it. On the face of it, this statement might appear quite commonplace. But let me tell you, the will to understand, the intense desire to understand, is far rarer than we think. Listen to the conversations of the world– the conversations between couples. I often call them the "dialogues of the deaf". Each one is anxious to set forth his own ideas, in order to justify himself, to defend his position, to make himself appear greater than he truly is, and to accuse others. There is scarcely a desire to understand the other person.

Think of the little things over which we quarrel. A wife said that she could not sleep until she had read something for a while. The husband said he could not sleep if the light was on. The wife switched on the light and the husband switched it off. This led to a quarrel, and the quarrel went on, until both of them felt tired and went off to sleep, with harsh, negative thoughts in their minds, ready to restart the war at the earliest opportunity, the next morning. The spirit of understanding was lacking.

The wife could have gotten a bedside table lamp, which would not disturb the husband in his sleep. The husband could have used an eye-shade. But there was an ego-problem, and the ego is something that will never give up asserting itself.

A couple came from New York and met me. The wife complained that her husband was so busy with his work that he could not find any time for her. She felt neglected and ignored. The husband did not defend his position. He said, "What she says is perfectly true. From now on, I promise to take her out every Wednesday evening, to the movies or wherever she chooses." That was a step in the right direction. Every Wednesday evening, he did take her out, but there was no attempt made by him to understand her. What his wife needed was understanding.

We may go out together every evening, we may live together for years, but if the spirit of understanding is lacking, we cannot draw close to each other. This is the situation in so many upper class, cultured, intelligent families, today. People of the very highest order– successful businessmen, big industrialists, learned professors– in their families, the spirit of understanding is lacking. It is understanding that will draw them closer and knit them into a unity which not all the changing vicissitudes of life may break.

Why do misunderstandings arise?

Women have come and said to me, "In the days of courtship, we seemed to understand each other. Our husbands said to us, we are made for each other. What has happened to us now? And why?"

The reason is a simple one. In the days of courtship, they talked to each other, they opened up to one another. They found great pleasure in understanding and in being understood.

Communication is the basis of good understanding!

Growing in the spirit of understanding

1. Learn to be a good listener! Listen more, talk less. We are made to listen. This is why we have been given only one mouth and two ears. If we were meant to talk more and listen less, we would have been given only one ear, right in front and two mouths on the two sides. How funny would we look! And, mind you, there is no door with which to close the ears– they are always open. They are meant to be open!

    Be a good listener. Therefore, listen not only with the ears, but also with the heart. Better than talking is listening. And better than listening is to enter the silence within.

2. Do not belittle another person. Do not make him feel small. Do not criticise him or find faults with him. No one likes to be criticised. Look for good qualities in others and

appreciate them. When you appreciate others, you draw out the best that is in them.

Never scold children. When you scold them, you stifle the life-force that is within them.

I asked a little boy, "My child, what is your name?" He answered, "At school, they call me Ramesh. At home, I am called Ramesh-don't."

I could not understand. And he explained: "At school they call me Ramesh. But whenever I am at home, they always tell me, Ramesh don't behave like this, Ramesh don't speak like this, Ramesh don't sit like this, Ramesh don't talk like this!"

Appreciate your children. Appreciate your spouse. Appreciate your friends, neighbours, and colleagues. Do not take people for granted!

The deeper your understanding is of people, the greater your appreciation will be of them. Your attitude towards them will be of respect and reverence. It is anger and intolerance which become the enemies of and hinder understanding.

3. When you find you cannot get along well with others, do not blame them. Find the fault in yourself. It is easy to blame others, but it does not help. When you find that things are not going well, ask yourself: What have I done? Where have I gone wrong? You will find that your relationship with others will immediately improve.

4. There can be no true understanding without the spirit of humility. It is only when you grow humble that you can truly understand. The word understand, says: "stand under". No one is prepared, today, to stand under anyone. Everybody wants to stand over everybody. This is the main cause of misunderstandings. This is why the man of humility will never misunderstand others. He will never give himself airs. He will never show that he is superior to others.

The conversation of so many of us is full of the pronoun, "I". I did this, I did that. I gave this, I gave that. I achieved this, I achieved that. The man of humility will rarely use the pronoun "I". His conversation is full of the pronouns, "we" and "you".

5. The man of understanding argues little. How true it is that no one ever wins an argument! When you think you have won an argument, sooner or later, you will discover that you have not convinced the other person. You have only worn him out. In the process, you may have lost a friend.

Understanding

6. The man of understanding knows what it is to agree, despite differences. Even when he does not agree, he respects the other person. He never indulges in backbiting. He does not compare himself or his partner with others. He forgets his ego. He practises what he preaches.

It is easy to give advice to others. It is very easy to tell your partner to do this or that. But if you do not practise what you preach, no one will pay attention to your advice.

7. The man of understanding is always on the lookout for opportunities to be of service to others.

I have found that people are indifferent to the needs of others. They are indifferent to the point of callousness. May I tell you what is the opposite of love? The opposite of love is not hatred, but apathy, indifference to the needs of those around you. If you wish to grow in the spirit of understanding, you must grow in the spirit of service. You must look out for opportunities to be of service to others.

One final thought...

"I wish you could understand me..."

Is this not the hunger of every human heart? Everyone wants someone to understand him or her. But here lies the great paradox= of understanding.

You will not receive understanding until first you forget yourself and learn to understand others. The understanding that you give to others will come back to you, for understanding moves in a circle.

It is the light of understanding that people need today. The man with an understanding heart, will not be easily angered, upset or disturbed. Of such a man the Lord says in the Bhagavad Gita:

In sorrow not dejected,
In joy not overjoyed!
Outside the influence of passion,
Of fear and anger,
Ever calm in sorrow and joy–
Such a one is wise, indeed!

Vegetarianism

The word vegetarianism is mostly used to refer to the commonly accepted meaning– a dietary practice that avoids the use of flesh foods. Vegetarianism is perhaps one of the most misunderstood concepts of our times. 'Grass eaters', 'salad eaters', freaks, eccentrics, cranks, and herbivores are some of the terms used with derision and affection alike to refer to vegetarians. Along with such attitudinal descriptions, misconceptions and prejudices are also attached to this much maligned dietary system.

Twenty or thirty years ago, it might have been difficult for us to find unbiased, systematic, comprehensive information on vegetarianism in the form of a book or a website. It was a time when vegetarianism was regarded as "the cult of the crazy". Today, however, the tide is turning. Apart from those who are born to a vegetarian lifestyle, several thousands of people in the East and West are turning to vegetarianism as a lifestyle that promotes health and well-being.

The diet for the new age

It is my firm belief that food of non-violence is the diet of the new age. Vegetarianism is the way of life for the 21st century– indeed, for the new millennium. Vegetarianism is no longer the diet of the neglected few, the freak or the eccentric. People all over the world are turning to a vegetarian diet, for reasons related to health, disease prevention, nutrition, lifestyle, ideology and philosophy.

The time has come when we must decide once and for all, that all types of exploitation, all types of human tyranny must cease, if we are to have lasting peace in the world. It is only through a shared reverence for all life that the dream of world peace can be turned into a realisable goal. A non-violent diet is the very basis of this ideal.

Vegetarianism: A brief history of the term

It is said that the Vegetarian Society of Britain, established in 1847, created the word vegetarian from the Latin *vegetus* meaning 'lively' (which is how these early vegetarians claimed their diet made them feel). This is how the term gained currency in the West. The records of the Vegetarian Society tell us that "the term was first formally used on September 30th of that year by Joseph Brotherton and others, at Northwood Villa in Kent, England, the occasion being the inaugural meeting of the Vegetarian Society of the United Kingdom…"

Vegetarian enthusiasts, with a sense of humour, note rather gleefully that the American vegetarian movement was initiated by two people named Cowherd and Metcalfe. It is presumed that their surnames engendered their sensitivity to the consumption of cows and calfs and other four-legged friends!

We are told too, that prior to 1847, non-meat eaters were generally known as "Pythagoreans", named after the Greek philosopher, Pythagoras. It is said that he followed a diet that avoided the slaughter of animals.

What are the marks of a 'true vegetarian'?

For me, vegetarianism is not just a diet, but a way of life. The true vegetarian, as I think of him, is filled through and through with reverence for life. He reveres life as a gift of God which no man can bestow and, therefore, must not destroy. Such a one has the following marks:

1. His heart is a flowing river of compassion and love. The basis of true compassion is a feeling of unity, of oneness with all creatures that breathe the breath of life. To the true vegetarian, therefore, each life-unit is as dear and precious as his own life.

2. The true vegetarian, in my belief, is a man of self-discipline. So many there are who do not eat flesh but, alas, they cannot resist the temptations of the flesh. They have not extinguished the fire of passion. The true vegetarian is unswayed by passion, unruffled by anger, unmoved by greed and gold.

3. The true vegetarian does not boast of his virtue. He is a man of humility. Deep in his heart he knows that he is not free from the sin of killing. For, to breathe is to kill the germs that are in the air around us. To talk is to kill, to walk is to kill. Indeed, to live is to kill.

4. Living in such a world, the true vegetarian becomes a worshipper, a man of prayer. He sees cruelty all around him. How many hearts can he touch? How many lives can he save? And so he turns to Him who is the one Saviour of all. The true vegetarian prays alike for the killer and the killed and he prays that he may become an instrument of

God's love in this world of anguish and pain.

5. The true vegetarian is a man of indomitable faith. He believes profoundly that life is entirely a gift of God. In periods of crisis, in times of famine and flood, his mind wavers not! He prefers starvation to eating impure food.

When we talk about a vegetarian lifestyle, we invariably tend to think of our diet. True, vegetarian food is perhaps the toughest choice that new 'converts' must make. But in an era when awareness and sensitivity are growing, we need to realise that a way of life that is based on *ahimsa* now embraces several issues, including the rejection of products tested on animals, or those which cause harm to animals, including pesticides, certain cosmetics and perfumes, and even personal accessories made from leather and silk.

Animals kill each other for food. So what is wrong if we kill them for our food?

This is the familiar excuse used by some people to justify the killing of animals for meat. Why should we be in such a hurry to descend from our evolved state as human beings to the not-so-evolved state of predators?

The goal of a thoughtful vegetarian is to eliminate direct, unnecessary suffering of animals at the hands of humans. He would not find it acceptable to kill any animal to satisfy his palate. It is as simple as that!

If all of us were to turn vegetarian, wouldn't earth be overrun with cows, pigs, lambs, sheep and chickens?

I am constantly amused by these pseudo-global concerns expressed by so many people who are reluctant to turn vegetarian! My friends told me about a book which blames agriculture rather than factory farming for destroying the environment!

The worldwide explosion in the population of slaughterhouse animals is due to the unhealthy and cruel practices of factory farming. If animals were to be bred naturally, we would not have such enormous numbers of meat-cattle at all. We are now using artificial methods, dangerous methods, to breed these animals. They are given growth hormones to gain flesh and increase their weight, so that they generate more money in the meat market.

Hens and cows are treated with steroids to increase reproduction.

Once these horrors are stopped, there will be no bio-problem of the sort you fear. Nature will take care of itself! It is only when we interfere with the laws of nature that we create problems, and the responsibility devolves on us to sort them out. Giving up meat is a humane and healthy choice. Do not complicate it by unnecessary considerations.

Hindu philosophy tells us that life can never be killed. It is the forms which perish. Why then must we feel sad if birds and animals are slaughtered?

Yes, it is true that life is eternal. Nonetheless, it is also true that the law of life is compassion and love. Out of love cometh joy and every other blessing. He who hath not experienced love hath not known what it is to live. All killing is a denial of love. For to kill or to eat what another has killed, is to rejoice in cruelty. And cruelty hardens our heart and blinds our vision– we see not that they whom we kill are our brothers and sisters in the one brotherhood of life. He who kills another, kills himself. He who feeds on death, himself becomes food for death. He who inflicts suffering upon another, brings suffering to himself. Such is the law!

What can we do to show to the world that it is a cruel offence to kill a helpless animal?

The *tapasya* of the tongue is very difficult. People are slaves to the tongue. Just to get a momentary pleasure of taste, people slay innocent creatures every day and devour their flesh. Even though meat eating has been proved injurious to health, in order to satisfy their palate, men become slaves to the tongue. We can influence the world, only through our own example, by refraining from all food of violence. Gradually the influence will keep on growing. It is like throwing a pebble in a pool of water which creates ripples. Likewise, a person who bears witness to an ideal in his daily life, creates ripples of influence.

To my mind, *ahimsa* is not a 'policy' that one can follow or drop strategically; it is a supreme virtue which is fundamental to my *dharma*– my duty and morality. Ultimately, I believe in the justice of *ahimsa*: it is morally and ethically wrong to inflict cruelty and pain on any living creature, directly or indirectly. It is this belief in rightness, this sense of innate justice, that will eventually make vegetarianism flourish.

Why choose vegetarianism?

The arguments in favour of a vegetarian diet fall under three categories:

1. Physiological: Flesh diet has been responsible for serious diseases such as cancer.

2. Moral and ethical: There is much to be said against the wanton cruelty inflicted upon dumb and defenceless animals.

3. Economic: It has been proved that equal or better nutrition can be obtained from vegetable foods more efficiently and economically than from flesh foods.

Vegetarianism as a philosophy of life

As a philosophy of life, vegetarianism is based on the following assumptions:

1. The principle of reverence for all life: All forms of life are equal and must be revered.

2. Animals are not resources to be exploited at man's will for food, attire, entertainment or sport.

3. As human beings, we are a part of the world of nature, not its owners or masters.

4. No life is superfluous, and we have no right to take a life away, since we can never give it back.

5. There is no 'hierarchy' in living beings that justifies the killing of certain creatures.

6. Cruelty, violence, and infliction of pain and suffering on another being is abominable and morally repugnant.

7. Peace, harmony, and progress cannot be achieved at the expense of violence, cruelty, and killing.

8. Compassion and benevolence are high humane values to be extended to all living beings.

9. The universe is interconnected. Everything that we do touches the world around us in one way or another. Each one of us is responsible for the protection and well-being of the environment in which we live.

10. The prime value of mindfulness, compassion, and reverence for all life should override all other aspects of custom, culture, tradition, taste, and convenience.

Why should a vegetarian be regarded as more spiritually inclined or spiritually evolved than a non-vegetarian?

My answer to this controversial question is: when I choose vegetarianism for economic or environmental or even charitable reasons, it becomes my ideology. But when I choose vegetarianism in the belief that all life is sacred; that my physical body is not just a mound of flesh and blood, but a temple wherein dwells the immortal spirit, the *atman*; that the same spark of Divine Life which animates the universe and all of Creation also animates me; that the so-called lesser creatures on this planet are my younger brothers and sisters in the OneFamily of God's Creation– then the choice to go vegetarian becomes an affair of the Spirit!

Myths about a vegetarian diet

Myth: Meat eating is not as cruel as some people make it out to be. The methods of the modern slaughterhouse are 'humane' and 'painless'.

Fact: In Sadhu Vaswani's words, if we wish to talk of 'humane' slaughter, we might as well speak of 'humane' murder! The truth is that slaughterhouses may have become clean and efficient in western countries, but the pain and cruelty inflicted on sentient creatures has not been minimised at all!

Myth: What applies to animals must also apply to plants; vegetarians also 'kill' plants to satisfy their cravings. Eating plants is also taking away a life.

Fact: While some people insist that eating animals is not morally different from eating plants, they nevertheless draw a distinction between animals consumed for meat and pet animals like cats, dogs, and horses. Thus, while they find it healthy, ethical, and civilised to consume sheep, lambs, pigs and chickens, they are repulsed by eating the meat of dogs, horses, or cats! To put it simply, they believe "some animals are more equal than others"!

When we pluck a vegetable, the pain caused to it is infinitesimally small as compared to the pain caused to an animal when it is slaughtered. Animals, like human beings, are five-sensed creatures and feel the pain as much as we do. Further, there are different degrees of sensitivity to pain. Plants cannot feel as much pain as animals do when they are uprooted because as was pointed out by Sir Jagdish Chandra Bose, plants have not developed a nervous system. Living on this earth-plane, we have to sustain our life, but our ideal must be to commit the least violence, cause the least pain to others. This can be accomplished when we live on vegetables instead of on animal flesh.

Myth: Meat is the only source of protein available to man. Thus, a flesh diet is the only one that satisfies our necessity for protein.

Fact: Meat has been mistakenly identified with protein. However, it has been amply demonstrated that sufficient protein can be obtained from *daals*, beans, nuts, and many other non-animal sources. In fact, a vegetarian diet has been proven to provide excellent quality protein, as well as the other nutritional constituents, at a very reasonable price.

Myth: A vegetarian diet lacks variety.

Fact: For the average family, an imaginative meatless diet of salads, soups, casseroles, loaves, stews, legumes, fresh breads, fruit and nuts, along with rice and bread offers an endless variety, especially when we include seasonal fruits and vegetables.

Myth: Vegetarians are week, sickly and malnourished.

Fact: Like their fellow human beings, vegetarians come in all shapes and sizes. Many famous sportspersons in India are vegetarians.

Myth: It is very difficult to be a vegetarian in the U.K. or U.S.A.

Fact: Not at all! Vegetarian foods are now freely available in supermarkets all over the world, and many customer friendly restaurants are ready to go out of their way to serve the most fastidious diners with their choice of meatless dishes.

Myth: Humans were meant to eat flesh food. God created animals for human consumption.

Fact: Human anatomy suggests otherwise! If you believe that animals are 'resources' for human exploitation, remember: the 19th century threw out a similar view about slaves as free labour resources; the 20th century dismissed the pernicious view of women as goods and chattels. I firmly believe that the present century will accord a similar status to animals as creatures with the right to live for themselves!

Myth: Vegetarians are people who have given up indulgences like good, appetising food.

Fact: Vegetarians are normal people with normal food cravings, who love good food and enjoy tasty delicacies! And they are hardly starved for choice when they are at home. Nowadays, good restaurants are also ready to serve them wholesome and appetising fare.

Myth: A vegetarian diet is at best a health compromise.

Fact: It is flesh food eaters who are choosing unhealthy animal products which are actually compromising their health! Misleading claims by the meat industry hold up the erroneous claim that a vegetarian diet is insufficient and nutritionally lacking. A poorly planned, ill-balanced diet may be a compromise, whether it is vegetarian or otherwise (for example, a plateful of french fries and fried chicken, or a full bowl of ice cream or a double beef burger). Most nutritionists and doctors will agree when I say that human beings flourish when eating a well-planned, plant-based diet.

Myth: Vegetarians make a hue and cry over the pain and suffering of animals. They care more for animals than their fellow human beings.

Fact: Vegetarians recognise that animals are sentient beings, and respect their right to live. Their aim is to cause minimal pain or suffering to all creatures and to avoid all killing in the name of food and nutrition.

How can I get started on a vegetarian diet?

If you are not a 'born' vegetarian, experts suggest the following steps:

1. Understand your reason for going vegetarian. Let your motives be clear to you.

2. Choose the type of vegetarianism you wish to adopt– with or without eggs, dairy products, etc.

3. Do your homework on the nutrition. Understand your own protein needs and how it

may be obtained from sources other than animals.

4. Start gradually, by reducing your meat and flesh consumption. Give up meat once a week or more often.

5. Find healthy, tasty substitutes for the foods you are cutting out. Do not resort to junk food to satisfy your cravings.

6. Invest in a good vegetarian cookbook. Try a variety of recipes with an assortment of fresh vegetables, cereals, and legumes!

One final thought...

People often ask me: How does a token Meatless Day, as advocated by the Sadhu Vaswani Mission help spread the cause of vegetarianism?

"One day at a time" is a good, easy way to begin for everyone. One day is all it takes to create awareness, to plant a seed of sensitivity in the minds of people in regard to the cruelties that are perpetrated on animals day after day.

On this one day– November 25– millions of brothers and sisters pledge to go meatless as a mark of tribute to Gurudev Sadhu Vaswani, who was the voice of the voiceless ones. On this one day, many organisations and offices go meatless. Slaughterhouses are closed in Maharashtra and other states. Is it not a worthwhile cause to save so many creatures at least on this one day?

Our Meatless Day and Animal Rights Day is a small step in that direction.

World Peace

The greatest need of humanity today is peace. The tortured, wounded soul of humanity has cried piteously for peace, age after age. World fellowship and world unity– in these two simple ideals is the panacea for all the social and political evils that afflict humanity. The world belongs neither to you nor to me! We are here as pilgrims on earth. Our stay here is but for a little while. The world belongs to God– He is our President. Under His sovereign rule we must establish a world union in which every nation lives as the sister of every other nation.

Peace may be fragile and vulnerable, but peace is possible, and peace is attainable, even in a turbulent world like ours.

The more I have thought of it, the more it seems to me that there are three things that are needed to create conditions for an enduring world peace. The first is the spirit of universal brotherhood, the spirit of fellowship. The second is the spirit of caring and sharing, of service. And the third is a new vision of life as a movement onward.

Is peace possible in our world?

The world today is passing through a period of crisis. Unrest in all countries is deepening and nations are moving in a jungle of darkness. Passion for power, lust for fame, greed of gold, are all growing from more to more. Humanity, today, stands on the brink of a precipice, on the point of annihilation. Humanity, today, is like an orphan crying in the night, crying for the light. It is the light of understanding that the nations need.

We have arrived at a stage where nations and individuals alike must learn to understand one another or perish. There is no other choice!

But there is hope for all of us! For thousands of years, nations have fought one another– and look at what man has made of man. Let us usher in a new age of love and peace, which will bring brotherhood among all nations and people.

When and how will this happen?

Let me tell you that within nature, there is only development. Time and space are human qualities. The new age will come when the old has lived to its fullest. First, a great broom will sweep out all old, outdated attitudes and beliefs– those that we are holding today– and new ones will arise in the hearts of men. Then the new age of love and peace will be established on earth.

How can we bring about peace on earth?

Wars will not leave the face of this earth until we have peace in our hearts.

"How can there be peace on earth when the hearts of men are a volcano?" said Sadhu Vaswani. Understanding and love are preconditions of world peace.

Just as some people are short-sighted or far-sighted, and their vision is clouded, similarly our vision is obscured from our very birth by prejudices of family, race and nation. We must break these barriers and realise the truth that all children of the earth are one. The key to peace is to love one another unconditionally. Love the world as your own nation, love every human being as your own sibling.

Universal brotherhood: Is this a practical ideal?

May I say to you, this is not a revolutionary idea that I am expressing! Our ancient rishis spoke thousands of years ago about the concept of *Vasudaiva Kutumbakam*– the world as one family. The Tamil Sangam poets of the 3rd Century A.D. sang, "Every place is my home; everyone is my relative!" No other world scripture expresses the spirit of universal brotherhood as beautifully as the Vedas:

Auspiciousness be unto all,
Perfect peace be unto all,
Fullness be unto all,
Prosperity be unto all.

I firmly believe that until we grow in this vision of brotherhood, world peace can never be a reality. "May we grow in the spirit of fellowship and understanding," say our ancient Hindu scriptures. And the *Rig Veda*, perhaps the oldest of all scriptures says: "Together walk ye, and together talk ye, and together know ye your minds!"

The world, I believe, is a garden of God. God is in all that is– in men and women, birds and animals, fish and fowl, worms and insects, trees and flowers, rivers and rocks, stones and stars, in this pen that scribbles, and even in the paper on which my moving finger writes, "Krishna! Krishna!" Krishna is in all, and we all are in Krishna! When we have this vision of the One-in-all and All-in-one, we will grow in the spirit of Brotherhood of all Creation!

How may we achieve this? Our hearts need to be saturated with love, for love is the light which will illumine the world. For this, developed brains are not needed; we need enlightened hearts that can behold the vision of fellowship, unity, and brotherhood. Love is what we need to build a new humanity, a new world of brotherhood and peace. We must eliminate the dark forces of greed, selfishness, prejudice and mistrust, and instead cultivate the power of love, which is the power of peace!

My vision of fellowship and brotherhood shows me a world in which the right to life is accorded to every creature that breathes the breath of life! How can wars cease until we stop all killing? How can we claim to seek world peace when we continue to slaughter sentient creatures? If a man kills an animal for food, he will not hesitate in killing a fellow man whom he regards as an enemy! Therefore I urge you, let us grow in the true spirit of brotherhood. Let us grow in the spirit of reverence for all life!

The spirit of caring and sharing

How can the world be peaceful and prosperous if only a fraction of its people live in luxury and opulence, while the majority live in poverty and deprivation? Therefore, we must all learn to share what we have with others! Let us set apart a portion– say one-tenth– of our earnings to be utilised in the service of God and His suffering Creation.

To some who are unable to make two ends meet, or live within their income, this may at first appear a very difficult principle to uphold! But we will find eventually, that in the measure in which we share what little we have with others, we will be truly blessed– andthis world will be a better place for our humble endeavours!

The seven musical notes of peace

Everywhere in God's good universe, peace prevails and the divine harmony of peace is played out as celestial music. Sadly, human beings trapped in their worldly affairs cannot hear it!

Without peace, life becomes full of discord, disharmony, strife, tempest, and tumult. Peace is the true, abiding music of life. I believe that if we so wish, we can create peace on earth through our own efforts.

Peace is harmony. Even as there are seven notes on the musical scale, so too, there are seven notes on the musical scale of peace– seven qualities that we must cultivate if we are to have peace.

What are the seven notes on the musical scale of peace?

Let us hear the sweet symphony, note by note.

The first note: Love

The very first note on the musical scale of peace is LOVE– love as in the Commandment: Thou shalt love thy neighbour as thyself. It is this spirit of love that is expressed in the universal bond of friendship. If we pick and choose and reject, then universal friendship does not have a chance! If we assess and evaluate and rate people, we have no time to love them. We must love all– not merely our family and friends, our kith and kin– we must love all Creation.

We must cultivate the fine art of friendship, for the permanent peace plan can only be a friendship plan. Therefore, we must go out and make friends with people belonging to different religions, communities, and nationalities. This is what friendship is all about– not just sticking to the people you know, your neighbours, your colleagues, or the people you grew up with.

Each one of us can become ambassadors of peace, harbingers of peace, merely by smiling the smile of friendship.

I repeat, the permanent peace plan can only be a friendship plan. Making friends is a win-win proposition. When we become friends with all, the world will be at peace. Befriend everyone, even your enemies. Extend your friendship and understanding even to those who are out to commit violence, and you are sure to find that they have hearts receptive to love. Go out to meet them, make an effort to understand them. Do not be afraid of them; do not avoid them or fight with them.

The second note: Equality

Equality always assumes a difference; it teaches all of us to remember our common humanity despite all the differences of class, race, creed, colour and religion. It reminds us of Sadhu Vaswani's clarion call: Children of the earth, ye all are one!

The third note: Tolerance

Tolerance, I would say, is a highly underrated virtue! While we elevate love, charity, and compassion to the status of saintly qualities, we do not appreciate the more basic and fundamental virtue of tolerance, without which peace is just not possible.

The Oxford Dictionary defines the verb tolerate as follows: to allow the existence or occurrence of something without authoritative interference; to leave something unmolested; to endure something with forbearance.

Tolerance is, in other words, the practice of allowing differences in religious opinion without discrimination. The truth may be one, but the ways to truth are many. You walk along one way; your neighbour, your friend, countless other strangers, may choose a different path. Allow them their freedom of choice!

Live and let live! This is tolerance at its best. Why should I force my neighbour to think, work, speak and worship as I do? Let me accept that all of us are different, and let me respect the difference. For all our differences, for all our diversity in language, culture and religion, we share but one world. Therefore, let us accept differences– nay, celebrate all differences, and take delight in them! In difference is variety, the spice of life. In diversity is strength.

The fourth note: Mutual respect between nations

When patriotism becomes fanatical and narrow, it is called jingoism. When nationalism becomes closed and restrictive, it degenerates into arrogance and hegemony. In a world that talks of superpowers and domination, let me say to you: What we need for lasting peace is mutual respect among people, mutual respect between nations.

Our own self-respect must lead us on to respect others. To retain a sense of proportion, to maintain a proper perspective on life, it is important to respect others.

As I said to you earlier, we may all be different, but we have just this one world to live in. Our skin colours may be white or black, brown or yellow; we might speak in Hindi,

Mandarin, French or Swahili. We may hail from Europe, Africa or New Zealand. But the fact of the matter is that we all need one another! We cannot live like islands, cut off from the rest of humanity. Therefore we must learn to respect other races, other people, and other nations and live and work amicably with them. Civility is as essential among nations as it is among people!

A memorable experience for me in recent times was my visit to the land of my birth, Sind, which is now in Pakistan. For over fifty years, several of my friends had not had the opportunity to go back to the land of our forefathers. Thanks to the new climate of trust and cooperation between India and Pakistan at that time, and the meaningful dialogues and exchange of visits which took place between the two countries, a new environment of trust and mutual respect was created. This enabled me to accept a kind invitation from my Alma Mater, D. J. Sind College, Karachi, and 'cross the border' that had divided our two countries in 1947.

Our visit to Pakistan was memorable, in every sense of the word. Above all, we were overwhelmed by the love, kindness, and courtesy extended to us by the generous people of a neighbouring country with whom we have been warring constantly!

Our visit showed us a new face of the thorny India-Pakistan relationship– the face of thousands of Indians and Pakistanis who had mutual respect for each other and believed sincerely that their future lay in cooperation, not confrontation.

Respect for each other opened wide the door of friendship between the two countries, making people-to-people contact a reality for the first time in fifty years.

Truth be told, the walls and fences we erect in our minds are perhaps far more formidable than exterior walls and boundaries. The political and emotional 'divide' among the people must be bridged by mutual respect, love, and understanding.

The fifth note: An end to racial discrimination

How can we ever hope to have world peace when any one race regards itself as superior to another? We must put an end to all forms of racial discrimination.

Harmonious integration of pluralistic, multi-cultural, multi-racial societies can only be achieved through relations based on racial equality. Racism, casteism, and all related practices must be condemned for the evils they perpetrate, including: discrimination against people founded on false notions of superiority and inferiority; discrimination on the grounds of descent, ethnicity, colour or physical characteristics; violent expressions of hostility, hate and bias; perpetuation of social injustice and inequality leading to intergenerational inequality.

Let us dream of a world where we will realise that all races were created by God, all races belong to God, and that there is no superior or inferior race!

In my secular vision of life, black and brown, yellow and white, are the colours of the one beautiful rainbow that we call 'humanity'.

In my spiritual vision of life, there is no segregation– only oneness and equality of all human beings, as children of God.

The sixth note: An end to all forms of exploitation

To exploit another is to take unfair advantage of him or her. 'Exploitation' acquired a political overtone in Marxist ideology, but it has always had its own moral and ethical significance in human discourse.

Several forms, several modes, several degrees of exploitation exist in our world today– exploitation of workers, hospital patients, women, children, and even the fragile ecosystem of this planet! Indeed, domestic/sexual violence against women, child abuse, and animal abuse are some of the worst forms of exploitation we have permitted to corrupt the moral basis of our society.

The world cannot be at peace until all forms of exploitation cease!

The seventh note: Compassion

The concept of compassion is at the core of all religions. The greatest form of compassion can only come by understanding the central concept of *Vedanta*– that all life is one. The life that sleeps in stones and minerals, the life that dreams in plants and trees, the life that stirs in animals and birds, is the same life that awakes and breathes in man. And this life is the very spark of the Life Universal.

Compassion binds the world together in a bond of unity and peace. In the words of the

Buddha: "In separateness lies the world's great misery, in compassion lies the world's true strength."

One final thought...

The task is to build a new world– a world without wars, a world without wants, a world in which peace and joy will be every man, woman, and child's birthright. The task is to create peace– or perish. The choice is ours.

The future must belong to a new civilisation where man will be a truly evolved super-being, who sees every human being as his equal, his friend, his brother, his sister.

Yoga

The word yoga is derived from the Sanskrit word *yug*, which means, to unite. Yoga, therefore, is the Science of Union. Through the practice of yoga, the soul is united with the Supreme Soul. Yoga is a divine science which teaches us how to disentangle the soul from the phenomenal world of sense objects and link it with the Absolute.

Yoga is not a theory or philosophy. Yoga is the essence of the revelation of sages and saints. Yoga is essentially a way of union.

Union with what?

Let us first realise that we live in a world of separation. We are separated from our Divine Source, that which, for want of a better word, we call God. Yoga unites man with God. Yoga unites man with the infinite storehouse of energy that is Divinity. Yoga is that which transforms man and makes him God-like.

Yoga is not escapism

Yoga does not ask us to run away from the world and retire into the depths of a *tapobana* or climb the peaks of a holy hill. Yoga is to be in the world, but not of the world. Yoga teaches us to live in the world– but not let worldliness live within us.

The Yoga Sutras of Patanajali

One of the great source-books which enshrines the teachings of yoga is named *The Yoga Sutra of Patanjali*.

We should note at first, what, according to Sage Patanjali, is yoga. He defines yoga beautifully as *chitta vritti nirodha*; *chitta* is consciousness; *vritti* is modification; *nirodha* is control. Yoga is *chitta vritti nirodha*– control of the restlessness of the mind. The mind is a stream of thoughts always going outwards. It has to be turned towards the self, the *atman*. The ceaseless wandering of the mind must be checked, controlled, restrained, if we would attain the only treasure that is worth having– *chitta shanti*, or peace of mind.

The eight steps of Patanjali's *Ashtanga Yoga*

1. The first step is *yama*, translated literally as control. Another word for *yama* is discipline. We must discipline our lives if we wish to advance spiritually. There are disciplines we must conform to– disciplines such as *ahimsa*, non-violence; *satya*, truthfulness; *asteya*, non-stealing; *aparigraha*, non-possession; and *brahmacharya*, chastity.

2. The second step is *niyama*, conformation to certain disciplines. Time and effort must be set aside for the pursuit of these *niyamas*– such as cleanliness, contentment, control of the flesh, study of the scriptures.

3. The third step is *asana*, posture control and exercises that are preparatory to meditation. These postures taught by Sage Patanjali promote good health. For, according to him, yoga is not for the weak, but for men and women of *shakti*.

4. The fourth step is *pranayama*, breath control. When breath is properly controlled, drawn in and let out, it helps to relax both the body and mind. *Prana* is a vital force in the air, with an enriching quality. *Pranic* energy can be conserved and utilised well by *pranayama*.

5. The fifth step is *pratyahara*, restraint from sense-enjoyment. If we wish to grow in yoga, we must resist indulgence of the senses.

6. The sixth step is *dharana*, concentration. The mind must be free from distraction and clean of everything except an all-pervading thought that helps you focus your concentration. This can be a mantra, an object or even an idea.

7. The seventh step is *dhyana*, or meditation. We turn inwards, making our minds open and receptive to a higher consciousness. We cross the distance between ourselves and the Universal Spirit. We attain a wonderful feeling of selflessness.

8. The eighth step is *samadhi*, the highest level of meditation, the supreme goal of yoga. It has been described as a state of super-consciousness. It is at-one-ment with the Universal Consciousness. *Samadhi* leads us into a world of new vision, the realisation of the One-in-all.

Abhyasis of yoga have described the *Ashtanga Yoga* of Sage Patanjali as "tuning into a higher awareness". According to the system so well defined by Patanjali, yoga is a strict discipline, a learning process involving, in order, proper preparation and attitude (*yama* and *niyama*) physical and breathing exercises (*asana* and *pranayama*), control of the senses (*pratihara*), concentration (*dharana*), contemplation (*dhyana*) and meditation (*samadhi*).

Different types of yoga

The first category of yoga is that which we call *Mantra Yoga*. *Mantra Yoga* teaches us how concentration can be achieved by the repetition of a single sacred word, set of words, or even a single syllable, which is symbolic of God or Truth.

The second category of yoga is *Raja Yoga*, which aims at the control of the breath and the mind. As the name indicates, *Raja Yoga* is royal yoga. It is the yoga of meditation.

According to the ancient philosophy of *Raja Yoga*, each one of us is blessed with infinite potential, laying open for us endless possibilities. So it is that Lord Krishna tells his dear disciple, Arjuna in the Bhagavad Gita:

The yogi is greater than the ascetic; the yogi is even greater than the Vedic scholar; the yogi is greater than the man of rituals. Therefore, do thou become a yogi, O Arjuna! And of all yogis, he who, full of faith adoreth Me, with his self abiding in Me– he is deemed by Me to be the most completely harmonised! Such a one is a Raja Yogi!

The next category of yoga is *Hatha Yoga*, or the yoga of physical culture. It is, in a sense, a branch of *Raja Yoga*. It is said to be a total and complete system of psycho-physical training, which helps to harmonise the mind and the body with the external world and the elements with which all Creation is composed.

Hatha Yoga is based on a system of exercises including: *asanas* or various postures, *pranayama* or breathing exercises, *mudras* or special gestures, *bandhas* or "ties" involving concentration, and *kriyas* or purification exercises. Exponents of *Hatha Yoga* claim that through exercises, concentration and meditation, the *kundalini shakti* (the coiled-up energy that lies dominant within us) can be unfolded, and ultimately, a union with the Divine achieved.

Laya Yoga teaches us to attain peace and serenity at the very core of the inner consciousness. The word *laya* signifies void or emptiness– the absolute dissolution of the ego. The symbol of *Laya Yoga* is a lotus of one thousand petals, with a void in the centre.

It is a system of meditation which all of us can practise. It is a process of spiritual ascent and descent, made by concentrating on the lotus in each *chakra* of the body and observing it with detachment.

Kundalini Yoga: In Sanskrit, *Kundalini* literally means "snake" or "snake power". This refers to the latent superior force in every human being, which is thought to lie curled at the base of the spine. This force is awakened from sleep through *Kundalini Yoga*, and it rises through a series of centres or *chakras* to attain spiritual awareness.

This is a highly technical process which can be learnt only at the feet of a competent guide.

Sahaj Yoga is the simple yoga. For yoga is nothing unnatural. Yoga is not foreign to us. Yoga is like the return of an intoxicated man to a life of sobriety. Having come to this world of allurements and entanglements, many of us have drunk the wine of *maya*. A veil of ignorance– *avidya*– clouds our minds. It is this ignorance that robs the intellect of its knowledge of discrimination. One begins to think that he is the body, the mind, the senses. One confounds the perishable body to be the Spirit and starts hankering after pleasure. In reality, this world of *maya* is nothing but a source of misery.

When we are satisfied by worldly pleasures, its possessions and its powers, we begin to live an existence similar to that of animals. From *maya*– intoxication, man has to attain God-intoxication. Ignorance has to be destroyed by the knowledge of the Self.

Yoga is integration of body, mind, and soul– a vital step to union with the Divine.

You are Not this Body: You are the Atman!

An infinite potential lies hid within us. We are unaware of it, because we think of ourselves as limited, restricted creatures. We have identified ourselves with a biochemical-mental organism, the body-mind complex that we inhabit to function on this material plane. Our true Self is the *atman. Tat Twam Asi!* That art thou!

Scholars or cobblers?

Raja Janaka, whom most of you know as the father of Sita in the *Ramayana,* was also renowned as a great philosopher-king. He often gathered sages and philosophers at his court, so that he could listen to their wise discourses.

At one such gathering, eminent rishis and scholars were made to sit on grand seats in the king's *darbar* when sage Ashtavakra entered.

This wise seer was called Ashtavakra, because his body was bent and twisted in eight different places due to a serious birth defect. As he hobbled into the hall, moving his crooked figure towards the conclave, the sages who were already seated burst out in derisive laughter. Ashtavakra paused, and then addressed the king. "I thought I was going to attend a meeting of philosophers," he said to Janaka. "But it would appear that I have walked into a gathering of cobblers!"

"How dare you!" protested one of the sages, rising to his feet in anger.

Raja Janaka replied in humility, "Please explain yourself, wise one."

"The men whom you have gathered here are looking at my flesh, my skin. What else can they be but cobblers? This physical body that I wear is but a shoe. These men are judging me by the shoes I wear. They do not realise that I am not this body. How can these men be philosophers?"

You are not the body, the mind, and the senses

Alas, the world judges people by outward appearances. Go anywhere, and you are judged by the clothes you wear, the car you drive, and even your hairstyle. Your exterior is what counts!

If you wish to understand your true Self, you must stop identifying yourself with the body, the mind, and the senses. You must move away from the "shoes" you wear. This is indeed the significance of the custom practised by Hindus of removing one's shoes before entering a temple or a holy place. This is symbolic of the idea that we move away from body-consciousness to walk upon the sanctified ground, which will help us move towards God-realisation.

Who am I?

We cannot literally cast off the body, but we can change our perspective by dwelling on the fact that we are not the bodies we wear– we are the immortal Spirits within. This brings about a tremendous change in our outlook!

The Bible tells us of a young man who approached Jesus and asked to be his follower. When Jesus spoke to him of the Ten Commandments, he assured the master that he had been observing them for several years. Then Jesus said to him, "If you wish to enter the Kingdom of Heaven, then sell everything you have, and come and follow me."

The young man was not prepared to do this. He backed away, but not without regret.

Selling everything one has is not to be interpreted literally. It too means moving away from the ego, from identification with the body.

So ask yourself again and again: who am I?

Realise the true Self

According to *Vedanta* philosophy, as human beings, all of us wear the garment of the physical body– our outer form of matter. This is the *annamaya kosha*. Within this outer sheath is the *prana*, or vital breath, which constitutes the *pranamaya kosha*. Our mind, or the instrument of cognition, along with the senses or the *indriyas*, constitutes the *manomaya kosha*. The ego and the intellect, together, constitute our *vijnanamaya kosha*. The consciousness of pure bliss is the innermost sheath, the *anandamaya kosha*. Folded in the centre of the five sheaths resides the true Self– That which Is. Caught up as we are in the

You are not this Body: You are the Atman

mire of worldly existence, most of us rarely experience this bliss or indeed become aware of the true Self within us.

The sad truth is most of the time we dwell in the consciousness of the body alone!

How we pamper our bodies from the cradle to the grave! We spend a fortune on clothes and accessories. We are fussy about the kind of food we like to eat. We go out of the way to procure exotic delicacies and expensive tidbits to please our taste buds. We get upset if our sleep is disturbed. We are conscious of every ache and pain in our limbs. We are constantly obsessed with looking good, feeling good, with our physical comforts, and with flavourful food. I might even go so far as to say that most of our activities are focussed on this obsession with the physical body!

The body is strong; the senses (*indriyas*) are powerful. But the mind (*manas*) is above them. Beyond and higher than the mind is the discriminatory faculty (*buddhi*) that helps us know right from wrong and beyond it all is the *atman*– the Spirit.

The body and its cognitive instruments, the mind and the senses, have been given to us with a purpose: that we may evolve towards self-realisation and perfection!

Glossary

Aahuti	Offering to a deity	*Asura sampadi*	Demonic qualities
Abhinivesha	Attachment	*Asuras*	Demons
Abhyasa	Practice	*Asuya*	Fear of losing what we have; resentment at others' happiness
Abhyasi	Spiritual seeker; one who practises		
Acharya	Spiritual teacher	*Atharva Veda*	One of the four Vedas, it addresses procedures and problems of daily life, diseases and their cure
Adharma	Wrongdoing; unrighteousness		
Adrishta	The unseen		
Agarbatti	Incense stick	*Atma shakti*	Spiritual strength; soul power
Aham Brahmasmi	I am Brahman		
Ahankara	Ego; egoism	*Atma vidya*	Spirituality; science knowledge of the soul; Spirit
Ahimsa	Non-violence		
Ajnana	Ignorance		
Akhanda Bharat	Greater India; undivided India	*Atman*	The soul
		Avatara	Divine incarnation
Amarphal	A mythical fruit that bestows immortality	*Avidya*	Ignorance
		Ayahs	Baby sitters
Amrit dhara	Literally, flow of nectar; refers to the teachings of saints	*Badshah*	King
		Bali	Sacrifice
		Bani	Guru's words of wisdom
Antah karan	Inner instrument	*Barkat*	Receiving more than one expects
Antaryami	Indweller		
Aparigraha	Non-possession	*Bhagavad sankalpa*	God's intention
Artha	Wealth	*Bhagwan*	God
Aryavarta	Ancient name of India	*Bhajans*	Devotional songs
Ashantasya Kutah Sukham	How can an agitated mind find comfort?	*Bhakta*	Devotee
		Bhakti	Devotion
		Bhakti marga	Path of devotion
Ashrama	A place of discipline; a house where a true Guru is living and teaching	*Bhakti Yoga*	Spiritual practice, focussed on loving devotion towards God
		Bharata	The nation of India
Ashtavakra Gita	A classical scripture, written as a dialogue between Sage Ashtavakra and King Janaka.	*Bharati*	The embodiment of the spirit of Bharata (India)

Bhav	Feeling; attitude	*Darshan*	Opportunity to have the vision of a holy person
Bhikkhus	Buddhist monk		
Bhudevi	Mother Earth	*Deenabandhu, Deenanath*	Friend of the poor
Bhumata	Mother Earth		
Brahma muhurt	Literally translated as "The Creator's Hour", an auspicious time for meditation; approximately 1.5 hours before sunrise	*Dharma*	Duty; righteousness
		Dharma Chakra	'The Wheel of Law', representing the Buddha's teachings
		Dholak	A folk instrument; drum
Brahmacharya	The first of the four stages in the life of a Hindu. It is the stage of celibacy of the student/ disciple	*Dhyana*	Meditation
		Doha	Stanzas of two rhyming lines
		Dosha	Anger; hostility; aversion
Brahman	The ultimate, unchanging, infinite reality; the supreme entity of the Universe, from which all things emanate and to which all return	*Dukha*	Suffering and misery
		Dwandas	Pairs of opposites; binaries
		Ekagrita	One-pointed focus
		Fakir (Urdu)	An ascetic in quest of God
		Gangajal	Holy waters of the River Ganga
Brahma jnani	A highly enlightened individual	*Ganja*	Opium
Brahmin	One of the Hindu castes; the priestly class	*Gayatri Mantra*	A highly revered Hindu prayer
Buddhi	Spiritual awareness, intellect	*Ghee*	Clarified butter made from milk
Chachera bhai	Paternal cousin	*Gherao*	Literally, 'encirclement'; picketing by union members or others surrounding a leader till their demands are met
Chakras	Energy centres in the body		
Daal	Lentils, pulses		
Daivi sampadi	Divine heritage		
Darbar	Court where kings and rulers had their formal and informal meetings		
		Ghurus	"Takers" in the Sindhi language
Dargah	Sufi shrine		
Daridra Narayana	The divine spirit in the poor; Lord of the poor and needy ones	*Gopis*	Cowherd girls from Brindavan with unconditional devotion for Lord Krishna

Grihasta	Householder	*Jignasu*	A seeker after truth; aspirant
Grihastha ashrama	Married state		
Gulab jamun	A milk-solid based Indian sweet	*Jilebi*	An Indian sweet; fried flour batter soaked in sugar syrup
Gurbani	The writings/ words of the Gurus	*Jitendriya*	One who has controlled and mastered his senses
Guru Granth Sahib	Primary volume of the Sikh scripture compiled by Guru Arjan Dev, which is revered as the last and Eternal Guru	*Jivan mukta*	One who has gained self-knowledge; a sage who is liberated while still living
		Jivatma	Individual soul
Guru kripa	Grace of the Guru	*Jivayajna*	A life-long saga of service and sacrifice for family and society
Guru-Bhakti Yoga	Devotional belief in Guru as God		
Gurudwara	A place of worship for Sikhs	*Jnana*	Wisdom; knowledge
		Jnana shakti	The power of wisdom, knowing
Gurukul	Schooling system in ancient India	*Jnana Yoga*	A difficult path to finding absolute truth through one's own effort and wisdom
Gwalas	Community of cowherds		
Hakim	Wise or learned man		
Holi	Festival of Colours; symbolises the victory of good over evil		
		Jnani	One who possess self-knowledge
Huzoor	A title of respect	*Kaabalikas*	Ascetic Shiva worshippers offering devotion with human skulls
Ichcha shakti	The freedom of choice; the power of desire, will, love		
Ishta devata	A worshipper's favourite deity	*Kaliyuga*	The fourth and present age of the world cycle, an age of darkness and conflict
Ishwara	A higher power		
Ishwara Pranidhana	Surrender to the Divine	*Kama*	Desire or longing
Jahanpanah	One who provides shelter to his subjects	*Kamini*	The personification of sense-indulgence
Janmas	Births	*Karma Yoga*	Path of selfless action
Japa	Constant repetition of a mantra or the Name Divine	*Kathopanishad*	A widely known Upanishad that represents a dialogue between an aspiring disciple and the Lord of Death, Yamaraj
Japji	First composition found in the Sacred *Guru Granth Sahib*; prayer of invocation of the Guru		
		Khandan	Family prestige

Khuda	God
Ki jai	Victory to
Kirtan	Chanting of devotional songs
Kismet	Fate
Klesha	Deadly sin
Krama mukti	Gradual or sequential liberation
Krishna Nama Sankirtan	Constant chanting of the Lord's Name
Kriya	Action
Kriya shakti	The power of action
Krodha	Fury; rage
Kshatriyas	Warriors
Kutiya	Hut
Leela	Divine play
Lobha	Greed
Loli/ koki	A typical Sindhi breakfast; spicy flatbread
Maasaat (Sindhi)	Maternal cousin
Mada	Ego
Mahavakya	Great saying of the Upanishad
Mantra japa	Silent chanting
Manusmriti	Laws of Manu; guidelines based on Hindu beliefs
Mata	Mother
Matsarya	Jealousy
Mausera bhai	First cousin (maternal)
Maya	Illusion
Moha	Desire or attachment
Moksha	Liberation
Mukti	Release
Mula priyaya	Main roots of evil
Mumukshatwa	The desire to attain liberation
Naam japa	Chanting of the Name Divine
Naam kirtan	Chanting the Name Divine
Naam smaran	Meditation on God's name
Naivaidya	Offering to God
Naraka/ naraka loka	A sort of a psychic, purgatorial quarantine where souls are cleansed
Nirvana	Liberation from the cycle of birth and death
Nishkama karma	Desire-less action
Niyamas	Dos or observances
Nuri	Sadhu Vaswani's nom-de-plume
Nuri Granth	A collection of over 4,000 songs and 2,000 *slokas* penned by Sadhu Vaswani
Ojas shakti	Sublimated sexual energy
Om Shanti Shanti Shanti	Mantra that is an invocation of peace
Paap	Sin
Padmasana	Seated posture with legs crossed and feet placed on opposite thighs
Paradharma	Others' duties
Paramartha	The ultimate goal of life
Paramatma	The Supreme Being (the Over Soul)
Parashakti	Pure consciousness
Parasmani	Stone that turns iron into gold
Pir	A Muslim saint or holy man
Pooja	Act of worship
Prahlada Charitra	The story of *Bhakta* Prahlada, supreme devotee of Lord Vishnu
Prakriti sangha	Fellowship with nature
Prana	The vital force of life; life of breath

Pranayama	Control of breath
Pranic	Relating to *prana*, the vital life force
Prarabdha Karma	Accumulated karma
Prasadam/ prasad	Devotional offering of food made to a Hindu god
Pratikriya	Reaction
Preya	The pleasurable, worldly path which leads to unhappiness
Punditry	Opinions and methods of pundits (scholar of Hinduism)
Punya	Virtue; moral deed
Puranas	Ancient Hindu texts
Puranic	Relating to the *puranas*
Purdah	Veil
Purusharthas	Goals of life according to the Hindu faith
Purushottama	Lord Supreme
Raas leela	The Divine play of Lord Krishna with the *Gopis*
Raga	Clinging
Rajas	Passion
Rajnigandha	Tuberose (fragrant flower)
Rakhi	Thread symbolising the bond of affection/ protection tied by sister on her brother's wrist
Raksha Bandhan	Hindu Festival celebrating the bond between brothers and sisters; *raksha* meaning protection and *bhandan* meaning bond
Ramayana	A Hindu epic about Lord Rama, whose wife Sita is abducted by Ravana
Riyaaz	Practice
Sadhaka	Seeker; spiritual aspirant
Sadhana	Spiritual discipline
Sadyah mukti	Instantaneous liberation
Sahaj Marg	An easy path
Sakhi Satsang	Spiritual fellowship of sisters
Samattva	State of indifference; equanimity
Sansaar	The cycle of death and rebirth to which life in the material world is bound
Samskara	Sacrament
Sanatana dharma	The eternal religion (Hinduism)
Sangha	Company; the people you associate with; fellowship
Sansaar sagar	The ocean of life
Sansaari jeeva	Living being who is caught in the cycle of rebirths
Sant	A saint
Sant Bani	Song of the Spirit
Santosha	Contentment
Sannyasa	Renunciation
Sanyasi	Hindu anchorite/ renunciate
Saranagati	Total surrender at the Lotus Feet of the Lord
Saranam	Surrender
Sashtang Namaskar	Salutation in which all *angas* (body parts) touch the ground
Sat Chit Ananda	The peace and bliss that no ending knows
Satguru	Lord; true teacher
Satpurkha	Saint
Satsang	Company of the highest truth; company of a guru; congregation of assimilating the truth

Satsangi	Follower of a *satsang*; seeker of truth	*Sloka*	Verse from a sacred text
Sattva	Detachment and dedication to God	*Smaran*	Act of remembrance of the Divine
Sattvic	Pure; fresh	*Sohum*	I am that (sacred statement from the Upanishads)
Satya	Truth		
Satya Yuga	The first age in the world cycle; age of truth, virtue, and righteousness	*Srimad Bhagavatam/ Srimad Bhagavata Purana*	A Hindu scripture which narrates the many incarnations of Lord Vishnu as a discourse between Rishi Shuka (son of Ved Vyasa) and King Parikshit
Satyagraha Movement	Nonviolent resistance employed by Mahatma Gandhi		
Satyapriya	Lover of truth	*Sukhmani Sahib*	Translated as "Pslam of Peace", it is a set of hymns by Guru Arjan Dev, which are part of the *Guru Granth Sahib*, the sacred Sikh scripture
Satya swaroopa	Embodiment of truth		
Saucha	Purification		
Saut (Sindhi)	Paternal cousin; cousin brother		
Sethia	A rich man; a wealthy trader		
		Surya- namaskar	A yoga practice of a sequence of postures offered in devotion to the Sun God
Seva	Service		
Sevaks	One who offers service to the master		
Shadaripus	Six enemies	*Swadharma*	Performance of one's own duty
Shakti	An energy that is of Eternity		
		Swadhyaya	Self-study
Shanti Suktam	A *Vedic* prayer for peace	*Swarga/ swarga loka*	The astral plane; Hindu idea of heaven
Shastras	A work of sacred scripture		
Shishu	Child of the guru	*Swasthya*	Health; to be oneself
Shishya	Disciple	*Taat*	Devotion; submission
Shraddha	Devotion	*Tamas*	Dullness
Shreya	The difficult, thorny path which leads to Ultimate Bliss	*Tapas*	Asceticism
		Tapasya	A test of sacrifice
		Tapobana	Forest of meditation
		Tarka	Philosophical debates
Shudras	One of the Hindu castes; service provider	*Tat Twam Asi*	That art thou! (Upanishad statement)
Siddhis	Spiritual or magical power		
Sika (Sindhi)	Longing	*Tateh kim*	What then?
Sipahis	Soldiers	*Tathastu*	So be it!

Trishna	Desire	*Vedanta*	Essence of the Vedas
Trishula	Trident	*Vedantic*	Of or relating to the *Vedanta* philosophy
Ukir (Sindhi)	Yearning		
Upadesh	Literally, homily; here, a discourse	*Vedic*	Relating to the Vedas
		Vidya	Knowledge
Vaasanas	Behavioural tendency	*Vidya dadati vinayam*	Knowledge generates humility
Vairagya	Detachment		
Vaishyas	One of the Hindu castes; traders	*Vishishtadvaita*	Non-dualistic school of *Vedanta* philosophy
Vanaprastha	Part of the *Vedic ashrama* system; leaving worldly luxuries and going to the *vana* (forest)	*Vishnu Purana*	An ancient text of Hinduism, centring around Lord Vishnu
		Vivaha	Marriage
Varaha	Avatar of Vishnu who takes the form of a boar to rescue Goddess Earth	*Viveka*	Discrimination between true and false
		Yajna	Offering; sacrifice
Varnas	Orders into which society is divided	*Yamas*	Restraints
		Yoga Vasistha	A sacred text by Valmiki; record of Sage Vasishtha's discourse to Sri Rama.
Vasudaiva Kutumbakam	Humanity is one family (from the Upanishads)		
Vatsalya bhava	Mode of affection for the Lord	*Yogic*	Of or pertaining to yoga

Books and Booklets by J.P. Vaswani

In English:

7 Commandments of the Bhagavad Gita
10 Commandments of a Successful Marriage
108 Pearls of Practical Wisdom
108 Simple Prayers of a Simple Man
108 Thoughts on Success
114 Thoughts on Love
A Little Book of Life
A Little Book of Wisdom
A Love that is Love Indeed!
A Simple and Easy Way to God
A Treasure of Quotes - Vol. I
A Treasure of Quotes - Vol. II
Around the Camp Fire
Be An Achiever
Be in the Driver's Seat
Begin the Day With God
Bhagavad Gita in a Nutshell
Burn Anger Before Anger Burns You
Comrades of God— Lives of Saints From East & West
Daily Appointment With God
Daily Inspiration (A Thought for Every Day of the Year)
Daily Inspiration
Dashavatara
Destination Happiness
Dewdrops of Love
Does God Have Favourites?
Ego Goes: Divinity Grows
Empower Yourself
Enrich Your Life - Desk Calendar
Face it With Love
Finding Peace of Mind
Formula for Prosperity
Friends Forever
Gateways to Heaven
God in Quest of Man
Good Parenting
Happily Ever After
How to Overcome Depression
I am a Sindhi
I Luv U, God!
India Awake
Jap Sahib - An Interpretation
Joy Peace Pills
Kill Fear Before Fear Kills You
Ladder of Abhyasa
Lessons Life Has Taught Me
Life After Death
Life and Teachings of Sadhu Vaswani
Life and Teachings of the Sikh Gurus: Ten Companions of God
Life is Beautiful: Live It Right!
Living in the Now
Management Moment by Moment
Mantra for the Modern Man
Mantras for Peace of Mind
Many Paths: One Goal
Many Scriptures: One Wisdom
Moment of Calm - Desk Calendar
Nearer, My God, to Thee!
New Education Can Make the World New
Peace or Perish
Practice the Presence of God
Positive Power of Thanksgiving
Questions Answered
Rainbow of Love
Saints for You and Me
Saints With a Difference
Say No to Negatives
Secrets of Health and Happiness
Seven Steps on the Path
Shake Hands With Life
Short Sketches of Saints Known & Unknown
Sketches of Saints Known & Unknown
Spirituality in Daily Life
Stay Connected
Stop Complaining: Start Thanking!
Swallow Irritation Before Irritation Swallows You
Switch on the Light
Teachers are Sculptors
The Endless Quest
The Goal of Life and How to Attain it
The Highway to Happiness
The Little Book of Freedom From Stress
The Little Book of Prayer
The Little Book of Service
The Little Book of Success
The Little Book of Yoga
The Magic of Forgiveness
The New Age Diet: Vegetarianism for You and Me
The Perfect Relationship: Guru and Disciple
The Simple Way
The Terror Within
The Way of Abhyasa (How to Meditate)
Thus Have I Been Taught
Tips for Teenagers
What Then?
What You Would Like to Know About Karma
What You Would Like to Know About Hinduism
What to Do When Difficulties Strike
Why Do Good People Suffer?
Why Be Sad?
Women: Where Would the World be Without You?
You Are Not Alone: God is With You!
You Can Change Your Life: Live— Don't Just Exist!

Story Books:

100 Stories You Will Never Forget
101 Stories for You and Me
25 Stories for Children and also for Teens
It's All a Matter of Attitude
Immortal Stories: Wisdom to Nourish Your Mind & Soul
Snacks for the Soul
More Snacks for the Soul
Stories With a Difference From the Bhagavata Purana

Break the Habit
The King of Kings
The One Thing Needful
The Patience of Purna
The Power of Good Deeds
The Power of Thought
Trust Me All in All or Not at All
Whom Do You Love the Most?
The Miracle of Forgiving
You Can Make a Difference

In Hindi:
Aadarsh Jeevan Ki Prerak Kahaniyaan
Aalwar Santon Ki Mahan Gaathaayen
Aapkay Karm, Aapkaa Bhaagya Banaatay Hein
Atmik Jalpaan
Atmik Poshan
Bhakton Ki Uljhanon Kaa Saral Upaai
Bhale Logon Ke Saath Bura Kyon?
Chaahat Hai Mujhe Ik Teri Teri
Dainik Prerna
Dar Se Mukti Paayen
Ishwar Tujhe Pranam
Khushaal Jeevan Ki Kahaniyaan
Krodh Ko Jalayen Swayam Ko Nahin
Laghu Kathayein
Mrityu Hai Dwar… Phir Kya?
Na Bhoolnewali 100 Kahaniyaan
Prarthana ki Shakti
Shama Karne Ki Aloukik Shakti
Sadhu Vaswani: Unkaa Jeevan Aur Shikshaayen
Safal Vivah Ke Dus Rahasya
Santon Ki Leela
Sarvottam Sambandh
Shama Karo Sukhi Raho
Srimad Bhagavad Gita: Gaagar Mein Saagar

In Arabic:
Daily Appointment With God

Daily Inspiration

In Bahasa:
A Little Book of Success
A Little Book of Wisdom
Burn Anger Before Anger Burns You
It's All a Matter of Attitude
Life After Death

In Chinese:
Daily Appointment With God

In Dutch:
Begin the Day With God
Women: Where Would the World be Without You?

In French:
Burn Anger Before Anger Burns You

In German:
Secrets of Health and Happiness

In Gujarati:
Daily Appointment With God
Flowers & Fruits
It's All a Matter of Attitude
Life After Death

In Kannada:
101 Stories for You and Me
Burn Anger Before Anger Burns You
Dada Answers
Life After Death
Tips for Teenagers
Why do Good People Suffer?

In Konkani:
Be in the Driver's Seat

In Letvian:
The Magic of Forgiveness

In Marathi:
10 Commandments of a Successful Marriage
101 Stories for You and Me
Burn Anger Before Anger Burns You
Life After Death
Management Moment by Moment
Questions Answered
Sadhu Vaswani: His Life and Teachings
Shake Hands With Life
The Magic of Forgiveness
What You Would Like to Know About Karma

In Oriya:
Be in the Driver's Seat
Burn Anger Before Anger Burns You
Empower Yourself
Kill Fear Before Fear Kills You
Life After Death
More Snacks for the Soul
Snacks for the Soul
The Little Book of Prayer
Why Do Good People Suffer?

In Russian:
Burn Anger Before Anger Burns You
What You Would Like to Know About Karma

In Sindhi:
Anjali Sangraha
Bhagavad Gita in a Nutshell
Bhaj Gobindam
Burn Anger Before Anger Burns You
Life After Death
Why Do Good People Suffer?

In Spanish:
10 Commandments of a Successful Marriage
101 Stories for You and Me
Begin the Day With God
Be In The Driver's Seat
Burn Anger Before Anger Burns You
Dada Answers
Daily Appointment With God
Daily Inspiration
Does God Have Favourites?
Formula for Prosperity
Good Parenting
I Luv U, God!
It's All a Matter of Attitude
Kill Fear Before Fear Kills You
Life After Death
Management Moment by Moment
More Dada Answers
More Snacks for the Soul
Nearer My God to Thee
Positive Power of Thanksgiving
Say No to Negatives
Shake Hands With Life
Snacks for the Soul
Stop Complaining Start Thanking
Spirituality in Daily Life
Swallow Irritation Before Irritation Swallows You
The Good You Do Returns
The Miracle of Forgiving
Thus have I Been Taught
What to do when Difficulties Strike
What You Would Like to Know About Karma
You Can Make a Difference

In Tamil:
10 Commandments of a Successful Marriage
Burn Anger Before Anger Burns You
Daily Appointment With God
It's All a Matter of Attitude
Kill Fear Before Fear Kills You
More Snacks for the Soul
Secrets of Health and Happiness
Snacks for the Soul
Why Do Good People Suffer?

In Telugu:
What You Would Like to Know About Karma

In Urdu:
Begin the Day With God
Steps to Happiness
Ticket to Heaven

Other Publications:

Books on J. P. Vaswani:
Dada J. P. Vaswani's Historic Visit to Sind
Dost Thou Keep Memory
How to Embrace Pain
Interviews and Innerviews
Jadhein Pireen Karay Tho Pandh
Jiski Jholi Mein Hai Pyaar
Dada J. P. Vaswani His Life and Teachings
Living Legend
Moments With a Master
Munhinjee Dil Te Lagee Laahootiyun Saan
Pyar Ka Masiha
Pilgrim of Love
Conversations With Dada Vaswani: A Perfect Disciple, A Reluctant Master
Guru of None, Disciple of All– The Life & Times of Dada J. P. Vaswani
Dada Vaswani: A Life in Spirituality
To Know Him... Is to Love Him